The Trickster Comes West

The Trickster Comes West

Pan-African Influence in Early Black Diasporan Narratives

Babacar M'Baye

University Press of Mississippi / *Jackson*

www.upress.state.ms.us

The University Press of Mississippi is a member
of the Association of American University Presses.

Copyright © 2009 by University Press of Mississippi
All rights reserved
Manufactured in the United States of America

First printing 2009

∞

Library of Congress Cataloging-in-Publication Data

M'Baye, Babacar, 1967–
 The trickster comes west : Pan-African influence in early Black Diasporan narratives / Babacar M'Baye.
   p. cm.
 Includes bibliographical references and index.
 ISBN 978-1-60473-233-7 (cloth : alk. paper) 1. Caribbean literature (English)—Black authors—History and criticism. 2. American literature—African American authors—History and criticism. 3. Blacks—Race identity—America. 4. Pan-Africanism in literature. 5. Slave narratives—History and criticism. 6. Tricksters in literature. 7. African diaspora in literature. 8. Slavery in literature. 9. America—Civilization—African influences. I. Title.

PR9205.05.M33 2009
810.9'8960729—dc22   2008045576

British Library Cataloging-in-Publication Data available

In memory of my mother, Fatou Wade

Contents

ix   Acknowledgments
3   Introduction

21   CHAPTER ONE
    African and Puritan Dimensions of Phillis Wheatley's Poems and Letters

69   CHAPTER TWO
    Pan-Africanism in Quobna Ottobah Cugoano's Liberation Discourse

105   CHAPTER THREE
    Pan-Africanism in Olaudah Equiano's *Interesting Narrative*

144   CHAPTER FOUR
    Africanism and Methodism in the Works of Elizabeth Hart Thwaites and Anne Hart Gilbert

178   CHAPTER FIVE
    African and Caribbean Patterns in Mary Prince's Resistance

207   Conclusion
211   Notes
219   Bibliography
241   Index

Acknowledgments

The genesis of this book goes back to the end of spring 2000 when I took my preliminary doctoral exam at Bowling Green State University. During my preparation for this exam, Sterling Stuckey's analysis of the relationships between the figure of Brer Rabbit, of African American folktales, and the character of Babo, of Herman Melville's 1855 tale *Benito Cereno*, inspired me to study further connections between black folktales and slave resistance. Under the guidance of Dr. Lillian Ashcraft-Eason, Dr. Michael A. Staub, and Dr. Donald McQuarie, I studied the African and diasporan survivals in Zora Neale Hurston's *Mules and Men*, James Baldwin's *Go Tell It on the Mountain* and Ishmael Reed's *Mumbo Jumbo* while keeping my scholarly interests in black folktales, reaffirming my conviction that a full understanding of African American literature and culture requires a study of both diasporan and African oral traditions. A fellowship from Bowling Green State University allowed me to collect many Pan-African folktales and analyze their resistance against slavery, imperialism, and sexism. Additional research grants from The Evergreen State College, Kent State University, and the NEH enabled me to gather and discuss Pan-African oral narratives from the Alderman Library of the University of Virginia, the *Institut Fondamental d'Afrique Noir* (IFAN) of Université Cheikh Anta Diop (in Senegal), and other libraries from around the world. I thank the librarians of Bowling Green State University, Evergreen State College, and Kent State University who have allowed me to borrow rare books of folktales from the African Studies resources of Indiana University, San Francisco State University, the University of Wisconsin, Ohio State University, and those of many other research institutions from around the United States.

I am especially grateful to the NEH for awarding me a stipend that allowed me to participate in the 2005 NEH Roots Summer Seminar of the Virginia Foundation for the Humanities. During that summer, I worked closely with the renowned historian Dr. Joseph C. Miller and used the exceptional resources of African history, literature, and oral traditions of the University of Virginia to enhance my study of Africa's relationships with the black diaspora. I would not have been able to complete this book without the influence that I received from "The Black Atlantic, 1500–1825: A Workshop of The Atlantic History Seminar" that was held at Harvard University on November 8, 2003. This seminar, in which key historians such as Dr. Bernard Bailyn, Dr. John Thornton, Dr. David Barry Gaspar, and Dr. Douglas Chambers were present, exposed me to new and creative ways of studying Africa's relationships with the black diaspora. I came from this seminar with an ardent desire to draw from my own expertise in American culture studies, folklore studies, and black Atlantic studies in an attempt to explore the connections between Pan-African folktales and literary narratives of slavery. Dr. Lillian Ashcraft-Eason and Dr. Michael J. Pfeifer gave me useful feedback on the proposal and direction of this book.

My academic goals would have been impossible to achieve without the support of many individuals such as Dr. Frances Novack, Dr. Baydallaye Kane, Dr. Simon J. Bronner, and Dr. Phillip G. Terrie, who trusted my academic skills and helped me pursue higher education in the United States. I thank these invaluable persons and my dear colleagues of the Africana Cultures and Policy Studies Institute (Dr. Zachery Williams, Dr. Seneca Vaught, and Dr. Robert Smith), whose moral succor and scholarly endeavors have sustained my academic motivations throughout the past decade. I also thank all my colleagues of the Department of English and the Department of Pan-African Studies of Kent State University, especially Dr. Wendy Wilson-Fall, Dr. Diedre L. Badejo, Dr. Amoaba Gooden, and Professor Mwatabu Okantah, whose scholarly collaborations have inspired me to refine my views of Pan-African cultures. Dr. Raymond Craig has provided me with useful advice during my negotiations for a book contract with the University Press of Mississippi. Finally, I thank my precious wife, Eriko Tanaka; my lovely daughters, Fatou and Amina; and my kind family in Senegal and Japan, whose patience and understanding made the completion of this book possible.

The Trickster Comes West

Introduction

Phillis Wheatley, Quobna Ottobah Cugoano, Olaudah Equiano, Elizabeth Hart Thwaites, Anne Hart Gilbert, and Mary Prince were pioneer writers of the black diaspora who identified with Africa and developed sustained criticisms against slavery, racism, and other oppression against blacks in the New World and Africa. In their works, they made strong Pan-Africanist and other nationalist references that allowed them to offset the occasional ambivalence that they expressed toward Africa. The black diasporan writers were part of a small elite group of Western-educated black intellectuals whose views on Africa did not represent those of all other black populations in the West. They received educations and eventually acquired freedom, experiences, and opportunities that were not available to most blacks in the United States and the Caribbean.[1] Yet they utilized their elite status and individuality by attacking Western slavery and linking their suffering to blacks in Africa and to the African diaspora, thereby becoming pioneers of Pan-Africanism. Recognizing this subversive quality of early black diasporan authors requires us to interpret their writings as Pan-African and radical texts that grappled with the racial, ideological, and political foundations of Western slavery and imperialism on the black world. As Anthony Bogues argues in *Black Heretics, Black Prophets: Radical Political Intellectuals* (2003), early black slave narratives reflect "discursive practices of slave criticism and critique that probed alternative meanings of racial slavery, natural liberty, and natural rights, and countered the dominant eighteenth-century ideas of racial plantation slavery. As documents of slave political criticism and critique, the narratives have a great deal to tell us about eighteenth-century social and political ideas, and form a central part of an Africana radical intellectual political tradition" (27).

Oral tradition had major roles in the critique of slavery and imperialism in early black diasporan narratives. These writings show how black writers overcame difficult personal, social, political, and economic conditions through appropriation and reconstruction of the resistance strategies of diasporan trickster figures such as Brer Rabbit, Nancy, and Bro' Boar-Hog, who remind us of West African prankster characters such as *Leuk* [the Rabbit], *Bouki* [Hyena], *Ananse* [Spider], *Mbe* [Tortoise], and other icons of black folklore. These trickster characters from various black cultures achieve freedom from alienating circumstances by using dexterous and creative resistance strategies and ideologies that are visible in the early literature of the black diaspora in which wits, kinship, communal support, verbal adeptness, and courage were necessary tools of rebellion against slave owners. These resistance tactics derived from traditional West African folktales in which tricksters represented multiple functions and worldviews. As John W. Roberts argues in *From Trickster to Badman: The Black Folk Hero in Slavery and Freedom* (1989), "Trickster tale traditions, especially those in which clever animals acted as humans, were ubiquitous in the cultures from which Africans enslaved in the United States had come. Therefore, it is not surprising that tales of trickery built around the exploits of anthropomorphized animals occupied a central position in the oral narrative performances of Africans enslaved in America" (17). Roberts's statement suggests the omnipresence of African trickster figures in African American slave culture.

Drawing from similar theories, such as those of Sterling Stuckey, Michael A. Gomez, Henry Louis Gates Jr., and many other scholars, this study explores the influence of Pan-Africanism and traditional African ideologies of resistance, communalism, and spirituality on selected African American, African British, and African Caribbean literary and historical writings produced between 1773 and 1831. The works discussed in the book include Phillis Wheatley's *Poems on Various Subjects, Religious and Moral* (1773), Quobna Ottobah Cugoano's *Thoughts and Sentiments on the Evil of Slavery* (1787), Olaudah Equiano's *The Interesting Narrative of the Life of Olaudah Equiano* (1795), Elizabeth Hart Thwaites's "History of Methodism" (1804), Anne Hart Gilbert's "History of Methodism" (1804), and Mary Prince's *The History of Mary Prince: A West Indian Slave, Related By Herself* (1831). These books reveal how pivotal writers of the black diaspora of the eighteenth and nineteenth centuries utilized African cultural, religious, and ideological symbols and concepts as means of resistance against oppression in their specific locations in the Western world. These writers drew from African ancestral traditions, Western Christian theology and spirituality, and secular philosophical and political thoughts that allowed them to establish connections with Africa.

My first reason for selecting the writings of Wheatley, Cugoano, Equiano, Thwaites, Gilbert, and Prince is that many of these writers remain unknown to most readers. For example, in his introduction to the 1999 edition of Cugoano's *Thoughts and Sentiments on the Evil of Slavery*, Vincent Carretta argues that Cugoano is one of the least studied authors of the black diaspora "because the least is known about his life" (ix). Cugoano's situation is not unique; the least studied authors of the black diaspora include Thwaites and Gilbert as well. Of the six authors I have selected, Thwaites and Gilbert are virtually unknown because their writings were inaccessible until very recently, when Moira Ferguson edited and published them in her volume, *The Hart Sisters: Early African Caribbean Writers, Evangelicals, and Radicals* (1993). Sandra Pouchet Paquet's review of *The Hart Sisters* (1995) describes the tremendous value of Thwaites's and Gilbert's writings: "The actual writings of the Hart sisters included in this volume are scant, but they give a rare glimpse into the lives of resistant, historically aware free black women at the turn of the nineteenth century" (518). By examining the representation of African and black diasporan cultures in the works of Thwaites and Gilbert, I want to see how the sisters coped with the same historical forces of alienation and oppression that Prince, Equiano, Cugoano, and Wheatley also experienced, and how they negotiated their double consciousness between African and European cultures.

My second reason for selecting to write about Wheatley, Cugoano, Equiano, Thwaites, Gilbert, and Prince is the neglect of their works in the scholarship on the black diaspora's relationships with Africa. Critics tend to focus on the individual and Western identities of these writers, overlooking the communal and African identities these writers created in their works. In *Middle Passages: African American Journeys to Africa, 1787–2005* (2006), James Campbell rightly argues that African American writers of the last 250 years have depicted Africa either as a continent with an "abiding presence in black political, intellectual, and imaginative life," a "'Dark Continent' crying out for Christian civilization" (xxiii), or a continent to which they deny any connection (xxiv). Yet Campbell does not show how these contradictory ways of relating to Africa are apparent in the writings of Wheatley, Cugoano, Equiano, Thwaites, Gilbert, and Prince. Campbell makes no mention of Prince, Gilbert, and Thwaites, whose writings reflect salient African spiritual, cultural, and ideological elements. Moreover, he does not refer to Cugoano, who, like Equiano, lived in Africa before he was enslaved into the Western world.

My third reason for selecting the books I have chosen is that these texts were written between 1773 and 1831. The year 1831 marks the end of a period when black diasporan cultures reflected more visible African influences than they did in succeeding decades. For instance, in *Exchanging Our Country Marks: The Transformation of African Identities in the Colonial and Antebellum*

South (1998), Michael A. Gomez represents 1830 as the period of transformation of blacks in the United States into African Americans through the forging of African "ethnicity" into "race" (11). By examining the African elements in black diasporan literature written prior to 1830, I show the significance of Pan-Africanism in this literature before the process that Gomez calls the "African Americanization" of slave culture that occurred in 1830 (11). My search for the Pan-Africanist influence in early slave culture is consistent with Gomez's argument that it was enslavement in the Americas that compelled "Africans of varying ethnicities, who had never considered their blackness a source of reflection," to seize it "as a principle of unity" (165). Yet, by focusing on the blend of African and Western sensibilities in New World black literature written before 1831, I show that the hybridity in slave culture began earlier than Gomez argues and that such diversity can be seen in the Christian and abolitionist sensibilities of Wheatley, Cugoano, Equiano, Thwaites, Gilbert, and Prince.

In an interview published in *The Journal of Pan-African Studies* (March 2008), the African American historian James Stewart asks, "While Black Atlantic Studies appropriately call for a broadening focus of 'diaspora' studies beyond Blacks in the U.S., how can the continent of Africa be left totally out of the discussion?" (91). In order to understand the importance of Africa in black Atlantic studies, it is vital to reinscribe the continent into the history of the black diaspora. This requires writing Africa into the global history of Pan-African resistance and tracing this history to early literature and cultures of the black diaspora. This process helps us see and acknowledge the subtle tactics that the enslaved Africans invented from the belly of the slave ships of the Middle Passage in order to resist European oppression and reconnect with Africa. As Gomez explains in *Reversing Sail: A History of the African Diaspora* (2005), Pan-African resistance began in "the belly of the whale" from which "the sons and daughters of Africa were dispersed all over the New World, occupying every conceivable place, performing every imaginable task" (79). This interpretation of the Middle Passage as a moment that marked the inception of black resistance through organization and invention of survival tactics needs to be expanded through an analysis of early black Atlantic literature in which traditional African folklore is an active agent. This folklore stands as a living testimony of Africa's permanent influence on the literary, political, cultural, and economic history of the black diaspora.

Moreover, in an attempt to validate the African background in early black diasporan literature, it is important to represent Africa as a site where specific cultures and ethnic groups existed for centuries before the beginning of the transatlantic slave trade. The homogenization of African cultures is detrimental because it overlooks the multifarious African civilizations from which the specific writers of the diaspora came or evolved. In "The African Diaspora" (2000), Colin Palmer urges contemporary scholars to emphasize the differences between African cultures by recognizing that "those people who resided on the African continent defined themselves solely in accordance with their ethnic group" (57).[2]

Like Palmer, Sidney W. Mintz and Richard Price, in *An Anthropological Approach to the Afro-American Past*, stress the specification of African customs and the importance of social-relational and cultural perspectives in understanding "the basic conditions under which the migrations of enslaved Africans occurred" (43). Using Mintz and Price's methodology, I examine the conditions that the early black writers experienced during the Middle Passage or after their arrival in the New World. Moreover, I explore the specific cultural contexts and social relationships that influenced the works and lives of these authors. This approach to literature consists of letting the texts talk in order to reveal the rich syncretism of African and European cultural elements that permeate them.

The dehomogenization of Africa helps us examine the exact African societies whose folklore, myths, religions, and worldviews permeate early black diasporan writings. By exploring these explicit African retentions, one can see how the pioneers of black Atlantic literature blended their African identities with their Western traditions to achieve admissibility and social and economic status in a world in which Europeans had equated the adjective "African" to inferiority and inhumanity. This Atlantic literature should be interpreted through an African-centered method that validates the importance of the multiple identities, positions, and ideas that early black writers developed in particular moments of their lives to strengthen or weaken their Pan-African consciousness. This method begins with an acknowledgment of the distinct African cultures from which the authors came and a validation of the contributions that the first black women writers of the diaspora made in the development of Pan-Africanism.

The recurring concepts in this study include folklore, tale-type, motif, parallel, analogue, Pan-Africanism, Africanism, black Atlantic, black diaspora, imperialism, and colonialism. Alan Dundes argues in *Mother Wit from the Laughing Barrel* (1973) that folklore is an indelible marker of human identity, which is "transmitted from person to person, often orally" (2). In a similar vein, Harold Courlander points out in "Africa's Marks in the Western Hemisphere" (1996) that folklore "includes narratives and traditions unique to particular communities as well as those that are shared by many or all" (6). According to Courlander, black folklore "refers to myths, tales, recollections, songs and other orally transmitted lore of the various, sometimes disparate, Negro cultures in the New World" (6).

In *African Oral Literature: Backgrounds, Character, and Continuity* (1992), Isidore Okpewho defines "tale type" as "a kind or class of tale that makes a particular point or deals with a specific issue (e.g., a tale of 'magic flight' or a 'werewolf' tale)" (168–69). As Stith Thompson remarks in *Folktale* (1946), a tale type also refers to "a traditional tale that has an independent existence" (415). Moreover, as Thompson argues, "a *motif* is the smallest element in a tale" that has "a power to persist in tradition" (415). The term "motif" derives from the word "motifeme" which is a concept that Dundes defines in "The Making and Breaking of Friendship as a Structural Frame in African Folk Tales" (1971) as the different functions of the trickster in an oral narrative (171). For Dundes, these functions include the establishment, end, testing, violation, and discovery of agreement or friendship (171–85).[3]

My definition of parallel and analogue is indebted to the meaning of the terms that May Augusta Klipple gives in *African Folktales with Foreign Analogues* (1992). As Klipple points out, "an analogue is a story similar to the one under consideration, but is not necessarily a retelling of the same story. Parallelism may rise from the fact that a well-knit story has a vitality which permits it to adjust itself to a new environment and yet to keep the basic kernel of the story unchanged even though specific details may be replaced by others, actors changed, incidents omitted or added" (xxxviii). Also, as Klipple says, "similar stories can spring up in various parts of the world and at different times because, since human nature is essentially the same irrespective of race, location, or time, similar things happen among different peoples and in places widely separated by distance and time" (xxxviii). In this sense, the West African and black diasporan folktales discussed in this book may have parallels in stories from other cultures and parts of the world, even if such analogues are not examined herein.

In his study of the history of collective resistance in the black diaspora, *The Pan-African Movement*, Immanuel Geiss shows that Pan-Africanism has been "one of the least known political movements or concepts of our time" because the term is still "vague," its history is "complicated and little explored," and "most writers have been more or less content with the short account by W. E. B. Du Bois and the more detailed work by George Padmore" (187). Though it focuses mainly on Du Bois, Padmore, Nnamdi Azikiwe, Kwame Nkrumah, and Léopold Sédar Senghor, Geiss's study of Pan-Africanism is crucial because it gives us a "provisional definition" of a concept that can serve as "a working tool for historical analysis."⁴ Discussing the theory that Pan-Africanism began either in the late eighteenth century or in 1900, Geiss argues that the history of the ideology "in the narrower sense begins with the Pan-African conference in London in 1900; that the broader sense goes back to the late eighteenth century" (8).⁵ J Ayodele Langley provides a theory that is quite different from Geiss's when he contends, in *Pan-Africanism and Nationalism in West Africa, 1900–1945*, that prior to 1900, Pan-Africanism in the diaspora "remained merely an 'informal organization of memories' among articulate members of the Black Diaspora" who used it in churches and in other organizations in order "to affirm positively their 'Africanity' or to reject it" (18). Langley's thesis minimizes the Pan-Africanism that strived in the diaspora during the eighteenth and nineteenth centuries.⁶

The term "Pan-Africanism" has two meanings in this book. First, it refers to the collective resistance of black populations from the United States, the Caribbean, and England against European slavery, imperialism, colonization, and racism from the 1770s through the end of the twentieth century. My definition of Pan-Africanism is indebted to Sterling Stuckey's interpretation of the concept in *Slave Culture: Nationalist Theory and the Foundations of Black America* (1987) as the idea of "total African liberation" that the African American abolitionist David Walker expressed in his *Appeal* in 1829 (134–35). According to Stuckey, Walker told African Americans: "I advance it therefore to you, not as a *problematical*, but as an unshaken and for ever immovable *fact*, that your full glory and happiness, as well as [those of] all other coloured people under Heaven, shall never be fully consummated, but with the *entire emancipation of your enslaved brethren all over the world*" (134–35).⁷ As Stuckey argues, Walker's statement suggests his Pan-Africanist conviction that "in the quest for African liberation, it is the duty of blacks, above all others, to take responsibility for the liberation of their people" (134). Walker's Pan-Africanism emphasizes his belief in the moral obligation of blacks of the diaspora to embrace their African traditions and work toward the political and economic liberation of all blacks. These pillars of Pan-Africanism are discernible in Stuckey's argument that "Walker's pride in blackness, his respect for the achievements of blacks in the ancient world, and his belief in African moral character and the need for African autonomy provided [vital] elements of cultural nationalism" (135).

The second meaning of Pan-Africanism in this book is the diffusion of African survivals (known as Africanisms) in different parts of the world, such as the spread of African cultural values, customs, and ideologies into the black diaspora since slavery. My use of the concept of Africanism is indebted to Amy K. Levin's *Africanism and Authenticity in African-American Women's Novels* (2003), which combines the methods of cultural anthropology, literary criticism, and intellectual history to analyze a variety of African influences in the writings of Gloria Naylor, Toni Morrison, Alice Walker, and Jamaica Kincaid, where they serve as metaphors of the cultural and social resistance of women of the black diaspora. As Levin defines it, the word "Africanism" refers to both African influences in the cultures of blacks of the New World (5) and to African Americans' perspectives "on or interpretation of African culture" (97). This definition is important because it allows me to conceptualize Africanism as a word that describes, at the same time, the early black writers' relations with Africa and their reflection of African patterns in their works. These influences are Pan-African, since they permeate the folklore of both the black diaspora and Africa.

Like the term "Pan-Africanism," the concepts of colonialism and imperialism mean different things depending on the historical context, region, and theory in consideration. As Robert J. C. Young argues in *Postcolonialism*, colonialism functioned as an activity on the periphery and was economically driven "from the home government's perspective," while imperialism operated from the center as a policy of state and was driven by the grandiose projects of power (17). Young writes: "Thus while imperialism is susceptible to analysis as a concept . . . colonialism needs to be analyzed primarily as a practice" (17). Another difference between colonialism and imperialism is the different time and forms in which they developed in different parts of the world (17).

The term "diaspora" comes from the Greek word *Diaspeirein* (to spread about). Originally referring to the dispersion of Jews outside Israel in the twentieth century, the concept of the diaspora has been enlarged to include the dispersal of Africans in New World societies by historical forces such as slavery, colonization, wars, and migrations.[8] My notion of the black diaspora is indebted to Michael L. Blakey's definition of diaspora (in "Bioarchaelogy of the African Diaspora in the Americas") as an idea that "assumes the character of a dynamic, continuous and complex phenomenon stretching across time, geography, class, and gender" (388). A useful discussion of the concept of the diaspora is Paul E. Lovejoy's 2000 essay "Identifying Enslaved Africans in the African Diaspora," which argues that the term "black diaspora" refers to the different places where people who view Africa as their homeland live (8–9). Lovejoy shows that the black diaspora "reflects layers of influences" and is wider than one could cover in a single book, since it includes black communities living in all the regions outside of Continental Africa (8–10). In light of Lovejoy's theory, this study uses the concept of the black diaspora to refer to the United States, the Caribbean, and England only, and not to all the other regions where African-descended people live.

The term "black Atlantic" became popular in academia when Paul Gilroy coined it in *The Black Atlantic: Modernity and Double Consciousness* (1993) to refer to the ambivalent representation of race and nationalism in the writings of nineteenth- and early twentieth-century African American and African British intellectuals such as Martin Robinson Delany, James Wedderburn, and W. E. B. Du Bois. In Gilroy's study, Africa is theorized in terms of dualities that reveal the diversity of modern black cultures (4). Although it broadens our understanding of the relations between the diaspora and Africa, Gilroy's theory is open to serious critique because it overemphasizes the antiessentialism, hybridity, individuality, and ambivalence of the early black writers of the diaspora towards Africa. Gilroy's vision of black cultures as fragmented overlooks the complex ways in which black writers of the diaspora have consistently perceived Africa in Pan-Africanist terms despite their fluctuating relations with Africa.

Moreover, Gilroy develops a rigid theory of hybridity that excludes Africa from the experiences of blacks of the diaspora. In *Against Race: Imagining Political Culture Beyond the Color Line* (2000), Gilroy contends that the works of Wheatley and Equiano "should not be valued only as means to observe the durability of African elements or dismissed as an inadequate mixture, doomed always to be something less than the supposed pure entities that first combined to produce it. Their legacy is most valuable as a mix, a hybrid. Its recombinant form is indebted to its 'parent' cultures but remains assertively and insubordinately a bastard" (117). Gilroy also argues that "neither he [Equiano] nor Wheatley ever returned to the African homelands from which their long journeys through slavery had begun" (116) and that Wheatley's poetry reflects "her personal transformation from African to American" (116).

By representing Equiano's and Wheatley's relations to Africa as an irreversible disconnection from the continent and total conversion into American cultures, Gilroy neglects how these writers bridged their physical distance from their homeland and attenuated their self-alteration through frequent appropriation of African identities. Gilroy's theory of hybridity assumes that this process of cultural and social mixing occurs only in the black diaspora, as if the African continent from which the enslaved blacks came was and continues to be a single, homogeneous, and pure entity.

The scholarship on Africanisms in eighteenth- and nineteenth-century black diasporan literature is scant. Although it does not explore African cultural influences in the early black literature, Houston Baker's *The Journey Back: Issues in Black Literature Criticism* (1980) somewhat suggests the spiritual significance of Africa for eighteenth-century black American writers such as Wheatley and Equiano. Baker identifies, in African American literature, a constant attachment (or spiritual journey) to Africa which produces a "double nomenclature" or the act of being "caught between two worlds" (3). He explains: "On the one hand, Africans were not free to be Africans; they found their traditional rituals and the instruments necessary for their performance suppressed by Whites. On the other hand, they were defined by law as outsiders and were excluded from the free, human community that the Puritans designated as a city of God in the New World" (3). My interpretation of the works of Wheatley, Cugoano, Equiano, Thwaites, Gilbert, and Prince provides a similar reading of early black diasporan literature. Yet I expand Baker's concept of a double bind in eighteenth-century African American literature by including the dualities of non-U.S. black authors such as Cugoano, Gilbert, Thwaites, and Prince about both the New World and Africa.

Sterling Stuckey's major study of eighteenth-century Pan-Africanism, *Slave Culture: Nationalist Theory and the Foundations of Black America* (1987), traces the birth of Pan-African resistance in the black diaspora to the period between 1800 and 1807 when slaves in South Carolina and the West Indies, "who had experienced the middle passage and had retained memories of the complexities of African culture" (44), were able to draw from shared experiences and cultures that influenced their political visions, religious outlook, and resistance against slavery (44). One example of Pan-Africanism in an early black diasporan community given by Stuckey is the ceremony of "election day" in eighteenth-century New England in which slaves chose a king who "carried himself as ruler and treated his [black] followers like subjects" and "controlled [their affairs] on behalf of others" (79). For Stuckey, the behavior of the black ruler and subjects during the parades of kings and governors in eighteenth-century New England reveals "the existence of elements of a Pan-African culture in New World slavery," especially since "substantial numbers of slaves in Cuba and North America came from essentially the same areas of Africa" (79).

Stuckey's arguments demonstrate the strong and pervasive impact of African culture on the traditions that the enslaved Africans invented in the diaspora. Discussing a Senegambian tale entitled, "The Hare Seeks Endowments from Allah," the collector Emil Magel writes: "The presence of the elephant in many Wolof stories attests to its former existence in the Senegambian savannah regions. In the early years of European trade with the Senegambian people, ivory was an important cash crop. Today, Wolof people know about elephants only through oral narratives" (181). The Senegambians, a displaced African community who were brought to the Atlantic world through this trade, carried these oral narratives or learned them from other African slaves during or shortly after the Middle Passage. This transplantation of African oral narratives allows us to make intertextual and comparative analyses between these tales and the narratives of African American slaves.

Like Stuckey, Herskovits explores the vital significance of African cultures in the early traditions of the black diaspora. In *The Myth of the Negro Past* (1941), Herskovits argues that most African worldviews such as "the river cult or, in broader terms, the cult of water spirits" have persisted in the New World (106–7). He demonstrates the evidence of such survivals "from the hint in the Dahomean data," which show the influence African priests had in their community even when they were considered as slaves (15). In a similar vein, Herskovits reports in *Suriname Folklore* (1936) that drumming fulfills three major functions among the Akan of the Gold Coast, such as "summoning the gods and the spirits of the ancestors to appear," "articulating the message of these supernatural beings when they arrive," and sending spirits of deities and ancestors "back to their habitats at the end of each ceremony" (520). The connection Herskovits establishes between Akan mythology and African American folklore helps me identify further relationships between the traditional worldviews of West African societies such as the Wolof, the Akan, and the Igbo and those of the black authors discussed in this book.

Herskovits's theory is expanded in *Slave Culture*, in which Stuckey argues that drumming has a mythological significance in African American culture. Discussing the traditional African American folktale entitled, "Bur Rabbit in Red Hill Churchyard," Stuckey points out that the fiddling of Brer Rabbit fulfills the same threefold mythological role that drumming accomplishes among the Akan (19). Stuckey's first example is a scene in which Brer Rabbit stops fiddling, wipes his face, and with Owl and Brer Mockingbird, bows in a circle before the grave of Simon (19). Stuckey writes: "De snow on the grave crack an' rise up, an' de grave open an' I see Simon rise up out er dat grave. I see him an' he look jest as natu'al as he don 'fore dey bury him" (19). Stuckey's second example is a scene in which Brer Mockingbird and Owl, who are keeping Brer Rabbit company at the cemetery and singing, speak to Simon, the dead man who had risen from his grave after hearing Brer Rabbit's music. Stuckey states: "An' he [Simon] look satisfy, an' he look he taken a great interest in Bur Rabbit an' de little beasts an' birds. An' he set down on de top of he own grave and carry on a long compersation wid all dem animals" (20). Stuckey's third example is a passage in which Brer Rabbit plays music until Simon returns to the spiritual world he came from. Stuckey writes: "But dat ain't all. Atter dey wored dey self out wid compersation, I see Bur Rabbit take he fiddle an' put it under he chin an' start to playin.' An' while I watch, I see Bur Rabbit step back on de grave an' Simon were gone" (20). Therefore, Rabbit plays the role of both *griot* and oracle in the New World, re-creating the multitalented functions of leader, musician, spiritual healer, and trickster figures in African cultures. Brer Rabbit, Owl, and Brer Mockinbird create a strong community in which members support each other and perform sacred rituals that are apparent in early slave writings and African cultures.

In *Going through the Storm: The Influence of African American Art in History* (1994), Stuckey describes other relations between African and African American folklore. He reveals the ties between the African American folk figure Brer Rabbit and the character of Babo in Herman Melville's 1855 tale *Benito Cereno*, whom he represents as a Senegalese. He writes: "The play of irony that informs Babo's activities on board the San Dominick is precisely that adopted by Brer Rabbit in his African American expression . . . What is certain is that Babo is so much like Brer Rabbit that it is perfectly logical that he should have come from Senegal, a thriving center for tales of the African hare, Brer Rabbit's ancestral model" (165). The evidence of the Senegalese folkloric influence on African American culture can be better understood through analysis of the numerous hare stories of the Senegambian region that can be accessed directly from the available collection of African folktales. The works of Senegambian folktales that are examined in this book include Ousmane Socé's *Contes et Légendes d'Afrique Noire* (1962), Léopold Sédar Senghor and Abdoulaye Sadji's *Les Aventures de Leuk-Le-Lièvre* (1975), David P. Gamble's *Wolof Stories from Senegambia Mainly From Old Published Sources* (1987), and Emil A. Magel's *Folktales from the Gambia: Wolof Fictional Narratives* (1984). I have translated the folktales of Senghor and Sadji, which were written in French, into English in order to compare them with the works of Wheatley, Cugoano, Equiano, Prince, Gilbert, and Thwaites.

The scholarship about the Wolof folk hero *Bouki* is scant. In *Three Tales from the French Folklore of Louisiana* (1943), Calvin Claudel and J. M. Carrière study the different theories about the origins of the word *Bouki* (also spelled *Bouqui, Bouki, Boukee, Boukie, Bookee,* or *Bouky*) and argue that the term "is common in the folklore of Louisiana, Missouri, the Bahamas, Haiti, the Dominican Republic, and Senegal" (38). According to Claudel and Carrière, the term *Bouki* is the Wolof word for "hyena."[9] The word *Bouki* has been associated with different human characteristics. In his *Philologie Créole* (1937), the Haitian scholar Jules Faine describes it as a derivation from "bookish" used in an ironical sense.[10] Yet storytellers in Louisiana, Missouri, and the West Indies "have generally no explanation to offer beyond the vague suggestion that it is the name of some greedy and stupid animal. A Louisiana informant consulted by Edward A. McIlhenny explains it, however, as meaning a deer."[11]

Like *Esu Elegbera*, the Yoruba-derived trickster and deity figure that Gates popularized in *The Signifying Monkey: A Theory of Afro-American Literary Criticism* (1988), the Wolof-derived trickster figure *Bouki* is a symbol of indeterminacy in black literature in which he dons different personas. *Bouki* appears, at the same time, as a bookish, greedy, stupid, and deerlike character because he is a metaphor of the disguise that allows African folkloric tricksters to represent different personalities and negotiate the relationships between opposites that are normally thought of as antithetical to each other.

In order to see the significant roles that *Bouki* plays in black literature, one must remove this character from the narrow binaries in which he is perceived as a foil of *Leuk*, which is the Wolof concept for Brer Rabbit.[12] One example is Cartwright's *Reading Africa into American Literature*, where *Bouki* is "characterized by inflexibility, ineptness, and the use of rules and power for selfish personal gain" in contrast to *Leuk* [the Hare] who "wields the ethically ambiguous 'wild' forces of 'intelligence, mobility, flexibility, unorthodox improvisation, and play'" (112). In African folklore, the Manichean Western opposition between *Bouki* and *Leuk* is merely temporal. The trickster characters in African folklore do not abide by strict conceptions of morality. As Mohamadou Kane argues in *Essai sur les contes d'Amadou Kumba* (1981), rigid oppositions between African prankster figures or speculations about honesty, morality, or religiosity of either one of the tricksters are unnecessary, because these characters all have flaws and play equally valid artistic roles that transpire through the creativity and personal style of the performer (17). In order to understand the creative roles of trickster figures in African folklore, one must avoid associating their personae with immorality. In so doing, one is able to perceive these characters as reflections of the unmistakable imprints that distinguish African folklore from others. As John Erickson posits,

> They [African trickster characters] bear the unmistakable imprint of oral tradition—the same formulae, ritualistic language, melodious rhythm suggestive of tribal instruments, tendency to "anecdotes, puns, digressions," and strong taste for the supernatural . . . The African "accepts genies, spirits and magic within the natural order of things," as contrasted to the Westerner who clearly distinguishes "objective and subjective reality" and relegates supernatural tales "to a childhood universe."[13]

Therefore, in order to identify African influences in black diasporan literature, one should use a new perspective in which African cosmology and ontology are represented as cultural universes where the traditional Western and

Manichean binaries between good/bad, beautiful/ugly, and moral/immoral are meaningless. As Peter Langford points out in *Modern Philosophies of Human Nature: Their Emergence from Christian Thought* (1986), the "Manichean view" of the world "perceives life as dominated by inhuman forces of good and evil" (190). African trickster characters, such as *Leuk, Ananse, Bouki*, or *Mbe* go beyond the limitations that Western dichotomies create in the interpretation of black literature. These trickster figures and the African folktales from which they came are the kinds of folklore to which the early writers of the black diaspora would have been exposed in Africa or in the West. In *Going through the Storm*, Stuckey portrays Brer Rabbit and Babo as characters who were "linked to a shared sense of moral righteousness, which leads them to become forces of retribution that unsentimentally punish the purveyors of greed and cruelty" (167). Stuckey's assertion underscores the common way in which enslaved Africans and their shared African trickster figures perceived themselves as symbols of faith, good, righteousness, and resistance against oppression and corruption. In attempting to uncover the traces of these figures, it is crucial to interpret the manner in which black writers of the diaspora appropriate the liminality and ambiguity in African oral tradition in order to resist domination and transgress boundaries.

Similar intimacies between black diasporan culture and African folktales are visible in works such as John W. Roberts's *From Trickster to Badman: The Black Folk Hero in Slavery and Freedom* (1989) and Walter C. Rucker's *The River Flows On: Black Resistance, Culture, and Identity Formation in Early America* (2006). Roberts examines "the folklore surrounding the trickster, conjurer, biblical figures, and the badman from the vantage point of African cultural values and forms as transformed under the conditions of slavery and in the sociocultural environment of the late nineteenth century" (13). By recognizing the influence of African oral traditions on the worldviews of nineteenth-century African Americans, Roberts allows us to examine the connections between the spirituality and resilience of trickster figures in African and black diasporan literature. Roberts's theory supports this study's representation of black diasporan slave narratives as extensions of cultural values and resistance strategies that evolved out of African folklore.

By comparing black diasporan narratives and African folk narratives, one can identify trickster figures and resistance traditions that are similar to those that permeated the cultures of both enslaved and free blacks of the diaspora. Such comparisons of black Atlantic narratives will reveal the relationships between the history of blacks of the diaspora and Africa. In *The River Flows On*, Rucker states: "If Brer Rabbit and other animal trickster characters are predated by African analogues, and if tales in Africa and the Americas serve some of the same functions and have similar meanings, then there would have to be some common social, political, and environmental circumstances in Africa and in the Americas" (204). By analyzing the Pan-African elements in early black literature, this book intends to suggest both the similarities and differences between the conditions of Africans and diasporan blacks during slavery.

The black populations in the New World were familiar with African-derived tricksters since the protagonists in their folktales have characters that resemble those in African folklore. Sheila S. Walker suggests in *African Roots/American Cultures* that the Rabbit and *Nancy* tales in the United States, the Compair Lapin stories of Louisiana, the Compé Lapin narratives of the Francophone Caribbean, as well as the Tio Conejo folktales of Colombia follow the same hare cycle from the Sahel area of West Africa (54). This similarity between African and New World folktales attests to the ubiquitous nature of African oral narratives in eighteenth-century black diasporan culture. In the introduction to *Anansesem: A Collection of Caribbean Folk Tales, Legends and Poems for Juniors* (1985), Velma Pollard writes: "Most of the folk tales, whether they are told in Jamaica or Trinidad, Curaçao or St. Lucia, came originally from the same source from Africa where most of our great great grandparents were born. Whether they ended up speaking Jamaican patwa or St. Lucia patois, they told their grandchildren the same stories" (vii). Pollard's assertion shows the sustained way in which blacks in the diaspora have preserved their African oral traditions since slavery.

Like the Wolof prankster figure *Leuk*, the Akan trickster character *Ananse* (also spelled as *Anansi*) is a Pan-African figure whose traces are found in the black diaspora. Like *Leuk*, *Anansi* performs complex tasks that reflect social relations influenced by traditional concepts of family, morality, and divinity, which are challenged by the transformations that slavery brought in African communities on both sides of the Atlantic. As I will show later, circumstances such as wars, fragmentation of families, poverty, forced exile, and other predicaments brought about by slavery are visible in both African and black diasporan folktales.

Discussing the origin of *Anansi*, Helen L. Flowers says: "The term, Annancy or Anansi, is the Tshi or Ashanti [word] for spider" (6). Yet, as Flowers contends, "the term, Anancy story, as applied to West Indian narrative, goes back at least to 'Monk' Lewis, who employed the distinctive term in his journal of 1816. As used by him, it included in addition to stories, also riddles and songs, and therefore seems to designate a diversified collection rather than a 'special class'" (6). *Anansi* plays multiple roles in both African oral traditions and Caribbean cultures.

Any study of the African background of black diasporan folklore should acknowledge Lawrence W. Levine's *Black Culture and Black Consciousness: African-American Folk Thought from Slavery to Freedom* (1977), Roger D. Abrahams's *Afro-American Folktales: Stories from Black Traditions in the New World* (1985), William Bascom's *African Folktales in the New World* (1992), and May Augusta Klipple's *African Folktales with Foreign Analogues* (1992). These studies have examined the African origin of New World folktales. In his preface to *Afro-American Folktales: Stories from Black Traditions in the New World* (1985), Abrahams argues that the tale-telling traditions of blacks in the New World came "directly or indirectly, from the places where the slaves' ancestors lived in the sub-Saharan area of the Old World. The major evidence for this is the relative consistency of the repertoire wherever Africans found themselves transported in the New World" (xix-xx).

Likewise, Bascom surveyed American and Caribbean folktales written before 1978 in search of tale types that originated from Africa. In *African Folktales in the New World*, Bascom found twenty-three African tale types such as "The Talking Animal Refuses to Talk" (found in Nigeria, Michigan, Arkansas, Texas, Mississippi, Alabama, and North Carolina) (29–30), and "Dogs Rescue Master in Tree Refuge" (discovered in Senegal, Ivory Coast, Mali, New England, Kentucky, the Bahamas, Jamaica, Haiti, and other areas) (156–95).[14] In a similar vein, May Augusta Klipple's *African Folktales with Foreign Analogues* contains African parallels of Western tales. In the book, Klipple says that the analogues she has collected "are limited to those found in Europe and Asia" and that her African versions come from societies living south of the Sahara desert (xxxviii). Both Klipple and Bascom give us pertinent examples of African tales to which I will refer as parallels of specific black diasporan tales.

Like the above works, Levine's *Black Culture and Black Consciousness* suggests the African origin of New World folklore. Discussing the African roots of tricksters in African American tales, Levine argues that it is in the animal trickster "that the most easily perceivable correspondence in form and usage between African and Afro-American tales can be found. In both cases the primary trickster figures of animal tales were weak, relatively powerless creatures who attain their ends through the application of native wit and guile rather than power or authority" (103). According to Levine, the African trickster figures that slaves preserved in their cultures include: "The Hare or Rabbit in East Africa, Angola, and parts of Nigeria; the Tortoise among the Yoruba, Ibo, and Edo peoples of Nigeria; the Spider throughout much of West Africa including Ghana, Liberia, and Sierra Leone; Brer Rabbit in the United States" (103).

Furthermore, Levine examines the factors that may have contributed to the retention of the African tales in the New World. He writes: "Comparison of slave tales with those guides to African tales that do exist reveals that a significant number were brought directly from Africa; a roughly similar percentage were tales common in both Africa and Europe, so that, while slaves may have brought the tale type with them, its place in their lore could well have been reinforced by their contact with whites" (82). In this sense, the numerous folktales discussed in this study could have parallels in European American folktales, which I would like to examine in a future research project.

It would be unfair not to acknowledge seminal works of black folklore such as John H. Johnson's "Folk-lore from Antigua, British West Indies" (1921), Elsie C. Parson's "Bermuda Folklore" (1925) and *Folk-lore of the Antilles, French and English* (1933), Zora Neale Hurston's *Mules and Men* (1935), Robert S. Rattray's *Akan-Ashanti Folk-Tales* (1930), Emil A. Magel's *Hare and Hyena: Symbols of Honor and Shame in the Oral Narratives of the Wolof of Senegambia* (1977) and *Folktales from the Gambia: Wolof Fictional Narratives* (1984), Léopold S. Senghor and Abdoulaye Sadji's *La Belle Histoire de Leuk-le-Lièvre* (1953), Birago Diop's *Les Nouveaux Contes D'Amadou Kumba* (1964), Helen L. Flowers's *A Classification of the Folktale of the West Indies by Types and Motifs* (1980), and David P. Gamble's *Wolof Stories from Senegambia Mainly From Old Published Sources* (1987). These works are priceless collections of black folktales that allow us to find African analogues of New World legends. Drawing from this wealth of black oral tradition, I have attempted to make a modest contribution to the "full-fledged history of African folktale research" that Alan Dundes describes in his introduction to Bascom's *African Folktales in the New World* as one of the major challenges of folklore studies (x).

Drawing from all the above perspectives, I analyze the strong influence of African cultures and Pan-Africanist spirit of resistance on the writings of Wheatley, Cugoano, Equiano, Gilbert, Thwaites, and Prince. In an attempt to reinscribe Africa in the study of black Atlantic literature, I will preface each section with a review of relevant scholarship and a brief summary of the historical context in which the writers lived in Africa or in the New World. This interweaving of history and literary analysis intends to show the Pan-African dimensions of these authors' works.

In the first chapter, I provide the historical contexts in which Wheatley was brought from West Africa to Boston, Massachusetts. In addition, I examine the ways in which Wheatley utilized her memory of Africa as a means for overcoming the experiences she faced as a slave and, later, as the first black woman poet of the United States. I trace Wheatley's origins in Senegambia and examine the strong influence of Senegambian Wolof folktales and specific African worldviews on her poetry and correspondences. Wheatley drew upon African oral narratives, worldviews, and figures of speech that seem to resonate with certain key ideas and rhetorics of Puritanism. The purpose of this comparison of Puritan and Wolof Islamic cosmogonies is not to force African values on African American literature but to give specific African theological and cultural contexts to the writings of Wheatley, which have so far been examined only in their Christian and Western contexts.

In the second chapter, I explore the foundational role that Cugoano played as one of the first writers in England of African descent. Tracing Cugoano's origins in Fantiland, in current Ghana, I provide a detailed analysis of the experiences Cugoano faced from the time he was captured in Africa to the time he became renowned as a black writer in England and an ardent fighter for abolition of slavery. As in the previous chapter, I show the strong influence of African folklore, cultures, and traditional religions on Cugoano's identity and writings. Cugoano's status as a leading Pan-Africanist is explored in detail. Also, I compare many African folktales with Cugoano's narrative.

In the third chapter, I trace Equiano's journey from his village of Essaka in Igboland to the New World, paying attention to his blend of African, Christian, and Judaic views about culture. I also compare numerous Igbo folktales with Equiano's narrative to show that Africa played a major part in Equiano's background. And I show the prominent roles that Equiano played in the Pan-Africanist intellectual tradition.

In the fourth chapter, I explore the specific African cultures and folklore that influenced the writings of Caribbean women authors such as Elizabeth Hart Thwaites and Anne Hart Gilbert, who were contemporaries of Prince. Discussing the folklore that influenced Antigua, where the Hart Sisters came from, I examine how these early women writers resisted racial, economic, and social oppression in the Caribbean in manners that are identical to the ways in which trickster figures in African and Caribbean folktales subvert similar forms of domination.

In the fifth chapter, I analyze Prince's narrative in the historical context of British colonization in the Caribbean and the transformations in Britain's attitudes towards slavery that led Prince to obtain her freedom in England. Placing a strong emphasis on Prince's struggles during her enslavement in Bermuda and Antigua, this chapter shows the ways in which African traditions allowed Prince to resist slavery, sexism, and other limitations that black women faced during the early nineteenth century. As in the previous chapters, this section compares Prince's narrative with African and Caribbean folktales.

CHAPTER ONE

African and Puritan Dimensions of Phillis Wheatley's Poems and Letters

Through her poems and letters, Wheatley identifies with Africa in complex and ambivalent terms that reflect her doubts and uncertainties about the continent. Yet her flawed, uncertain, and ambiguous relationship with Africa does not prevent her from using subtle Pan-African folklore and ideas as means of denouncing the oppressions Europeans perpetrated against Africans during the Atlantic slave trade. In her criticism of slavery, Wheatley uses verbal and ideological tactics that evolved from the resistance strategies that trickster figures from both African and African American folktales employ in order to liberate themselves from domination and achieve equality. By comparing Senegambian Wolof folktales, praise poetry, and satire with Wheatley's poems and letters and other African American narratives drawn from slave culture, I suggest in this chapter the subtle ways in which Wheatley used Pan-African resistance strategies in order to weaken her ambivalence about Africa, affirm her connections with Africans, and denounce European oppression of blacks. I also suggest the ways in which Wheatley used the resilience and adaptability of the trickster icons of African and African American folktales as means of establishing intimate relationships with a selected group of blacks and whites in colonial New England and developing salient Pan-African, Puritan, and abolitionist rhetorics against slavery.

In *The Black Aesthetic Unbound: Theorizing the Dilemma of Eighteenth-Century African American Literature* (2008), April C. E. Langley writes: "Through Wheatley's use of Afro-British American ways—grounded in culturally specific African knowledge—she is able to travel through and unpack thousands of years of African women's history within an African frame of reference . . . Wheatley's recovery of Africa is exemplified in the tradition of the Sankofa-Bird, or bird of passage, which constantly moves forward to the future even as it continually looks behind to its past" (59). As Langley suggests, one method of studying Wheatley's recovery of Africa is to compare African American rhetorical devices, such as "speaking in tongues" and "signifying," with the West African Wolof poetics of *taasu* (66). Lisa McKnee's "The Black and the White: Race and Oral Poetry in Mauritania" (2001) defines "*taasu*" as a Senegalese Wolof form of poetry "to be performed among women at festivities or in private" as a means of parodying people in erotic and indirect ways (131–32), questioning simple binary models (127), and (in the case of its Mauritanian rhetorical version called *tebra' e*) attempting to "break the conspiracy of silence in a male-oriented morality" (132). According to McKnee, the poetics of *taasu* "mark the subject positions of an individual agent, but provide a discursive space of negotiating relationships between participants at these events during and through the exchange of gifts" (*Selfish Gifts*, 47–48).

Expanding McKnee's theorizing of *taasu*, Langley interprets this oral tradition as a West African "way of knowing that provides the foundational grounding" for "Senegalese poetics" (48). Langley's concept of "Senegalese poetics" broadly refers to "forms of writing, formalized interpretations of literature, and cultural interventions that privilege a synthesis of culturally specific African ways of knowing such as *taasu* and alongside a more generalized (but equally rich) composite of Afro-/Afra-Western ways of knowing" (49). Using similar theories, I will examine the Pan-African, Puritan, and abolitionist elements in Wheatley's poems and letters.

Constructing a coherent biography of Phillis Wheatley is problematic because certain key experiences such as the events that led to her enslavement from the Senegambian coast of Africa and the predicaments that she faced as a child during the Middle Passage remain unknown. Another difficulty in tracing the early details of her life is the lack of information regarding the interactions that she had in her early career with her white critics. In *The Trials of Phillis Wheatley: America's First Black Poet and Her Encounters with the Founding Fathers* (2003), Henry Louis Gates Jr. writes: "We have no transcript of the exchanges that occurred between Miss Wheatley and her eighteen examiners" (29). The only document available is the "Letter of Attestation," which serves as prefatory matter in her 1773 *Poems*.

In *Memoir and Poems of Phillis Wheatley: A Native of Africa and a Slave* (1834), Margarita Matilda Odell argues that Wheatley did not "seem to have preserved any remembrance of the place of her nativity, or of her parents, excepting the simple circumstance that her mother *poured water before the sun at his rising*—in reference, no doubt, to an ancient African custom" (30). Odell's description of the mother's pouring of water before the sun as a "simple circumstance" ignores the deeper significance of a practice that, as Katherine

Clay Bassard suggests in *Spiritual Interrogations: Culture, Gender, and Community in Early African American Women's Writing* (1999), could be part of "ritual libations for the ancestors" (34). Pouring water in the direction of the rising sun is the first thing that elderly Senegambian women do in the morning at the door of their house before talking to anyone in anticipation of a good day. This Senegambian tradition of pouring water on the ground is consistent with other West African practice of decanting water, milk, or wine on the earth as liquid offering to the spirits.[1] These rituals are antecedents to the practice of libation in African American religious ceremonies.[2]

On the other hand, the African idea of worshipping the sun that Wheatley remembered is consistent with a representation of sunrise in African American and Senegambian cultures. This connection is visible in the Wolof-derived concept of "day clean" that Lorenzo D. Turner found in the dialect of the Gullah people of the United States. In *Africanisms in the Gullah Dialect* (1949), Turner argues that the Gullah expression "*de klin* 'dawn,' i.e., 'day clean,'" is "a translation of the Wolof expression *bər bu sɛt* 'dawn,' lit. 'the day clean'" (232). Both the Wolof and African American expressions for "dawn" represent sunrise as a time of hope and rebirth, which are suggested in the sun worship ritual of Wheatley's mother.

Furthermore, Odell's representation of Wheatley's remembrance of the sun ritual as a simple memory reflects her denial of Wheatley's connection with Africa, which has unfortunately affected much of the scholarship on Wheatley. As Bassard argues, Odell's "portrait of Wheatley's near-amnesia about her African past has since become cliché, used by scholars to prove everything from the wretchedness of enslavement to the much-held view of the total 'whitewashing' of Wheatley, resulting, the theory goes, in a body of poetry with no racial consciousness" (34). The denial of Wheatley's intimacy with Africa and her racial consciousness is also evident in the opinions of Barbara Christian and Amiri Baraka about the early black writer. For example, in *Black Feminist Criticism: Perspectives on Black Women Writers* (1985), Christian claims that Wheatley's poetry "reflects little of her identity either as a black or a woman, except in a few of her poems where she attempted to justify slavery, since through it, many Africans were introduced to Christianity" (120). Christian's argument echoes sentiments that Baraka expresses in "The Revolutionary Tradition in Afro-American Literature" (1999): he says that "Ms. Wheatley writing in the eighteenth century is simply an imitator of Alexander Pope" and accuses her for "evincing gratitude at slavery" (333). Christian's and Baraka's arguments overlook how Wheatley fought for the freedom of blacks within liminal spaces where she had to assume multiple identities, which included

Christianity, interracial alliance, and African womanism. As Nah Dove argues in "African Womanism: An Afrocentric Theory" (1998), the concept of African womanism urges critics to study the experiences of black women living in Europeanized societies within African paradigms (515).[3] This African-centered feminism emphasizes the bonding between black women who resist similar race, class, and gender-based oppressions.

In her poetry, Wheatley developed her own form of black womanism by using the verbal skills of the African *griottes* and tricksters in order to negotiate her freedom within an eighteenth-century New England culture in which Puritanism and Methodism were predominant.[4] *Griotte* is the female equivalent of the word *griot*, which is a term for traditional African historian, lyricist, storyteller, diviner, advisor, and healer. As Thomas A. Hale argues in *Griots and Griottes: Masters of the Word* (1998), the functions that *griots* and *griottes* carry out in Africa include praise-singing; advising; diplomacy; performing instrumental music; and creating poetry, songs, tales, epics, and other verbal and nonverbal art forms (18). According to Hale, since the beginning of the Harlem Renaissance, African Americans have adopted the concept of *griots* "as a sign of respect for those who know about the past, are artists in various media, or are simply high achievers" (4). By identifying Wheatley as a *griotte*, I want to suggest the major role that this pioneer black writer from Senegal had in a Pan-African literature that praised Puritan and Methodist Christianity and American patriotism in order to achieve freedom for the enslaved Africans.

In her poetry, Wheatley displayed her status as a Christian and a unique and unmatched sense of religious fervor that was noticeable in her conversion to Puritanism in 1771 in the Old South Meeting House of Boston.[5] Yet her Christianity was not a self-defeating, self-serving, or self-destructive act of worship. It was a genuine, yet calculated, strategy to create a Pan-African identity that allowed her to reconnect with both her African American and African roots. In order to uncover the hidden legacy of Phillis Wheatley, one should heed William H. Robinson's optimistic statement in *Phillis Wheatley in the Black American Beginnings* (1975) that "exhaustive research and textual analysis will one day reveal Phillis Wheatley to have been a cleverly disguised, badly misunderstood, militantly assertive Black woman" (30).

Discussing the Christian influence in her work, Samuel J. Rogal, in "Phillis Wheatley's Methodist Connection" (1987), argues that while Wheatley's visitations to England, her discussions with the Countess of Huntingdon, and her correspondences with Voltaire are common knowledge, little is known about "her loose ties to British Methodism and the recognition by certain

British Methodists (as well as by those friendly towards this religious organization) of her skill as a serious poet" (85). Though Wheatley's relations with England and Voltaire are common knowledge, those she had with Africa are not. While there have been extant studies about Wheatley's life, religious beliefs, and social connections, they have not been African-centered, since they do not show how Wheatley's networking through letters, poems, and other forms of communications in the Atlantic world were Pan-Africanist. In other words, the extant studies about Wheatley do not show how her writings project a humane image of Africa and blacks that dismantles the yoke of slavery and misrepresentation. Yet, in spite of the scant data about her biography, Wheatley's relationships with Africa can be examined through analysis of her representations of the continent in her poems and letters. Speaking to this effect, James A. Rawley writes in "The World of Phillis Wheatley": "These letters add important details to our meager knowledge of Phillis, such as her relations with the major influence upon her life, Susanna Wheatley; her religious outlook; her attitude toward returning to her native Africa, as well as a negative clue to her African origin" (665).

Wheatley, the first African American to publish a book in English, was born along the Senegambian coast in or around 1753 and was brought to the United States as a slave when she was seven or eight years old.[6] In *The Trials of Phillis Wheatley*, Gates posits, "It's a fair guess that she [Wheatley] would have been a native Wolof speaker from the Senegambian coast" (17). Wheatley's Senegambian origin is also evident in John C. Shield's rationale that her high forehead and her small nose remind us of the elegant features of the Fulani people, who inhabited the Gambia-Senegal region in the eighteenth century ("Wheatley," 1251). Whichever ethnic group Wheatley came from, it is certain that she was a Senegambian. Wheatley arrived in Boston on July 11, 1761, on a schooner called the *Phillis*. Susanna Wheatley, the wife of a rich merchant from Boston, bought her that year. Thanks to her precocious mastery of the English language and of major biblical texts, Phillis Wheatley began to write poetry at an early age. At fourteen, she composed her first extant elegy, "On Messrs. Hussey and Coffin," which was published in December 1767 in Newport, Rhode Island.[7] In that same year, she also wrote a dirge that was put to press some three years later under the title, "A Poem by Phillis Wheatley, a Negro Girl, on the Death of Reverend Whitefield." At the age of seventeen, Wheatley was already a local celebrity in Boston. She was, however, subjected to the acerbic and racist scrutiny of eighteen white Boston dignitaries, who summoned her to the courthouse one day in the spring of 1772 to question the authenticity of her poems. Wheatley came out victorious from this examination with a document that attested to her ability to write literature. A passage of the Attestation from the dignitaries of Boston reads:

> We, whose names are under-written, do assure the World, that the Poems specified in the following page* were (as we verily believe) written by Phillis, a young Negro girl, who was but a few years since brought an uncultivated barbarian from Africa, and has ever since been, and now is, under the disadvantage of serving as a slave in a family in this Town. She has been examined by some of the best judges, and is thought qualified to write them. (*To The Public*, x)

As the attestation also suggests, the white dignitaries patronized Wheatley in depreciating and demonizing ways by representing her as a slave who was qualified to write literature while continuing to perceive her as "an uncultivated barbarian from Africa" (x). Such an ambiguous assessment reflects the white elite's racist and sexist bias toward Wheatley despite their depiction of her as a "Negro girl" who is "under the disadvantage of serving as a slave" (x).

Thanks to the support of Susanna Wheatley, Phillis Wheatley traveled to England in 1773, where thirty-eight of her verses were published under the title *Poems on Various Subjects, Religious and Moral*. The publication of *Poems* was a result of collaborations that Kirstin Wilcox describes as "the efforts of a white transatlantic circle of supporters who became adept at marketing Wheatley" (2). Moreover, as Wilcox argues, *Poems* was published in 1773 "with Archibald Bell in London, under the patronage of Selina Hastings, Countess of Huntingdon," who was a close friend of Susanna (3). The publication of *Poems* in 1773 was a pivotal moment in the history of African American literature. As Gates suggests in *The Trials of Phillis Wheatley*, *Poems* is "the first book of poetry published by a person of African descent in the English language, marking the beginning of an African-American literary tradition" (31). According to Benjamin Bussey Thatcher, in England, Wheatley was received by dignitaries such as her patron, Lady Huntingdon, and Lord Dartmouth and was on the point of meeting the young monarch George III when she decided to return to Boston so that "she might once more behold her beloved protégée [Susanna]" (25–26). The dignified welcome Wheatley received in England contrasted with the shameful manner in which she was treated in North America. Susanna Wheatley was a prime figure among Wheatley's supporters, since she allowed the African American poet to make the acquaintance of Reverend George Whitefield, the pioneer Methodist about whom Wheatley wrote in "A Poem by Phillis Wheatley, A Negro Girl, On the Death of Reverend Whitefield." As

Rawley suggests, Susanna knew Whitefield and often entertained his sympathizers, called "the connection," in her home (668).

Wheatley's last years were marked by a blend of happiness and sorrow. Sometime between September 13 and October 18, 1773, Susanna Wheatley freed her. Philipa Kafka writes in *The Great White Way* that, on April 1, 1778, she married John Peters, an African American man that she described in a letter to Obour Tanner, dated October 30, 1770, as being "clever," "complaisant," and "agreeable" (40).[8] Six months after she granted Wheatley her freedom, Susanna died on March 3, 1774.[9] Wheatley suffered much from Susanna's death since this decease ended the vital support that she used to receive from one of the distinguished women of Boston. In addition, Wheatley had frail health that was aggravated by the harsh, damp, climate of New England. One cold day on December 5, 1784, Wheatley, who had also become poor and traumatized by the death of two of her children, was found dead in a room with the body of her third child lying on her breast.[10] But there is more to Wheatley's story, such as her African roots and the intimate relations between her poems and the folktales of her Senegambian homeland.

A brief analysis of extant research on slavery in Senegambia helps us understand the history of the Wolof ethnic group from which Wheatley came. The history of the Wolof predates the Atlantic Slave Trade. The Wolof came to Senegambia prior to the tenth century A.D. from the eastern part of Africa and were part of ancient ethnic groups from the Nile valley who founded Egyptian civilization.[11] Between the end of the twelfth century and the beginning of the thirteenth century A.D., the Wolof founded their first empire under the leadership of a philosopher called Ndiadian N'Diaye.[12] In the next centuries, the Wolof developed good relationships with the northern inhabitants of Senegal they later called "Tukulër," following the Portuguese pronunciation of the Arabic word "Takrûr" as "Tucharor."[13] The contact between the Wolof and the Tukulër led to intense social, ethnic, and cultural mixing and exchange that reflected a major trend across the sub-Saharan region.[14] As a result of amalgamation between ethnic groups, the Wolof became a diverse entity that shared similar characteristics of language, caste system, and worldviews.[15] By the seventeenth and eighteenth centuries, the Wolof had a highly stratified society in which people were classified according to occupation and social position.[16] Between 1753 and 1755, the time during which Wheatley's enslavement in Senegambia occurred, many of the kingdoms in Senegambia were heavily impacted by the Atlantic slave trade. In *West African Slavery and Atlantic Commerce: The Senegal River Valley, 1700–1860* (1993), James Searing discusses a French slave trader's description of the enslavement of Wolof women from

Senegambia in 1752, which is a year before Wheatley was brought to America. Searing writes:

> "We hardly buy anything in the Senegal river except these blacks from the Wolof nations [*de nations yolofs*]; their women are highly valued in our colonies, where they are all employed as nannies [*nourrices*] or as servants. These negroes are very nimble, and hardworking, and have attractive features and are tall." Later, Pruneau noted that "Gorée yearly draws out 220 to 250 slaves from the kingdoms of Cayor, Baol, and Sin." More specific sale of slaves in this same period, but before the famine of 1753, indicated a relatively small-scale trade. (31)

This assertion clarifies the origins of the elegance, beauty, and diligence that Wheatley brought from her Wolof ancestry. Yet the passage also elucidates the historical context in which Wheatley would have been kidnapped and sold to Europeans. Thus, the year 1753, which is the time when Wheatley was enslaved, was a precarious one during which powerless Wolof families suffered from famine. They also suffered from insecurity and slave raiding, which prevailed in their territory as the result of the European incitement of slavery.[17]

Wheatley's relations to African and African American cultures can be ascertained through her intimacy with Obour Tanner, one of the persons who helped her stay in contact with her African past and her African American community. Obour Tanner's major role in Wheatley's relations with Africa is suggested in Shields's argument that this woman was "Wheatley's close black friend ('sister') and her possible cohabitor on the ship during the terrible Middle Passage from Africa to America" (*Collected Works*, 317). As Robin S. Doak points out, "Wheatley may have even visited Obour at her home in Newport, Rhode Island" (*Phillis Wheatley*, 24). This meeting between Wheatley and Obour occurred during the summer of 1770 in Newport, where their owners were on vacation.[18]

Both Obour and Wheatley would have known about African folktales from their memory of their homelands and their contacts with other Africans of New England. As Chiji Akoma argues in *Foklore in New World Black Fiction: Writing and the Oral Traditional Aesthetics* (2008), Africans brought in as slaves to work the plantations in the New World strove to maintain their religious and cultural bearings by relying on their memories of folk traditions in their various homelands and transforming them to usable and passable forms in the hostile Europeanized environment of the New World" (4). Wheatley was not isolated from these Africans, since, as William Robinson suggests, the former slave called John Peters whom she married on April 1, 1778, lived in Boston for most of his life and moved to the South after she died (*Black New England Letters*, 35, 38). John Peters was another intimate person who would have taught Wheatley about black folktales, since his complex personality mirrored the ambiguity, mobility, and independence of the tricksters in these legends. In her introduction to *The Poems of Phillis Wheatley* (1989), Julian D. Mason describes Peters as a man who "was free, thought well of himself, tried various occupations, often had financial difficulties, and remains an enigma" (10). These are the exact traits of African-derived folk heroes such as Brer Rabbit and Brer Lion that John Peters, Obour Tanner, and Phillis Wheatley would have known through their familiarity with slave culture.

Obour Tanner, John Peters, and Phillis Wheatley were in contact with African culture through the folklore that slaves developed in colonial New England. In *Black Yankees: The Development of an Afro-American Subculture in Eighteenth-Century New England* (1988), William D. Piersen shows the tremendous impact that African folklore from Senegambia had on the culture of colonial New England. Piersen writes: "Thomas Hazard, a great Yankee yarn-spinner in his own right, never forgot the 'splendid stories those old nigs, gathered from all quarters of Narragansett [for the Christmas holidays] used to tell me and the six little nigs and niggeresses.' Many a time he sat 'scrootched up' in the kitchen corner 'trembling all over with fear, listening to their stories of big lion, and giants, in Guinea'" (107). During the Atlantic slave trade, the word "Guinea" referred to the "Guinea Coast" which was a region that included the territories stretching from Senegambia to Cape Mount.[19] As Piersen argues, in eighteenth-century New England, "new slaves of African origin were only vaguely noted as 'from Guinea' or 'from the Gold Coast.' Slaves from the 'Windward Coast' and from the island of Goree off Senegal were also specifically mentioned in New England's advertisements" (6). The tales about big lions and scary giants that Thomas Hazard used to hear from old slave men and women were the kinds of African tales that Senegambians brought to eighteenth-century New England. These folktales might have come from Senegambia since a large number of slaves in the Americas came from this region. In *Transformations in Slavery: A History of Slavery in Africa* (2000), Paul E. Lovejoy shows that the Senegambian basin supplied most of the slaves who were transported into the Americas, averaging "less than 1,000 slaves per year early in the [eighteenth] century to highs of 5,000 per year in 1751–1780" (60). In a similar vein, Boubacar Barry argues in *Senegambia and the Atlantic Slave Trade* (1998) that from the fifteenth to the seventeenth century, the "Wolofs made up nearly 20 percent of slaves exported from Senegambia" into the Americas (40).

Moreover, Senegambia was the origin of a large part of the slave population in the United States between the early seventeenth century and the end of the eighteenth century. As Gwendolyn Midlo Hall suggests in *Africans in Colonial Louisiana: The Development of Afro-Creole Culture in the Eighteenth Century* (1992), "two-thirds of the slaves brought to Louisiana by the French slave trade came from Senegambia" (29). As Hall points out, Senegambia referred to the West African territories between the Senegal and the Gambia rivers and included people speaking languages such as Wolof, Sereer, Pulaar, and Malinke (29). The Senegambian presence in the Americas preceded the Atlantic slave trade, since, according to Diana Baird N'Diaye and Gorgui N'Diaye, Emperor Aboubacar II of thirteenth-century Mali "set out in the direction of the Americas from the West African coast with 2000 boats navigated by experienced sailors" (98). As the two authors suggest, "the impetus of the journey may have been similar to that of Portuguese-funded Columbus—the discovery of new trade routes and new trading partners" (98).

The Trans-Atlantic Slave Trade database estimates the total slave population brought from Senegambia to the Americas to be 243,503.[20] In *Black Yankees*, Piersen says that slaves from the island of Gorée located off Senegal were "specifically mentioned in New England's advertisements," because Gambia slaves were considered to be "much more robust and tractable than any other slaves from the coast of Guinea" and "more capable of undergoing the severity of the winter seasons in the North American colonies" (6). The New England slave-owners' preference for Senegambians led to the transplantation of strong Senegambian folklore in the colony. In *The Negro in Colonial New England* (1968), Lorenzo Johnston Greene gives two pertinent examples of this retention of Senegambian oral tradition in colonial New England: "Many Negroes amused themselves and gratified their listeners by regaling them with stories of Africa. Lucy Terry built up an enviable reputation as a raconteur and her home, following her marriage to a free Negro, is said to have become a favorite gathering place for young people who found pleasure in her stories. Most famous of all the Negro story tellers of the Narragansett section was Senegambia [,] whose brand of tales, which are said to have been reminiscent of Aesop, are still familiar to South Country residents" (248).

The West African influence in colonial New England is further evident in Piersen's argument in *Black Yankees* that Senegambia had a good memory of his African homeland. Piersen says: "Thus, Senegambia, an African-born slave, in North Kingston, Rhode Island, was known to brag that his own father, who he claimed was a Gambian king, was beautifully dressed in white man's clothes, given as some of the innumerable presents handed out to him by British slaving captains" (11). This story is doubly important. First, it reflects the economic relationship between Europeans and Africans on the Senegambian coastal region that led to the prosperity of a few Africans and the enslavement of many of them. Second, the anecdote reveals the cultural context from which the enslaved Africans came. As is apparent in Senegambia's praise of his father's elegance and wealth, these Africans brought into the Americas oral tradition, verbal eloquence, and noble deportment that derived from either the royal or *griot* classes of Africa. This linguistic and artistic heritage was the cultural wealth that allowed slaves in New England to construct their real or imagined memory of Africa in the West.

The kinds of stories that Senegambia and other Africans told in New England would have allowed Wheatley and other African Americans of her generation to survive the trauma of oppression. As Piersen argues in *Black Yankees*, in colonial New England, "Folk narratives joined folk songs as part of the moral armament of the slave population. In African fashion blacks used the tales for instruction of their own and their master's children, as well as relishing the stories for their entertainment value" (106). Another major African influence that Wheatley would have received from New England's slave culture would have been the African rhetorical strategies that survived in African American language. One example is the survival of African storytelling techniques on African American folk narratives. This African retention is noticeable in the tales in Zora Neale Hurston's book of folklore, *Mules and Men*, (1935) where the narrators use formulaic expressions to begin their stories. One example of opening formula is the canto that John French tells in the beginning of "How Jack Beat the Devil":

> Ah got to say a piece of litery [literary] fust to git mah wind on.
> Well Ah went up on dat meat-skin
> And Ah come down on dat bone
> And Ah grabbed dat piece of corn-bread
> And Ah made dat biscuit moan. (47)

In the stanza, John lets the audience know that he is a talented orator. In saying "Ah got to say a piece of litery [literary] fust to git mah wind on," John seeks to impress the listeners by showing off his verbal and poetic creativity. By describing how he took the meat-skin, bone, cornbread, and biscuit, John wants to awaken the audience and invite them to listen to his story. John's verbal play allows him to establish a good rapport with his listeners.

The opening device that John uses may have a parallel in African American oral performance. In *Talking and Testifying*, Geneva Smitherman argues that the African American rapper, comedian, and preacher may begin his/her performance by saying, "Y'all don't want to hear dat so I'm gone leave it lone!" to which the audience responds, "Naw, tell it, Reb! Tell it! Tell it!" (96). The automatic and improvised verbal exchange between the African American orator and his/her listeners allows the audience to participate actively in the oral performance. The African American verbal exchange is similar to the call-and-response pattern in Wolof storytelling. In *Folktales from the Gambia: Wolof Fictional Narratives* (1984), Emil Magel argues that the Wolof storyteller begins a narrative by saying, "*leb-on*" (there was a story) to which the audience responds by uttering, "*lup-on*," [our legs are crossed] (8). The formula "*leb-on*" helps the Wolof narrator to create a moment during which he can tell the audience the context in which the story took place. In this sense, "*leb on*" is the first step that the storyteller must take before beginning a narration. As Ayi Kwei Armah suggests in *The Healers* (1979), every African storyteller should be asked the following questions: "Did you remember to tell your listeners of what time, what age you rushed so fast to speak? Or did you leave the listener floundering in endless time, abandoned to suppose your story belonged to any confusing age? Is it a story of yesterday, or is it of last year? Is it of that marvelous black time before the desert was turned desert?" (2).

Moreover, the formula "*leb-on*" allows the speaker to spark the audience with normal volume and pitch, while "*lup-on*" helps the teller find out if the audience is ready to listen to the story and participate in its telling through exclamation, gesture, and facial expressions. As Magel suggests in *Folktales from the Gambia*, when a good rapport between speaker and listener is established, the narrator, then, utters the clause, "*Am-on a fi*" [it happened here] to which the audience responds by saying, "*da na am*" [it was so] (8). Yet every African community constructs their opening formula differently. Lilyan Kesteloot argues in *Contes et Mythes du Sénégal* (1972) that the Fulani of Niger begin a story by saying, "*taalol tal talde!*" [a story to tell!] (5). Similarly, Jan Knappert remarks in *Myth and Legends of the Congo* (1971) that the Alur people of Uganda initiate a tale by saying, "In the days of this story" (2) or "In the old days" (20). These opening formulas are different in length, syntax structure, and style. Yet they all suggest that the story occurred in the past. They all indicate the sense of anteriority that one notes in the classic English formula "Once upon a time."

Drawing from the above poetics of African folklore, I will examine Wheatley's relations with Africa and the ways in which she used her African background to gain freedom and achieve self-actualization in a colonial New England culture that had many affinities with her African heritage. In an attempt to understand how Wheatley conceptualized her cultural heritage and freedom, this chapter will first begin with an analysis of her relations to Africa. Wheatley discusses her relations to Africa in dualistic terms. The ambiguity in her relations with Africa is visible in how she expresses a desire both to reconnect with and to sever her relationships from Africa. On the one hand, she wanted to return to Africa, where she hoped to live with people she viewed as having rich cultures. On the other hand, she was reluctant to go to Africa because she regarded the continent as a land that reminded her of the brutal oppression of slavery. Consequently, as Phillipe Wamba argues, Wheatley often represents Africa in negative terms even when she continues to depict the continent in Ethiopianistic terms (84). In a letter to Sir John Thornton, a merchant of London, dated October 30, 1774, she declines an invitation to serve as a missionary in the village of the Anamoboe ethnic group of Ghana. In the letter, she says that she is happy to be free and ready to work as a "*servant of Christ*" (184). Yet in the letter, she raises a slight concern that belies her willingness to go to Africa. She writes:

> But why do you hond'd sir, wish those poor men so much trouble as to carry me so long a voyage? Upon my arrival, how like a Barbarian shou'd I look to the Natives; I can promise that my tongue shall be quiet/for a strong reason indeed/being an utter stranger to the language of Anamaboe. Now to be serious, this undertaking appears too hazardous, and not sufficiently Eligible, to go—and leave my British & American Friends. (184)

The expression "Now to be serious" is a teasing remark that indicates the facetious nature of Wheatley's earlier statements and the irony and duality in her representation of Africa. First, she perceives Africa as a distant place to which she was not ready to travel perhaps because she did not want to cause inconvenience to the black men who would have accompanied her there. As Rawley shows in "The World of Phillis Wheatley" (1772), these men were "Bristol Yamma and John Quamine, members of the Newport, Rhode Island congregation of the Reverend Samuel Hopkins, who had formulated a plan to colonize American Negroes" and return them to Africa as missionaries (674). Wheatley opposes this attempt to colonize American blacks to Africa by suggesting how she would have been expected by Sir Thornton to keep her tongue "quiet" (184). Wheatley's emphasis on this silence reveals her opposition to a colonization project that would have compelled her to remain oblivious to the harmful impact of imperialism on Africans. Her reference to how she would have been "an utter stranger to the language of Anamaboe" shows her fear of offending, not Africans, whose language she could not speak, but Sir Thornton, who has invited her to be a missionary in Africa.

Yet, the semblance of respect Wheatley seems to have for Africans belies her condescension for their culture. Wheatley's fear of being looked on as a "Barbarian" who is unfamiliar with the language of the Anamaboe suggests serious hesitancy in her desire to go to Africa. While she does not want to cast Africa out of her memory, Wheatley is periodically unwilling to go to a region where she feared being in contact with black peoples and cultures that would corrupt her Christianity. Thus, as Terrence Collins argues, Wheatley sometimes affirms "the very indictment she seeks to refute. That is, she does not [always] attempt to discredit the myth that the black man's color reflects a special moral inheritance from Cain the murderer" who was "marked by God in Genesis as a sign of his fratricide" (83). According to Collins, in believing this myth, Wheatley accepts a European representation of "African origins" as "an essentially corrupt moral nature specifically related to the mere fact of blackness" (83)

Wheatley's concern about the time and the distance that it would take her to travel to the village of the Anamaboe indicates her reluctance to go to Africa. Her fear of being severed from her "British & American Friends" by the journey to Africa indicates her attempt to conceal her unwillingness to go through this voyage. These ambiguous attitudes about Africa convey her unconsciousness about the equal effects that colonization of blacks on both sides of the Atlantic Ocean was going to have on her life. In "Phillis Wheatley's Vocation and the Paradox of the 'Afric Muse'" (1998), Paula Bennett asserts: "What she [Wheatley] could not know was that remaining in the colonies as a 'free' African woman would silence her anyway. Cut off from her British friends by the Revolution (and her commitment to it) and from the members of her white 'family,' who were dead or dispersed, Wheatley died in poverty in 1784, without having gathered sufficient subscribers to publish her second book" (73). In this sense, Wheatley did not know that her resistance against colonization would have been stronger if she had traveled to Africa. Had she gone to the land of the Anamaboe, she would have been able to expand her resistance against the oppression of blacks in colonial America which, as Paula Bennett suggests, she redeemed "by making it the source of her religious response to God and by making God, with whom she identifies both freedom and the sublime, the power that liberates her speech" (66).

Additionally, many of the poems in which Wheatley mentions Africa reflect hesitancy toward African peoples and cultures. One example is the poem

"On Being Brought from Africa to America" (1773) in which she represents Africans as "*Pagans*" who "May be refin'd," and made to "join th' angelic train" (18). She states:

> 'Twas mercy brought me from my *Pagan land*,
> Taught my benighted soul to understand
> That there's a God, that there's a *Saviour* too:
> Once I redemption neither sought nor knew.
> Some view our sable race with scornful eye,
> "Their colour is a diabolic die."
> Remember, *Christians*, *Negros*, black as *Cain*,
> May be refin'd, and join th' angelic train. (18)

This much-written-about poem reveals paradoxes in Wheatley's relations with Africa.[21] When she calls Africa her "*Pagan* land" with people who "May be refin'd, and join th' angelic train," she may be saying that the conditions of continental Africans could be improved by the same Christianity that allowed European Americans and African Americans to gain spiritual freedom. As Sondra O'Neale argues in "A Slave's Subtle War: Phillis Wheatley's Use of Biblical Myth and Symbol" (1986), Wheatley uses the image of the "angelic train" to symbolize "the purity that evangelicals assumed for themselves both in time and in eternity" (147). Wheatley wanted blacks to be given the same opportunity to enter this threshold of Christian purity to which whites aspired by faith. The way in which Wheatley uses the endearing possessive pronoun "my" to identify Africa as her "*Pagan land*" may indicate her nationalist and resolute attempt to claim Africa and appropriate the distorted images that Europeans created about the continent in order to correct them on her own. In this sense, Wheatley sought to create a new form of "black otherness" by accepting the African identity Europe rejected and transforming it into an identity that allows blacks to be liberated from European oppression and primitivistic representations of Africa.

Yet, there is a serious problem in Wheatley's representation of Africa in the poem, which is its repetition of European stereotypes about Africa. The Christianity that Wheatley praises is the Christianity that white missionaries brought to slaves in the United States and later wanted blacks of Africa to embrace unquestionably. While Christianity was a strong and legitimate spiritual resource and tool of resistance for Wheatley and many black populations, the missionaries that spread the Judeo-Christian tradition in Africa assumed that African traditional religions were "dark," "pagan," and "heathen."[22]

While she does not clearly express this bias, Wheatley somewhat conveys it in her depiction of Africa as a "*Pagan land*" and her idea that Africans will be "refin'd" by Christianity. This dimension contradicts the pride that Wheatley expresses when she describes herself as a descendant of a "sable race," revealing her unresolved double consciousness toward Africa. In *Kinship: A Family's Journey in Africa and America* (1999), Philippe Wamba analyzes this dilemma as follows: "For Wheatley, reconciling her historical ties to Africa with her adoptive American culture became an effort to transcend her African identity; she acknowledged the inferiority of her background, but reminded her readers that it was a circumstantial, not innate, condition and had not prevented her from finding religious salvation and rising in civilized American society, and would not prevent others like her from doing the same" (84). Wheatley's representation of her "inferiority" as being not "innate" shows that she considered herself as being a privileged individual who had been saved into civilization from savagery. Her perception of blacks as being inferior shows that she was heavily impacted by the Western misrepresentation of Africa as backward. As Jerome Klinkowitz suggests in "Early Writers," "It was the influence of New England Christian values rather than her own native disposition that made her seem to feel superior to her African heritage" (13).

Yet despite the pervasive influence of Western stereotypes on her poetry, Wheatley continued to identify herself as an African. In poems such as "Mæcenas," "Afric," and "Ethiop," she referred to herself as an African. In "Mæcenas," she writes:

> The happier *Terence* all the choir inspir'd,
> His soul replenish'd, and his bosom fir'd;
> But say, ye *Muses*, why this partial grace,
> To one alone of *Afric*'s sable race;
> From age to age transmitting thus his name
> With the first glory in the rolls of fame? (11)

Wheatley felt great admiration and pride in Terence's literary achievements, because she saw him as a Roman poet of African descent, who was able to use his oratorical skills in order to achieve his freedom and inspire the world.[23]

Wheatley's description of Terence as a product of "*Afric*'s sable race" attributes Terence's choiring abilities and "grace" to his African origins, thus letting it be known that she was proud of her African heritage and of the fact that both she and Terrence were poets of African descent who had demonstrated through their literary work an uncontested power of imagination and love for mankind. Her attempt to know why the *"Muses"* favored Terence alone, by giving him the glory that many poets of African descent want, shows that she perceived herself as one of the talented African artists. In "Phillis Wheatley and the Black American Revolution" (1993), Betsy Erkkila asserts: "Self-consciously placing herself and her poems within a specifically African tradition, Wheatley registers her own ambitious desire to share—or perhaps transcend—the 'first glory' of her African forbear in a poetics of ascent" (231–32).[24]

In other verses, Wheatley appropriates the African identity that she admires in Terence in order to promote her own poetic self. In "Hymn to Humanity. To S.P.G. Esq," she calls herself "Afric's muse," who honors her friends and works to move their "tender human heart" (97). In a similar vein, Wheatley identifies herself as "Afric's damsel" in a broadside on the evangelist Reverend George Whitfield, in which she asks, "Shall [Whitefield's] due praises be so loudly sung / By a young Afric damsel[']s virgin tongue? / And I be silent!"[25] The literary scholar Gay Gibson Cima interprets Wheatley's identification of herself as "Afric's damsel" as a representation that shows that "she was a proud 'Africana [woman]' who demanded the acknowledgement of her talents" and the education and freedom of enslaved blacks in colonial America ("Black and Unmarked," 483). In this sense, Wheatley's recognition of her African background was an ideological instrument that empowered her to resist European domination of blacks. A similar use of African origins as a tool of liberation from racial oppression is apparent in Wheatley's act of calling herself "*Afric's* muse," which attests to her desire to draw on her African background as a means of opposing slavery and appreciating her racial identity. In *The Heath Anthology of American Literature* (1990), William H. Robinson and Phillip M. Richards describe her representation of herself as "Afric's muse" as an expression of her "racial self-consciousness" (1060).

Yet, given the elusive nature of Wheatley's rhetoric, one continues to wonder if her imagery of "*Afric's* muse" and "*Afric's* damsel" derived from a genuine sense of African consciousness or from a strategy of deception. As Houston Baker contends in *The Journey Back*, "One pauses to ask if her reference to nationality was calculated merely to win added admiration from or to shock a white public that sometimes argued that the human heartbeat is not a property of the black world, or whether it is actually an indication of an extended African consciousness" (11). There are instances in which Wheatley's identification with Africa seems to be sincere. One example occurs in the poem "To the University of Cambridge" in which she expresses a strong desire to be seen as a woman of *Ethiop* [Africa]. She views herself as "An *Ethiop*" whose mission is to tell Americans that slavery or "the sable monster," which prevails in the "sable land," is the greatest sin of all (196–97).

Wheatley's reference to herself as "An *Ethiop*" conveys her desire to be regarded as an African who emphasizes her blackness to denounce the barbaric institution that oppressed blacks of both sides of the Atlantic Ocean. Her self-depiction as an "Ethiop" deserves recognition, even if it might have been driven by her attempt to differentiate herself from Europeans and making it seem that she, the African, could write good poetry. Even if a strategic quest for literary notoriety and fame may have led Wheatley to represent herself as "*Ethiop*" or "*Afric*," the simple fact that she called herself an African registers a strong degree of black racial consciousness and African identity.

Ultimately, the question as to whether Wheatley viewed herself as an African or not does not undermine the fact that she drew from the African rhetorical strategies to develop subversive ways of fighting against slavery. She garners the support she received from her adoptive parents in Boston to resist slavery and its exploitation of Africans. She combines Puritan and African religious worldviews while using a poetic language that mirrors the cosmology and verbal strategies that one finds in Wolof society and folklore. For instance, in certain letters she wrote to her benefactors, Wheatley reflects a hybrid-like influence of Calvinistic Methodism, Puritan faith, and Senegambian religious traditions. In her letter "To the Rt. Hon'ble the Countess of Huntingdon," written in Boston on October 25, 1770, she expresses her sympathies to the Countess on the passing of Reverend Whitefield, while interspersing comments about her African identity. She represents herself as an "untutor'd African" whose poetry cannot suffice to depict the fascinating qualities of Reverend Whitefield, who is "this Citizen of Zion!" (162).

Within this letter, Wheatley infuses into her Calvinistic religion poetics elements that derive from both European and African cultures. Her representation of Reverend Whitefield as a "worthy chaplain" (162) whose passing is a "Greater gain" (162) for himself reflects a worldview that some whites and blacks in America shared. This "Greater gain" signals that the death of a saint is a blessing in disguise, because it emanates from divine will, which brings peace to both the deceased and the living while simultaneously maintaining harmonious relationships between the two parties. This Puritan concept of death is evident in Wheatley's Calvinist representation of the Countess as a person whose actions of kindness, faith, and fairness mirror those of the Divine Benefactor (God) that the Reverend has rejoined in heaven. This ideology about death is also consistent with the African conception of life and death as two related parts of a cycle that join the living and the deceased eternally through continual worship. Commenting on the theme of death in Wheatley's poetry, Shields writes in "Phillis Wheatley's Struggle for Freedom" (1988):

> Expectedly, her elegies resemble the Puritan funeral elegy. This poetic form contains first a portrait or biography of the deceased, whose life is divided into three stages: vocation or conversion, sanctification or evidence of good works, and glorification or treatment of the deceased's joyous reception into heavenly reward. The second section of the Puritan funeral elegy, called exhortation, urges the living to put off mourning and to concentrate on earning for themselves a reward similar to that of the deceased. (246)

Many elements of the Puritan funeral elegy are similar to those found in the Senegambian Islamic and Wolof funeral elegies in which, upon news of the deceased person, the community gathers to perform three major rites: testify to the good deeds and the moral character of the individual before the burial; mourn the individual for only a limited length of time, usually during the first hours or days after the passing; and, finally, urge the family and friends of the deceased who are most affected by the death to please the departed by ceasing to cry and demonstrating in their lifetime that they will perform good and noble deeds that will please the individual who has passed into heaven. The representation of heaven in Senegambian-Islamic worldview as a place of tranquility is evident in Lucie Gallistel Colvin's article, "Islam and the State of Kajoor: A Case of Successful Resistance to Jihad" (1974), in which the author discusses how, in the 1770s, the Almamy [Head Cleric] Abdul Kadir of the Empire of Futa Toro, in northern Senegal, attempted to convert many inhabitants from the Empire of Waalo and Jolof, in northwest and central Senegal, into the Islamic faith through both force and persuasion (599–600). According to Colvin, "The Almamy issued the call to jihād, bringing in men, women, and children, old, lame, and blind, each anxious to secure his place in heaven through this religious military service" (601).

By the end of the eighteenth and the beginning of the nineteenth centuries, many of the slaves that were brought from Senegambia into the United States were Muslims who shared these values. As Sylviane Diouf points out in *Servants of Allah: African Muslims Enslaved in the Americas* (1998), during both the eighteenth and nineteenth centuries numerous Islamic religious teachers, leaders, students, judges, and memorizers of the Koran shared an Islamic cleric-warrior tradition in which those who were killed in war "rejoice in the Bounty Provided by Allah [God]" (31). According to Diouf, the Muslim clerics were "among the captives from Senegambia and Guinea who were sent to America" as slaves (31). This assertion attests to the religious essentialism that Senegambians carried with them into the New World. These Muslims shared an essentialist representation of heaven as a place of eternal reward and quiescence. Yet this absolutist belief in heaven was not particular to the African Muslims since it was also prevalent in Judeo-Christian worldviews. For instance, the belief in the sanctity of heaven was evident in the orthodox terms in which Puritans and Protestants represented the New World as God's heavenly province on earth. As Sacvan Bercovitch points out in *The Puritan Origins of the American Self* (1975), John Winthrop viewed New Englanders as "Israelites" whom God preserved "with water from the rock and manna from heaven" (38). According to Bercovitch, Roger Williams and other forthcoming Protestants appropriated the early Puritan vision of the New England colony as God's paradise on earth in order to represent their own settlements as terrestrial extensions of heaven (137–38). Jonathan Edwards, an eighteenth-century Puritan from Connecticut, perceived New England in similar ways. In "Learning the Language of God: Jonathan Edwards and the Typology of Nature" (1991), Janice Knight writes: "Edwards drew an analogy between God's providence and 'a large and long river, having innumerable branches beginning in different regions, and at a great distance one from another, and all conspiring to one common issue.' Just as all dispensations of providence and all historical prefigurations flow from God as source or fountain, so they converge in Christ, who is the living water. The cycle is completed both in nature and in history with the passage to the 'great ocean'" (538). Knight's rationale reflects a Judeo-Christian image of heaven as a well of life and happiness that resonates with the Senegambian Islamic representation of paradise as a fount of existence and pleasure.

Though David P. Gamble describes the mourning period in Wolof Senegambian society as lasting for months, in *The Wolof of Senegambia* (1967), the author skillfully identifies the following elements of Wolof funeral traditions that are consistent with the patterns of Puritan elegy. These aspects include the announcement of the deceased's name, the testimony of relatives and friends on what they know about the departed, and a mourning period that can last four months (69). The elements of Wolof mourning traditions seem quite similar to their equivalents in the Puritan elegy in Wheatley's writings. Both customs attach a primary importance to public witnessing and testimony of the deeds that the departed performed during their lifetime. Also, both traditions attach a major significance to the spoken word as a means for strengthening the faith and the wisdom of a community in the process of mourning the deceased. In this sense, as Mary McAleer Balkun argues, Wheatley was working within a Puritan tradition that privileged the linguistic aspect of the redemption experience or "the power of words" ("Phillis Wheatley's Construction of Otherness," 124). This linguistic aspect is African as well, since African societies and their descendants in the Americas value what they call "*Nommo*," or "the power of words" as a fundamental element of their rhetorics. In "Paradigm for Classical African Orature" (1991), Adetokumbo F. Knowles-Borishade points out: "In African orature, the Word (*Nommo*) gains in power and effectiveness in direct proportion with the moral character, strength and commitment, and vision of the Caller (the person who initiates the speech ritual) as well as the skills s/he exhibits. This requires what Thompson calls a 'double admonition of arts and goodness'" (490). This African valuation of the power of words to convey a double voice and a morality is retained in African American culture, in which, as Barbara J. Marshall argues in "Kitchen Table Talk," "the power of the word" is a "generative power" which is "African in both a historical and spiritual context" (94).

Wheatley uses *Nommo* to bless the memory of her deceased benefactors while implicitly trying to influence those who were alive to help her in the ways the former did. In the letter she wrote to Obour Tanner of Newport on March 21, 1774, Wheatley thanks Susanna for adopting her when she was "a poor little outcast & a stranger" and treating her "more like her child than her servant" (178). Revealing her respect for commitment, knowledge, and faith, Wheatley shows appreciation for the invaluable teachings she received from Susanna's dedication to alleviate the sorrows of the outcast and fortify "the upper courts of the Lord" (178). Within this correspondence, Wheatley intertwines Puritan and African religious beliefs and poetics by making a public testimony about the departed while praying for the sanctification of the living. The letter also shows Wheatley's capacity to use *Nommo* to express a dual innuendo that is parallel to the double voice Gates identifies as the Signifyin(g) device in African American literature (*Signifying Monkey*, 81). Wheatley uses this double voice to persuade her reader indirectly. When she praises Susanna for having adopted her when she was "poor little outcast & a stranger," Wheatley testifies the moral worth of this benefactor while encouraging citizens of Boston to learn from Susanna's tenderness and engagement in the betterment of the life of an orphan black girl.

Wheatley's representation of Susanna as a savior resonates with the way in which the Wolof *griots* praise the deceased people who had helped them during their lifetime. These kinds of Wolof praises are songs and poems known as *tagg*. In "Mariama Bâ" (1998), Siga Fatima Jagne defines *tagg* as the "poetic act" of the Wolof *griots*, goldsmiths, and *laobes* (timbermen) "of extolling virtues" from a person "with their honeyed language" (64–65) and is shared "in public" or broadcast over the radio to make the person "feel important and accepted in 'high society'" (65). As Jagne points out, *tagg* "operates as a way to show thanks and appreciation, to goad one to release money, to praise one's ancestry, and to ensure that things move smoothly at public functions" (65). This form of praise poetry that Kenneth W. Harrow describes in *Faces of Islam in African Literature* (1991) as a form of "praise poem/song which is pre-islamic" (165) is one of the elements that African slaves brought to the Americas.

Yet the Wolof do not praise people during happy occasions only since their traditional historians also eulogize individuals who have passed away. One example of this kind of Wolof praise poetry is apparent in Tijan M. Sallah's book *Wolof* (1996). Sallah cites the poem as follows:

> Samba Njai was so good,
> The man with the three hearts.
> When Samba Njai died,
> Even the Europeans mourned. (44)

According to Sallah this *taga* is entitled "Samba Njai Ya Bakhone" [Samba Njai was a good person] and is "a praise poem for a dead person" (44). Moreover, Sallah says that the poem "employs flattery and exaggeration to praise a person who has rendered noble service to the society" (44). This poem is similar to Wheatley's tribute for Susanna. Like the Wolof narrator, Wheatley stresses the unique goodness of a person independently of their race. Wheatley describes Susanna as a parent and a devout Christian that people of all races should remember. In a similar vein, Wheatley mourns, in "To His Honour the Lieutenant-Governor, on the Death of his Lady" (March 23, 1773), the loss of a departed friend's wife and calls herself "the *Afric* muse" who brings "heav'nly tidings" to a grieving husband. In order to bring solace to the bereaved husband, Wheatley assures that his wife is waiting in paradise. Wheatley tells the husband:

> There sits, illustrious Sir, thy beauteous spouse;
> A gem-blaz'd circle beaming on her brows.
> Hail'd with acclaim among the heav'nly choirs,
> Her soul new-kindling with seraphic fires,
> To notes divine she tunes the vocal strings,
> While heav'n's high concave with the music rings.
> *Virtue*'s rewards can mortal pencil paint?

> No—all descriptive arts, and eloquence are faint;
> Nor canst thou, *Oliver*, assent refuse
> To heav'nly tidings from the *Afric* muse. (117)

The way in which Wheatley describes *Oliver*'s deceased wife as a spirit that is being welcome in heaven with music and praise shows that she mastered the traditional African poet's art of actualizing the past in mythical, vivid, theatrical, and lifelike images. This device is similar to the narrative strategy that Anthony Graham-White describes in *The Drama of Black Africa* as the storyteller's impersonation of the character of the epic "as dramatically as possible" (27). Wheatley employs this type of impersonation as she adorns the prophetic role of an "*Afric* muse" whose status as emissary of deities allows her to crisscross the worlds of the living and the dead and bring the solace of music, artistry, and "heav'nly tidings" to a bereaved spouse. In this sense, Wheatley was an early African seer and *griotte* who mastered the African storyteller's art of narrating poignant accounts about life in a manner that captivates listeners. Discussing Wheatley's invocation of the power of the "*Afric* muse" in "Who Can Speak?" G. Michelle Collins-Sibley argues that Wheatley recognizes "values and principles that inform her own West African storytelling tradition. The obligation of the storyteller is not so much the invention of new and original tales as it is to retell stories in ways that make the truths they contain lively and pertinent to the audience. The test of the storyteller is to make the tale his or her own in a unique performance, dependent upon not only teller and tale but audience involvement as well" (n.p.).

Moreover, Wheatley's Pan-Africanism is apparent in her letter to Obour Tanner dated on March 21, 1774, which shows her intertwining of the Puritan and Wolof concept of upward mobility from disgrace to fame. In the letter, Wheatley writes:

> Her [Susanna's] exemplary life was a greater monitor than all her precepts and instruction; thus we may observe of how much greater force example is than instruction. To alleviate our sorrows we had the satisfaction to see her depart in inexpressible raptures, earnest longings, & impatient thirstings for the upper courts of the Lord. Do, my dear friend, remember me & this family in your closet, that this afflicting dispensation may be sanctify'd to us. (177–78)

Wheatley acknowledges the priceless support Susanna gave her by empowering her to draw from the "force" of an "exemplary life," which is a "greater monitor" than all "precepts and instruction[s]," as a source of behaviorial and spiritual resilience that can bless, guide, and help to liberate enslaved Africans from slavery. Earlier in this letter, Wheatley says, "I presently became a sharer in her most tender affections. I was treated by her more like her child than her servant; no opportunity was left unimproved of giving me the best of advice; but in terms how tender! how engaging! This I hope ever to keep in remembrance" (178). By recognizing the affection, care, and opportunities (such as religious education and patronage) that she received from Susanna, Wheatley shows how her benefactor's backing can enable her to rise from humble beginnings to success, conveying the Puritan's valuation of humility and spirituality as means for rising above humiliation. In *God's Caress: The Psychology of Puritan Religious Experience* (1986), Charles Lloyd-Cohen discusses how Puritans transmuted humiliation into a catalyst for power and survival through "a potent fusion of humility and strength, the grace of love transfigured into iron willfulness" (274).

One finds a similar transmutation of humiliation into power in Senegambian oral narratives. For instance, like Wheatley, the character of Kumba in the Wolof tale, "Kumba the Orphan Girl," suggests the power to transform disgrace into success. In the tale that appears in Emil Magel's *Folktales from the Gambia*, a young Wolof woman named Kumba is forced by her stepmother to go to the Sea of Denyal to wash a cup that has indelible stains (93). After long walks, unsuccessful attempts, and hunger, Kumba meets a woman whose children are lions, tigers, and hyenas (93). Kumba does whatever the woman asks of her, such as putting an old bone and a grain of rice in an empty pot and cooking. The next day, the woman gives Kumba three eggs and tells her to break them on her way home (93). When she breaks the eggs, a herd of cattle, a flock of goats and numerous servants begin to follow her. Kumba has remained free and victorious from that day on (92–93).

This story represents the human capacity to overcome the trauma of exile through the power of faith that attracted many New World slaves to Christianity. Referring to the biblical figure of Moses in the narratives of Harriet Tubman, Roberts writes: "The Life and deeds of Moses were the most reminiscent of those of African epic heroes: he was born under unusual circumstances, was exiled, and grew up away from his people, underwent great trials and tests, and acquired the spiritual knowledge and power to affect his community's destiny" (148). Roberts's quotation suggests the influence of Judeo-Christian mythology on the worldviews of African Americans for whom the truth, wisdom, and fulfillment of biblical stories of redemption from the agony of exodus are similar to those of African fables. As is apparent in the following comparison of

Wheatley's poetry and "Kumba the Orphan Girl," both African Americans and Africans use spirituality and solidarity as means to re-create a fragmented community and appease the agony of exile. Wheatley knew about Senegambian folktales since, as Michelle Collins-Sibley argues, "the practice of [West African] story telling and its associated ways of knowing framed and informed" her efforts "to survive the Middle Passage and beyond" (n.p.).

Moreover, the Senegalese tale represents an African conception of freedom as a status that comes from hard trials, resilience, and the ability to negotiate with strangers and show kindness to them. Like Wheatley, Kumba survives forced exile from her homeland and other hardships with a polite demeanor, a strong spirit of resilience, and a persistent belief in the possibility of divine intervention and social justice. Kumba has faith in a divine benefactor who is similar to the Calvinist God of Wheatley, and she receives wealth from God and the kindness of strangers. Kumba has material success that parallels the spiritual growth that Wheatley gained from her benefactors in America.

Furthermore, both Wheatley and Kumba achieve spiritual strength, freedom, and success thanks to the kindness of a stranger who adopts them as outcasts. Wheatley's former status as "a poor little outcast & a stranger" who was added to Susanna's family is similar to Kumba's early position as an outsider who was included into a woman's family of "lions, tigers, and hyenas." The elderly woman who rescues Koumba as one of the outcast members of her family is synonymous to Susanna, who felt a genuine desire to protect Wheatley from suffering. Susanna demonstrated this affection in the lifetime support and nurture she provided to Wheatley. The black poet extended this support to other Africans by developing a female solidarity that predated the Pan-Africanism that Levin describes in *Africanism and Authenticity* as a major feature of African American women's novels (7). By including "what is black and female" in Pan-African cultures (7), Levin gives new meaning to the word "Africanism," associating it with a theory of "Gendered Africanism," which is a study of the tradition of black women writers who appropriate the status of leaders and priestesses of African mothers in order to resist oppression. Levin states: "Often these magical qualities and heritages are particularly evident in female characters who are leaders, many of whom possess special skills for healing the spirit or body" (7). Like the black woman in the Senegambian tale, Wheatley participated in this "Gendered Africanism" since she used her poetry as a means to shield vulnerable blacks such as herself and Tanner, who were similar to Kumba in their forced exile from their homeland, from being victims of oppression.

Moreover, both Wheatley and Kumba exemplify humility toward the mother figures that nurture them so that they can turn an oceanic journey into an experience of glory, freedom, and recognition. Kumba's faith and the support of the old woman figure allow her to avoid being eaten by lions, tigers, and hyenas, in the same way Wheatley's religious conviction and network of female supporters allow her to achieve success and gain her freedom in America. Wheatley's primary mother figure was Susanna, who opened the doors of international success to her. In "The World of Phillis Wheatley" (1977), Rawley writes: "Susanna directly influenced the girl's religious life, and was responsible for the poet's dedication of her book to the Countess of Huntingdon, and Phillis' poems about Whitefield and the Earl of Dartmouth. It was Susanna who planned for the publications of the *Poems*, and in England enabled the poet to meet distinguished personages, and ultimately secured the slave's freedom" (668). Therefore, Susanna had an important role of mother figure in Wheatley's life that is analogous to the significant role of grandmother that the goddess character in the Senegambian tale has in Kumba's existence. Both personas are symbolic female parents of an orphan black girl to whom they provide vital emotional, spiritual, and material support. The resemblance between Wheatley and Kumba helps us understand the similarity between Wheatley and Obour Tanner, since the two African American women shared a common experience of forced exile from their homeland to the Western world that resonates with Koumba's compulsory alienation from her home to the sea of Denyal. Like Kumba, Wheatley and Obour Tanner used this brutal separation from their homeland as an urge to create a female community based upon companionship and unity.

The friendship and solidarity that Wheatley and Obour Tanner created out of their shared experience of the Middle Passage reflects a Pan-African philosophy known as the experiential communality of blacks. Communality refers to the collective history and identity between the members of a society. In "African Philosophy Foundations for Black Psychology" (1972), Wade W. Nobles defines the concept of "Communality" as "the sharing of a particular experience by a group of people" (15). Nobles uses the term "experiential communality" as a concept that "helps to determine how the people will be, and concurrently, what ethos, or set of guiding beliefs, a people will follow. These guiding beliefs, in turn, dictate the creation and adoption of the values and customs, which in the final analysis determine what social behavior a people will express in common—their cultural configuration" (15). One example of communality is evident in a Senegambian story entitled "The Donkeys of Jolof," in which the inhabitants of a village find out that a man who lives in their community is a donkey. The story occurs in the village of Bati Hai located in the Gambia, where a man called *Fari* has a wife and five children. As the narrator says, one day, a group of people from the Wolof kingdom of Jolof, in Senegal, comes to Bati Hai to look for this man (156). When the people arrive at Bati Hai, they go right to the middle of the village and begin to sing

> FARI, WHERE IS HE? WHERE IS HE? NAXE-NAXE, THE GOOD DONKEY IS LOST. FARI-MBAM, THE LOST DONKEY, FARI-MBAM. (156)

As the narrator says,

> After that *Fari* got up. He went to the center of his compound, then walked to his gate. He said to his wife, "I heard something confusing. Those are my relatives. When I hear their singing, my hair tingles from my head to my feet. But I won't go to see them yet." He went back to the compound. Soon the people began to sing . . . After he heard that, *Fari* went into the house of his wife and said, "It's alright, I'm going in Peace."
>
> He went and stood by the side of the ring and began to stamp his foot REK-REK-REK and a donkey's foot appeared. Then the crowd sang. (156)

According to the storyteller, the oldest child of Fari heard the drum calling and told his mother, "My father has turned into a donkey. Is he going away with his relatives?" (156). As the storyteller remarks, the mother said, "Yes, but if you go too, I will be very lonely in this empty house" (156). This tale reflects the kind of African solidarity that allowed the transplanted blacks to create Pan-African unity from similar experiences such as racial, physical, or economic isolations in dominant host cultures. This communality is evident in the affection and devotion that the inhabitants of Fari's village express to him. Fari's neighbors travel far to look for him, demonstrating their loyalty to a person they consider as both their leader and kin. The effort of Fari's people to bring their king back home and the kindness of strangers they receive as they search for the village of Bati Hai reflect the communality of Senegambian culture. This communality is analogous to the unity that Obour Tanner, Bristol Yamma, and John Quamine expressed toward one another by creating a subtle Pan-African community in colonial New England in an attempt to protect slaves in the diaspora and Africa from further oppression.

Obour Tanner was Wheatley's primary link to the Pan-African community in colonial New England. For instance, she helped Wheatley know two African freed slaves (Bristol Yamma and John Quamine) who wanted to go back to Africa to do missionary work. In "Samuel Hopkins and His Doctrine of Benevolence" (1935), Oliver Wendell Elsbree writes: "Quamine was the son of a wealthy African who sent him on a voyage to England to receive an education, but the person in charge of the boy politely sold him to a Newport slave-merchant. Both Quamine and Yamma had purchased their own freedom and had acquired an education through the assistance of friends. They came under the influence of [Samuel] Hopkins and wished to go to Africa as missionaries. Hopkins sent them to Princeton to study theology under Dr. Witherspoon for one year, but neither of them went to Africa because the Revolutionary War interrupted the labors of Stiles and Hopkins and prevented the raising of funds" (544). Elsbree's assertion suggests the communality that educated Africans in colonial New England such as Bristol Yamma and John Quamine showed in their desire to help Africa. As Julian D. Mason indicates in *The Poems of Phillis Wheatley* (1989), Bristol Yamma and John Quamine "had been brought to Newport from Africa as Children" but "had retained their native language" (202). The black philanthropic inclination toward Africa and Bristol Yamma and John Quamine's retention of their African languages would have allowed New England blacks such as Wheatley to learn about and stay connected to their African heritage.

Wheatley's relations with Bristol Yamma and John Quamine are also suggested in her correspondence with Obour Tanner. In her letter to the Reverend Samuel Hopkins of Newport, on February 9, 1774, Wheatley shows how her correspondence with Obour Tanner might have allowed her to learn about Bristol Yamma and John Quamine's plans to go to Africa. She writes:

> I received some time ago 20s sterling upon them [copies of her book], by the hands of your son, in a letter from Abour Tanner. I received at the same time a paper, by which I understand there are two negro men, who are desirous of returning to their native country. to preach the Gospel, but being much indisposed by the return of my asthmatic complaint, besides the sickness of my mistress, who has been long confined to her bed, and is not expected to live a great while; all these things render it impracticable for me to do anything at present with regard to that paper, but what I can do in influencing my Christian friends and acquaintances, to promote this laudable design, shall not be wanting. (175)

Wheatley's representation of the ambition of the "two negro men, who are desirous of returning to their native country" as a "laudable design" attests to her solidarity with blacks of the diaspora who were trying to help Africa. The letter shows that Wheatley was in contact with the work of African Americans who intended to go to Africa. William H. Robinson underscores, in *Phillis Wheatley in the Black American Beginnings* (1975), the poet's deep concerns for other black Americans and "her cooperation in helping to fund what was likely the first Black American back-to-Africa attempt" (62). As Robinson suggests in "On Phillis Wheatley and Her Boston" (1984), when she received hundreds of copies of her *Poems* from London in May 1774, Wheatley sold many of them to her white friends in Boston and Newport because she fully understood "that Hopkins badly needed the prestige of her name and fame to help him in his attempts to raise funds for the education of" Yamma and Quamine "at the College of New Jersey (Princeton University) for pioneering African missionary work" (44). Wheatley monitored the progress of Yamma and Quamine: she says in her letter to Sir John Thornton, dated October 30, 1774, that "the reverend gentleman who under [ta]kes their Education has repeatedly inform'd me by Letters of their prospect in learning" (184). Wheatley's interest in the instruction of Yamma and Quamine attests to her Pan-Africanism that is also evident near the end of her letter to the Reverend Samuel Hopkins of Newport (who is mentioned above as the "reverend gentleman"), where she states: "I hope that which the divine royal Psalmist says by inspiration is now on the point of being accomplished, namely, Ethiopia shall soon stretch forth her hands unto God. Of this, Abour Tanner, and I trust many others within your knowledge, are living witnesses. Please to give my love to her, and I intend to write her soon" (176).

Wheatley's biblical imagery of Ethiopia as a being that "shall soon stretch forth her hands unto God" reflects a Pan-Africanist sentiment that is apparent in her representation of Ethiopia as a symbol of both her prospective and liberated self and the future nation of free people of African descent in which she will be a part when slavery ends. African American writers have frequently used this image as a means to stress their Ethiopianism. In *Black on Black: Twentieth-Century Writing about Africa* (2000), John Cullen Gruesser asserts: "African American literary depictions of Africa published between 1902 and 1982 either invoke or react against one or more aspects of Ethiopianism, the teleological and uniquely African American view of history inspired by the Psalms verse 'princes shall come out of Egypt, Ethiopia shall soon stretch forth her hands unto God'" (1). Wheatley was a precursor to this African American Ethiopianism, since she was one of the first black American poets to express it in writing. Wheatley's eminent place in Ethiopianism is apparent in the endearing ways in which the African American poet Jupiter Hammon entitled his 1778 eulogy for her "*An Address to Miss Phillis Wheatley [sic], Ethiopian Poetess, in Boston, who came from Africa at eight years of age, and soon became acquainted with the gospel of Jesus Christ*" (3). In this poem, Hammon tells Wheatley that

> The humble soul shall fly to God,
> And leave the things of time,
> Start forth as 'twere at the first word,
> To taste things more divine. (7)

Hammon's tribute to Wheatley participates in the Pan-Africanism that the black woman poet engineered naturally by inspiring other African Americans to admire her intellectual and spiritual ability to "stretch forth" to "God." In this sense, Wheatley was able to overcome her physical distance from Africans and blacks of the diaspora with spiritual intimacy and guidance. Wheatley was a forerunner of the Ethiopianist intellectual tradition, in which Shirley W. Logan places the nineteenth-century African American writer Maria Stewart, that reminded African Americans "of their origins and of the promise that 'Ethiopia might stretch forth her hand unto God'" (*We Are Coming*, 35).

In addition, the ending of Wheatley's letter to the Reverend Samuel Hopkins of Newport suggests her intimate relationships with Obour Tanner, as apparent in her representation of this woman as one of the "living witnesses" of Ethiopia's inclination toward God (176). Wheatley's description attests to her admiration and love for Obour Tanner's religiosity and humanity. The strong feelings that Wheatley had for Obour Tanner are not surprising since the two women came from the same continent and had similar religious inclinations. In "A Phillis Wheatley Letter" (1949), Benjamin Quarles writes: "Living in Newport, Obour Tanner was a close friend of Phillis. Very likely (as may be deduced from internal evidence in the closing sentences of this letter) Obour, like Phillis, had been born in Africa. Like Phillis also, Obour was of a deeply religious bent" (463).

Another important theme in Wheatley's poetry is that of atheism. This theme is apparent in a 1767 poem appropriately entitled "Atheism." Here Wheatley begins a spiritual representation of blackness when she confronts atheist philosophers of her time by asking, "Where now shall I begin this Spacious Field / To tell what curses unbelief doth yield?" (129). These lines follow the traditional African storyteller's way of introducing an oral narrative with questions and moral parables to both himself/herself and the listeners.[26] Wheatley follows this narrative process by letting the reader know that her story is about the Judeo-Christian time and the chaos that will prevail in the world if there is no belief in a higher power that gives hope to people. She asks the reader, "If there's no heaven whither wilt thou go?" (129).

In the rest of the poem, Wheatley uses metaphors for darkness such as "the Shades below" and "the deepest hell" in order to represent hell as the abode of those who use secular or ancient philosophical learning to oppose the divine knowledge and wisdom of "the Book of praise" (130), the Bible. Wheatley's concept of darkness appropriates both Puritan and African symbols. The Puritan element is perceptible in her insistence on the moral chaos that results from a break of God's divine plan. For her, this plan is

> That covenant [which] was made for to ensure
> Made to establish lasting to endure. (130)

Wheatley's idea of the "covenant" stresses not only the belief in the "essence of God" but also in the sustenance of this "essence" through unselfish love. In this sense, Wheatley places human equality at the center of her theology in order to show her critics that the slaves, who had been treated inhumanly in violation of the principle of the "covenant," have earned the right to be free and rehabilitated spiritually and intellectually. Therefore, Wheatley utilizes Puritan rhetoric as a means for developing an underground form of rebellion. As Baker writes in *The Journey Back*, Wheatley "seized for herself a place among those who claimed poetry as their particular 'calling,' an important word in the vocabulary of American Puritanism" (10).

The Puritanism that influenced Wheatley had worldviews that are similar to those of Senegambian cultures. In "Types of Puritan" (1987), Gerald C. Brauer states: "They [Puritans] asserted that human beings were created by God, in the very image of God in a state of innocence, but that in Adam and Eve they fell from this state into sin and so were cut off, estranged at enmity with God their creator, and with their fellow human beings. Puritans believed that only God could bridge that gulf that stood between human beings and the divine" (43). Wheatley's concept of sin derives from this Puritan and Christian Protestant philosophy in which the world is represented as a stable cosmos regulated by divine will and good until it was corrupted with the original sins of Adam and Eve. This Puritan cosmology is comparable to the worldview of the Murid of Senegal in which the holy city of *Tuba*, identified in the figure of "The Lote Tree," stands as the link between the divine, human beings, and the underworld. In "Touba: A Spiritual Metropolis in the Modern World" (1995), Eric Ross describes *Tuba* as "a cosmological symbol—the *axis mundi*, transcending the earthly and heavenly spheres" (223) and represents "The Lote Tree" that identifies it as a medium that assures "proper passage through judgment and into paradise" (223). Ross's semiotic construct indicates the duality in the African conception of the world as a cosmos that is composed of two antithetical forces (the earth and the heavens), which are mediated by individuals who are sanctified by the divine.

Wheatley's subtle resistance is also apparent in her use of "Signifying" as a means for disguising her views against the immorality of slavery through criticisms of atheism. In *The Signifying Monkey*, Gates argues that "to Signify" is to use indirection in rhetorical strategy and play with "the figurative difference between the literal and the metaphorical, between surface and latent meaning" (82). "Signifying" is apparent in how Wheatley uses the concept of "Atheists" not to refer to the popular meaning of the term but to identify slave traders who "daily feel his [God's] hand and rod / And dare deny the essence of a god" (129). Wheatley's "Atheists" are the slaveowners that she saw as "unbelievers" who were not afraid of keeping human beings in servitude and losing the opportunity to go to heaven. By talking about sin in spiritual ways, Wheatley used the Jeremiad as a tool of resistance. As Vincent Carretta defines it, in "Three West Indian Writers of the 1780s Revisited and Revised" (1998), the Jeremiad is a genre of "political sermon, denouncing the sins of the community and warning of divine retribution should the evil behavior continue (7).

Drawing from Christian rhetoric of sin and forgiveness, Wheatley substitutes the meaning of blackness from the racial innuendo that was traditionally attached to it with a nonracial one in which the color "black" signifies the spiritual perdition of those who keep their fellow human beings in bondage. Why was Wheatley ostensibly indirect toward white Americans when she meant to criticize them? One answer could be William H. Robinson's argument that when Wheatley seemed to be praising white America or Christian America, she was "much aware of the hypocrisy of whites who falsely professed the religion" (33).[27] Another answer could be that she preferred to signify this hypocrisy rather than confront it directly because she did not want to alienate the whites who supported her work and abolitionist cause. Both hypotheses contradict the charge that Wheatley pandered to whites, since they suggest Wheatley's use of "Signifying" as a trickster strategy that allows her to gain acceptance among elite whites whose knowledge and power she appropriates in order to fight for the freedom and humanity of blacks. Wheatley's use of "Signifying" resonates with the "weapon of the weak" that James C. Scott theorizes in *Weapons of the Weak* as the strategy of "hidden transcript" that oppressed individuals use to resist the domination of the elite classes of merchants and property owners. According to Scott, reliance on "hidden transcript" identifies instances when a subordinate group enacts neutrality, passive accommodation into the elite's society, or adaptation to the customs of the intruder as an outward means of maintaining a semblance of order while covertly resisting oppression (xviii, 317).

Wheatley's use of "Signifying" as an indirect tool of resistance has equivalents in Wolof folklore in which *Leuk* makes subtle and disguised criticisms against authority. One example is the Wolof tale, "The Hyena Engages the Hare as a Gewel," in which *Leuk* uses indirection as a means for resisting the power and retaliation of *Bouki*. In this tale that appears in Magel's *Folktales from the Gambia*, *Leuk* escapes death after *Bouki* has burned the fields of the mythic country of Guijanxa and has confined him without food (53–54). *Leuk* runs away from the confinement through a small hole in the back fence of the compound (53–54). As the narrator suggests, after his escape, *Leuk* travels to *Guijanxa*, where the king of the country resides, and tells him, "King, I have seen the one who has done it [the burning of the fields]" (55). According to the narrator, the King responds, "Then go and tell him that I want him to come here with his whole family. Tell him that he should come here with drums, having his wives and cousins singing an appropriate song" (55). When *Bouki* sees *Leuk* return to his compound, he asks him, "Did you go to the King?" and *Leuk* replies, "Yes" (55). *Bouki* asks, "What did the King say?" and *Leuk* responds, "The king said in the morning you should come with all of your wives and relatives dressed up in your finest clothes. You too should dress in your finest outfit. You must arrive with the tama beating and your people singing a song which, you know, tells of your burning of the fields" (55–56).

In the passage, *Leuk* employs "Signifying" by criticizing *Bouki*'s burning of the fields indirectly. In order to protect himself against *Bouki*'s violence, *Leuk* pretends to speak only about what *Bouki* wants to hear while making understated criticisms against him. *Leuk* employs the Wolof rhetorical device known as "Wax," which is analogous to the African American "Signifying." "Wax" is a Wolof term that Abdoulaye Dial defines in *Apprentissage Rapide Du Wolof: Jàng Wolof* (1994) as "parler" [to speak] (65). My capitalization of the "w" in "Wax" serves to distinguish the art of speaking indirectly from the act of speaking directly. In this sense, the act of performing "Wax" is a form of communication in which the speaker conveys multiple and profound meaning in an utterance and is able to manipulate the significance of words. One example of such manipulation of meaning is noticeable in "The Ethnography of Speaking" (1975) in which Richard Bauman and Joel Sherzer say that "within the basic structure of an obligatory dyadic greeting exchange in the Wolof greeting there is room for strategic manipulation in which two individuals can affect their own rank and especially the nature of their subsequent interaction" (110). The Wolof's manipulation of the meaning of words occurs in a discourse in which subtle strategies of communication such as disguise, pretense, pun, and indirect allusions are employed in order to appear polite and nonconfrontational even in the midst of difficulties. For instance, in the introduction to Birago Diop's *The Tales of Ahmadou Kumba* (1989), Dorothy Blair points out the Wolof people's custom of greeting one another with the polite formula "*Djâma rek!*" [the house is at peace] at all times, even when there may be no peace or food in the house (xiv).

Wheatley employs the Wolof form of indirection since she does not want to offend the oppressive hegemonic power of white America that she criticizes. She attempts to please her white readers and appear inoffensive to them even when she remains adamantly critical of their tolerance of slavery. One instance is the poem "On Imagination" in which she disguises her frustration with America through complaints about the cold weather of Boston. She writes:

> *Winter* austere forbids me to aspire,
> And northern tempests damp the rising fire,
> They chill the tides of *Fancy*'s flowing sea,
> Cease then, my song, cease the unequal lay. (68)

Wheatley intersperses a criticism of slavery in a silent lamentation of the cold winter season of Boston. Wheatley's references to the severe climate that "forbids me to aspire" and the heavy storms that "damp the rising fire" are examples of "Wax," since they indirectly signify the effects of slavery on her life and work. This institution prevents her imagination from flowing and suffocates her ability to use her poetry to bring change. Wheatley's suffocation from slavery in America is similar to that which *Leuk* experiences in a narrative in which he is kidnapped by strangers and put in bondage. This story is told by Léopold Sédar Senghor and Abdoulaye Sadji in their classic Senegalese book, *Les Aventures de Leuk-Le-Lièvre* [*The Adventures of Leuk-The-Rabbit*] (1975). In the tale, *Leuk* witnesses violence, separation of families, and realizes that freedom is a fleeting illusion as long as one human being is kept in servitude. He says: "What I have just seen is not self-reassuring! The man who has kept my cousin *N'Diombor* in slavery must be able to do the same to me" (24).

Leuk's depiction of slavery in the mythical land of *Ndoumbélane* is similar to Wheatley's representation of slavery in the United States. Both Wheatley and *Leuk* confront a form of slavery that disrupts the stability of their homeland and separates families from their kin. Both resist the evil system through oblique subversion in the same way the African slaves and folkloric tricksters who came to the United States rebelled against the evil system during the Middle Passage. Being a Wolof and a Senegalese, Wheatley was certainly familiar with these folkloric icons. She would have been exposed to the African American folk tricksters Cunning Rabbit and Brer Rabbit, who were commonly known among African slaves in America, and who were both descendants of *Leuk*. In *Folk Beliefs of the Southern Negro* (1926), Newbell Niles Puckett argues that "Cunnie Rabbit," who was "so-called by the African natives," was the favorite prankster of the slaves, because he represented their inferior social position in America (34). Puckett writes: "This little creature is very difficult to capture and its shyness, fleetness and cunning have led the natives to invest it with a sort of veneration. It may be that the similarity of proper names have led the slave to invest the American hare with the qualities of their Cunning Rabbit, since 'it certainly requires a very friendly eye to see in the hare all the mental acumen accredited by the Negroes to Brer Rabbit'" (34). Puckett's rationale shows that African slaves in America were aware of the virtues of *Leuk*, Brer Rabbit, and Cunnie Rabbit. Knowingly or unknowingly, Wheatley preserved their skills in her writings to gain spiritual force, resilience, and the knowledge to denounce and survive subjugation. She used the shyness, intelligence, sagacity, and poetic deftness of these characters to remain alive. As Kafka writes, "with Wheatley and other enslaved Africans, their very survival depended on mastering appearances, of appearing humble. The assumption of acquiescent masks to appease their captors was a matter of life and death" (44).

In her poetry, Wheatley also plays a dual role of Christian prophet and African diviner. In "An Address to the Deist," written in 1767, she suggests the chaos that whites who were going to Africa to buy slaves faced by pointing at the "black despair" that await those who question the existence of "th' Almighty monarch" (132). Pointing at the sinners, Wheatley implores them to "Attend to Reason whispering in thine ear / Seek the Eternal while he is so near" (132). This passage registers Wheatley's double status as a Christian prophet and an African seer. As a Christian prophet, she carried the responsibility to warn against the deceitfulness of evil. As an African diviner, she performed the priestess's duty to predict that such disaster was imminent unless slavery was abolished. Using the Jeremiad, she invokes the theme of Christ's sacrifice in order to expose the suffering and price that blacks have paid for shielding their fellow human beings from destruction. She writes:

> "Father forgive them," thus the Saviour pray'd
> Nail'd was king Jesus on the cross for us
> For our transgressions he sustain'd the Curse. (132)

The figure of Jesus in this poem is a metaphor for the slave who endured incommensurable pain that allowed whites to achieve wealth and the illusion of spiritual well-being. In return, blacks have never been paid for the suffering they experienced during the accumulation of this wealth. In the poem "An Address to the Deist," Wheatley addresses this contradiction by demanding equal treatment, freedom, and economic advancement for blacks in America. According to her, immense social, political, and economic work must be done in America before the nation can benefit from the sacrifices of the African slaves who gave their lives, in martyrdom, in the name of liberty. Wheatley asks white America a straightforward question: "Must Ethiopians be employ'd for you?" (131). This question attests the right of the Africans to be free from the demeaning labor of slavery. As R. Lynn Matson points out in "Phillis Wheatley—Soul Sister" (1972), Wheatley was not devoid of racial consciousness and sympathy for the plight of the Africans since "she protested slavery, after her fashion, often implicitly" (223).

Wheatley's search for freedom for African Americans is evident in her poem "AMERICA," in which she creates an implicit analogy between the freedom of the New England colony from Britain and that of African Americans from slavery (134). Using indirection, she could demonize slavery without alienating the abolitionists who supported her work. For instance, she describes slavery as a system that will be defeated by the powers of "Liberty" and the voices of the "weak" and of the "Ethiopians" (134). This poem reflects Wheatley's belief that "Liberty" can overcome slavery in the same way New England's colony tamed a "wilderness" in order to exist (134). Here, she creates analogy between slavery and wilderness in order to demonize the moral darkness of the whites who held the Africans in bondage. This subtle denunciation of slavery shows Wheatley's ability, as Paula Bennett describes in "Phillis Wheatley's Vocation and the Paradox of the 'Afric Muse'" (1998), "to placate her superiors" while stressing "her race-based subordination—a subordination whose constitutive inferiority she refuses to internalize" (64).

Wheatley's ability to demonize slaveowners in her writings shows her possible appropriation of the tricksters' capacity to humiliate their opponents indirectly. In *Black Culture and Black Consciousness*, Levine shows the relationship between African American slave culture and trickster icons when he says that slaves' animal and human trickster tales "placed the same emphasis upon tactics of trickery and indirection, took the same delight in seeing the weak outwit and humiliate the strong, manifested in the lack of idealization, and served the same dual function which included the expression of repressed feelings and inculcation of the tactics of survival" (131). These tactics of trickery in African

American tales are subversive strategies of deception that are also apparent in African tales. This presence is manifest in how the characters in the African American folktale "Big Talk" and in the Senegambian tale "The Monkey and the Dog Court the Same Girl" use rhetorical tactics such as indirection and bad-mouthing to resist the oppressive planter. "Big Talk" is about a slave who explains how he cusses his wicked master every time he gets the chance to do so. The tale appears in Zora Neale Hurston's *Mules and Men* (1935). According to the narrator, one slave told another slave, "Ole Massa made me so mad yistiddy till Ah give 'im uh good cussin' out. Man, Ah called 'im everything wid uh handle on it" (77). As the storyteller suggests, the other slave said,

"You didn't cuss *Ole Massa*, didja? Good God! Whut did he do tuh you?"
"He didn't do *nothin'*, an' man, Ah laid one cussin' on 'im! Ah'm uh man lak dis, Ah won't stan' no hunchin'. Ah betcha he won't bother *me* no mo'." (77)

As the narrator says, the next day the first slave did something and "Ole Massa got in behind 'im and he turnt 'round an' give Ole Massa one good cussin' and Ole Massa had 'im took down and whipped nearly tuh death" (77). According to the storyteller, the next time they saw each other again, the first slave told the second one, "Thought you tole me, you cussed Ole Massa out and he never opened his mouf" (77). As the narrator suggests, the second slave responded,

"Ah did."
"Well, how come he never did nothin' tuh yuh? Ah did it an' he come nigh uh killin' *me*."
"Man, you didn't go cuss 'im tuh his face, didja?"
"Sho Ah did. Ain't dat whut you tole me you done?"
"Naw, Ah didn't say Ah cussed 'im tuh his face. You sho is crazy. Ah thought you had mo' sense than dat. When Ah cussed Ole Massa he wuz settin' on de front porch an' Ah wuz down at de big gate." (77–78)

In this tale, a slave bad-mouths a cruel planter by giving him a "good cussin' out" behind his back and "down at de big gate," signifying his ability to counter the slaveowner's violence with indirect verbal resistance. Bad-mouthing helped the slave to resist the restriction and oppression that plantation life represented. As noticeable in the breach between the master and the protagonist, verbal insults allowed the slave to squelch the anger and frustration that he/she felt as a victim of the master's violence. The slave's use of bad-mouthing as a means for resisting the master's brutality is consistent with the "weapon of the weak" that James C. Scott theorizes, in *Domination and the Arts of Resistance: Hidden Transcripts* (1990), as the aggressive language that a subordinate individual develops against the public humiliation of his/her employer (115). Scott describes how "a subordinate [person] who has just received a public dressing down from his superior during which he behaved deferentially, and who now finds himself among his peers may curse his superior, make physical gestures of aggression, and talk about what he would like to say next time" (115). The slave's bad-mouthing of the master is a hidden transcript, because it represents his/her subtle way of confronting the tyrannical authority and dominance of the master without facing immediate reprisal.

The practice of bad-mouthing is a major characteristic of African American vernacular. In *Talking Back* (1976), Roger D. Abrahams argues that bad-mouthing is a common discursive practice in which a group of black Americans gossip approvingly or disapprovingly about somebody's business (77). One example of bad-mouthing that Abrahams gives is as follows: "One notorious Georgia planter, Bill Mattox, liked to tell of the song his slaves used to sing about him. Once when he heard someone singing it he asked the singer who was the subject of the song. The singer replied, "'Master, . . . ain't you nebber heared of old Bill Mattox!' 'Dats de meanest man dey is!'" (111). This slave singer bad-mouths his cruel master by implicitly calling him the "meanest man" in the world while pretending to talk about "old Bill Mattox."

The practice of bad-mouthing in slave culture is a discursive strategy that is traceable to Senegambian folktales in which the trickster figure of *Golo* [Monkey] distinguishes himself as the master of satire and indirection. One example is the Wolof story "The Monkey and the Dog Court the Same Girl," in which *Golo* competes against his rival *Xaath* [Dog] for the love of a woman. In this tale, which appears in Magel's *Folktales from the Gambia*, *Golo* meets his future daughter-in law as he is going to the house of the woman he loves (75). As the narrator suggests, *Golo* waits until the tobacco that he is chewing is settled in his mouth and says, "'Ah my daughter-in-law, where is that dog? When did he last come here? . . . Honestly, if I ever meet him here, I will kill him. You know his ass looks like a bitter tomato" (75). The satirical and dissident quality of *Golo*'s language suggests his status as the indisputable master of bad-mouthing. As Birago Diop suggests in *Mother Crocodile* [Maman-Caïman] (1961), the spiteful nature of *Golo*'s language is also apparent when he says, "Of all the animals that fly in the air, walk on the earth, or swim in the water, the craziest must be the crocodiles, who creep on the earth and walk on the bottoms of rivers" (3). When the children of *Diassigue* [Alligator] hear about *Golo*'s derision of their mother and go to see him, the monkey answers, "Old talk is crazy talk" (19), revealing his denial of the mischievous language he had used against their parent. This *Golo* figure is the source of the bad-mouthing, indirection, satire, and irony in African American folktales. *Golo* is a cousin of the African American folk figure of the Signifying Monkey who permeates African American tales. Discussing the connection between the monkey figures in African and African American folktales, Hurston writes in *Dust Tracks on a Road* (1942):

> There were many other tales, equally ludicrous, in which the Negro, sometimes symbolized by the monkey, and sometimes named outright, ran off with the wrong understanding of what he had seen and heard. . .
>
> There was a general acceptance of the monkey as kinfolks. Perhaps it was some distant memory of tribal monkey reverence from Africa that had been forgotten in the main, but remembered in some vague way. Perhaps it was an acknowledgement of our talent for mimicry with the monkey as a symbol. (163)

Hurston's representation of black tradition shows that the Signifying Monkey in African American folktales is a descendant of the monkey figure in African oral literature. Slaves in the United States often resorted to the indirect resistance strategies of these monkey tricksters to counter the punitive plantation system that tended to perceive their resilience as misbehavior directed toward the master. Alternatively, slaves concealed their indirection and bad-mouthing strategies into their songs in order to hide their rebelliousness from the planter and his overseers. Moreover, as Roger D. Abrahams notes in *Singing the Master: The Emergence of African-American Culture in the Plantation South* (1992), slaves often followed African bardic traditions by bad-mouthing their masters in songs, which made the offense more subtle and difficult to detect (110). This use of bad-mouthing is an equivalent of the Wolof use of "*Xass*" as a means to criticize somebody indirectly. As Jagne argues, even within a *tagg*, a Wolof *griot* woman may use the "*xas*" as a style "that shows contempt for the person receiving the *xas*" (64). Wheatley retained such rhetorical styles in her poems, where one finds the use of indirection and subtle criticisms that attest to the survival of African culture in black American vernacular tradition.

In her poems, Wheatley mimics the African and African American trickster figures' use of indirection and bad-mouthing in order to demonize slavery. Her use of these trickster rhetorical styles is apparent in the poem "AMERICA" in which she views New England's victory from English rule as incomplete unless it contains provisions guaranteeing the freedom of African Americans to work, move, and express themselves as they see fit. A gifted African storyteller, she criticized the limitations slavery imposed on blacks by relating the myth of a woman [Britannia] who "laid some taxes on her darling son [America]" and turned "a senseless ear" to his cry for liberty (134). This poem, one very critical of Britain's tyrannical stronghold over New England during colonial times, walks the fine line between satire and praise while stressing the right of the colony to prosper like its mother country. While it appealed to the reason of both American and British troops, Wheatley's statement, "O Britain See / By this New England will increase like thee" (135), stresses the right Americans had to be independent from British colonial tyranny. Later, Wheatley tells white Americans that African Americans want the same freedom that America was demanding from England. In "To the Right Honourable William [Legge], Earl of Dartmouth, His Majesty's Principal Secretary of State for North America," she conveys her logic by describing slavery as a system that is inimical to the ideals of justice and freedom that America represents. She writes:

> No more, *America*, in mournful strain
> Of wrongs, and grievance unredress'd complain,
> No longer shall thou dread the iron chain,
> Which wanton *Tyranny* with lawless hand
> Had made, and with it meant t' enslave the land. (74)

The imagery of "the iron chain" helps Wheatley suggest the horror of slavery and call for its abolition. Coupled with her allusion to the "*Tyranny* with lawless hand" which is "meant t' enslave the land," the "iron chain" becomes Wheatley's means to vilify slavery indirectly as the trickster figures bad-mouth their oppressors obliquely for fear of punishment. For her, ending slavery would have allowed America to become a free nation where justice and law prevail. As James A. Levernier suggests in "Phillis Wheatley and the New England Clergy" (1991), in making America's freedom contingent upon the emancipation of the slaves, she develops a rhetoric that appeals to clergymen and abolitionists in both England and America (24).

Wheatley's writings are also Pan-Africanist in their frequent and assertive invocation of Africa as a place where peace and freedom need to be restored. In response to the poem "The Answer [By the Gentleman of the Navy]" in which the author calls her "The lovely daughter of the Affric shore" (141), Wheatley wrote "PHILLIS'S REPLY TO THE ANSWER," in which she proudly represents Africa in romantic terms as her land of origin. She depicts the Gambia as the pleasing land where her soul wishes to return "with native grace in spring's luxuriant reign" (144). Later, she gives a picture of the scenic view of "Afric's blissful plain" and "the warm limits of the land and main" (144).

In this poem written on December 5, 1774, Wheatley describes the Gambia, which is part of the Senegambian region where she came from. As evident in her portrayal of the Gambia as an idyllic place of birth that had splendor equal to that of Britain's shores, Wheatley desired to return to Africa, at least from a spiritual vantage point. Wheatley did, then, present a positive image of Africa, even while she often contradicted this portrayal in some parts of her writing. By representing Africa in positive terms, she perhaps sought to compensate for her errors and prejudices towards Africa. Alternatively, she might have wanted to gain the same type of recognition that Homer, Milton, and Isaac Newton, whom she describes as "Those bards whose fame in deathless strain arise" (143–44), received for presenting beautiful images of European society. From this perspective, she wanted to create a poetic tradition that was equal or superior to those of European authors. Therefore, Wheatley's writing was both African and American since it had a larger goal of asserting not just her rights as a gifted American author but also her privileges as a talented writer of African descent who was conscious about Africa.

As visible in her memory of the Gambia, Wheatley remembered her African origins. Yet her reminiscence of Africa was more than just a search for cultural authenticity; it was a strategy that prepared Wheatley for addressing the demons and contradictions of American slavery. In numerous poems that she wrote in the form of letters, she attempted to convince white American dignitaries such as General Washington of the injustice of holding Africans in bondage. In "To His Excellency General Washington," written on October 26, 1775, she mixes a tribute for Washington and a critique of his involvement in the slave institution that she viewed as contradictory to the ideals of liberty and democracy that America was supposed to embody. First, as a skilled literary *griotte*, she made a ravishing praise-song for Washington by describing his successful actions in patriotic battles. She praises the muses who,

> In bright array they seek the work of war,
> Where high unfurl'd the ensign waves in air.
> Shall I to Washington their praise recite?
> Enough thou know'st them in the fields of fight.
> Thee, first in peace and honours,—we demand
> The grace and glory of thy martial band.
> Fam'd for thy valour, for thy virtues more,
> Hear every tongue thy guardian aid implore! (145–46)

Wheatley's eulogy for Washington and his army resonates with the kinds of tributes that *griots* and *griottes* used to give to their kings who came back home from victorious wars, suggesting the strong influence of traditional Wolof narrative techniques on early African American poetics. This survival of the Wolof storytelling devices in the Americas is evident in Wheatley's eloquent praise [known in Senegambia as *tagg*] of the "grace" and "glory" of Washington's army and her tribute to the "valour" and "virtues" of Washington (146). A Wolof analogue of this praise poem is the Senegambian *tagg* in Emil Magel's *Hare and Hyena: Symbols of Honor and Shame in the Oral Narratives of the Wolof of the Senegambia*. According to Magel, the song was recorded by a woman griot named Haja Mbana Diop in Richard Toll, Senegal (58). As Magel points out, Haja Mbana Diop narrated this praise poem as follows:

> This is how my aunt sang him:
> Brave Mbabaa!
> Brave Mbabaa! Yaram Joop.
> Fara Penda Aadam Sal.
> That Tuesday you crossed the river at Dagana,
> You spent the day at Ngor Madd
> You distributed the ammunitions among your men at Barey-Kaat.
> You left in the afternoon for Arbuum where you spent the night.
> There, you killed Ahmet Faal, you killed Maalik Klis and their slave Wulnaasiri. (62)

In this poem, the Wolof *Griotte* Haja Mbana Diop sings the prowess of a Senegalese king (Mbabaa) by describing his actions in battle in incremental ways, and suggesting each of the glorious steps that led to his victory. The narrator's use of the expression "This is how my aunt sang him" to begin her praise poem lets the audience know that her eulogy is a story that has been passed down to her family from generation to generation. Drawing from a vast register of Wolof oral poetry, Haja Mbana Diop uses the *griot*'s unmatched art of storytelling, singing, and praising in order to suggest, through embellishing terms, the extraordinary actions that demonstrate Mbabaa's title of "Brave" ruler. Haja Mbana Diop's African song is also a praise poem because the two genres are interdependent in African oral tradition. As Samba Diop points out in *The Oral History and Literature of the Wolof People of Waalo, Northern Senegal* (1995), "it is impossible to separate African oral poetry from singing" or a "poem" from a "tale" since these terms are "relevant in the specific context of Wolof oral poetry" (125).

Moreover, Haja Mbana Diop's narrative depicts the victory of Mbabaa's army against the Moors as a relentless power that evokes the unconquerable potency of nature. As is apparent in her reference to the "river at Dagana" and, later, to "The wind of MaSamba Xosifor" (62), the Wolof *griotte* is able to create the same kinds of analogies between nature's invincible fury and a chief warrior's unconquerable wrath that Wheatley also creates in her tribute to George Washington. Haja Mbana Diop's *tagg* of Mbabaa is similar to the following section of "AMERICA" in which Wheatley praises Washington as follows:

> Muse! Bow propitious while my pen relates
> How pour her armies through a thousand gates,
> As when Eolus heaven's fair face deforms,
> Enwrapp'd in tempest and a night of storms;
> The Refluent surges beat the sounding of shore;
> Or thick as leaves in Autumn's golden reign,
> Such, and so many, moves the warrior's train. (145)

Like the Wolof *griotte*, Wheatley pays attention to the different actions that suggest the progression of a chief warrior toward victory. Wheatley's narrative shows the deployment of America's army "through a thousand gates" and then describes how these soldiers were "Enwrapp'd in tempest and a night of storms" before their "Refluent surges" started to "beat the sounding of shores" (145). Wheatley's allusion to "storms," "shores," and a "tempest" are ecological terms that allow her to represent the victories of Washington's army against the British as unstoppable environmental forces that recall the indomitable strength of nature and of the Muse of Eolus (145). In this sense, Wheatley's and Haja Mbana Diop's tributes to their respective heroes share a relentless admiration for leaders that are worthy of praise and a persistent belief in nature's resonance of these rulers' power to liberate people from oppression. Later, Haja Mbana Diop says:

> Brave Mbabaa!
> You are worth singing
> Fara Kumba, Mataar Naar.
> Ooh Jaajee!
> Brave Mbabaa.
> Brave Mbabaa, Yaram Joop. (62)

Here, the Wolof *griotte* stresses her intent to eulogize Mbabaa's victory from the Moors in ecstatic terms. Her representation of Mbabaa as the king who is "worth singing" and the exclamation that accompanies her depiction of this ruler as the "Brave Mbabaa!" and the "Jaajee!" are consistent with Wheatley's portrayal of Washington as a classic ruler who merits to be chanted in "every tongue thy guardian aid implore!" (146). Wheatley's use of an exclamation point accentuates her ardent desire to "recite" the Muse's praises of Washington (145) and "relate" through her "pen" how America's armies fought for liberation from British colonialism. Both eulogies show the key characteristics of African oral poetry, which are visible in the use of exclamatory lines, the gradual and sequential order of the description of events, and the direct and emotionally driven praise of a hero who is almost larger than life. These rhetorical strategies are common in traditional African poetics where *griots* use them in the epics of Sunjata Keita, Chaka Zulu, Njajaan Njaaye to praise royalties and other famed individuals.[28] In this sense, Wheatley could be considered as one of the first African American writers to infuse *griottes* poetics within African American literature.

In a similar vein, Wheatley's "AMERICA" indicates centeredness on black freedom, which, however, does not always equate to African consciousness. This contradiction is evident in the first stanza of the poem where she delicately suggests the dilemma she faced as an elite black poet who wanted to express admiration for a white American male leader who nonetheless was tied to the system of slavery (145). This paradox reflects Wheatley's disillusionment with a system of oppression that had direct impact on her life. As Betsy Erkkila points out in "Revolutionary Women" (1987), "For Wheatley, drawing upon the same Old Testament image to describe the captivity of her people to 'our Modern Egyptians,' the language of bondage and freedom was no longer metaphoric but real. Knowing the truth of slavery as part of her daily experience as the slave of a prosperous Boston merchant, she, too, pointed out the contradiction between rhetoric and reality in America" (201).

Moreover, Wheatley mimics the Senegambian tricksters' use of diplomacy as a means for gaining freedom from domineering systems of oppression. Like the trickster figures, Wheatley subverts domination by denouncing it in a forceful and unyielding language that mirrors the strength and resilience that *Leuk* and Brer Rabbit exhibit as they resist authoritarian forces such as *Bouki* or the Elephant. One Senegambian tale in which *Leuk* plays the role of diplomat is the Wolof narrative entitled "Le Lapin devant Dieu" [The Rabbit Standing Before God], which appears in David P. Gamble's *Wolof Stories From Senegambia Mainly From Old Published Sources* (1987). According to the storyteller, *Leuk* comes to God and asks him to increase his intelligence. God tells him, "Very well, but go first and fill me this goat skin [bag] with living birds"

(68). *Leuk* walks into the forest and finds many birds that are perched on top of a tree and tells them, "I made a bet, [and] it was said you were not numerous enough to fill this skin" (68). Trying to prove *Leuk* wrong, the birds dive into the goatskin bag. *Leuk* closes the bag and takes his prey to God, who asks him to go and fill another bag with vultures (68). *Leuk* plays a similar trick and succeeds (68). Then God asks him to go and bring him the brain of an elephant. *Leuk* gets a bunch of hay and sits at the side of a patch frequented by elephants (68). The story continues:

> One of them [elephants] was passing, he [*Leuk*] asked him to carry him and his hay. The elephant agreed, and the hare, after having taken the precaution of attaching the hay to his back, climbed up. The elephant had not taken ten steps before the hare set fire to the hay and jumped down. The elephant was burnt alive. A Laobe [timberman] was passing with his ax. The hare begged him to open the skull of the largest of the land animals, and carried its brain to God. (68)

This Wolof story, which explains how *Leuk* received his cleverness from God through the victorious performance of difficult and sacrificial tasks, suggests that it is inappropriate to represent *Leuk* as either a saint or a contrast of *Bouki*. *Leuk* sometimes misbehaves like his alter ego *Bouki*, whose weaknesses he subconsciously conveys. As the narrator suggests, *Leuk* receives special favor of God, which consists of intelligence symbolized by "a white spot on his forehead" (68). Here, *Leuk*'s intelligence gives him the power to manipulate the strength of *Bouki*. Yet *Leuk* can preserve this power only when his actions appropriate *Bouki*'s unyielding determination and subversion. While his privileged rank symbolizes purity and intelligence, it is achieved through means that defy Western moral conventions. In the tale, *Leuk* got a special rank only after he/she had burnt an elephant (known as *ñey* or *ñay* in Wolof) and brought the latter's brain to God, who had requested it.

A traditional African American folktale that is similar to "The Rabbit Standing Before God," appears in Abigail M. H. Christensen's *Afro-American Folk Lore* (1971). This folktale, "DE RABBIT AN' DE ELEPHAN' TUSHES," presents an anarchic and highly competitive social and political universe that mirrors the context in which *Leuk* lived in Africa. In the African American tale, Brer Rabbit, who is a descendant of *Leuk*, dupes the elephant into breaking his own tush during an uneven race that the Rabbit has spoiled. Not knowing that the Rabbit has put okra on the pavement where he has agreed to run with him, the elephant slips so badly that he breaks his first tush. Seeking revenge, the elephant promises to give all his property to his son if he can catch the Rabbit. The son goes to see the Rabbit and asks him to come help bury his father. At his arrival at the Elephant's house, the Rabbit says: "'How Elephan' dead?' So 'e stood fur off from Elephan an' say, 'When my ol' fader was dead 'e groan.' So Elephan' say, 'Hm-m-hm-m!' Den Rabbit say, 'Dere now, I nebber yeardy dead man groan in my life. Fe! Fe! Boy, tink you kin catch me, but you can't catch me!'" (22).

The two stories about a rabbit figure that tricks an elephant character reveal an adversarial historical context in which both tricksters fight for survival through desperate tools that allow them to defeat a large enemy and regain power and proper social status. In the African context, the Rabbit hurts the elephant to receive divine favor of God. In the American context, he harms the elephant to free himself from tyranny. In both worlds, the Rabbit fights for his freedom. This interpretation allows us to see the elephant figure in the African American tale as a parody of the slaveowner who keeps the enslaved Africans in bondage. This oppression is visible in the material wealth and power to keep his son in slavery that the elephant shows when he tells him, "Ef you kin catch Br'er Rabbit I'll gi' you all my proputy and set you free" (22). This statement mirrors the arbitrary world in which the enslaved Africans lived in the West under captivity. In order to free themselves, the enslaved Africans had recourse to the power of their traditional African trickster figures such as *Leuk*, *Golo*, and *Bouki*, which strengthened their resistance against slavery and racism.

In similar ways, Wheatley uses diplomacy and intellect in order to raise some awareness of the evils of slavery. This is evident in the first stanza of "To His Excellency General Washington," where she suggests the dilemma she faced as an elite black poet who expressed admiration for a white leader who nonetheless was tied to the demonic system of slavery. Using the metaphor of "Columbia" as a means for signifying her abomination of slavery, she expresses the paradox she felt toward an American Declaration of Independence that tolerated the capture and exploitation of human beings. She writes

>   Celestial choir! Enthron'd in realms of light,
>   Columbia's scenes of glorious toils I write.
>   While freedom's cause her anxious breast alarms,
>   She flashes dreadful in refulgent arms.
>   See mother earth her offspring's fate bemoan,
>   And nations gaze at scenes before unknown!
>   See the bright beams of heaven's revolving light
>   Involved in sorrows and veil of night! (145)

This passage personifies Columbia, the name for America, as a goddess who epitomizes freedom, motherhood, and life sustenance for all Americans that Wheatley perceived as "nations" gazing "at scenes before unknown!" (145). The narrator's reference to the divine light that is "involved in sorrows and veil of night" foregrounds the moral darkness in which slavery put the American people, revealing a dilemma that could have been overcome only through acceptance of and surrender to the freedom from "Anon Britannia" that Columbia stands for. Later, Wheatley describes how the "eyes of nations" remain fixed on Columbia's War of Revolution while "round increase the rising hills of dead" (146). The example shows that Wheatley's major goal in writing about General Washington was to help him see the contradiction of the American patriots' fight to defeat the British, during the War of American Revolution, at a time when blacks and other groups in America were taken away from their homeland(s). Wheatley uses the clause, "cruel blindness to Columbia's state," which describes Britain's disgraceful role of oppressor during the Revolutionary War, to signify America's sightlessness towards the predicament of blacks within "Columbia's state." By critiquing this tyranny, national silence, and passivity toward injustice through her reference to the peoples' "cruel blindness to Columbia's state" (146), Wheatley was able to intersperse into her poetry a subtle denunciation of the political leadership that Washington represented without alienating the man behind the General whom she continued to admire and support personally. Wheatley's high regard for Washington is transparent in the belief of many critics such as Thomas J. Steele, Kenny J. Williams, Marie Rose Napierkowski, and Vera Camden that she anticipated the patriotic legend of Washington as "the father of his country."[29]

In the final section of "To His Excellency General [George] Washington," Wheatley tells Washington that he should continue his war for freedom and expect, as rewards, "a crown, a mission, and a throne that shine" (146). This passage reveals the strong and continuous esteem that Wheatley held for Washington despite her disapproval of his complicity in the treatment of enslaved blacks, which she conveyed in the subtext of her eulogy. Therefore, Wheatley was a conscious and tactful black intellectual who used her high literary and social status in order to criticize, though implicitly, the oppression of slavery to an elite white audience that she could reach on intellectual, emotional, and patriotic levels. This denunciation is further visible in her poem "On the Death of General Wooster," written in July 1778, in which she takes advantage of her privileged status as a renowned poet in order to defend the cause of enslaved African people. Recounting General Wooster's "warlike deeds" in terms that recall her depiction of Washington's, she directly attacks the institution of slavery and demands African American freedom. In her poem about General Wooster, she asserts:

> But how, presumptuous shall we hope to find
> Divine acceptance with th' Almighty mind—
> While yet (O deed Ungenerous!) they disgrace
> And hold in bondage Afric's blameless race? (149–50)

Wheatley's poem reflects a spirit of explicit and unflinching resistance that she affirms by suggesting the paradox that African Americans experienced by living in a freedom-seeking American nation in which they were denied the respect, equality, and freedom that were given to whites. Therefore, Wheatley was strongly committed to the improvement of the conditions of African Americans despite her privileged status.

By implicitly criticizing the impact of slavery on the enslaved Africans, Wheatley used her African-influenced poetic skills as weapons of resistance against slavery. In so doing, she developed a tremendously strong tradition of Pan-Africanist analysis of the predicament of people of African descent during slavery that deserves more attention than it has so far received. This consciousness about Africa that Wheatley, Bristol Yamma, John Quamine, and Obour Tanner had is a Pan-African enthusiasm that resonates with the willingness of the king figure in "The Donkeys of Jolof" to accept his African heritage and to return to his homeland. Like this king, Wheatley and her black friends overcame their alienation in the West by revealing through their relationships with one another the existence of a tight African community in colonial New England. This united black community in Colonial New England suggests the influence of the communality of early Senegambian culture on early black diasporan culture.

CHAPTER TWO

Pan-Africanism in Quobna Ottobah Cugoano's Liberation Discourse

Quobna Ottobah Cugoano was a leading Pan-Africanist among the first writers of the black diaspora. He played a major role in the Pan-Africanist intellectual tradition of resistance through his sustained condemnation of the impact of the transatlantic slave trade on blacks of Africa, England, and the Caribbean during the last quarter of the eighteenth century. Anticipating the strong impact of racism and unequal distribution of resources on blacks of Africa and of the diaspora, he vehemently denounced these forms of oppression and urged the Western world to participate in the rehabilitation of the human rights of blacks and the improvement of their conditions. In his Pan-Africanist resistance against oppression, Cugoano developed strategies that are similar to those that trickster figures in the folklore of his Fanti homeland, in current Ghana, employ to struggle against subjugation. Moreover, in his Pan-Africanist liberation discourse, Cugoano drew from biblical and philosophical themes to resist oppression. He was aware of the importance of alliance with abolitionists in England, the United States, and the rest of the world in the fight against slavery. This consciousness led him to describe the predicaments of the enslaved Africans in terms that reflect the horror of slavery and the need to offset its effects on blacks. His representation of slavery sets the standards of an unprecedented and radical Pan-Africanism that attacks racist theories about blacks.

Cugoano was an early African British abolitionist and the author of *Thoughts and Sentiments on the Evil of Slavery*. This book was first published in 1787 under the title *Thoughts and Sentiments on the Evil and Wicked Traffic of the Slavery and Commerce of the Human Species, Humbly Submitted to the Inhabitants of Great Britain*.[1] As Hakim Adi and Marika Sherwood point out in *Pan-African History: Political Figures from Africa and the Diaspora Since 1787* (2003), this book is "at the present time the main source for biographical information about its author" (26). One early study of Cugoano's work is "Three West African Writers of the 1780s" (1985), in which Paul Edwards introduced the British audience and the rest of the world to pioneer black writers of the eighteenth century such as Cugoano and Equiano. As Vincent Carretta argues in his tribute to Edwards in "Three West Indian Writers of the 1780s Revisited and Revised" (1994), Edwards "made many readers aware for the first time that Britain had a tradition of writers of African descent dating back to the eighteenth century" (74).

In his essay, Edwards represents Cugoano as a less talented writer than Equiano was and argues that the first author would have been unable to write *Thoughts and Sentiments* without the second author's assistance (183). Edwards bases his reasoning on what he views as the poor grammar and rhetorical style in Cugoano's book. Edwards writes: "Turning to the book, the reader will see that its frequently elevated rhetorical manner must reflect the work of a writer having greater control of the language than Cugoano. All the same, we must allow for the difference between writing a casual letter and settling down to produce a book. One feature of the book which would support the case for its authenticity is the occurrence of a number of grammatical errors similar to those of the letter, but in concealed positions where they might be more likely to be missed by an editor or reviser" (183–84). Indeed, Cugoano's *Thoughts and Sentiments* has a few grammatical errors that the author could have avoided through proper editing. Yet these errors, which I have reproduced in this study as they appear in Cugoano's narrative, do not reduce the significance of Cugoano's book since they remind us of harsh times when blacks had little educational privilege in the West. As Norbert J. Gossman points out, in the eighteenth century, "few blacks obtained anything in the way of education" ("William Cuffay," 57). In this sense, Cugoano's *Thoughts and Sentiments* is the product of a difficult stage of black literature in the West that critics should reevaluate on the basis of literary aspects beyond the author's writing style and grammar. Moreover, as Carretta suggests, in order to be fair to Cugoano, critics should point out not only "that his surviving holograph letters are not significantly less polished than those of Equiano" but also "that many of the formal qualities of Cugoano's *Thoughts and Sentiments* that strike readers as ungrammatical, repetitive, imitative, and lacking in narrative force may be explained by approaching the text from the oral as well as the written tradition" ("Three West Indian Writers" 83).

Reestablishing Cugoano's prominent role in Pan-African literature requires an acknowledgement of the African folklore and political ideologies in his work and a critique of the minimization that early black Atlantic writers experienced in the eighteenth century, when many white readers considered them incapable to produce literature. As Gossman has shown, readers in eighteenth-century England perceived the narratives of Cugoano, Equiano, and Sancho as "suspect" because "it was assumed that these books or pamphlets were actually written by someone else" (56–57). Studying Cugoano's contribution to Pan-Africanism is a complicated task, because most of the extant studies about him overlook his relationships to Africa and interpret his work as a struggle against slavery and racism in the West only, rather than as a resistance against European oppression in both Africa and the West. Though such works are pertinent explorations of Cugoano's views on slavery and his relations to the Western world, they ignore the author's consciousness about and connections with his African homeland, history, and folklore, his Pan-Africanist discourse against European imperialism, and his theories about the spread of European civilization to Africa.

Three extant studies of Cugoano's representation of slavery are Roxann Wheeler's "Betrayed By Some of My Own Complexion" (2001), Carretta's introduction to *Unchained Voices: An Anthology of Black Authors in the English-Speaking World of the 18th Century* (2004), and Adi and Sherwood's *Pan-African History: Political Figures from Africa and the Diaspora Since 1787* (2003). Wheeler argues that Cugoano's *Thoughts and Sentiments* "engages typical religious and secular arguments marshaled to justify slavery and examines some of the major institutions of his day in terms of their alleviating or worsening the situation of slaves" (17). In a similar vein, Carretta contends that *Thoughts and Sentiments* "remains the most overt African-British challenge to the slave trade and slavery ever published" (11). Resonating with Carretta's theory, Adi and Sherwood represent *Thoughts and Sentiments* as "one of the earliest written challenges by an African to slavery and the trans-Atlantic slave trade" (26).

Likewise, Paul Edwards and David Dabydeen's introduction to *Black Writers in Britain 1760–1890: An Anthology* (1994) and Anthony Bogues's "The Political Thought of Quobna Cugoano: Radicalized Natural Liberty" in *Black Heretics, Black Propehts* (2003) underscore Cugoano's critique of Western slavery. According to Edwards and Dabydeen, "though he [Cugoano] abhors the practice of slavery and asks for legislation 'to hinder and prohibit all men under British government to traffic either in buying or selling men,' he assumes pessimistically and with reason too that slave ownership will continue in the British colonies, suspecting that the establishment of the Freetown colony for freed slaves in 1787 to be yet another piece of white duplicity" (39–40). Edwards and Dabydeen's perspectives resonate with Adi and Sherwood's arguments that "He [Cugoano] was the first published African critic of the trans-Atlantic slave trade and the first African to publicly demand the abolition of the trade and the freeing of all slaves at a time when few other abolitionists made such demands" (27). In a similar vein, Bogues argues that "Cugoano centers the Atlantic slave trade as a focal point of eighteenth century European civilization" (33).

To my knowledge, the only work about Cugoano that emphasizes the African background of the author is Chris Kwame Awuyah's "Nationalism and Pan-Africanism in Ghanaian Writing: The Examples of Ottobah Cugoano, Joseph E. Casely-Hayford, and Ayi Kwei Armah" (1998). Awuyah considers Cugoano as a black author who inaugurated the tradition of protest writing in Ghanaian literature (203) and represents *Thoughts and Sentiments* as "some of the early chapters missing from the literary history of Ghana" (209). Awuyah's representation of Cugoano as a pioneer Ghanaian writer stresses the African origin and identity of the author, allowing us to examine the strong influences of traditional Ghanaian folklore on early black diasporan cultures. This African background is evident in Captain Robert Sutherland Rattray's work, *Akan-Ashanti Folktales* (1930), in which the author argues that slavery was an important factor in the dissemination of African folktales into the rest of the world (viii). One example of this African survival in the New World is the strong retention of Akan folklore in the Americas. In "Carrying Our Spirit with Us: Gold Coast Spiritual Continuities in Eighteenth-Century Suriname and North America" (2005), Zawadi Iyanjura Barskile writes: "Anansi spider stories are important elements of the folk culture of Akan people in present-day Ghana. These same stories were told in the same manner in parts of the Americas during the eighteenth century and still exist throughout the African Diaspora" (2–3).

The Akan folklore that has survived in the New World includes narratives about the Pan-African hero *Anancy*, whose struggles in exile and dislocation the enslaved blacks carried into the West Indies, North America, and Europe. As Pietro Deandrea argues in *Fertile Crossings: Metamorphoses of Genre in Anglophone West African Literature* (2002), *Anancy* is "a figure that survived the Middle Passage experience and still appears in Caribbean folktales" (95). According to Deandra, *Anancy* can be a half-spirit, half-human, and spider within Akan-lore (61). These hybrid qualities of *Anancy* in Akan oral tradition are similar to those he/she had in the slave folklore of the Americas. As Sheila S. Walker points out in *African Roots/American Cultures*, in the Americas, *Anancy* could be half-human and half-spider and could transform himself into "a trickster boy and man, as well as [into a] powerful, controlling half-spider woman" (54). According to Walker, in Grenada, *Anancy* could be a man who had "shapeshifter abilities" (54). Walker's representation of *Anancy* as a multifaceted figure in the Americas suggests the retention of Akan folklore in the Americas. Walker's representation of Grenada as one of the sites where *Anancy* possessed shapeshifter abilities is fascinating, since this British colony was the settlement where Cugoano faced the most atrocious part of his servitude and began to develop liberation strategies similar to those of *Anancy*. The relationship between Cugoano and *Anancy* is evident in the positions towards society that both icons symbolize.

Deandrea identifies the *Ananse* figure in Akan-Ashanti tales as the symbol of "wicked humour and penchant for pranks and taboo-breaking" (75) and the propensity "to act against the rigidity of tradition, continuously redrawing its boundaries 'not so much in defiance as in a new ordering of their limits'" (76), and as a key image in the interpretation of transgressiveness (94). As I will show in this chapter, Cugoano reflected similar trickster qualities as an Akan writer who resisted noninclusiveness in the West through wit and alteration of conventions. The strong survival of Akan folklore in the New World is not surprising since the Akan were a large part of the African population in the Americas. As Barskile points out, between 1601 and 1700, "52.5% of Gold Coast Africans brought to the Americas disembarked in Barbados" (54). Furthermore, as Rucker shows in *The River Flows On*, "between 1601 and 1800, roughly 80 to 85 percent of all Gold Coast Africans involved in the slave trade were embarked on ships destined for British, Dutch, and Danish colonies" (30). These statistics demonstrate the strong presence of Gold Coast inhabitants in the New World slave population during the seventeenth and eighteenth centuries.

Cugoano was born about 1757 in the Fanti coastal village of Agimaque or Adjumako, in current Ghana.[2] He was kidnapped in 1770 on the coast, when he was about thirteen years old, and sold into slavery.[3] According to Jerome S. Handler, "He was later transported from Cape Coast Castle to the Caribbean island of Grenada, where he spent eight or nine months; then for about a year he was taken to other places in the West Indies" ("Survivors of the Middle Passage," 44). He was eventually brought to England in 1772, where he was purchased and renamed John Stuart in 1773.[4] As Francis D. Adams and Barry Sanders argue, "Exactly how he [Cugoano] gained his freedom is not clear, but by the 1780s he was a free man, actively involved in the problems of the black men and women" ("Ottobah Cugoano," 43). In order to know who Cugoano was, it is important first to study the history of the Fanti ethnic group of eighteenth-century Ghana from which he came and the relationships between this society and the institution of slavery in Africa that influenced his early life. As John Kofi Fynn argues in *Oral Traditions of Fante States* (1974), the term "Fanti" (also pronounced "Fante") is an umbrella term referring to about twenty-two Twi-speaking groups of people who once inhabited the Gold Coast from West to East.[5] According to Fynn, the Fanti are an Akan ethnic group occupying the stretch of the Ghana coast from the estuary of the river Pra to the borders of Accra (a distance of more than one hundred miles) (*Fante of Ghana*, 1). The Fanti are one of the twi-speaking groups including the Asante (also called Ashanti), Assin, Akwapim, Brong, and Kwahu, which inhabit the southern part of Ghana. Nana Abarry writes: "They [the Fanti] speak dialects of the same language, Akan, and interact socially, religiously, and politically. Although they are not strictly homogeneous, enough cultural correspondences exist among them to warrant a meaningful generalization concerning the nature and forms of their oral literature" ("Teaching Akan Oral Literature," 310).

In the early eighteenth century, the Ashanti state, which had become the most powerful in Ghana, was competing for the domination of a slave trade that Europeans had begun in current Ghana from about 1471. A major point of encounter and conflict between the Fanti, the Ashanti, and Europeans was El Mina Castle, which, as Christopher R. DeCorse shows in *An Archeology of Elmina*, "was founded 10 years prior to Columbus's first voyage to the Americas" (90). In 1701, the Ashanti fought against the Denkyera and defeated them, mainly thanks to people from Wasa and Adom who, as Larry W. Yarak argues, were reported "to have imposed trade embargoes on military goods to their nominal overlords, in effect aiding the Asante revolt" ("Kingdom of Wasa," 144). In addition to fortifying their cultural influence on the region, the Ashanti expanded their influence on the other Akan groups, except the Fanti, who had always remained resistant to external domination. So, according to J. D. Fage, by the end of the eighteenth century, "the Ashanti Union had become the dominant power in the forest west of Akim and north of the Fante states and had extended to a considerable distance north of the forest, incorporating Bono and Banda and imposing tribute on Gonja and Dagomba. Then in 1807, Ashanti embarked on the first of a series of invasions of the Fante and Gã coastal states" (54–55). The disputes between Ashanti and Akan did not occur in a historical vacuum. They were brought about by the competition that Europeans created among the ethnic groups in Ghana by weakening local alliances and disrupting the increasingly unstable authority that each social entity had over the commerce of slaves.

The Fanti were so dependent on Europeans that they believed that they could not exist without their protection against the Ashanti. This apprehension is noticeable in a letter dated August 11, 1772, where Major John Joseph Crooks describes a council held at Cape Coast Castle between English military and Fanti dignitaries. In the letter, Crooks states: "Whereas there is the greatest reason to believe that the Ashantees intend to come down upon the Fantees and other inhabitants of the water side in a hostile manner and Deputies from the Heads of the Fantees having been sent here to know what part we propose to take in case they are attacked by their enemies and to request our assistance in supplying them with Gunpowder and Guns" (*Records*, 37). The British could not have shielded the Fanti from the hegemonic forces that developed across Africa because of the Atlantic trade. One of such forces was the Ashanti kingdom, which was so powerful during the eighteenth century that it had incorporated all the forest states except the Fanti states.[6] Like the Gã, the Fanti, and the other groups who had dominated the entrepreneurship with Europeans in earlier times, the Ashanti wanted to be integrated in the commercial economy of the trade. The Ashanti also wanted to be in control of certain parts of the coastal trade on which the Fanti had a monopoly for a long period. Clyde Chantler writes: "The Ashantis were an inland people and had for many years wanted direct access to a trading station on the coast. European goods were only obtainable at high prices owing to the middleman's activities. The Ashantis needed imported goods and resented having to trade through the Fante and Elmina middlemen" (*Ghana Story*, 80). Alternatively, the Ashanti used full offensive to displace the Fanti. As Chantler points out, "In 1805 the Ashanti armies invaded the Fante country. They attacked a small British fort near Cape Coast—it was probably Anomabu fort—where 2,000 Fantes had fled for safety" (80).

The tensions between the Fanti and the Ashanti provide the historical context leading to Cugoano's enslavement into the West. These conflicts led to the bondage of millions of people from the Cape Coast of Africa. They anticipate the nightmares that later confronted not just the Fanti and the Ashanti but all the populations of western and central Africa as the slave trade became stronger and more devastating. The terrible effects of slavery in Africa are visible in Cugoano's *Thoughts and Sentiments*, which is a Pan-Africanist and abolitionist treatise against the evil institution. The book participates in the colonial intellectual debate on the legal and moral validity of slavery, which, as David Brion Davis indicates in *The Problem of Slavery in Western Culture* (1966), "was a troublesome question in European thoughts from the time of Aristotle to the time of Locke" (13). Fighting for the antislavery movement, Cugoano presented and attacked the perspectives of the advocates of slavery, showing his awareness of the history of the slave trade and its effects on blacks.

Cugoano knew which part of Africa he came from. In his narrative, he says: "I was born in the city of Agimaque, on the coast of Fantyn; my father was a companion to the chief in that part of the country of Fantee, and when the old king died I was left in his house with his family" (12). The royal family's disposition to allow Cugoano to live among them shows the fluidity of social status in Fanti society. Here, both slaves and servants could live within the confines of the monarchy and rise to the privileged positions of leaders and advisors in their adoptive societies. Cugoano remembered his previous and honored social class in this African society and the customs of people who valued the extended nature of a family. His past royal status is hinted at in the passage where he explains his African playmates' reaction to him when he refuses to go with them into the woods to gather fruits and catch birds: "I refused to go with the rest, being rather apprehensive that something might happen to us; till one of my play-fellows said to me, because you belong to the great men, you are afraid to venture your carcase, or else of the *bounsam*, which is the devil" (12–13). The passage has a triple meaning. First, it shows that Cugoano had not forgotten the language and mythology of the Fanti. In *Double Descent among the Fanti* (1954), James Boyd Christensen defines the Fanti word "*Bonsam*" as meaning "men having power of evil magic" (140). This definition of evil is similar to the one Cugoano might have ascribed to the word "*bounsam*." Both definitions reveal the material connotation that the word "evil" possesses in Fanti culture, especially during the late eighteenth and early nineteenth centuries, when the slave trade brought on the southern coast of Ghana serious insecurities such as the eventuality of kidnapping and the prevalence of violence between ethnic groups. In *History of the Gold Coast and Asante* (1895), Ghanaian pastor Reverend Carl Christian Reindorf describes the state of Ghana during this period as being characterized by "pillage," "man-stealing," and "murder" in every district that Europeans witnessed "for their own benefit" (145). The kidnapping from this violence is the material "devil" to which Cugoano alludes in his account.

The association of the word "*bounsam*" with kidnapping and death is further evident in the Fanti people's fear of the folk figure of the *Sasabonsum*. As Verna Aardema argues, "The Ashanti kept children in their huts at night by telling them that if they went out, Sasabonsum [the Boogey Man] would grab them in his long arms and fly off with them . . . And the San hushed their children's cries by telling them, 'Whitemouth will hear you, and he'll come and swallow you whole!'" (*Once upon a Time Tales*, 23). The assertion shows that Africans used their belief in the existence of the folk character of the *Sasabonsum* in order to express their fear of European invasion of their villages and kidnapping of their people. This folk belief illustrates the Africans' awareness of the presence of Europeans in the interior of West Africa. During the Atlantic slave trade, Africans called the Europeans they saw on their coast "devils" because they viewed them as strangers and cannibals in a physical and psychological sense.[7] In *Black Legacy: America's Hidden Heritage* (1993), William D. Piersen analyzes oral narratives in which Africans on the coast reversed the stereotypes of white slavers by "believing that it was whites who were the cannibals, buying slaves in order to eat them. The tradition of insatiable white man-eaters explained why no one ever returned after being purchased on the coast" (4).

The African folklore about white man-eaters is evident in *Thoughts and Sentiments* when Cugoano describes the people that he saw near the seaside where an African guide and kidnapper had taken him to sell him to Europeans. Cugoano says: "I saw several white people, which made me afraid that they would eat me, according to our notion as children in the inland parts of the country. This made me rest very uneasy all the night" (14). Cugoano is petrified because his Fanti tradition, which associates whiteness with cannibalism, leads him to believe that the Europeans will devour him. The belief in the cannibalism of whites derived from two competing African ideologies that were responding to the presence of Europeans. First, it was maintained by the African captives who were on the verge of being sold to European slavers. In his report of the trip in which he accompanied the Slave Coffle in West Africa in 1797, the Scottish explorer Mungo Park describes the terror of the enslaved Africans he talked with in Kamalia, a town near the Niger River: "They were all inquisitive, but they viewed me at first with looks of horror and repeatedly asked if my countrymen were cannibals. They were very desirous to know what became of the slaves after they had crossed the salt water. I told them that they were employed in cultivating the land, but they would not believe me" ("Document 2," 111–12). This statement reveals the social and material reality of the Africans' belief in the cannibalism of European slavers and the traumatic psychological and physical impact it had on them. These Africans were as much worried about being "eaten" literally as about being kidnapped and sold into slavery and forced to work in alien lands. Their refusal to believe that the slaves who "had crossed the salt water" were alive reveals their conviction that the latter might have been devoured by the Europeans who had taken them away. Their attitude also shows their real fear of being captured and consumed by the inhumane labor system of these Europeans.

According to Joseph C. Miller, the tradition of insatiable white man-eaters was also a myth that grew out of the wealthy African slavers' attempts to offset unpredictable loss of investment from the capitalistic and exploitative trading relationships that Europeans had established with them (*Way of Death*, 157–58). For example, African slavers used the preexisting African magical, mythopoetic, and folkloric beliefs about the existence of witches as means for deterring kidnapped slaves from escaping. Piersen writes: "Terrifying rumors of foreign man-eating may also have been used by African slave merchants to placate new captives by pointing out that their present situation was not so bad when compared to the fate they could suffer among alien masters" (*Black Legacy*, 8). From this perspective, Cugoano's representation of the Europeans as cannibals resonates with the folk belief about alien man-eaters that Fanti slave traders might have spread among their captives in order to reduce the eventuality of slaves' escapes on their coastal region.

The myth of alien man-eaters was beneficial to both African and European traders, since it gave them the license to enslave any vulnerable person without regard to class, age, creed, religion, sex, or politics. Cugoano describes the Africans' fear of strangers as a consequence of the insecurity that the commerce of human beings created on the Gold Coast. This insecurity is visible when, after agreeing to go to the woods with his playmates, Cugoano and his friends are kidnapped by local strangers. Cugoano writes: "We had not been above two hours before our troubles began, when several great ruffians came upon us suddenly, and said we had committed a fault against their lord, and we must go and answer for it ourselves before him" (13). This citation shows that the Atlantic slave trade had created an extremely dangerous situation in Africa in which being a "stranger" marked someone as a potential criminal or abductor, as was the case for the people who snatched Cugoano and all his young companions and forcibly brought them to the Western world.

In his narration of the circumstances of his kidnapping and transportation into the West, Cugoano reflects a series of trickster motifs in the rhetoric of his assailants, such as the use of "smooth-talking," "pretense to do good in order to be rescued," "incremental tricks," and "lies," which finally make him realize he is betrayed by people who look like him. After being taken to an unfamiliar territory with the complicity of a black man who pretends "to be more friendly than the others," and who later disappears, Cugoano wakes up the next morning and finds himself surrounded by three other men whose languages differ from his (13). When he asks about his friends, he is told that "they were gone to the sea side to bring home some rum, guns and powder, and that some of my companions were gone with them, and that some were gone to the fields to do something or the other. This gave me strong suspicion that there was some treachery in the case, and I began to think that any hopes of returning home again were all over" (13–14). Therefore, Cugoano's separation from his homeland occurred in the context of active commercial transactions between African local traders and European merchants. The sight of white traders, a ship, and of "many of my miserable countrymen chained two and two, some hand-cuffed, and some with their hands tied behind" (14) confirmed Cugoano's increasing realization of his being trapped into bondage.

Cugoano's awareness of his dire plight reflects the terrible dilemma Africans faced during the Atlantic slave trade when Europeans established their imperial hegemony in Africa through kidnapping and trickery. As Daniel Tetteh Osabu-Kle points out in "The African Reparation Cry: Rationale, Estimate, Prospects, and Strategies" (2000), "the character of the [imperialist] process was European raid of African villages to obtain captives to sell to fellow Europeans in Africa, Europe, or the Americas. Europeans in Europe, Africa, and the Americas created the demand, and Europeans in Africa created the supply through a combination of their superior military might and trickery" (338). Using emotionally wrenching tone and diction, Cugoano depicts the barbarity of this enslavement: "I was soon conducted to a prison, for three days, where I heard the groans and cries of many, and saw some of my fellow-captives. But when a vessel arrived to conduct us away to the ship, it was a most horrible scene; there was nothing to be heard but rattling of chains, smacking of whips, and the groans and cries of our fellow-men" (14–15). The violence that Cugoano and other kidnapped Africans experienced on the European slave ships led to the formation of the first Pan-African and transethnic solidarity in the black diaspora. As Stuckey argues in *Slave Culture*, "during the process of their becoming a single people, Yorubas, Akans, Ibos, Angolans, and others were present on slave ships" to the Americas and "experienced a common horror—unearthly moans and piercing shrieks, the smell of filth and the stench of death, all during the violent rhythms and quiet coursings of ships at sea. As such, slave ships were the first real incubators of slave unity across cultural lines, cruelly revealing irreducible links from one ethnic group to the other, fostering resistance thousands of miles before the shores of the new land appeared on the horizon—" (3).

In the genre of captivity narratives, Cugoano's is unparalleled in its testimonial quality and its description of the atrocity of slavery. His account reveals a partnership of African and European traders in his enslavement. As visible in his portrayal of his guide, he abhors the greed and corruption that led African traders to sell their fellow Africans to Europeans. Yet he places the responsibility of this enslavement on Europeans rather than on Africans, because he believes that the former were the ones who profited most from the trade.

Cugoano asserts: "I must own, to the shame of my own countrymen, that I was first kid-napped and betrayed by some of my own complexion, who were the first cause of my exile and slavery; but if there were no buyers there would be no sellers" (16). Cugoano's perspective reflects the inhumane conditions that developed from the Atlantic slave trade while illustrating the arguments of Oliver Ransford, Keith Richburg, and Carretta that Africans were also to blame for the enslavement of their own people.[8]

Corroborating the theories of Claude Meillassoux, Paul E. Lovejoy, and John Thornton on the particular types of slavery that existed in African societies before the Atlantic trade began, Cugoano shows that Africans had slaves but that their system of bondage was far different from the one that Europeans introduced in Africa.[9] Key differences were: 1) in Africa, slaves could return home and had more means to go back home even if they might lose rights in their native society; 2) fleeing from slavery in Africa presented fewer risks than was the case in the Americas, because in Africa the system of slavery was rarely enforced and nearby societies were sometimes not slavers; 3) unlike in the Americas, in Africa a slave could marry a free person and join their lineage, and he was allowed to be a soldier.[10] These flexible forms of slavery, which existed in Africa before the Europeans' arrival, appear in Cugoano's following description: "So far as I can remember, some of the Africans in my country keep slaves, which they take in war, or for debt; but those which they keep are well fed, and good care taken of them, and treated well; and, as to their cloathing [clothing], they differ according to the custom of the country. But I may safely say, that all the poverty and misery that any of the inhabitants of Africa meet with among themselves, is far inferior to those inhospitable regions of misery which they meet with in the West Indies, where their hard-hearted overseers have neither regard to the laws of God, nor the life of their fellow-men" (16–17).

Cugoano's description of African domestic slavery provides a counterpoint to the inhumane slavery systems Europeans introduced on both sides of the Atlantic. His emphasis on the opportunities that slaves in Africa had in contrast to "the poverty and misery" of their counterparts in the Americas shows that the Africans' systems of servitude were more humane than those of Europeans. Before Europeans arrived in Africa, most of the people who were put in servitude in the continent were pawns. J. D. Fage defines the term "pawn" as the pledge of a slave or a kinsman or even himself "as security for a debt" (48). As Fage posits, before the advent of Europeans, this pawn system did not produce a large-scale trade in slaves in the West African forests and coastal lands including the Gold Coast (48).

Contrary to the Europeans' system in which slaves were regarded as a nonentity that could be eliminated when they were deemed to be unproductive, the African system of pawnship allowed slaves to preserve their humanity. In African pawnship, the slave was regarded as a symbolic economic investment that could be replaced with useful material good. In *Way of Death: Merchant Capitalism and the Angolan Slave Trade, 1730–1830* (1988), Joseph Miller describes how traditional Africans viewed a slave as a person one could buy "as a gift to the seller of the slave (or receiver of the goods), who thereby assigned his compensating dependency onto a substitute, a member of his kin group or a dependent in his entourage" (52). The relational and communal nature of pawnship in traditional Africa was a stark contrast to the individualistic and capitalistic features of slavery in the New World. Unlike Europeans, who viewed a slave as a degraded commodity, Africans considered a slave to be an untarnished human being who could regain freedom and be reinserted into a community without prejudice.[11]

Furthermore, Cugoano debunks a series of racist myths that Europeans developed about Africans. One of these views was the belief "that an African is not entitled to any competent degree of knowledge, or capable of imbibing any sentiments of probity; and that nature designed him for some inferior link in the chain, fitted only to be a slave" (11–12). Here, Cugoano creates a subtle analogy between the chain around the feet of the kidnapped Africans and the "Chain of Being" metaphor in eighteenth-century philosophy. The English referred to this chain to classify people in a hierarchical order in which servants and subjects were placed in a position below that of the monarchs.[12] This hierarchal order is similar to the social stratification in American and European societies in which blacks were perceived as inferior to whites. The ideology of white supremacy was strongly held in the works of eighteenth-century Western political philosophers such as the Scot David Hume and the Germans Immanuel Kant and George Friedrich Hegel, who, as Emmanuel Chukwudi Eze contends in *Race and the Enlightenment* (1997), "played a strong role in articulating Europe's sense not only of its cultural but also racial superiority" (5). Along with the American Thomas Jefferson, these early Western thinkers believed in the universal power of reason while denying black people's ability to have it.[13]

The connection between the chain around the feet of Africans and the European "Chain of Being" that Cugoano makes in *Thoughts and Sentiments* reveals his ability to use elements of philosophy as a means for resisting slavery. As Anthony Bogues argues, Cugoano "is refuting the system of slavery at the level of logic, reason, and religion" (*Black Heretics*, 33). Using these fundamentals of philosophy that Western intellectual tradition cherished, Cugoano participated in the revolutionary Pan-African intellectual tradition that Bogues identifies as a political discourse that is "preoccupied with the nature of natural liberty and natural rights as 'common rights'" (33).[14] Yet Cugoano does not limit his political discourse to philosophy and religion; he also draws on history in order to stress the humanity and natural rights of blacks. This emphasis on the humanity of blacks is visible when he shifts the notion of darkness that has been associated to the curse of Ham by employing it as a signifier for the ignobility of slavery. Reinterpreting the Judeo-Christian story about the curse of Cain, he represents the "wicked" generation of slaveholders in the West Indies as the descendants of "the Canaanites who fled away in the Time of Joshua" (32).[15] Cugoano develops his hypothesis by saying, "For if the curse of God ever rested upon them [Canaanites], or upon any other men, the only visible mark thereof was always upon those who committed the most outrageous acts of violence and oppression. But colour and complexion has nothing to do with that mark; every wicked man, and the enslavers of others, bear the stamp of their own iniquity, and that mark which was set upon Cain" (33). By making an analogy between slavery and darkness, Cugoano removes the negative racial stigma that Western intellectual history associated with Africans and identifies it as a useful symbol of human oppression against other humans. In this sense, Cugoano emphasizes the humanity of Africans and, as Anthony Bogues points out, creates a "positive self-affirmation of blackness in an anti-black racist world" (45).[16] Bogues continues: "Cugoano's dethronement of blackness as curse and badge of inferiority was astonishing for its time, given the normative weight of hegemonic whiteness naturalized as the universal self . . . this would separate him from many of the white abolitionists who argued against slavery but felt that Africans were uncivilized" (45).

Another instance in which Cugoano uses history as a tool for dismantling racist European accounts about Africans is the passage in *Thoughts and Sentiments* where he reinterprets the Judeo-Christian narrative about the curse of Ham from a Pan-African perspective. He discusses the situation of Cush and Nimrod, the descendants of the other three sons of Ham who "were not included under the curse of his father" (33). According to Cugoano, Cush, the oldest descendant of Ham, settled in the southwest of Arabia; Nimrod, one of the sons of Cush, founded the kingdom of Babylon in Asia, and the others "made their descent southward, by the Red Sea, and came over to Abyssinia and Ethiopia, and, likely, dispersed themselves throughout all the southern and interior parts of Africa" (33). Thus, Cugoano was conscious of his African origins and was able to trace African history as far back as it was possible for him to do. In providing this brief analysis, he helps bring Africa back into a historiography that ignores the heterogeneity of the civilizations of the continent. His attempt to reinscribe Africa into history is suggested when he describes the word "Africa" in terms that register his strong Pan-Africanist consciousness. He writes:

> And, as they [the Cushites] lived mostly under the torrid zone, or near the tropics, they became black, as being natural to the inhabitants of those sultry hot climates; and, in that case, their complexion bears the signification of the name of their original progenitor, Cush, as known to the Hebrews by that name, both on the east and on the west, beyond the Red Sea; but the Greeks called them Ethiopians, or black faced people. (33)

Cugoano seems to attach primary importance to the words "Ethiopia" and "Ethiopians," which are Pan-Africanist terms that many early black writers of the West used to identify with Africans on the continent and abroad. Earlier in the book, he describes blacks in the diaspora as "Ethiopians" (70), conveying his perception of the term "Ethiopians" as a word that expresses the diaspora's strong attraction to Africa. In *The Struggle for Freedom: A History of African Americans* (2005), Clayborne Carson, Emma J. Lapsansky-Werner, and Gary B. Nash say that the late nineteenth-century Pan-Africanist Edward Blyden had a program known as "*Ethiopianism*," which "called attention to the biblical story in which Ethiopia commanded a divinely protected empire" (307). Cugoano's references to Ethiopia predated the Ethiopianism of the late nineteenth century while participating in a Pan-African intellectual framework that other nineteenth-century black diasporan writers such as Blyden, Henry McNeal Turner, and Martin R. Delany also used to defend Africa against Western oppression. For instance, Delany perceived Africa as the promised land of blacks where free slaves would find all the rights and privileges that whites denied them in the United States. In the *Official Report of the Niger Valley Exploring Party* (1860), Delany describes the colony of Liberia that he visited in 1859 as follows: "On the African coast already exists a thriving and prosperous Republic. It is the native home of the African race; and there he can enjoy the dignity of manhood, the rights of citizenship, and all the advantages of civilization and freedom. Every colored man in this country will be welcome there as a free citizen: and there he can not only prosper, and secure his own comfort and happiness, but become a teacher and benefactor of his kindred races" (35). Delany's representation of Liberia suggests that he supported the idea of a nation in Africa that all blacks could call "home." He envisioned this nation as a country where blacks in Africa and abroad could have the autonomy and independence that were necessary for their social and economic development. Delany's representation of Africa as "the native home" where free blacks will enjoy "the advantages of civilization and freedom" resuscitated the Ethiopianist portrayal of Africa that Cugoano provided in 1787.

Additionally, by drawing from the beliefs in the universality and nonracial basis of reason and the power of writing against fanaticism, which were intrinsic in the tenets of the philosophers of the Enlightenment, Cugoano opposes Western racism toward blacks by revealing its falsities and paradoxes. Cugoano says: "Some pretend that the Africans, in general, are a set of poor, ignorant, dispersed, unsociable people; and that they think it no crime to sell one another, and even their own wives and children; therefore they bring them away to a situation where many of them may arrive to a better state than ever they could obtain in their own native country" (22–23). Cugoano's statement attacks the pathologizing of blacks that was intrinsic in Enlightenment philosophy.[17] According to Carretta, the quotation might have been a summary of a view that David Hume expressed in "Of National Characters" in *Three Essays: Moral and Political* (1748), saying: "You may obtain any thing of the NEGROES by offering them strong drink; and may easily prevail with them to sell, not only their children, but their wives and mistresses, for a cask of brandy" ("Explanatory Notes" 156). Opposing Hume's theory, Cugoano writes: "This specious pretence is without any shadow of justice and truth, and, if the argument was even true, it could afford no just and warrantable matter for any society of men to hold slaves. But the argument is false; there can be no ignorance, dispersion, or unsociableness so found among them, which can be made better by bringing them away to a state of a degree equal to that of a cow or a horse" (23). Cugoano uses two keywords that show the criteria by which he assesses the value of a theory: justice and truth. Since Hume's rationale provides no means for reaching the three goals, Cugoano dismisses its racism without, however, denying that there were some "ignorance, dispersion, or unsociableness" among slaves. Cugoano's acceptance of the existence of unawareness, fragmentation, and disorganization among slaves does not repeat Eurocentric racism. It rather stresses his idea that improving the lives of slaves required the promotion of education, unity, and conviviality among them rather than the development of unconsciousness, division, and hostility between them. By representing slaves in such humane terms, Cugoano counters the racist ideas Europeans developed about them. As Adi and Sherwood point out, "In his writing Cugoano demolishes all the principal pro-slavery arguments which questioned the humanity of Africans or preached the benevolence of the trade" ("Quobna Ottobah Cugoano," 27).

Moreover, Cugoano criticized Hume's perception of slaves as ignorant by saying: "But let their ignorance in some things (in which the Europeans have greatly the advantage of them) be what it will, it is not the intention of those who bring them away to make them better by it; nor is the design of slave-holders of any other intention, but that they may serve them as a kind of engines and beasts of burden" (23). In this statement, Cugoano shows that it was unfair for Europeans to bring Africans to the West, deprive them of all opportunities for advancement, and expect them to have the same level of education, cohesion, and social structure that the privileged whites possessed. Appealing to the basic tenets of Enlightenment philosophy, he describes legal freedom and education as better ways of improving the lives of blacks. He says: "By the benevolence of some, a few [slaves] may get their liberty, and by their own industry and ingenuity, may acquire some learning, mechanical trades, or useful business; and some may be brought away by different gentlemen to free countries, where they get their liberty, but no thanks to slave-holders for it" (23). Here, Cugoano undermines Hume's theory that inferiority was inherent in the natural environmental or climatological characteristics of Africa. Dismantling Hume's notion that Africans who were enslaved into the New World had become "civilized," Cugoano shows that the West corrupted the humanity of these Africans. In this sense, he perceived Africa as being a far better place than the world slaves found in the West. His positive view of Africa stemmed from his knowledge of the privileges that slaves had there before the arrival of Europeans. Having been reared in Akan cultural and intellectual traditions, Cugoano knew that slaves in Akan society enjoyed social and political securities that mitigated their legal status as slaves.

Though they were categorized, slaves in Akan society benefited from communal supervisions that guaranteed their integration into society when their slave status was removed. In *Chieftaincy in Ghana* (2000), A. Kodzo Paaku Kludze describes how among the Ewe of Ghana, "where only the maternal side of the candidate is tainted with slave blood, such a candidate may be elected to occupy the stool if his other qualities are outstanding" (160). This tolerance of maternal slave ancestry also existed in Akan society where, as James Christensen argues, enforced servitude was cosmologically explained as a consequence of not just a single line of descent and the tracing of one's paternal ancestry with one's left hand, suggesting that the slave could be reintegrated into society for his/her other qualities as long as his/her patrilineal line of descent was not compromised (38).

In Fanti society, slaves were an integral part of the community even if they were placed at the bottom of a distinct hierarchy. The community protected enslaved persons by guaranteeing that they could regain their rightful place in society once the debts they owed for their symbolic servitude were paid. As James Christensen argues, even a free Fanti who accidentally got immediate slave status, instead of death penalty, for insulting a chief, could regain his/her status if the debt was paid at the normal rate of interest on a loan, which amounted to 50 percent with a certain percentage added each year for a renewal (39). In this sense, the Fanti did not keep their slaves in eternal bondage and did not apply any racial categories on their status and nature. The Fanti had a social system that guaranteed the enslaved certain prerogatives that demonstrated their knowledge of law, communal supervision, and ethical fairness. Cugoano's familiarity with this Fanti culture allowed him to resist racism and promote the abolition of slavery in the West. Using his knowledge of Africa, he shows that slaves in Africa were better treated than those in the West. In so doing, he represents slavery in the New World as a corruptive and heathen system that distanced blacks in the diaspora from the virtues of their traditional African culture. Thus, Cugoano viewed knowledge of Africa as a fundamental part of Pan-African consciousness that demonstrates the diaspora's recognition of the significance of homeland in its racial awareness and transnational identities. In this sense, as Kadiatu Kanneh suggests, "discourses of Africa," such as those of Pan-Africanism, "are important in relation to the politics of Black identities and cultures in the African Diaspora" (*African Identities*, 1).

Although he denounces Western stereotypes of Africans, Cugoano does not reject his Western identity. Being conscious of the ruptures that slavery has brought into his identity, he creates a harmonious syncretism between his traditional African culture and his new Western customs. He maintains this balance even though he is occasionally ambivalent toward both Africa and the West. Early in his book, Cugoano celebrates his Western cultures without demeaning his African traditions. Expressing his gratitude to the education that he received in the West, he represents it as knowledge that helped him survive the atrocity of slavery. He says: "Thanks be to God, I was delivered from Grenada, and that horrible brutal slavery.—A gentleman coming to England, took me for his servant, and brought me away, where I found my situation become more agreeable. After coming to England, and seeing others write and read, I had a strong desire to learn, and getting what assistance I could, I applied myself to learn reading and writing" (17). This statement suggests Cugoano's perception of diligent quest of Western knowledge as a vital tool for Pan-African resistance and survival. Recognizing the significance of hybridism in

Pan-Africanism, Kanneh writes: "The movement between African and European contexts reveals how Africa and its identities have been crucially informed by the impact of knowledges and interests from *outside* the continent" (1).

Later, Cugoano celebrates the Christianity he embraced in the West. Identifying himself as a personification of the prophet Joseph, whom God saved from the betrayal of his brothers, he states: "I may say with Joseph, as he did with respect to the evil of his brethren, when they sold him into Egypt, that whatever evil intentions and bad motives those insidious robbers had in carrying me away from my native country and friends, I trust, was what the Lord intended for my good" (17). He continues:

> I am highly indebted to many a good people of England for learning and principles unknown to the people of my native country. But, above all, what have I obtained from the Lord God of Hosts, the God of the Christians! in that divine revelation of the only true God, and the Saviour of men, what a treasure of wisdom and blessings are involved? How wonderful is the divine goodness displayed in those invaluable books the Old and New Testaments, that inestimable compilation of books, the Bible? And, O what a treasure to have, and one of the greatest advantages to be able to read therein, and a divine blessing to understand! (17–18)

Thus, African culture and spirituality had a strong impact on the Christian beliefs that Cugoano espoused in the diaspora. This Christianity integrates African conceptions of God and diplomacy that are traceable to Cugoano's Fanti traditions. His depiction of God as "the only true God, and the Saviour of men" reflects a Christian worldview that is influenced by the Fanti's conception of divinity as the incarnation of ultimate spirituality to which all the personal, religious, and ancestral spirits converge. This representation of God as a "meta-spirit" is evident in the Fanti's perception of their orators or historians [*griots*] as diplomats or emissaries of God whose major duty is to make sure that necessary personal rites are performed so that the intimacies between the Supreme Being and individuals are protected. As James Christensen points out, the Fanti use the word "*Nyankupon*" to refer to God and the term "*Asaase Efua*" to identify the "earth goddess" (34). This supreme Fanti/Akan God and the Christian God fulfill the same function as arbiters of tensions that individuals and emissaries of divinities must resolve together in consultation with the higher power. In a similar vein, Sidney G. Williamson argues that the Akan see the "Supreme Being" (also called *Onyame* or *Onyankopon*) as a "personal" God who is the dependable, trustworthy, all-creating, and all-seeing one (86–87). This notion of a personal and monotheistic Supreme Being has survived in the Christianity of Cugoano, in which God is conceptualized as the reliable bearer of all truth. Cugoano writes: "God hath promised to fill the world with a knowledge of himself, and he hath set up his bow, in the rational heavens, as well as in the clouds, as a token that he will stop the proud ways of error and delusion, that hitherto they may come, and no farther. The holy arch of truth is to be seen in the azure paths of the pious and the wise" (108). In such praise of the Judeo-Christian God, Cugoano creates a religious ideology in which traditional Akan representation of God as a personable deity blends with the Western Judeo-Christian view of God as a friendly divinity.[18]

Yet Cugoano's representation of Christianity is permeated with occasional condescension toward Africans. Repeating the Europeans' stereotyping of Africans as inferior, he calls for the conversion of Africans to Christianity. He states:

> And should it please the Divine goodness to visit some of the poor dark Africans, even in the brutal stall of slavery, and from thence to instal[l] them among the princes of his grace, and to invest them with a robe of honor that will hang about their necks for ever; but who can then suppose, that it will be well pleasing unto him to find them subjected there in that dejected state? Or can the slave-holders think that the Universal Father and Sovereign of Mankind will be well pleased with them, for the brutal transgression of his law, in bowing down the necks of those to the yoke of their cruel bondage? (24)

By perceiving the Africans' conversion to Christianity as a good situation that can repair the evil of their enslavement into the West, Cugoano somewhat repeats the Western bias that views Christianity as the only source of spiritual and moral uplift for Africans. This perspective is grounded on the prejudiced idea that Africans have no worthy religions and traditions that are equal to those of the West.

Another instance in which Cugoano reveals his condescension toward Africans is visible when he denounces Britain's involvement in the slave trade as a history that belied the Europeans' claim to bringing "reformation" and "civilization" to Africans (88). He writes: "The greater that any reformation and civilization is obtained by any nation, if they do not maintain righteousness, but carry on any course of wickedness and oppression, it makes them appear only the more inconsistent, and their tyranny and oppression the more conspicuous" (88). This statement carries a double argument. The first one is Cugoano's perception of British civilization as a culture that has achieved a "greater" stage of development that he wants to enhance through a substitution of fair trade with slavery. Myra Jehlen and Michael Warner write: "By putting an end to slavery, the English will profit not only in virtue but in cash. Promising through freedom ten times the profits of slavery, Cugoano, for all his invocation of Christianity, seems to have few illusions about the motives of European society" (880).

While Cugoano viewed European society to be imperialist towards Africa and accused Britain of joining other Western nations to rob Africa (88), he tolerated English cultural imperialism toward Africa. This contradiction is evident when Cugoano exhorts the British government to go on a cultural and Christian mission in Africa. He writes: "And this should be expected, wherever a Christian government is extended, and the true religion is embraced, that the blessings of liberty should be extended likewise, and that it should diffuse its influences first to fertilize the mind, and then the effects of its benignity would extend, and arise with exuberant blessings and advantages from all its operations" (92). By asking Britain to extend the blessings of its liberty and religion to Africa, Cugoano becomes a writer who is somewhat coopted by the Western government that he criticizes. He transforms himself into a diffusionist who believes that civilization spreads from the West to Africa. This ideology is also apparent in the *Official Report of the Niger Valley Exploring Party* (1860) where Delany represents Africa as a promised land where every free black of the West will become "an agent in carrying civilization and Christianity to a benighted continent" (35). Like Cugoano's, Delany's representation of Africa reflects the ideology of Western diffusionism that Tunde Adeleke describes eloquently in *UnAfrican Americans: Nineteenth-Century Black Nationalists and the Civilizing Mission* (1998). Adeleke provides a useful definition of this diffusionism when he writes:

> Power and its ideological underpinning radiated from two potent and idiosyncratic European concepts: Eurocentrism, the proclamation of Europe's superiority over non-Europe, and diffusionism, the attribution of cultural change and innovations to external interventions, i.e., to the diffusion of ideas and values from elsewhere. Eurocentric diffusionism, therefore, negated the theory of independent invention or parallel development, projecting "development," "change," and "civilization" as products of the infusion/diffusion of superior European ideas and institutions. (15)

Cugoano participated in European diffusionism by revealing the racist, stereotypical, disparaging, and patronizing notion that Africans need Western civilization in order to develop from a primitive or inferior status. This prejudice was common among New World blacks during the late eighteenth and early nineteenth centuries. As Nemata Amelia Blyden points out in *West Indians in West Africa, 1808–1880: The African Diaspora in Reverse* (2000), "In the eighteenth and nineteenth centuries, New World blacks' perceptions of Africa were framed by the negative images and stereotypes espoused by their captors. During the period of the slave trade and into the nineteenth century, Africa was depicted as a place of savagery and darkness. Blacks in the New World internalized the belief that they were more privileged than their counterparts in Africa" (52). The veracity of Nemata Blyden's theory is evident in the ways in which Cugoano represents Africa as a desolate land that Europeans could rescue by sending educated black Westerners there to elevate Africans from barbarism. Discussing his reasons for proposing that Britain send its educated blacks to Africa, Cugoano says:

> It might be another necessary duty for Christians, in the course of that time, to make enquiry concerning some of their friends and relations in Africa; and if they found any intelligent persons amongst them, to give them as good education as they could, and find out a way of recourse to their friends; that as soon as they had made any progress in useful learning and the knowledge of the Christian religion, they might be sent back to Africa, to be made useful there as soon, and as many of them as could be made fit for instructing others. (99)

Cugoano was therefore one of the eighteenth-century black intellectuals who believed that Africans needed to be religiously and culturally salvaged by the West through the intercession of elite blacks of the West. This attitude is consistent with Cugoano's portrayal of Africans as ignorant and heathen. Describing Africans, he says that they are "a set of distressed poor ignorant people" who could become "refined and established in light of knowledge" and allowed to "imitate their noble British friends, to improve their lands, and make use of that industry as the nature of their country might require" (101). Cugoano's portrayal of Africans exposes the deep-seated feeling of superiority over Africans that Western blacks of the eighteenth and nineteenth centuries had. As Nemata Blyden points out these blacks "viewed indigenous African cultures as inferior and saw themselves as missionaries, both spiritual and cultural. New World blacks 'considered themselves peculiarly suited to the task of uplifting and civilizing those Africans who had never left their native shores'" (52). These blacks perceived themselves as outsiders who acted simply as intermediaries between the West and Africa for the benefit of Western cultural and economic imperialism.

Focusing on the writings of nineteenth-century African American nationalists such as Alexander Crummel and Martin R. Delany, Adeleke describes these blacks as Pan-Africanists who "appropriated the values and idiosyncrasies that distinguished Euro-American nationalism and expansionism" (13). The product of this Western expansionism was the idea of the "civilizing mission," which operated in terms of dichotomies. Adeleke writes: "Scientific, historical, and ideological postulations legitimized the 'civilizing mission' and defended a Manichean construction of the world. The world was conceived as consisting of an advanced, civilized European sector and a primitive, backward, non-European sector" (13–14). Cugoano partly shared this Manichean view of the world, since he occasionally perceived Africa as a primitive land where he expected Europeans to bring civilization. In this sense, Cugoano has conflicting relationships with Africa since his Pan-Africanism upheld the dangerous Western perception of Africans as culturally inferior that he occasionally rejected in *Thoughts and Sentiments*.

Another paradox in Cugoano's perception of Africa is visible in his call for black emigration to Sierra Leone, which reflected imperialistic tendencies that somewhat compromised his Pan-Africanism. This contradiction is apparent in how he views the establishment of British colonies in Africa as positive as long as such colonies are used to help blacks living in England settle there. In an attempt to convince blacks of the diaspora to become "residentors in the African colonies," Cugoano describes the latter as territories "where there might be employment enough given to all free people, with suitable wages according to their usefulness, in the improvement of land," the "encouragement" of "agriculture" and "every other branch of industry," and the increase of inhabitants, "without which any country, however blessed by nature, must continue poor" (99–100). Cugoano's statement mixes a Eurocentric imagery of Africa as colonies, where blacks of the diaspora can achieve their individual economic dreams, with a Pan-Africanist representation of Africa as land where these blacks can also fulfill their collective desire to provide the necessary workforce and technological knowledge that will allow the continent to develop.

The idea of resettling these blacks in Africa started in the late 1780s when thousands of blacks living in England were encouraged by English abolitionists and government officials to go to Africa and help alleviate the damage slavery had brought about there. As Carretta suggests, in 1786, an association called

Committee for the Relief of the Black Poor was founded by a group of humanitarian English businessmen to help "provide relief, health care, clothing, food, and jobs to needed blacks" who were working with the East India Company as sailors.[19] According to A. Adu. Boahen, in 1787, many Englishmen perceived Liberia as a product of their humanitarian, abolitionist, and antiracist campaigns of the period, just in the same way the Americans who founded Liberia in 1820 imagined it for similar purposes (*African Perspectives*, 7–8). Celebrating what he views as the positive impact of the emigration of blacks of England to Sierra Leone, Cugoano writes: "According to the plan, humanity hath made its appearance in a more honorable way of colonization, than any Christian nation have ever done before, and may be productive of much good, if they continue to encourage and support them" (104). Cugoano's description of the emigration project as an "honorable way of colonization" suggests the transitory and imperialistic motivation that partly led him to support the relocation of blacks to Sierra Leone. Cugoano legitimizes the establishment of Sierra Leone as a colony when he knows that such validation implicitly supports British colonization of African land. He legitimizes English colonization of African land by describing it as a good deed from a distinguished "Christian nation," thereby forgetting the atrocities that England perpetrated against Africa.

Yet, by the end of his narrative, Cugoano counters his imperialistic motivation toward Africa when he raises serious doubts about the feasibility of the black emigration project. He writes: "But after all, there is some doubt whether their own flattering expectation in the manner as set forth to them, and the hope of their friends may not be that they never will be settled as intended, in any permanent and peaceable way at Sierra Leona" (104). Cugoano gives many reasons that the project was unsuccessful. First, he notes that the emigration idea "has neither altogether met with the credulous approbation of the Africans here, nor yet been sought after with any prudent and right plan by the promoters of it." Second, he posits that the European organizers made no "treaty of agreement" with the inhabitants of Africa and they failed to point out "the terms and nature of such a settlement fixed upon, and its situation and boundary." Third, he argues that the organizers hurried unconvinced blacks from England into delayed ships, where most of them died from cold and other "disorders." Fourth, he contends that several of these blacks who were among "the most intelligent" of the participants were prevented by the jealous governors of the mission from going on the journey. In a satirical tone, Cugoano describes Western blacks who had been obliged to go but who plunged into the water to get ashore because they feared the trip's prospect of misery, difficulty, and surrounding danger (105). These blacks' perception of

Africa as a prospect of looming desolation, challenge, and danger repeats the Western falsification of the continent that Cugoano himself shared.

Yet, while it reflects disrespectful remarks about Africans, Cugoano's narrative reveals his appropriation of distinctive Pan-African cultural elements that weaken his persistent stereotypes of Africans. His story exposes the strong influence of Fanti religious outlook on his worldviews. This impact is noticeable in his belief in the power of the Akan and Christian Gods to intervene in human affairs and punish wrongdoers such as slaveholders. Having Africanized the Bible by speaking about the Akan God through allusions to the Christian God, Cugoano performs the function of the traditional Akan priest whose duty is to mediate harmonious relationships between the heavenly/sacred spheres and the earthly/secular worlds. In order to play this role of divine mediator, he takes the position of the orator who asks fundamental rhetorical questions about slavery that Europeans were avoiding. He says: "If the blood of one man unjustly shed cries with so loud a voice for the Divine vengeance, how shall the cries and groans of an hundred thousand men annually murdered ascend the celestial mansions, and bring down that punishment such enormities deserve?" (76). This question recalls the prayers the Fanti/Akan diviner says to *Nyankupon* (God) through the medium of ancestors by imploring them, with libation, to protect the community against chaos.[20] In this sense, Cugoano was a Pan-Africanist despite his problematic views about Christianity's civilizing role in Africa. Edwards and Dabydeen write: "though he acknowledges the good fortune that attended him under divine benevolence after his enslavement, he [Cugoano] never allows his argument to slip into the common hypocrisy of the slave owners, and some churchmen, even of some slaves, that the benefits of Christian conversion outweighed the sufferings of slavery, and that slavery was itself part of a divine scheme of benevolence" (39).

Additionally, Cugoano develops a discourse of supernatural Chaos that serves as a warning against the consequences of slavery and imperialism on humanity. He uses metaphors that convey the pain and disorder that European oppression of Africans brought about. Using the imagery of the crying and groaning of "an hundred thousand men" who ascend "the celestial mansions, and bring down that punishment such enormities deserve" (76), he invokes supernatural upheavals in a poetic and dramatic manner that recalls the oral strategy that the Fanti diviner uses in order to warn the community against potential harm or evil. Drawing from such traditions, Cugoano asks Europeans who enslaved Africans to imagine what they would think if the same thing was done to them. He writes: "Were the inhabitants of Great Britain to hear tell of any other nation that murdered one hundred thousand innocent people annually, they would think them an exceeding inhuman, barbarous, and wicked people indeed, and that they would be surely punished by some signal judgment of Almighty God" (76). Here, Cugoano develops an African-influenced rhetoric of supernatural chaos that allows him to implicitly denounce the Europeans' participation in slavery.

Moreover, Cugoano develops a discourse that represents Africans in positive ways. He stresses that Africans are as human as Europeans because the survival and destiny of both groups depend on respect for "Divine clemency," "Sovereign goodness," and the universal right of each group to achieve high learning and freedom (24). The latter can be propagated only through unselfish sharing of religious and universal goodness. Speaking like a teacher who introduces Western readers to the diversity in Africa, he asserts: "And now, as to the Africans being dispersed and unsociable, if it was so, that could be no warrant for the Europeans to enslave them; and even though they may have different feuds and bad practices among them, the continent of Africa is of vast extent, and the numerous inhabitants are divided into several kingdoms and principalities, which are governed by their respective kings and princes, and those are absolutely maintained by their free subjects" (25). Cugoano's history lesson is an informative portrayal of late eighteenth-century Africa as a geographically and politically diverse continent. Its description of autonomous "kingdoms" and "principalities" governed by "kings and princes" shows Cugoano's reverence for and knowledge of Africa. This positive representation of precolonial Africa contradicts Hume's negative representation of Africans as "dispersed" and "unsociable." Cugoano proves Hume wrong by showing that the continent is composed of sophisticated societies that, like Europe, had empires and dominions. Responding to Hume's theory that Africans would sell their wives and children without remorse, Cugoano states: "Nothing can distress them [Africans] more, than to part with any of their relations and friends. Such are the tender feelings of parents for their children, that, for the loss of a child, they seldom can be rendered happy, even with the intercourse and enjoyment of their friends, for years" (27).

Cugoano's Pan-Africanist rhetoric reflects the Fanti's respect for filial bonds and their grieving for the enslavement of their children as an irreparable loss. The reluctance to put one's family in bondage is a central element in Fanti folktales where the trickster *Kwaku Anansi*, the spider, has complex social, ideological, and cultural functions that are similar to those that Cugoano has in the West. *Anansi* and his neighbors of the Akan folkloric kingdom reveal anxieties in Fanti society while utilizing the subtle tools of resistance Africans such as Cugoano, who were victims of slavery, used to survive and overcome their predicament. One Akan folktale in which *Anansi* uses a trickster strategy in order to resist oppression is the story, "How it Came that Wisdom Came among the Tribe," in which he spreads his god-given intelligence to his community when he finds out that his son has become smarter than he is. In this folktale, *Anansi* is a wise father who preserves strong filial bonds, demonstrating his conformity with Akan norms of patrilineality. As the storyteller tells us, *Anansi* kept the wisdom God gave him in a gourd and tied the latter around his waist. According to the narrator, "He [*Anansi*] then declared that he would climb a tree and go and hang it on it, so that all wisdom on earth would be finished."[21] When *Anansi* failed numerous times in his attempts to climb the tree, his son recommended he place the gourd on his back. Having tried this method with success, *Anansi* said,

> "I, Kwaku Ananse, by the lesser god, Afio! I might as well be dead, my child who is so small, so small, so small—there was I, I collected all wisdom (so I thought) in one place, yet some remained which even I did not perceive, and lo! my child, this still-sucking infant, has shown [it] to me." Then he seized that gourd, and there was a sound of rending, *tintini*! and he cast it away, and there was a sound of scattering, *tesee*! (5)

The Akan story reveals the sense of community building that *Anansi* develops by climbing a tree and collecting wisdom for the survival of his people. In a similar way, Cugoano attempted to bring blacks of the diaspora together to free their enslaved brothers and sisters in the New World. This trickster-inspired Pan-Africanism is apparent in the political work that Cugoano did with Equiano and other early blacks of the diaspora in order to create the "Sons of Africa" organization that aimed at liberating slaves in the diaspora and taking them to Africa. Cugoano was a member of the "Sons of Africa," a group of black abolitionists, including Equiano, Ignatius Sancho, and Francis Barber, who vehemently campaigned in England against the slave trade during the 1780s and who attempted to pressure Britain to improve the conditions of poor blacks of London by helping them emigrate to Sierra Leone.[22] In 1786, Cugoano informed the British abolitionist and lawyer Granville Sharp of the unjust treatment of a slave named Harry Demane, who had been waylaid and tied to the mast of a ship that was bound for the West Indies.[23] As Carretta suggests in his introduction to *Thoughts and Sentiments on the Evil of Slavery* (1999), "with Equiano and other 'Sons of Africa,' Cugoano continued the struggle against slavery with published letters to newspapers" (xvii–xix).

Moreover, Cugoano was an active member of the Committee for the Relief of the Black Poor. In the notes to *Thoughts and Sentiments*, Carretta tells us that the Committee for the Relief of the Black Poor was a London-based group that was "organized by humanitarian businessmen in early 1786 to offer aid to indigent East India sailors . . . Since Black referred to complexion rather than ethnicity or origin, the recipients of the committee's charity soon included people of African descent" (173). Carretta continues: "The committee raised more than £1,000 to provide relief, health care, clothing, food, and jobs to needy Blacks" (173). Moreover, the committee played an important role in the idea of helping carry out the plan to settle poor London blacks to Sierra Leone (Cugoano, *Thoughts*, 104).

The work of the committee was connected to that of the "Sons of Africa," since both organizations aimed at toppling slavery by drawing from the subversive resistance tactics of slaves in the Americas. In "Black Resistance to Slavery and Racism" (1992), Douglas A. Lorimer writes: "The Black poor, who were involved in the Sierra Leone enterprise of 1786–7, either as recipients of relief or as participants in the settlement, have left a record of their demands and organization which bears some similarity to the tactics of the fugitive slaves of the mid[eighteenth]-century" (73). Discussing these tactics, Lorimer writes: "The fugitive slaves of the mid-century exposed the contradiction between English proclamations of liberty and the reality of oppression in slavery. Seizing hold of this opportunity many slaves achieved their own liberation" (76). The Black Poor and the fugitive slaves' use of communal gathering as a means for obtaining freedom from whites is consistent with the way in which *Anansi* climbs a tree to collect wisdom for the survival of his people. Though he dwells in Akan folktales, *Anansi* is the living force that inspired the black revolutionaries of the diaspora to gather strength from all sides of their societies for the liberation of their people. As Zawadi Iyanjura Barskile argues in *Carrying Our Spirit With Us: Gold Coast Spiritual Continuities in Eighteenth-Century Suriname and North America* (2005), "the Strength in the spirit of Kwaku Anansi spider stories that existed in South Carolina and Georgia can also be seen in the practice of obeah men and women" who "played significant roles in numerous Akan slave revolts throughout the Americas" (109). According to Barskile, the Obeah men and women's "knowledge of medicinal herbs was not only used in slave rebellions, but also to help heal ailments throughout the slave community and avert evil forces" (109). *Anansi* and Cugoano had similar role of Obeah doctors, since they both used either a tree or a book to seek wisdom that could end the suffering of their community.

Another similarity between *Anansi* and Cugoano is the way in which they both draw from logic and intelligence as tools of liberation. *Anansi*'s good judgment is apparent in his respect for the intelligence of his child and his recognition of the filial and spiritual relationship he has with his son. *Anansi*'s valuation of the importance of his son attests to the sacred bonds that the Fanti establish between fathers and their children in order to guarantee the progression of ancestral spirituality and leadership within their nucleus family and society.[24] This worldview validates Cugoano's sentiment that the Fanti never wanted their children to be taken away from them. Corroborating the Akan's abhorrence of the enslavement of their own people, Cugoano wonders if there is any "man of feeling [who] can help lamenting the loss of parents, friends, liberty, and perhaps property and other valuable and dear connections" (27). In this statement, Cugoano shows the immeasurable sense of loss that Africans experienced from their forced transplantation into the New World. Giving an example of the "liberty" that was snatched from the Africans, he paints an image of an African society that was exemplary in its social, political, and economic organizational structure. He writes: "Those people annually brought away from Guinea, are born as free, and are brought up with as great a predilection for their own country, freedom and liberty, as the sons and daughters of fair Britain. Their free subjects are trained up to a kind of military service, not so much by the desire of the chief, as by their own voluntary inclination. It is looked upon as the greatest respect they can shew to the king, to stand up for his and their own defence in time of need" (27). Thus, the Fanti attached a central importance to the notion of individual power within a collective concept of intellectual freedom, leadership, and responsibility. In this African society, the individual is expected to fulfill important duties. Yet he/she has a lot of space, freedom, and agency to rationalize and perform these responsibilities.

As noticeable in Cugoano's statement, the male individuals in Fanti society are prepared through training to work for the survival of their country. Like the *ceddo* warrior soldiers of precolonial Wolof society, the Fanti men preserved the safety of the royalty by serving in its army and guarantying the financial stability of the rulers.[25] As James Christensen suggests, the Fanti man's ability to preserve his *abusa*, or "the localized matrilineal clan whose members recognize collective responsibility," partly depends on his family's sustenance of the army of the country (4, 137). The Fanti's allegiance to the supremacy of the collective good over the individual good is an ideology about which Cugoano is ambivalent. While he praises its capacity to strengthen the ties between families and society, Cugoano condemns this ideology's contribution to his enslavement. When he was being taken to the coast for sale, Cugoano could not suspect what was happening to him until the time when the last man who accompanied him showed him that he was being sold to white people (14). His inability to predict his fate was a result of his respect for elders and the idea of the collective good, which prompted him and his kidnapped friends to follow their captors without resistance. He could not then realize that the men were tricksters who were on the verge of selling him out. He says:

> Some of us attempted in vain to run away, but pistols and cutlasses were soon introduced, threatening, that if we offered to stir we should all lie dead on the spot. One of them pretended to be more friendly than the rest, and said, that he would speak to their lord to get us clear, and desired that we should follow him; we were then immediately divided into different parties, and drove after him. We were soon led out of the way which we knew, and towards the evening, as we came in sight of a town, they told us that this great man of theirs lived there, but pretended it was too late to go and see him that night. (13)

Cugoano's and his playmates' submission to the will of the captors, after a brief attempt at resistance, stems less from fear of being killed than from that of offending neighboring dignitaries who were considered part of the extended Akan community. The detainees' behavior derives from their desire to abide by the Akan respect for the preeminence of the will of chiefs and elders over those of the individual. In *Akan Ethics* (1988), Christian A. Ackah says that the Akan use the term "Nana," which "ordinarily means grandfather or grandmother or any ancestor" as "the same word which is used as the appellation of a chief" (121). This designation of the chief shows how he/she is considered in Akan society as an integral part of the chain of being linking God, the *abusa*, the deities, the army, and all the divinities and institutions that preserved the stability of the country.

The community of African slave traders that Cugoano describes reflects central elements of Akan culture in their attempts to please Cugoano and his comrades. These patterns include the use of verbal negotiations to settle potential disputes or decide on the fate of an individual and the extension of hospitality to strangers. In this cultural context, Cugoano and his friends have no power to decide what will happen to them, because they are excluded from the private consultations that the African captors, who are their elders, are having among themselves before they bring the young people to other Africans, who are going to sell them to the Europeans on the Ghanaian seaside. When he was being taken to the coast, Cugoano was taken to a house where he stayed for a few days. He writes: "I was kept about six days at this man's house, and in the evening there was another man came and talked with him a good while, and I heard the one say to the other he must go, and the other said the sooner the better; that man came out and told me that he knew my relations at Agimaque, and that we must set out to-morrow morning, and he would convey me there" (14). The secretive nature of the captors' meeting and language reflects the importance of conversation in Akan culture where the adults decide the position of the individual. Such consultations are important elements of African cultures. In *African Spirituality: On Becoming Ancestors* (1997), Anthony Ephirim-Donkor explains how consultations among elders, which Eurocentric interpretation might misconstrue as authoritarianism or the stifling of individuality, has intrinsic democratic elements such as the elders' use of critical reflection and thoughtfulness to preserve resources of wisdom and inculcate in succeeding generations the virtues of humility. According to Ephirim-Donkor, "This process of deliberation and adjudication is [a] quintessential Akan practice and characteristically African" (118).

As is apparent in the instance in which Cugoano and his friends were allowed to choose either to run away and be killed or to cooperate and live, the Akans did not alienate the individual in their deliberation process even if the latter might have been excluded from certain proceedings that were determined by age or other categories. More important, the Akan did not seclude the individual to the point that he/she might choose suicide, as was the case on the slave ships of the Middle Passage. Cugoano describes how his African captors attempted to keep their slaves happy before they were taken to the Europeans:

> We asked our keepers what these men had been saying to them, and they answered, that they had been asking them, and us together, to go and feast with them that day, and that we must put off seeing the great man till after; little thinking that our doom was so nigh, or that these villains meant to feast on us as their prey. We went with them again about half a day's journey, and came to a great multitude of people, having different music playing; and all the day after we got there, we were very merry with the music, dancing and singing. Towards the evening, we were again persuaded that we could not get back to where the great man lived till next day; and when bedtime came, we were separated into different houses with different people. (13)

Thus, Cugoano and his countrymen were being systematically tricked into slavery through entertainment and diversion without their knowing. Cugoano's representation of his captors as people who were using his friends and him as their "prey" reveals his perception of the detainers as despicable individuals. Yet his portrayal of the cultural atmosphere that these keepers create around the detainees as being joyful shows that he valued what he saw as normal hospitality that foreclosed any possibility of evildoing. It was not until he arrived in the West and had the experience to write about this episode that Cugoano realized that his watchmen had done irreparable damage to him. Yet, when he was in Africa, he knew that his captors had tamed him and his friends not so much with physical restraint as with Akan customs that presented the youngsters with attractive, yet dubious, images of hospitality, generosity, and sociableness in return for their total cooperation. These values, which are part of the standards of reciprocity, generosity, and moral duties in Akan culture, are stronger than the individuation that Cugoano finally expresses toward his evil captors. The captor's deception of Cugoano reveals dynamics that are similar to the process in which *Kwaku Anansi* dupes many animals in Akan folktales where he plays a dual role. One the one hand, *Anansi* is a trickster who commits all sorts of evil acts that satirize the detrimental tactics that traders used to enslave Africans. On the other hand, he performs noble acts that celebrate the strategies that African slaves used to resist slave catchers.

In order to understand *Anansi*'s actions and motivations as they relate to Cugoano's narrative, one needs to stress the Akan cultural and ideological contexts that inform the resistance strategies of both figures. These contexts are visible in a folktale entitled, "How Ananse, The Spider, Became Poor," which was published in 1930 by Rattray. According to the narrator, *Anansi* goes off to Nyankonpon, the Sky-god, and says, "Give me a single grain of corn and let me bring you a whole village of people (in exchange)" (257). As the storyteller suggests, the Sky-god says, "You are not able" and the Spider replies, "Should I be unable, I swear by your mother, Nsia, then I shall pay for the violation of my oath with my head" (257). The Sky-god says, "Receive it (the grain of corn) and be off" (257). Later, *Anansi* goes to the house of a wealthy man with the body of a dead man that he claims to be his son. When a group of children discover the body, *Anansi* accuses them of having killed his son. The children's father tells *Anansi* to take the children away to replace his loss. *Anansi* refuses to settle for that option and requests that all the people in the village go with him to the Sky-God to defend their case (257–58). As the narrator shows, *Anansi* then begin to march with the people while singing victoriously:

> 'Ananse, alas, alas, I got a single grain of corn to go and gain a fowl.
> Ananse, alas, alas, I took the fowl to go and receive a sheep.
> I took the sheep and went and got a cow,
> I took the cow and went and got a corpse,

I took the corpse and got the people of a town.'
Every one said, 'Do you hear the song which
Ananse is singing?' Ananse raised his song once more. (261)

When *Anansi* arrives at Nyankonpon with the people he has promised to gather, the Sky-God says: "'Praise him.' (They shouted,) 'E! e! e!' The Sky-god said, 'What must I give you as a thank-offering?' The Spider said, 'I do not desire anything; (a place) on the rafters is all I want.' The Sky-god said, 'Oh, oh! this subject (of mine), you will die in poverty, you, who went and brought much, yet say you do not desire anything.' That is why poverty will never pass Ananse by" (261).

This tale shows the role of defender and opposer of traditions that *Anansi* plays in Akan folklore. He defies social binaries and conventions while proposing alternative ways of creating substance out of small things such as "a single grain of corn." The achievement he makes out of a humble beginning suggests the power of Akan folklore in which tricksters embody success through creativity and resilience. His success mirrors that of exiled Africans such as Cugoano, who defied the institution of slavery. Through reasoning and negotiation with white abolitionists such as Granville Sharp and Thomas Clarkson, who were part of Britain's leading progressive thinkers and legal authorities during the last quarter of the eighteenth century, Cugoano and the other members of "Sons of Africa" and the Black Poor were able to receive substantial support from whites who fought to end slavery. Sharp and Clarkson's support of the black writers is apparent in the introduction to *Black Atlantic Writers of the Eighteenth Century* (1995), where Adam Potkay and Sandra Burr assert: "While their legal status remained uncertain, London's free blacks could still expect spiritual encouragement as well as some material assistance from men such as Granville Sharp and Thomas Clarkson, both of whom became founding members of the Society for the Abolition of the Slave Trade in May 1787" (4).

As Lorimer argues, the credit for the end of slavery in Britain in 1807 should not be given only to "the libertarian tradition of English law and the unstinting efforts of Granville Sharp and other [white] abolitionists" (76). According to Lorimer, the credit should also be given to the subdued black voices of eighteenth-century Britain who made "a decisive contribution in helping launch the global assault on slavery" through "their resistance to slavery and oppression" (76). Yet it is important to recognize how English libertarians such as Sharp and Clarkson allowed the resistance of the slaves to become politically visible by developing an antislavery movement that emphasized the common suffering of Britain's black and poor white populations during the late eighteenth century that justified the end of corrupt labor systems. While many of these blacks had been freed by their owners or had purchased their freedom by the 1780s, many of them could not find any use for their newly gained liberty since they were continuously discriminated against in England. In "The Evolution of Black London" (2004), Judith Bryan describes the conditions of blacks living in London around 1783 as follows: "While some [free blacks] were able to continue their trades, such as cookshop owners and shoemakers, the vast majority joined the London poor as beggars and street musicians, being deprived of even Army back pay and compensation for war injuries, and denied work due to prejudice" (64). These harsh conditions of poor blacks and whites in late eighteenth-century Britain were major forces that also motivated the English abolitionists to fight for the end of slavery.

Finally, Cugoano, like *Anansi*, overcame the challenges placed before him by relying on his own wits and survival skills. The two figures exemplify the accomplishment of "the seemingly impossible by trickery rather than by supernatural aid" that John Roberts identifies as the key survival strategy of the black folk hero in slavery and freedom (27). This survival strategy is visible in the *Anansi*-influenced determination to escape confinement by any means necessary that Cugoano and the other Africans who were forced into a Western slave ship showed against their captors. Describing this brutal experience, Cugoano says that "a plan was concerted amongst us, that we might burn and blow up the ship, and to perish all together in the flames; but we were betrayed by one of our own countrywomen, who slept with some of the head men of the ship, for it was common for the dirty filthy sailors to take the African women and lie upon their bodies; but the men were chained and pent up in holes" (15). The thwarted plot Cugoano describes is what Jerome Handler portrays as "what may be the only reference to a revolt by enslaved Africans in all of the slave-trade literature" (34). The uprising attempt reveals the strong impact of the African sense of collective responsibility on Cugoano and the other slaves on the ship. Like *Anansi*, these Africans carried a sense of pride and honor that was shamefully affected by the inhumane and agonizing hardships European slavers made them go through.

Cugoano was particularly hurt because the Akans group to which he belonged viewed captivity as one of the most dishonorable conditions. Christian Abraham Ackah describes the concept "*mfehoekyir*" as a word that expresses the sense of "regret" that the Akan feels when he/she is put in shameful situations such as confinement (113). Ackah explains: "If a person steals and is caught and *subjected* to disgraceful treatment such as beating and imprisonment, his feeling is one of *mfehoekyir*. This is a case where the agent is sorry for his misdeed, not because he had remorse or any pangs of conscience, but only because he did not expect to be caught and would not have stolen on that occasion if he knew or had any reason to suspect he would be caught. There is nothing morally praiseworthy about this" (113). Ackah's observation reflects the deep sense of shame, loss, and grief that the enslaved Africans might have felt on European ships as they were being subjected to all forms of sexual, psychological, physical, and moral violence that they could resist only by relying on the resilience of their own wits and traditions. Like *Anansi*, who resorts to stealing a fowl, a cow, and a dead slave in order to please the Sky-god, Cugoano and his comrades organized their escape in secretive, systematic, and rational ways in an attempt to be free.

In this process of revolution, the sexual and physical submission of slaves to the evil desires of their captors should be perceived as conscious activities that subvert the oppression of European slavers. While representing the pain they felt in the ships, Cugoano shows the collective identity slaves shared as a group of oppressed and exiled Africans. He writes: "When we were put into the ship, we saw several black merchants coming on board, but we were all drove into our holes, and not suffered to speak to any of them. In this situation we continued several days in sight of our native land" (15). The silence of these slaves anticipates a rebellion that could have occurred in the vessel had the plot not been discovered. The foreshadowing of the slave resistance demonstrates the Africans' capacity to maneuver their way toward freedom through valuation of the Pan-African principles of tacit and mutual cooperation and collective responsibility in a relational and social framework. The collective pronouns "we" and "our" that Cugoano uses to describe the slaves' last sight of Africa signify the shared consciousness and destiny that united these Africans in the slave ships as they were being taken away from their homeland. Discussing how blacks of the diaspora have survived their own traumatic history, Gomez, writes in *Reversing Sail*: "for all of the horror of the transatlantic slave trade, it did not completely rupture ties to the homeland. Africa would remain a central consideration in the hearts and minds of many, the dream of reconnection, of reversing sail, one of the Diaspora's central challenges" (79). Physical disconnection from Africa thus did not prevent blacks of the diaspora from identifying with Africa spiritually, culturally, and in other ways. One stark example of this unbroken link between the diaspora and Africa is Cugoano's ability to recollect and write about his traditional society and the feelings of collective identification and destiny that other kidnapped Africans and he had shared since their fateful union in the slave ships.

Cugoano's *Thoughts and Sentiments on the Evil of Slavery* is an essential

Pan-Africanist exploration of the meaning of race and resistance in the black diaspora during the last quarter of the eighteenth century. Using the knowledge of his own education in Africa and in England, Cugoano was able to re-create images of his upbringing among the Fanti, his capture and transportation, and his struggles against oppression. Like the Akan trickster *Anansi*, Cugoano was also able to devise strategic means of overcoming obstacles and demand justice and equality for his people. In this sense, Cugoano was a Pan-Africanist in both his liberation discourse and his consciousness about Africa's cultural heritage.

CHAPTER THREE

Pan-Africanism in Olaudah Equiano's *Interesting Narrative*

The Interesting Narrative of the Life of Olaudah Equiano, Written by Himself (1795) is the most celebrated autobiography of a black writer from the West. In *The Classic Slave Narratives* (1987), Henry Louis Gates Jr. canonizes it as "the prototype of the nineteenth-century slave narrative" (xiv). A decade later, Caryl Phillips describes it in *Extravagant Strangers: A Literature of Belonging* (1997) as "the first authentic account in English of the life of an African slave" (9). Adebayo William's "Of Human Bondage and Literary Triumph: Hannah Crafts and the Morphology of the Slave Narrative" (2003) reestablishes the pivotal place of Equiano in black literature. Comparing Equiano's narrative with those of Cugoano and Sancho, Williams says, "Of the three, Equiano was the most politically important and by far the most talented" (143).

More recently, Vincent Carretta depicts the book as being "motivated by a combination of factors," including "a desire to recount his spiritual autobiography, and an interest in outlawing the African slave trade."[1] Carretta neglects the place of Equiano's narrative in Pan-African history, however, since he believes that Equiano was not born in Africa.[2] In *Equiano The African: Biography of a Self-Made Man* (2005), Carretta contends that Equiano "may have invented rather than reclaimed an African identity" and that he may have also "invented his African childhood and his much-quoted account of the Middle Passage on a slave ship" (xiv). Carretta further claims: "The accounts of Africa and the Middle Passage in *The Interesting Narrative* were constructed" (xiv). Carretta's thesis was recently challenged by G. Ugo Nwokeji's revelation that "Equiano's baptism in January 1759, arranged by his owner and his relatives, happened more than three years after his slave name and purported Carolina birthplace had appeared on record for the first time through the handiwork of his naval officer master, Michael Henry Paschal" (Review of *Equiano the African*, 840). Therefore, Equiano's possible birthplace in England is less relevant than the

African origin and identity that he presents in his narrative since, as Nwokeji posits, "Essentially, the choice is between Equiano's own claim and documents his master was instrumental in creating" (840–41). While Equiano's life in the diaspora reveals certain ruptures from his homeland and his inventions of new identities in the West, there is no conclusive evidence that he was completely disconnected, alienated, or deracinated from Africa.

Olaudah Equiano played pivotal roles in the Pan-Africanist tradition of resistance against Western stereotyping and economic exploitation of blacks. Expressing ambivalent positions toward Africa and the West, he fulfills the complex and double functions that trickster figures in Igbo folklore perform as mediators between individuals and ancestors and as negotiators for the people's acquisition of agency and power. Although it is replete with dualities that are visible in how the author positions himself between Africa and the West, Equiano's narrative is distinctively Pan-Africanist. Equiano's memoir reflects both the radical ideas of resistance of black intellectuals of his generation and the humanitarian concepts of freedom of abolitionists of his time.

According to his autobiography, Equiano was born in 1745 in Essaka, an Igbo agricultural province located in present-day southeastern Nigeria.[3] One day in 1756, when his parents had gone to the farms, two persons came to their home and kidnapped Equiano and his sister. Six months later, he was taken to Barbados, from where he was sold to many slave traders who made him work as a seaman in England, the British Caribbean, and the United States.[4] In 1757, Michael Henry Pascal, a British navy lieutenant, purchased Equiano from Mr. Campbell, in Virginia, and took him to the West Indies and to England (60). Pascal named him Gustavus Vassa, after a sixteenth-century Swedish patriot. With Pascal, Equiano traveled to the Americas, Turkey, and the Mediterranean and participated in the renowned Seven Years' War.

When he was not at sea, Equiano spent most of his time reading, writing, and learning arithmetic. In 1762, Pascal refused to set him free and sold him into West Indian slavery. In 1766, Equiano, who had become a very skilled sailor, soldier, and trader, bought his freedom from a Quaker called Robert King, and began to work for the abolition of the slave trade.[5] In the last part of his life, he traveled to England, North America, continental Europe, the Middle East, and Central America, and went on an adventurous expedition to find a northeast passage to the North Pole.[6] He then returned to England to convert to evangelical Christianity and work for the British government's effort to abolish slavery.

In order to understand the influence of Igbo folklore in Equiano's work, one should study the author's biography and the relationships between his

Igbo culture and the former English colony of Virginia where he spent a part of his life. Virginia, like South Carolina, was a settlement where Igbo populations from Africa brought pervasive Africanisms during the Atlantic slave trade. In *Equiano The African*, Carretta posits: "As a slave brought from the hinterland Biafra, he [Equiano] would most likely have been brought to the port of Bonny on the Bight of Biafra" (30). As Gomez points out in *Exchanging Our Country Marks* (1998), "the Bight of Biafra, the Igbo's region of origin, accounted for nearly one-quarter of the total number of Africans imported into North America, placing it in a virtual first-place tie with West Central Africa" (114–15). According to Carretta, the ship *Ogden* that left the coast of Biafra and sailed for Barbados in March 1754 was the schooner that carried Equiano to the New World (*African*, 30–31). As Carretta suggests, the sloop *Nancy* brought Equiano to the York River in Virginia on June 13, 1754, two weeks after Equiano arrived in Barbados (37). Virginia was then a colony in which Igbo culture and people were more predominant than those from other parts of Africa. In a similar vein, Douglas Chambers points out in *Murder at Montpellier: Igbo Africans in Virginia* (2005) that the "Igbo presence in eighteenth-century Virginia was pervasive, especially in the interior Tidewater and Piedmont counties on the upper reaches of the James, York, and Rappahannock Rivers" (13).

The high proportion of Igbo culture in Virginia is also evident in *Exchanging Our Country Marks*, in which Gomez argues that, during the middle of the eighteenth century, the Chesapeake was "the preserve of the Igbo" even if the Akans of the Gold Coast and the Senegambians accounted for a substantial part of this settlement's population.[7] In this sense, Igbo folklore in colonial America was a creolized culture because it coexisted with the traditions of the Akans, the Senegambians, and other Africans. In *Generations of Captivity: A History of African-American Slaves* (2003), Ira Berlin writes: "Although the presence—and rumored presence—of slaves from Africa provided a connection to an African homeland, too few Africans entered the interior to reafricanize the slave population. The vast majority of immigrants were African Americans, drawn from all over the North American continent" (170). Although he underscores the mixing of African traditions in North American slave cultures, Berlin seems to deny the consistency that existed in these cultures. While they borrowed folklore and worldviews from one another, Africans who invented these slave cultures preserved their particular ethnic characteristics that allowed them to develop a distinct black diasporic identity. Responding to Berlin's thesis, Chambers argues that even if Africans from other ethnic backgrounds were in Virginia in the mid-eighteenth century and continued to arrive in the 1760s and early 1770s, "the historical world the creolizing slaves created in Virginia seems to have developed largely from a diasporic Igbo base. By drawing on their ancestral material, social, ideological, and other resources to adapt to slavery and make sense of their new lives, communities of Igboized Creole slaves created a distinctive culture informed by 'Eboe' or Igboesque principles and paraphernalia" (11). Therefore, the Igbo diasporic legacy in Virginia and other parts of the United States was consistent despite its hybridity. Moreover, as Chambers suggests in his essay "Tracing the Igbo into the African Diaspora" (2000), in order to understand the continental Igbo heritage in the New World, one needs "to follow Eboan African (Igbo) peoples and history *from* the hinterland *into* the diaspora" (58). It is from this viewpoint that I examine the survival of Igbo folklore in the New World as oral tradition that Equiano and other early Igbo migrants brought with themselves. In order to trace this folklore from Africa to the diaspora, one must examine its survival in modern Igbo culture in order to be able to trace its roots in early black Atlantic traditions.

The influence of Igbo folklore in the New World is noticeable in the stories of captivity and resistance that the descendants of the Igbo in both the black diaspora and Africa tell in an attempt to understand the plight of their ancestors. In *The Igbo Roots of Olaudah Equiano: An Anthropological Approach* (1989), Catherine Obianuju Acholonu uses oral history as a means for retracing the origins of Equiano and collect numerous stories about the black writer's enslavement in Africa. Acholonu conducted numerous interviews with descendants of Equiano that suggest the importance of storytelling in Igbo culture. In one of the interviews, Igwe Agbaka tells Acholonu the following narrative that explains the origin of the Igbo people's belief in the "Big God in the Sky":

> There is a people called the Aros of Arochukwu. In the olden days, as we were told, these Arochukwu people used to come. They were associated with the *Igwe k'ala* (*Igwe ka ala*, which means 'Sky supersedes the Earth') of Umunneoha, an oracle, situated some forty or so miles away from Isseke. The *Igwe* (Sky) people from Umunneoha used to bring those Arochukwu people. In our land, if a person was considered a misfit or a trouble-maker and was to be sold, we would invite the Arochukwu people. They would take the person away and our people would say that Chukwu (the Big God in the Sky) had eaten him. This is the God we knew about before this recent Christianity. (74)

The Igbo religious mythology is a commentary on social and economic relationships that engendered the alienation or enslavement of numerous members of Igbo society during the Atlantic slave trade. The historical importance of the Igbo spiritual legend is evident in the narrator's representation of the other world where the "trouble-makers" were taken as the land of Chukwu, suggesting the Igbo's ability to use their religion as a means for appeasing the trauma that enslavement created in their community. Even if it does not appear in the above text, the enslavement of these Igbo was the result of a collaboration between European slave traders and some local Igbo individuals who influenced the Arochukwu to sell their neighbors to them. This partnership is apparent in the following story that Acholonu has collected from her interview with Ambrose:

> Apart from the fact that the Aro people came here to kidnap people, there was a woman who lived in the neighborhood who was noted for her long basket with which she carried away children and sold them to the Aros. Her name was *Ucheime Nwankwo*. She always carried a large basket (abọ). She was a native of Arochukwu who came to live among us. And she was a kind of contact person for the slave-traders in the place. From Arochukwu the slaves were sold to Azumili—the riverain area between Cross River and Arochukwu and Bende districts. (48)

This story reveals the Aro's involvement in a type of slavery that was prevalent in Equiano's homeland during the time when he was kidnapped in Africa. The references to the woman who carries children away in baskets and the contact person of slave traders are preludes to the story of Igbo enslavement into the diaspora. These allusions implicitly criticize the Aro's involvement in a slave commerce that Europeans instigated. As Gomez suggests in *Exchanging our Country Marks*, in the middle of the seventeenth century, the Aro responded to the tremendous demand of slaves in the Biafra by raiding and kidnapping other subgroups in exchange for European textiles, manufactures, firearms, tobacco, alcohol, and ornaments (132–33). Because of this trade, the Aro transformed the sacred Igbo land of the "Big God in the Sky" into a passage into slavery in the West. As Gomez remarks, "The Oracle of Arochukwu 'became an instrument of exploitation among the Igbo' in that the autochthonous system of justice was altered in order to advance slaving interests" (133).

Furthermore, Igbo oral tradition represents differences of social class and plight among Igbo people during the Atlantic slave trade, epitomizing the connection between religious myth and economic materialism. In *Murder at Montpelier: Igbo Africans in Virginia*, Chambers argues that the people of Elem Kalibari, Nigeria, have oral traditions in which they say that "Bonny stole the

Europeans from them. They describe the conflict in terms of struggle in spiritland between the tutelary gods of each group" (30). This oral history reveals the economic decline and loss of power that slavery brought among the inhabitants of Igboland. Chambers's representation of "spiritland" as a contested terrain for diverse Igbo spiritual entities suggests the power that homeland would later have on the transplanted Africans as a signifier for a lost diasporic identity they wanted to recuperate. In *Caliban's Reason: Introducing Afro-Caribbean Philosophy* (2000), Paget Henry represents oral narratives as stories that "atavistic cultures have consistently created to intuit and transform a creation of the world into a myth," affirm "the focus of their collective existence" (23), and "confirm their identity and their rights to the land they occupied" (24). This affirmation of right to homeland and origins is evident in the oral stories that the descendants of the Igbo people have created in the diaspora to understand their past. The oral tradition is evident in Julie Dash's book *Daughters of the Dust* (1997), adapted from a film of the same title. This narrative describes how a group of Igbo African slaves walked in the sea to go back home when they arrived in the United States and realized the dire fate that awaited them there. The character Paymore suggests that the Igbo were displeased with the harsh treatment of white slaveowners:

> Dey put de Ibo men to work in de fields, but it no good. Dey lay down an not get up even when dey beat half to death. It like dey want to die, and dey help demselves to it. Dey put dem to all kinds of work, but dey no good for nuttin. Dey set de Ibo women to work in de yard, and it not much better. De other captives mad wit dem cause when de Boss Man mad wit dey, it bad for everbody. Paymore him tell de Boss Man dey fair builders, an de Boss Man put dem to work carryin de wood for de new landing....
>
> When de Boss Man say dey finished, de Ibo start wailin an carryin on. Cryin so dat de birds in de trees stop de callin, de animals in de woods run for cover, all de work stop cause de cryin hurt so bad. (104)

Physical, psychological, and emotional suffering thus prompted the Igbo to resist the subversion of their white owners by deliberately refusing to perform the tasks they were assigned to do. The dire plight of the Igbo in the diaspora is apparent in the image of slaves who are "wailin and carryin on" and "cryin so dat de birds in de trees stop de callin, de animals in de woods run for cover" (104). Paymore's reference to animal and vegetable beings reflects his attempt to appease the pain of his Igbo ancestors. The fact that the Igbo workers continued their chores despite the agony of enslavement contradicts the way in which the scholarly literature depicts them as people of weak constitution. In *Equiano, the African*, Carretta traces this stereotypical portrayal of the "melancholy reflections," "depression of spirits," and "constitutional timidity" of the Igbo to Bryan Edwards's *The History, Civil and Commercial, of the British Colonies in the West Indies*, written in 1793 (32). The evidence in *Daughters of the Dust* shows that Edwards was wrong to view the Igbo as weak people. These Igbo walk away from the brutality of their masters and disappear in the sea not as an act of "suicide" but as a defiance of the authority of white slave owners. Giving an example of Igbo resistance against their white oppressors, Paymore says:

> Dey stop dey cryin all de sudden. Everting stay quiet! All de Ibo start to walk to down de landing headed to dey home. De Boss Man try to stop dey, but dey walk right through he! Das what Paymore say! Dey go through he like dey a summer breeze. Him holler for de others to come help he, but de other captives can see de Ibo walk right in he front an come out he back. Dey aint messin wit dat! Oh, no! Dey step off de landing an start to walk cross de water, head for home. De other captives run to see the Ibo walk de water. Dey walkin all right! Caint nobody say dey aint walkin de water. De Boss Man hair turn white as cotton when him see dem walk de water. Now dey get aways out, an de other captives dey run to follow dem, but when dey step off de landin dey fall in de water. Dey pull some of de captives from de water, but some just gone like dat! Everbody watch dem Ibos cross de water til dey couldn't see dem no more. (104–5)

Paymore's story reflects the strong spirit of resistance against slavery and its tyrannies that the Igbo slaves in America developed against their white oppressors.[8] These Igbo preferred death to a continuation of life in misery, humiliation, and deprivation, showing a great sense of honor and moral and physical strength. In the same vein, they demonstrated a great spirit of solidarity that is visible in the collective way in which they planned and implemented their spiritual return home. The Igbo's spiritual return home resonates with the sacred effort that Dash and her African American community make by remembering the history of their black ancestors who had been forcefully brought to the diaspora. As Sheila Smith McKoy points out, Dash attempts to preserve the knowledge of some semblance of home, or "the knowledge of what could be the mast of the slave ship that brought his [Eli's] ancestors to Daughter Island" ("Limbo Contest," 220).

The survival of Igbo folklore in the United States is also apparent in *When Roots Die: Endangered Traditions on the Sea Islands* (1987) in which Patricia Jones-Jackson identifies correspondence between the Igbo tale "Nnabe and the Fruits" and the Sea Island narrative "Ber Rabbit, Ber Wolf, and the Butter" (113). According to Jones-Jackson, the similarity between these stories is visible in the manner in which "Nnabe is able to defraud a whole host of animals" while "Brer Rabbit outwits Brer Wolf" (113). Later, Jones-Jackson identifies another parallel between Igbo and American tales:

> The spider, tortoise, and hare are shown to be inferior to and answerable only to a higher immortal being, Chineke in Igbo and the Lord in Sea Island tales. Here, for example, Nnabe and Ber Rabbit seek more knowledge from their creator in "Nnabe and Chineke" and "Ber Rabbit and the Lord." While both animals are revered for their wit and ingenuity, both are kicked out of heaven when they attempt to cheat God. Both continue to bear the scars of God's wrath: Nnabe has a broken shell as a result of his fall, and Ber Rabbit has a white tail as a reminder that God threw a cup of milk at him as he was ejected. (113)

Here I provide similar analyses of the relationships between African and New World folktales by interpreting their influences in Equiano's narrative, revealing parallels in the ways in which Equiano and Pan-African trickster characters resist oppression and achieve liberation.

Equiano's *Interesting Narrative* played key roles in the development of Pan-Africanism. On the one hand, it takes part in the black diaspora's cultural and intellectual reconnection with Africa by showing how an enslaved African reconstructs his ancestral African traditions and worldviews from the New World. On the other hand, the story belongs in the black diaspora's political and economic denunciation of slavery and imperialism. Understanding the diverse contributions of Equiano's narrative in Pan-Africanism requires a change of the lenses through which it is interpreted. This alteration requires an African-centered approach that removes the narrative from the reductive epistemologies through which Western critics tend to analyze it. This decentering necessitates an African criticism that interprets black literature in its African context. In *Belated Modernity and Aesthetic Culture: Inventing National Literature* (1991), Gregory Jusdanis writes: "An African criticism will situate works in the traditions of its African audience and illuminate the social and philosophical conditions that the works address. The only alternative is for Africans to develop discourses that are as embedded in their own 'plot of history and mythology' as European theories are defined by European perspectives" (10).

First, Equiano's narrative is a recollection of the Igbo culture from which slavery had severed him. His memory of this culture is noticeable in his depiction of the social, political, economic, and cultural characteristics of life in his village. He writes: "When our people go out to till their land, they not only go in a body, but generally take their arms with them for fear of a surprise; and when they apprehend an invasion, they guard the avenues to their dwellings, by driving sticks into the ground, which are so sharp at one end as to pierce the foot, and are generally dipt in poison" (39–40). The villagers' willingness to give up their own lives to protect their territory reflects the paramount importance that the Igbo give to their land.[9] By forming a group and taking their weapons to defend their land, Equiano's African community reveals the Igbo sense of communal identity in which the preservation of a shared territory was perceived as the expression of an extended sense of kinship between the inhabitants of the society. As U. D. Anyanwu argues, the Igbo perceive communal spirit or solidarity as the "union of living blood relatives, the dead relatives and the gods of the community—a sort of spiritual commonwealth" ("Gender Question," 31) that the term *Erima* describes (34). This spiritualistic view of communal identity is the root of the sense of togetherness and determination that Equiano's people demonstrate in their protection of their land.

Equiano's narrative is also a study of the effects of the Atlantic slave trade on Africa. Describing insecurities that the trade brought into the Igbo community and the corruption it created in their society by influencing the local inhabitants to become involved in the sale of human beings, Equiano writes: "From what I can recollect of these battles, they appear to have been irruptions of one little state or district on the other, to obtain prisoners or booty. Perhaps they were incited to this by those traders who brought European goods I mentioned, amongst us. Such a mode of obtaining slaves in Africa is common; and I believe more are procured this way, and by kidnapping, than any other" (40). Equiano's views show the manner in which slaves in Igboland and in other parts of Africa were obtained during wars and kidnappings. His opinions reflect a harsh and complex dynamic of enslavement that must be placed in its proper historical context before it is misunderstood as simply an evidence of Africans' enslavement of Africans in traditional Igbo society. The Igbo practiced slavery. But their system of servitude was not as brutal as the one that the enslaved Africans experienced in the West. First, slavery in Igbo society was not the racialized and hegemonic system of domination that was particular to the Western world. Instead of being an economic system based on the torture of members of one racial group, slavery in Igbo society was a burden that fell indiscriminately on any people who allegedly failed to protect their patrilineal and matrilineal lineages. Victor C. Uchendu says: "As they [the Igbo] conceive their statuses, a slave was a man whose links with his lineage had been severed forever" ("Igbo of Southeast Nigeria," 88). In this sense, slavery in Igbo society was rationalized as the effect of personal disconnections from ancestral lines, and not as the result of racial inferiority.

Another peculiarity of the Igbo servitude system was that it allowed slaves to gain social, political, and economic advancement. Regarding the conditions of the Igbo called *Osu* (also spelled as *Ohu*), Daniel A. Offiong says that these slaves were allowed to achieve upward mobility through marriage with members of noncasted groups ("Status of Slaves," 32–33).[10] According to Offiong, the Igbo also permitted the *Osu* to become "judges, lawyers, beauty queens, academicians and magistrates" (50). Uchendu describes this process of upward mobility in Igbo society as "absorption," that is, the manner in which the slaves became the companions of their masters into whose lineage they were generally absorbed (88). In this sense, the Igbo did not view the *Osu* as people who inherited a permanent low status.

The literature on slavery in Igbo society shows a massive increase of this slavery that resulted from frequent wars and conflicts between ethnic groups that were fueled by the presence of Europeans in search of slaves. As a consequence of this European influence, many Igbo became victims of slave raids and were captured for sale to Europeans. As Gomez shows in *Exchanging our Country Marks*, by the 1670s, the cities of Bonny and Elem Kalabari had become major suppliers of captives to Europeans (132). According to Gomez, this trade led to the enslavement of nearly one million people from the Bight of Biafra, most of whom were caught in the area of Arochuku, where a powerful "Oracle" resided (133). These numbers show the devastation that the Atlantic trade created on an Igbo society in which slavery was part of social relations based on African principles of trust, communal bonds, and individual achievements rather than on the war and violence that Europeans instigated in Africa.[11]

Moreover, Equiano's narrative is a study of the community, culture, and family from which he came. He tells us that his birthplace is "one of the most remote and fertile" provinces of the kingdom of Benin, then situated in current Nigeria (34). He depicts Essaka as a region where there is strong individual freedom and collective social and economic responsibility. He admires the high social and judicial status his father had for being an *Embrenche*, a term "importing the highest distinction, and signifying in our language *a mark of* grandeur" (34). Validating the practice of scarification, common in many parts of Africa, he relishes the fact that he was expected to receive a mark from the top of his forehead down to his eyebrow, just as judges and one of his brothers had already borne (34).

Yet, reflecting ambivalence about Africa, he exhibits double consciousness toward his Ibo culture by recollecting an instance when "a woman was convicted before the judges of adultery, and delivered over, as the custom was, to her husband, to be punished. Accordingly he [the husband] determined to put her to death; but it being found, just before her execution, that she had an infant at her breast, and no woman being prevailed on to perform the part of a nurse, she was spared on account of the child" (35). Though the Embrenches' leadership fascinates him, Equiano is outraged by their arbitrary use of the law. While he is impressed with the fact that they spared the life of a nursing woman who had committed adultery, he is put off by their punishment of the women's adultery with slavery or death while the men are allowed to "indulge in a plurality" of sexual relationships without necessarily facing any penalties (35).

Moreover, he criticizes the corruption of customary law that supported the practice of slavery in Africa. He writes: "I remember a man was brought before my father, and the other judges, for kidnapping a boy; and, although he was the son of a chief or senator, he was condemned to make recompense by a man or a woman slave" (35). Here, Equiano is uncertain as to whether he should condemn the African practice of domestic slavery or not. Being reluctant to condemn this slavery system for fear that his white readers would use it to justify their participation in the Atlantic trade, he tactfully makes an implicit censure of African slavery without likening it with its brutal counterparts in the Americas.

Equiano's censure of African forms of servitude is further noticeable when, referring to Richard (Dick) Baker, who was one of his white friends and shipmates, he states: "From what I could understand by him of this God, and in seeing these white people did not sell one another as we did, I was much pleased; and in this I thought they were much happier than we Africans" (63). This passage contradicts Equiano's early argument that the African form of slavery was less traumatic than its Western counterpart (37). He says that people from Essaka occasionally sold slaves who were mainly prisoners of war or people who had been convicted of kidnapping, adultery, or other crimes (38). Yet he points out that these slaves received better treatment than they did in the Americas (40–41). He compares the Igbo system of slavery with that of the Caribbean, in which slaves did constant hard work, ate and were fed differently than were their owners, and had no "slaves under them as their own property, and for their own use. (41)

Furthermore, Equiano indicates the difference between slavery in Igboland and that in the West by portraying the terrible experiences he had in Virginia and on the West Indian Island of Montserrat, where he was a slave. He remembers his experience in Virginia as a "dreadful review to my mind," which "displayed nothing but misery, stripes, and chains" (89). Resonating the Africans' preference of death over shame, he asserts: "I called upon God's thunder, and his avenging power, to direct the stroke of death to me, rather than permit me to become a slave, and be sold from lord to lord" (89).

In the same vein, he recalls the terrible experiences of slaves on the Island of Montserrat, where Captain Doran sold him to Robert King (90–91). Although he represents King as an owner who was initially kind to him and who fed his slaves properly, Equiano describes the masters on the Island as generally violent toward their slaves (90–91). Identifying with the suffering of these slaves, he depicts the predicament of "a countryman of mine who once did not bring the weekly money directly that it was earned; and, though he brought it the same day to his master, yet he was staked to the ground for his pretended negligence, and was just going to receive a hundred lashes, but for a gentleman who begged him off with fifty" (91). Equiano continues: "This poor man was very industrious; and by his frugality, had saved so much money by working on ship-board, that he had got a white man to buy him a boat, unknown to his master" (91–92). Thus, Equiano abhorred the degrading conditions in which slaves were kept in the West.

Despite his denunciation of slavery, Equiano was engaged in this institution at some point in his life. His involvement in the slave trade began at the time when he belonged to Mr. King, who employed him in "supplying the place of a clerk," "receiving and delivering cargoes" to ships, "tending stores," and "delivering goods" (92–93). As Jennifer Margulis notes in her review of James Walvin's biography of Equiano, his participation in slavery suggests a major contradiction in his resistance to this institution, because it allowed him to profit from the trade that he abhorred (175). Yet, Equiano's involvement in slavery was not a self-defeating enterprise since it allowed him to obtain the knowledge that he needed to have in order to acquire his freedom and help other Africans. While it included transporting and selling slaves, Equiano's role as a trader taught him important business-keeping and moneymaking skills that an entrepreneur like himself needed to have in order to succeed in the capitalistic economy of the Atlantic world in which slavery was a major part. Discussing Equiano's relationships with this economy, Lynn M. Festa observes in *Sentimental Figures of Empire in Eighteenth-Century Britain and France* (2006) that Equiano is "a self-made man in the more colloquial sense of the expression: in his business transactions. The kind of reversal permitted by the acquisition of literacy—the reflexive construction of self as subject and object—reappears in Equiano's doubling of self as slave and trader. Equiano as a slave is a form of merchandise, but he incorporates himself into the system as an agent, trading goods in voyages that included transporting slaves" (143). On the one hand, Equiano uses his "double" status of slave and trader as a means for garnering ideological and material strength that can liberate him from slavery. As Houston Baker points out in *Blues, Ideology and Afro-American Literature* (1984), "the pure product of trade," Equiano "becomes a trader, turning from spiritual meditations to canny speculations on the increase of a well acquired and husbanded store" (35).

On the other hand, Equiano uses his position of trader as a means of assimilating into the institution of slavery and gathering daunting facts on its inhumane treatment of Africans. Describing the Europeans' appaling treatment of Africans in the ships that were bound to the West Indies, he writes: "While I was thus employed by my master [Mr. King], I was often a witness to cruelties of every kind, which were exercised on my unhappy fellow slaves. I used frequently to have different cargoes of new Negroes in my care for sale; and it was almost a constant practice with our clerks, and other whites, to commit violent depredations on the chastity of the female slaves; and these I was, though with reluctance, obliged to submit to at all times, being unable to help them" (93). Equiano's description of the "violent depredations" of white clerks on the "chastity of the female slaves" suggests his continuous abhorrence of the brutal trade in which Mr. King had compelled him to be a merchant. In an attempt to compensate for his involuntary and debilitating role as a trader, he uses this status as a tool for developing secret connections with other enslaved Africans to whom he shows "diligence" and "care" (94). This strategy helps him to dissuade Mr. King from selling him to other traders and to develop a tacit solidarity with Africans.

Furthermore, Equiano's involvement in slavery enabled him to resist the capitalistic commodification of Africans as properties. Vilifying the ways in which the capitalistic economy of slavery exploited the labor of Africans to the benefit of a wealthy class of white merchants and antiabolitionists, he observes: "I have known many slaves whose masters would not take a thousand pounds current for them. But surely this assertion refutes itself; for, if it be true, why do the planters and merchants pay such a price for slaves? And, above all, why do those who make this assertion exclaim the most loudly against the abolition of the slave trade? So much are men blinded, and to such inconsistent arguments are they driven by mistaken interest!" (93). Equiano's rationale suggests his ability to use his insider knowledge of the barbarity of the slave trade as a basis for promoting the development of a new and fair labor system that safeguards the African workers' right to provide voluntary and paid "service" to others (93).

Equiano would have been unable to understand capitalism if he had not been a slave trader. Being a merchant helped him to infiltrate the economy of slavery in an attempt to replace it with an equitable and entrepreneurial system in which free service, not forced labor, is the basic means of exchange of products. Equiano's alternative to capitalist economy of slavery is apparent in Ross J. Pudaloff's argument that "despite his own enslavement, Equiano celebrates commerce and exchange because they make the self a product of exchange. He gains his freedom by purchasing himself and implies that the exchange of money for self can lead to a new and better identity" (501). This "new and better identity" is antithetical to slavery's commodification and alienation of Africans, since it stresses the primacy of independence and entrepreneurship that Equiano invoked as a means of conveying a subtle Pan-Africanist message of liberation from oppression.

Moreover, being a slave trader allowed Equiano to travel to many continents and gain a cosmopolitan knowledge of the world. According to Leyla Keough, "Even after he bought his freedom in 1766, Equiano elected to remain at sea for several years. He voyaged to the Arctic as a surgeon's assistant and to the Mediterranean as a gentleman's valet, and for a time lived among the Moskito Indians of Nicaragua" ("Equiano," 684). When he was free, Equiano continued to work as a slave trader in an attempt to make some economic profit and be more familiar with the world. In February 1768, he hired himself to Dr. Charles Irving of Palmall, England, who paid him a low wage of twelve pounds a year (140). As James Arthur argues, between 1773 and 1777, Equiano joined Charles Irving again to "help [him] set up a plantation in Central America. He [Equiano] purchased slaves for the plantation and acted as an overseer. Eventually he returned to London" ("Slave, Subject and Citizen," 154).

Although it included selling human beings, Equiano's voluntary employment as a traveling slave trader helped him to develop a cosmopolitan knowledge of the world. This cosmopolitanism is apparent when he says: "We sailed from England in July following, and our voyage was extremely pleasant. We went to Villa Franca, Nice, and Leghorn; and in all these places I was charmed with the richness and beauty of the countries, and struck with the elegant buildings with which they abound" (141). Equiano's travels exposed him to many cultures and gave him reasons to stay alive and fight for the liberation of his fellow Africans who deserved to have the same opportunities of freedom and mobility that he had. "Equiano," as Christopher Apap points out, was then "an enlightened, cosmopolitan, and staunchly abolitionist African" (6). Equiano's cosmopolitanism was a form of Pan-Africanism, since it aimed to inspire the Western world to treat Africans and other peoples as equals. As Christine Levecq argues in "Sentiment and cosmopolitanism in Olaudah Equiano's *Narrative*" (2008), "in the representation of his relationship to Africa, Equiano sought to establish more equalized and less exploitative international relations" (13).

Yet Equiano naively believed that there was such a thing as a "kind master." This myth delayed his subversive resistance against slavery and his destruction of his mirage of the illusive power of the white man. This transformation was latent because Equiano continued to romanticize whiteness and believe in superstitions that his white owners had embedded in his mind for a long time. Early in the book, white traders made him believe that they were going to take the other African slaves and him to a land where they were going to eat them (57). Also, he once believed that the picture he saw in a room of a slaveowner "was something relative to magic" (60). The two examples show how Equiano was a victim of the slaveholders' use of superstition as a means for instilling fear among slaves in order to exploit them further. During this period, Equiano suffered from the same conditions that Betsy Erkkila describes in "Ethnicity, Literary Theory, and the Grounds of Resistance" (1995) as situations in which he became a silenced property of his kidnappers (576). According to Erkkila, in Africa "Equiano is kidnapped from his people and his country, transformed into goods, and transported and sold as property. This forced seizure from family, people, home, and land is accompanied by an act of literal silencing by his 'kidnappers'" (576). Equiano's belief in the existence of a "kind master" and his mirage of the power of whiteness exemplify a similar silencing of his humanity by slave owners.

Another example of the impact of the white man's superstition on Equiano is when he describes Europeans as superior to Africans. Recalling the first three years he spent in England with Pascal, his owner, Equiano states: "I could now speak English tolerably well, and I perfectly understood everything that was said. I not only felt myself quite easy with these new countrymen, but relished their society and manners. I no longer looked upon them as spirits, but as men superior to us; and therefore I had the stronger desire to resemble them, to imbibe their spirit, and imitate their manners" (72). Equiano's use of a trickster strategy allows him to assume a low status while implicitly fighting to reach a higher one. Appropriating the trickster tactics of *Mbe*, the Tortoise, he puts on a mask as an indirect means for struggling against oppression. As Wilfred Samuel argues in "Disguised Voice in the Interesting Narrative of Olaudah Equiano, or Gustavus Vassa, the African" (1985), Equiano creates "a self whose muted voice veils covert intentions that lie hidden behind the façade—the mask, with which he disguises himself" (65). Equiano's use of the mask as a means of resistance resonates with Igbo cosmology in which this object is the main tool that the exiled person who has been away from "the seven seas" into "the land of the dead" can use to preserve connections with "the land of the living" from which he/she came and with ancestors.[12] The mask is Equiano's tool for acquiring incremental power in English society without having his Igbo identity crushed by whites. By speaking the language of the English, absorbing their spirit, and imitating their lifestyle, he puts on a mask that helps him copy acceptable social behaviors in the West while remembering and preserving the ancestral heritage from which whites were trying to sever him. In this sense, he was a trickster who successfully assimilated into the world of whites in order to seek ways to free blacks from their oppression.

Putting on the mask is an initial stage where Equiano pretends to adopt some of the ideologies of the hegemony in order to gain strength in an environment where integration into mainstream society and appropriation of knowledge and power are strategic tools of resistance. His appropriation of power would have been impossible if he had not rejected the myth of the superiority of whites over blacks. His strength and self-awareness evolve out of the brutal wars in which he saw white soldiers become vulnerable like him. In the summer of 1757, Captain Michael Henry Pascal, who had just been appointed as first lieutenant of his Majesty's ship the Roebuck, bought Equiano from Virginia and took him to many parts of the world, where he fought for England and learned many things (64). At that time, Equiano was twelve years old and described himself as being "at a great loss" and filled with "an endless field of inquiries" about most of the things that immigrants ask when they first come to the snowy parts of the West (63–64). He is graciously told that the white mass covering the earth is called snow, not salt; that the amazing voices he hears in a church is a worship of God; that the demeanor of the slender English women in the streets of Falmouth might not invoke the immodesty or the shame-ridden conscience of the Igbo woman (63–64). Listening to his American friend Dick Baker, who interprets English culture for him, he develops a thirst for discovering the books where whites preserve their knowledge. He writes: "I had often seen my master and Dick employed in reading; and I had a great curiosity to talk to the books as I thought they did, and so to learn how all things had a beginning. For that purpose I have often taken up a book, and have talked to it, and then put my ears to it, when alone, in hopes it would answer me; and I have been very much concerned when I found it remained silent" (64).

In the passage, Equiano interprets the Bible as a book that contains images of a Saint (Jesus Christ) whose benevolence and sacrifices are similar to those of African deities. Being aware of the importance of books in his subversion of the power of whites, he Africanizes the Bible, reflecting the Igbo trickster's use of spirituality as a means for achieving freedom and power. While tricksters such as the Rabbit, the Dog, and *Usu* (the bat) appear in Igbo oral narratives, *Mbe* (the tortoise) is the master prankster in these folktales. *Mbe* epitomizes the African sense of resilience, adaptability, diplomacy, and refusal to be manipulated in challenging situation. Yet *Mbe* also exemplifies the individual's capacity to be creative and able to absorb new knowledge in order to survive oppression. Characterizing *Mbe*, E. Nolue Emenanjo points out: "Down-to-earth and as selfish as Mbe might be, and occasionally trapped to stew in his own juice, he always exploits his wisdom and the folly of his co-animals to wriggle out of the tightest corners. Mbe is rarely killed. The greatest punishment he gets is that he is thrown out of the company of the animals from above" (xvi). In this sense, *Mbe* epitomizes a fluidity of behaviors and identities that defies the good versus evil binary that characterizes the European concept of morality and order.

One example of *Mbe*'s resilience is the Igbo tale, "The Food Drum," in which he lived in a society that used to be stable and peaceful until famine forced him to be exiled in a foreign land, where he established relationships with a spirit that provided him with the food and sustenance he needed in order to stay alive. The tale has two central episodes. The first one is the scene in which *Mbe* establishes connection with a providential spirit. The storyteller writes: "Suddenly, Mbe awoke and was terribly scared. He quickly drew his head inside his shell and waited for the worst to happen. The spirit, however, was friendly, and as the amazed Mbe looked on, he stretched out his thin hand and took one of the many drums hanging from the high roof of his house" (Okeke 31). The tale continues: "He [the spirit] hit one side of the drum, and Mbe's favorite treat, bread-fruit meal, appeared! Mbe's mouth watered, but he was cautious. Could this be a trick? he wondered. The spirit invited him to eat. Mbe could not resist. He fell to it as though it was his last meal, and ate and ate and ate" (31). Later, "he [the spirit] understood that Mbe must return to his family. As a farewell gift, the spirit presented Mbe with one of his drums, and also gave him lessons on how to use and keep it" (32). *Mbe*'s acquisition of the spirit's drum is an allegory for the ways in which Equiano negotiates his relations with Christianity and the spirits within the Bible in order to gain the intellectual and spiritual power he needed in order to survive the famine of the "land of death" that slavery represented for the Igbo in bondage. Had he not Africanized the Christian god of his oppressors in the way *Mbe* had appropriated the power of the alien spirit, Equiano would have chosen death like most Igbo slaves did before or after they arrived in the West.[13] Like *Mbe*, Equiano chooses life and receives the knowledge that allows him to return to the land of his ancestors without passing through death. By taking the Bible as his own, he domesticates its knowledge in the same way *Mbe* appropriates the Igbo spirit's drum.

Brought into London by Pascal, Equiano and his American friend Dick Baker are conscripted into the British navy by force to fight for England (65). Equiano represents his enrollment as an experience that allows him to work as a human being equal to others. He asserts: "This was the first time I ever fought with a white boy; and I never knew what it was to have a bloody nose before" (65). This war experience allows Equiano to rid himself of his inferiority complex incrementally. After fighting in long battles against the French in 1759 around the area off Cape Logas in Portugal, he describes the atrocity of war that, paradoxically, helps him realize his equality to whites who, he initially believed, overcame death. He writes: "My station during the engagement was on the middle deck, where I was quartered with another boy, to bring powder to the aftermost gun; and here I was a witness of the dreadful fate of many of my companions, who, in the twinkling of an eye, were dashed into pieces, and launched into eternity. Happily I escaped unhurt, though the shot and splinters flew thick about me during the whole fight" (76–77). Therefore, war experience helps Equiano realize his equality to whites and allow him to confront Western prejudice, discrimination, and exploitation. On the moving ships where he is assigned to work, he counters the racism of European slaveowners with the spirit of tolerance and solidarity that he learns from life, books, church attendance, and his white friend Dick Baker. Describing the time when he is insulted in one of these ships, he writes: "Sometimes, he [Pascal] would say to me—the black people were not good to eat, and would ask me if we did not eat people in my country. I said, No; then he said he would kill Dick (as he always called him) first, and afterwards me" (62). Dick died, probably from hanging, during a battle that occurred before Equiano's fleet moved to Gibraltar. Equiano describes how he found out about Dick's death: "I learned from the boat's crew that the dear youth was dead! and that they had brought his chest, and all his other things, to my master. These he afterwards gave to me, and I regarded them as a memorial of my friend, whom I loved, and grieved for, as a brother" (73–74). By expressing sadness about the death of Dick, Equiano expresses humanism toward a fellow shipmate he admired as both a friend and a teacher who introduced him to Christianity and English culture. Recollecting Dick's special qualities, Equiano writes: "I lost at once a kind interpreter, an agreeable companion, and a faithful friend; who, at the age of fifteen, discovered a mind superior to prejudice; and who was not ashamed to notice, to associate with, and to be the friend and instructor of one who was ignorant, a stranger, of a different complexion, and a slave!" (61–62). As Robert J. Allison suggests in "Olaudah Equiano: An African in Slavery and Freedom" (1999), Dick was one of the Europeans, such as the Guerin sisters, who helped Equiano learn to read (about Christianity), write, and "feel more at home" in the New World (296).

The knowledge that Equiano gained from Africa, his personal experiences, and his white friends allowed him to begin a "marronage," or a banding and bonding between slaves for survival and resistance against domination. Inspired by an interpretation of Alain L. Locke's *The New Negro* (1925), Houston Baker defines the concept of "marronage" from a literary/philosophical perspective as a field of "national interests of a black community [set] in direct opposition to the general political and theological tenets of a racist land" (*Modernism*, 77).[14] According to Baker, the work of "marronage" is, in itself, a communal project drawing on resources, talents, sounds, images, rhythms of a marooned society or nation existing on the frontiers or margins of all promise, profit, and modes of production (77).

Although it is often used to identify the Jamaican Maroons who resisted the British until the latter signed their independence treaty in 1739, the term "marronage" (also spelled as "maronnage") is applicable to slave resistance in both the West Indies and the United States.[15] The major characteristic of "marronage" is its covert, passive, and subversive forms of resistance. Parallels of these tactics are the strategies that James C. Scott describes in *Weapons of the Weak: Everyday Forms of Peasant Resistance* (1985). Using the example of the South Asian peasantry's subtle resistance against the dominance of their states and landowners, Scott identifies confrontation tactics that may pass unseen owing to their informal nature. A few examples of these subversive strategies that powerless groups utilize are "foot dragging, dissimulation, false compliance, pilfering, feigned ignorance, slander, arson, sabotage, and so forth." These "weapons of the weak" help peasants to confront the exploitation they face (29–30).

In similar ways, slaves in the Americas used covert hidden transcripts such as the invisible bonding of kinship, intra-ethnic solidarity, and flight as subtle means of resistance against their masters.[16] Discussing the liberation strategies of the African slaves in the Atlantic world, Chambers writes in *Murder at Montpellier: Igbo Africans in Virginia*: "Poison, arson, and running away were generic 'weapons of the weak,' and particularly effective ones for enslaved people resisting their oppression in a kind of asymmetric opposition to the hegemonic power of the masters expressed both individually as owners and collectively as the state itself" (13–14). Yet understanding "marronage" as a transnational resistance strategy that may not be physically implemented—as the use of arson or poison is—, helps us recognize the power of black literature as a subversive intellectual and ideological tool of resistance against oppression. From this perspective, Equiano's discrete remarks, feelings, and actions are not accidents. They are conscious tactics of resistance against slavery. This resistance is blatant in a passage from Milton's *Paradise Lost* that Equiano uses to describe the horrible things he saw on the ships in which he worked or fought:

> Regions of sorrow, doleful shades, where peace
> And rest can rarely dwell. Hope never comes
> That comes to all, but torture without end
> Still surges. (89)

Equiano's use of the poem expresses his sadness and loneliness in a land corrupted by slavery that can be equated to the "land of death" in Igbo folklore. This world is a "no man's land" of uncertainty and ambiguity that is devoid of life and spirit, where the survival of individuals depends on their ability to invoke and use the wisdom of the African pranksters. One example is Okolo, the hero of the Igbo tale "The Twin Gongs," who finds himself in a "no man's land" where tradition is the spiritual food that allows the individual to overcome the trauma of exile and violence. In this tale, a wicked chief is so jealous of Okolo, the leading wrestler of the village, that, upon hearing of his exploits such as the killing of a leopard, he decides to get rid of him (Okeke 23). As the narrator says, one day, the wicked chief orders Okolo to go to a smithy who lives in the "land of the dead" and bring back the famous twin gongs (23).

Having crossed seven stretches of grass-woodland, Okolo found himself in the borderland between the "land of the living" and the "land of the dead," the latter being *Agbano* (the no-man-no-spirit's land) (24). He quickly crossed the borderland and reached the land of the dead where everything was strange (24). The forced exile of Okolo is parallel to the enslavement of Equiano. Both exiles are allegories for the forced displacement of people from Africa into alien lands following drastic circumstances such as wars, famine, and disarray brought about by the Europeans' presence on Africa's coasts for slaves. These tragedies involved the responsibility of local African chiefs who often got rid of individuals in order to maximize profits from the commerce of slaves that Europeans were promoting and controlling.[17]

As the narrator suggests, Okolo overcame the challenges he faced in "the land of the dead" by using the secrets that he learned during his journey. When he arrived in "the land of the dead," Okolo found Uzummuo, a smithy who was a frightful but hospitable creature. Having been allowed to stay in the smithy's room, Okolo realized that he was going to be burnt soon. When the smithy was asleep, Okolo "ran as fast as his legs could carry him," passed *Agbano*, and reached "the land of the living" where "all the villagers rushed out to welcome him and dance to the music from the gong. Thus the envious chief was completely defeated!"[18]

This narrative attests to Okolo's ability to return to his lost community by taking advantage of the liminal space given to him in an alien and violent world. Equiano epitomized such heroic acts because he was able to take advantage of the negligible freedom of movement and association that his owners gave him in a fragmented world in order to fight for his autonomy and that of blacks on both sides of the Atlantic. Equiano never returned to Igboland physically. Yet he was spiritually and culturally connected with this homeland, since that is where his resistance strategies derived in Igbo folktales. He used this knowledge to protect himself from white violence, become educated, and achieve freedom in the West.

In order to understand how Equiano appropriates the Igbo trickster's survival tactics, it is important to chart how he employs the weapons that were accessible to him in order to resist slavery. He condemns the moral and economic impact of slavery on blacks and the ill-treatment slaves experienced on Western ships: "I was made to help unload and load the ship. And, to comfort me in my distress in that time, two of the sailors robbed me of all my money, and ran away from the ship" (89). Later, he describes how he incrementally negotiates his freedom in difficult conditions. First, he rejects the language, myth, and ideas about supposed differences between blacks and whites. Second, he reconstructs his status by perceiving himself not as a slave but as a laborer who is forced to subsist in a racist, materialistic, and hierarchical society. When Captain Doran sells him to Mr. King, he negotiates the transaction with the Quaker and delights in working for a person who respects the fundamental role slaves played in the plantation economy. Equiano writes: "If any of his slaves behaved amiss he did not beat or use them ill, but parted with them. This made them afraid of disobliging him; and as he treated his slaves better than any other man on the island, so he was better and more faithfully served by them in return. By this kind treatment I did at last endeavor to compose myself; and with fortitude, though moneyless, determined to face whatever fate had decreed for me. Mr. King soon asked me what I could do; and at the same time said he did not mean to treat me as a common slave" (90).

Thus, Equiano perceives the plantation system as a business institution in which his survival depends on his ability to snatch an extent of freedom from the planter and expand it by his own efforts. This tactic recalls the strategic way in which Okolo survived in the "land of death" by avoiding the smithy's wrath. As the storyteller tells us, when Uzummuo, the smithy, pretended to sleep, Okolo realized that he was being tricked and "Hid in a corner beside the door. Soon afterwards he was able to observe the Uzummuo roll over, and pull out his sword and strike at where Okolo was lying" (25). The moral of the story is that one should not be too comfortable with the hospitality of strangers. This parable is a metaphor for the ways in which Equiano could not rely on his owners, because he knew that they could sell him any time, as the Chief in the village had done to Okolo, or kill him, as the smithy tried to do to Okolo, if he became visibly subversive toward them. Knowing that his relationships with his owners were precarious and unpredictable, Equiano relied, as Okolo did, on his own wits.

In order to resist the subtle oppression of his owners, Equiano needed to appropriate the oratory skills of the Igbo trickster Tortoise, including the use of sweet-talking and indirections. These two devices are traceable to the Igbo verbal expression of implicit meaning that Dubem Okafor represents as a combination of "satire," "irony," and "a contradictory mode—[of] saying one thing and meaning another, praising and damning in one breath" ("'Overdetermined,'" 92). The use of satire and irony in Equiano's narrative is apparent in the trickster tactics he employs in order to criticize slavery even when he appeared not to be doing so. One example occurs when Equiano represents Mr. King as a person who sometimes considered slaves as workers who needed educational opportunities, decent pay, and care. He describes how Mr. King arranged for one of his clerks to teach him how to gauge (measure) after the latter told him that "I knew something of seamanship, and could shave and dress hair pretty well; and I could refine wines, which I had learned on shipboard, where I had often done it; and that I could write, and understood arithmetic tolerably well, as far as the Rule of Three" (90). By representing Mr. King in such glowing ways, Equiano was "singing the master" by appealing to his sense of paternalism and benevolence, which could be satisfied only through undeserved praises and thankfulness. In *Singing the Master* (1993), Roger D. Abrahams discusses how slaves in the Plantation South sang their masters through various activities such as chanting, dancing, and corn-shucking festivals, which emerged "as forms of active resistance, not in the sense that they attacked the system but rather in the ways in which they maintained alternative perspectives toward time, work, and status" (xix-xxii). The term "alternative perspectives" is essential in the theorizing of the master-slave relationships, because it shows that the slaves' major goal in singing the master was to denounce the harsh conditions of their existence that the planter could not see because of his egotism and paternalism.

Developing "alternative perspectives," Equiano denounces the injustices he faced when he worked as temporary cargo receiver and deliverer, clerk, and horseman without receiving any part of the hundred pounds he saved Mr. King each year (93). Connecting the injustice he experienced to the predicament of other slaves, Equiano says: "I have sometimes heard it asserted that a Negro cannot earn his master the first cost; but nothing can be further from the truth . . . I grant, indeed, that slaves are sometimes, by half-feeding, half-clothing, over-working, and stripes, reduced so low, that they are turned out as unfit for service, and left to perish in the woods, or expire on a dung-hill" (93). Equiano's rationale counters Thomas Carlyle's racist claim in *The Nigger Question* (1849) that slavery was beneficial to the enslaved Africans rather than to their European exploiters.[19] Mr. King's act of giving his slaves the opportunity to improve their skills was a way of increasing the slaves' dependence on him rather than of making them be equal partners in the economy of slavery. Mr. King was then a trickster who gave slaves minimal freedom while expecting from them more labor in return. This subtle exploitation of slave labor was what motivated some planters to concede a degree of freedom to slaves in some quarters. In *The Slave Community* (1979), John Blassingame writes: "The planters generally had little concern about the recreational activities in the quarters. They did not, however, want their slaves carousing all over the country and wearing themselves out before the day's labor commenced" (107). In this sense, planters conceded a limited and necessary degree of cultural freedom to slaves in order to maintain an indirect, patronizing, and hegemonic dominance over them.[20] As is visible in the following Igbo folktale and Equiano's narrative, authoritarian masters, such as Leopard and the planter, did not assign much value to the freedom of subordinate entities, such as slaves and Tortoise.

In the Igbo folktale narrated by Victor C. Uchendu, Tortoise was trying his best to avoid being the prey of the leopard by using all the weapons of the weak including patience, wisdom, sagacity, and cunning. As Uchendu tells us, one day, "at the height of a famine season, when all the animals were starving, the tortoise encountered a leopard that had been preying on other animals, a fact well known to the tortoise. As the tortoise was passing the leopard's gate, he was invited to come in for kola nut. When the tortoise refused this hospitality, the following dialogue with the leopard began:

> "Come in for kola nut, my dear friend," requested the leopard.
> "No thank you. Nobody eats my kola nuts at home," replied tortoise.
> "Come in for a drink," insisted the leopard.
> "My liquor at home is growing sour for want of guests," said the tortoise.
> . . . .
>
> As the tortoise anticipated, the leopard hunted for him along the "clean" path while he moved safely through the grove path. The moral of this little tale is that the recipient of hospitality should have his wits about him. (*Igbo of Southeast Nigeria*, 72)

The verbal indirection that Tortoise uses in order to protect himself against the Leopard's deviousness is parallel to the signifying oratory that Equiano employs in order to defend himself against his white oppressors. When a white man in St. Eustatius wanted his money back for a pig he had sold him, Equiano said: "Had the cruel man struck me I certainly should have defended myself at the hazard of my life; for what is life to a man thus oppressed?" (97). This statement suggests Equiano's use of trickster language as a means for representing the powerlessness that he feels, just as Tortoise does when his life and humanity are endangered.

Equiano knew that his weapons of resistance needed to be subtle and mental, not physical. When he became legally free, he maximized his reliance on his wits by becoming a man of justice and peace who wanted to fight for the liberation of the enslaved Africans. Using the self-taught education he gained from his life experiences and from reading books such as the Bible and the *Guide to the Indians*, which he describes as "the two books I love above all others" (104), he challenged the servitude of blacks as antithetical to Western ideas of freedom. He writes: "I will not suppose that the dealers in slaves are born worded than other men—No; such is the fatality of this mistaken avarice that it corrupts the milk of human kindness and turns it into gall. And, had the pursuits of those men been different, they might have been as generous, as tender-hearted and just, as they are unfeeling, rapacious, and cruel" (99).

Equiano's rhetoric against slavery illustrates the influence of Tortoise's verbal dexterity and diplomacy in his resistance tactics. Tortoise's influence is apparent in the adept word play that Equiano uses to reflect the dual intention of his oratory, which is to condemn slavery without alienating the support of "generous" white readers that he wanted as allies in his fight against slavery. Katalin Orban's "Dominant and Submerged Discourses in The Life of Olaudah Equiano (or Gustavus Vassa?)" (1993) identifies the major challenges that Equiano and other African slave narrators faced in their attempt to express a genuine authorial voice to their audience. Orban says: "Their authorial freedom was complicated by a number of special concerns, such as their serious responsibilities to a community or the expectations of a likely audience. The most important complication is related to the fictional liberties the authors of slave narratives are (not) allowed to take" (655).

Having been raised in Igboland until he was eleven years old, Equiano was able to empower his complicated authorial voice. He retained in his writing the importance that the Igbo give to the use of rhetoric as a tool for helping an individual establish successful connections with others and survive in a community. Equiano reflects this tradition in many ways. First, from a linguistic point of view, he is the epitome of the gifted orator. As Robin Sabino and Jennifer Hall point out, the name "Olaudah" itself is traceable to either "Olaude," which describes a "ring with a sonorous sound," or "Ola-uda," which identifies "a ring with a loud sound." In Igbo, these words signify "vicissitude or fortunate; also, one favoured and having a loud voice and well spoken" ("Path Not Taken," 13).

In addition to being an Igbo symbol of the loud sound, Equiano is also a figure of the black diasporan trope of the "Talking Book." According to Gates, "the Talking Book" is the project in which black Atlantic writers attempt "to establish a collective black voice through the sublime example of an individual text" in which there is "a paradox of containing the oral within the written" (*Pioneers*, 4). The "Talking Book" is a radical black literary and intellectual tradition, because it also describes the continuous Pan-African canon of denunciation of injustices against blacks in which Equiano participated.

Because he was not allowed to have a voice in the West, Equiano used the trickster's covert diplomacy in order to intersperse his feelings about Africa in a language in which he was attacking slavery and singing the benevolence of the abolitionists he admired. As Wilfred D. Samuels suggests, Equiano's "anticipation of some negative response," "his awareness of the importance of audience," and his avoidance of censure led him "to assure his audience that his purpose throughout is not to offend or alienate" (64). In spite of his caution, Equiano was able to represent the predicament of slaves and depict his Igbo traditions positively and, thereby, resuscitate the silenced black voice in his narrative. This restoration of Equiano's voice is crucial in the Pan-African struggle against colonization. Discussing the import of Equiano's new voice, Betsy Erkkila says, in "Ethnicity, Literary Theory, and the Grounds of Resistance" that "the unstopped black mouth, the black subject who thinks, speaks, writes, and creates back becomes integral to the process of transforming the black person's material and symbolic status as 'cargo,' slave, and other within the imperialist narratives and representational practices of white Euro-American history" (576).

The significance of Equiano's unsilenced black voice is apparent in the ways in which he uses it to show how slavery contradicted the invaluable notion of liberty in Western society. One example is when he prefaces a poem about his African homeland with a complaint about the injustice done to free blacks who are "thus villainously trepanned and held in bondage" (107). Right after this passage, Equiano directs his voice towards the Quaker abolitionists of Philadelphia whose "benevolence" has helped "many of the sable race, who now breathe the air of liberty" (107). Next, he emphasizes his Pan-Africanism when he says that black freedom will be uncertain till the day when the courts treat blacks as equals of whites, when there is evidence that the word "liberty" is not merely "nominal" but a reality (107). Following his strategic appeals to abolitionist support with a celebration of his homeland, he writes:

> With thoughts like these, my anxious boding mind
> Recall'd those pleasing scenes I left behind;
> Scenes, where fair liberty, in bright array,
> Makes darkness bright, and e'en illumines day;
> Where, nor complexion, wealth, or station, can
> Protect the wretch who makes a slave of man. (107)

By romanticizing Igboland as an idyllic place with a "pleasing" and unforgettable landscape, Equiano attempts to create respect and recognition for his Igbo heritage in a Western world in which he perceived himself to be living only temporarily with the expectation of returning home. Anticipating the nationalist language that Du Bois and other black writers of the diaspora used some two hundred years later to describe parts of Africa, Equiano was then a pioneer in a black Atlantic literary tradition of representation of this continent as a land with civilizations equal to those of Europe. Equiano knew that if he returned to Essaka, his people would assess his experience in the West on the basis of his success or failure to bring back home what he learned from his journey.

In order to understand Equiano's tight bonds with Africa, one should also interpret them in relation to the ontological and metaphysical realities of Igbo folktales. For example, in the folktale, "The Food Drum," one can see the ways in which the Igbo individual values his community even when he/she is forced by incidental reasons to be far away from it. In the story, *Mbe* finds himself in a world far from his homeland where he had been asked to go to find the necessary food that could save his people from dying from the effects of a famine. In this story, *Mbe* considers himself as an agent who has been given the mission of bringing something specific to an Igbo community that prized the individual's capacity to do good for the whole society. When he comes home with the magic drum that provides food when it is beaten, *Mbe* is welcomed with the utmost joy and pride of the people: "The square was crowded with people. *Mbe* made a long speech full of boasts about his adventures and told the hungry village he was going to feed them all." Paradoxically, in "The Gift of Fire," *Mbe* comes empty-handed from his journey and notices the silence of his people toward him. He receives no public recognition, not because he failed to bring food but because, after he flew to the land of Chukwu (God), he misbehaved toward the divine spirit. As the storyteller says, "When he got to Chukwu's great gate, he knocked on the door and waited. There were no answers. *Mbe* became impatient and started to drum on the door. Then he heard a loud voice from the inside curse, 'Let those hands that knock stick to the door.' *Mbe* retorted angrily, 'Let those words stick in your mouth.' The gate remained closed. *Mbe* could not see Chukwu, so he returned empty-handed."[21]

Mbe's failure to fulfill the mission his community gave him is a situation that a self-conscious Igbo such as Equiano would have dreaded for obvious reasons, such as the fear of alienation and ridicule that awaits the person who disrespects Chukwu and fails to provide the nourishment he was expected to bring home. From this perspective, Equiano was very conscious of the responsibility that the individual Igbo has for his/her community. In "The Writer and His Community" (1984), Chinua Achebe describes the Igbo representation of the relations between the individual and the community as a dynamic in which the individual always subsumes his worth below that of the group (38–39). According to Achebe, the Igbo refuse the Western egocentric representation of the self that is epitomized by Renee Descartes's "*Cogito ergo sum.* I think therefore I am!" (35) and "set about balancing this extraordinary specialness, this unsurpassed individuality, by setting limits to its expression. The first limit is the democratic one which subordinates the person to the group in practical, social matters. And the other is a moral taboo on excess which sets a limit to personal ambition, surrounding it with powerful cautionary tales" (39). Achebe's remarks corroborate the significance of the subordination of the individual's will to that of the community, which is salient in the worldviews of both Equiano and *Mbe*.

Furthermore, Equiano appropriates Igbo tradition by playing the role of diviner, discarder of omen, and protector of societal values that the oracle in Igbo society plays. This oracle is the religious institution that preserves the relationships between the land of the living and the land of ancestors and of Chukwu (God) through constant communication. Each Igbo subgroup has an oracle. Uchendu explains: "The common characteristics of the Igbo oracles are their secret operations, the institutionalization of an 'intelligence service' and the attraction of clients through a chain of contact agents. Their geographical locations indicate a regional influence or sphere of authority" (100). A central part of the oracle is the blend of oratory and diplomatic skills that the Dibia [diviner], who mediates the relationships between the intertwined worlds of the living, ancestors, and God, employs. Another key element of the oracle is the mixture of religious and secular rationality that the Dibia exhibits in his conception of the power of God. In this worldview, God is both a powerful being to fear and a personable deity to whom the individual can relate on reciprocal terms. Uchendu writes: "The Igbo attitude toward the gods is not one of fear but one of friendship, a friendship that lasts as long as the reciprocal obligations are kept. This contractual quality in the man-spirit relationship is based on the recognition of the inadequacy of either party. Only the high god is self-sufficient. Nowhere is the contractual relationship between man and spirit better illustrated than in the Igbo attitude toward the ancestors" (101).

The Igbo concept of a personable "high god" is apparent in *The Igbo Roots of Olaudah Equiano* where Acholonu suggests how some Igbo represent Chukwu as "the Big God in the Sky" who smokes as the people do (75). In his narrative, Equiano represents his Igbo God as the "Creator of all things" who "lives in the sun" and "smokes a pipe, which is our favorite luxury" (41). The image of a divinity who likes the same things that human beings enjoy attests to the Igbo's view of God as a pleasant and casual deity. The Igbo perception of God as a personable spirit is also evident in what the Igwe of Orlu tells Acholonu, "Glory be to God on the Highest, and on earth, peace to men of goodwill" (168). The Igwe of Orlu also tells Acholonu, "You have unravelled what has baffled the ancient gods" (173), which is a statement that refers to the history and fate of Equiano (173). These quotations underscore the Igbo's belief in the capacity of human beings to intrude in the divine realm and resolve mysteries for their people. Yet the Igbo people's ability to enter the divine sphere and resolve problems depends on their continual relationships with God and ancestors. This permanent intimacy between people and sacred spirits is suggested in Acholonu's argument that in Equiano's homeland (Esseke), "There is a continuity between the past and present generations; between the past and the present, the present and the future, the dead and the living" (40). Acholonu's assertion emphasizes the Igbo's continuous ties with their reachable ancestors and gods who shape their lives and customs.

The notion of personable and accessible gods and ancestors who give people the power to do social good is an Igbo ideology that Equiano blends harmoniously with his Western Christian worldview. The Pan-African influence in his cosmology is noticeable in the ways in which he appropriates the *Dibia*'s rhetorical skills to preach for the end of the slave trade to a Western audience that he knew was as religious as the Igbo in Essaka were. In an attempt to convince readers of the inhumanness of slavery, he uses the imagery of human beings that society has corrupted by taking them from their homeland and bringing them into a world in which stratifications based on race and social status had replaced individual freedom.

From the moment he gains his freedom (121), Equiano becomes a Christlike figure who talks about the importance of atonement for one's sins. Looking at the waving water from the deck of a ship, he says: "All my sins stared me in the face; and, especially, I thought that God had hurled his direct vengeance on my guilty head for cursing the vessel on which my life depended. My spirits at this forsook me, and I expected every moment to go to the bottom. I determined if I should still be saved, that I would never swear again" (127). In this passage, he is using the genre of spiritual autobiography in order to talk about his own sin. Yet because his rhetoric appropriates the verbal ambiguity of both *Mbe* and the *Dibia*, Equiano's reference to his sin also signifies the whites' necessity to acknowledge the transgressions they committed against God by enslaving other human beings. Equiano's allusion to such sins is possible, because his words have a double meaning and direction that allow him to attack slaveowners implicitly without making himself vulnerable to their violence.

In addition, Equiano's narrative is distinguished by its ambivalent representation of Africa. On the one hand, Equiano was attracted to an Africa that he romanticized in order to show his nostalgia for his homeland. On the other hand, he was repulsed by an Africa that he vituperated in Eurocentric and ethnocentric terms in order to reveal his occasional lack of longing for his ancestral home. His duality toward Africa is traceable to the Igbo tricksters' shifting attitudes about life.

One positive representation of Africa in Equiano's book is the stanza from "Miscellaneous Verses" that describes the narrator's sorrow about his bondage. This section invokes the image of the free and innocent African person who was snatched from his/her homeland. Equiano writes:

> Unhappy more than some on earth,
> I thought the place that gave me birth—
> Strange thoughts oppress'd—while I replied
> "Why not in Ethiopia died?"
>
> And why thus spar'd when nigh to hell?—
> God only knew—I could not tell!
> "A tott'ring fence a bowing wall,"
> "I thought myself ere since the fall." (163)

This poem reveals Equiano's agony that he had been taken from his African homeland and brought into a world where misery and oppression compromised a freedom he could only dream of. The poem resonates with sentiments that Wheatley expressed in "To The Right Honourable William Legge, Earl of Dartmouth," published in Boston on October 10, 1772, where she describes her love for freedom as stemming

> From native Clime, when seeming cruel Fate
> Me snatch'd from Afric's fancy'd happy Seat,
> Impetuous—Ah! what bitter Pangs molest,
> What Sorrows labour'd in the Parent Breast?
> *That*, more than Stone, ne'er soft Compassion mov'd,
> Who from its Father seiz'd his much belov'd. (218)

Both writers describe the heavy and immeasurable price they paid for having been snatched from Africa and oppressed through captivity, confinement, and what Equiano summarizes as a descent into "hell" and which Wheatley synopsizes as a "cruel Fate." The two authors convey, through their "Talking Book," the horror that slavery brought into their personal and collective lives. Equiano, like Wheatley and Cugoano, was, then, a pioneer black Atlantic writer.

Equiano's ambivalence toward Africa is traceable to Igbo folklore in which duality is a common theme. A representation of doubleness in Igbo folklore is the tale "Usu (the Bat)" in which the protagonist allies himself with both birds and other animals for protection. As the storyteller says, "When, [during] the winged race, the birds appeared to be winning, Usu moved to their sides." In response to the birds' victory, "the animals regrouped and pulled down all the trees in the world, thus forcing the birds to remain constantly in flight. They had nowhere to perch. At this stage, Usu joined the animals."[22] The moral of this story is the belief in the inseparability of dual entities or qualities of life such as good/bad, tall/short, and beautiful/ugly that Western discourse categorizes. In *Toward an Igbo Metaphysics* (1985), Emmanuel M. P. Edeh explains the Igbo theory of duality as the idea that "for all beings in the material universe, existence is a dual and interrelated phenomenon. Whatever exists in a sensible form in this world does not exist solely in this way. It has a dual existence, dual in the sense that the reality of its existence is a phenomenon in the visible world and also a reality in the invisible world" (77). The Igbo theory of duality helps us explain the frequent change in Equiano's perception of Africa in ambivalent ways. Like Usu, Equiano pretends to be neutral when he visibly casts very critical eyes on Africa as if he does not want to reconnect with his homeland. Yet, at the same time, he is noticeably appreciative of Africa and wants to renew ties with his native land. It is therefore impossible to interpret Equiano's relations with Africa in monolithic ways, since his memory of cultural practices and political values in his homeland is ambivalent. Equiano's ambivalence toward Africa is an early sign of the "double-consciousness," or the intricate attempt of black Atlantic writers to blend their African and Western selves that Gruesser identifies in *Black on Black* (2000) as a major characteristic of twentieth-century African American literature (21–22).[23]

Equiano's representation of African culture was influenced by his disappointment and reproachful attitudes toward Africans whose involvement in his captivity he could neither understand nor pardon. Referring to Richard (Dick) Baker and his other white friends and shipmates, he states: "From what I could understand by him of this God, and seeing these white people did not sell one another as we did, I was pleased; and in this I thought they were much happier than we Africans" (63). Equiano's criticism of African culture was, therefore, influenced by his disillusionment with Africans' participation in his captivity.

Equiano's duality toward Africa is not permanent since he is able to look back to Africa in order to transcend the confusion that slavery created in his life. As F. Abiola Irele points out in *The African Imagination: Literature in Africa and the Black Diaspora* (2001), Equiano recovers from his anxieties by reversing the language of Western misrepresentation of Africans, "which he is able to grasp as a function both of his essential human condition and of his African antecedents" (48). This self-recovery allows Equiano to transcend his grudge toward Africans by his romantic celebration of his homeland of Essaka, where mostly his mother reared him and where matriarchy has a different meaning than that which applies to Western women.[24] For the sake of avoiding the pitfalls of Western feminist interpretations, which, as Filomina Chioma Steady argues, "have often been projections of male/female antagonisms that derive from Western middle-class experiences" with "very little concern shown for the oppression by world economic systems on African *men* as well as women" ("Black Women Cross-Culturally," 28), it is imperative to understand the complex matrilineal gender and class-based structures of the Igbo society from which Equiano came. In Igbo society, women have social and economic means that put them in egalitarian and complimentary relationships with men. In *Igbo Roots of Olaudah Equiano*, Acholonu records the statement of Egwuatu Onwuezike about the important status of women in traditional Igbo society in Esseke: "Our women, according to the stories we were told, were very cooperative. If the men were returning from war, the women would join together and go to meet them rejoicing. Also according to the stories we heard, if there was war in our village or town, our women would join forces with the men and go to war . . . if they stayed home they would still give their support to the men" (71–72). In a similar vein, Equiano gives a list of activities in which women in Essaka have absolute control. For instance, before a wedding, the relatives of both the bridegroom and the bride give a dowry that "generally consists of portions of land, slaves, and cattle, household goods, and implements of husbandry" (35).

Moreover, as Equiano suggests, in Essaka women are involved in economic transactions that require them to travel long distances, as evident in the case of the woman who helped two men capture Equiano and her sister and sell the siblings to a "chieftain" "in a very pleasant country" (48). This instance suggests the important economic and social role Igbo women have as forces that guarantee the well-being of their community by working in both external and internal spheres of life. In *Male Daughters, Female Husbands: Gender and Sex in an African Society* (1987), Ifi Amadiume says that Igbo women "could combine power derived from their control of subsistence farming and family sustenance, as they were the food producers and crop growers" and "their organizational ability, for effective mass action against a particular village or all the village group, until their demands were met" (182). According to Amadiume, these elements show that Igbo women's "strong economic position made up for their lack of formal political authority" (182).

Later, Equiano tells us that he was sold to a wealthy widow he later saw at a town he calls Tinmah (51). The editor of Equiano's narrative, Robert J. Allison, says that the town may be Utuma, Utu Etim, or Tinan, which are villages located between Ibo and Ibibio (51). In fact, it is also possible that the town Equiano calls Tinmah refers to the region in Central Sierra Leone where the Temne (Atemne or Timne) people lived. In *Senegambia and the Atlantic Slave Trade* (1998), Boubacar Barry describes the Temne territory as one of the Southern Rivers regions of West Africa that also included Susu, Bullam, and Baga, where large numbers of slaves (about 70 percent of the population of these regions) caught from the hinterlands were concentrated (122). The region was located on the route from the land of the Igbo in southeast Nigeria to the Guinea coast where Equiano would have been taken for sale into the Americas. It is then probable that the wealthy widow Equiano mentions identifies the prosperous class of African women traders whose functions in striving local and transatlantic networks of slave commerce have been examined by Lillian Ashcraft-Eason ("She Voluntarily Hath Come," 202–21).

The women Equiano describes also have power in the arena of sexuality. On his forced journey to the African west coast, Equiano describes a country where "women were not so modest as ours [in Essaka], for they ate, and drank, and slept with their men" (52). The sexual freedom is in contrast with the sexual restraint in Essaka (39), but it fits into the general pattern of equal roles between genders that exists in Equiano's community, especially in aspects of resistance against enemy invaders. He writes: "Even our women are warriors, and march boldly out to fight along with the men. Our whole district is a kind of a militia: on a certain signal given, such as the firing of a gun at night, they all rise in arms and rush upon their enemy. It is perhaps something remarkable, that when our people march to the field a red flag or banner is borne before them" (40). The striking element in Equiano's description of Igbo women is the complementary nature of their work and the important role these women played in the maintenance of the peace and order of their society. Rather than being the alleged victims of African men that Western scholars perceive them to be, women in Igbo society were strong and worked in harmonious ways with their men for the development of the community. In "Gender Question in Igbo Politics" (1993), U. D. Anyanwu says: "Men and women had specific roles but these were complementary. Men generally were the leaders or heads at all levels of the Igbo political structure. Women did not have equal access to power and authority with men. Yet women were not second-class citizens" (119). Anyanwu's statement contradicts the Western critics' tendency to represent gender relations in Igbo society in terms of antinomies between the discrete power of men and women.

Equiano also represents Africa through his depiction of Essaka as a place where artistic talent and creativity flourished. He states: "We are almost a nation of dancers, musicians, and poets. Thus every great event, such as a triumphant return from a battle or other cause of public rejoicing, is celebrated in public dances, which are accompanied with songs and music suited to the occasion" (36). Here, Equiano affirms his pride in an African tradition that he could remember so vividly in the West. His depiction of the inhabitants of Essaka as happy and sophisticated people registers his African consciousness and stands as a big contract to Wheatley's early misrepresentation of Africans as "*Pagans*." In this sense, one may agree with Femi Ojo Ade's argument that the experience of being in the West did not lead Equiano to neglect his African heritage (4).

Equiano's remembrance of African culture is also evident in his description of the allocation of space in his homeland according to gender and marital status. He tells us that in Essaka, men and women sleep separately unless they are married. The male-head of the family "has a large square piece of ground, surrounded with a moat or fence" (37). In the middle of the house stands a "principal building" [*Obi*] that is "appropriated to the sole use of the master consisting of two apartments" (37). He also tells us that the head of the family has "a distinct apartment in which he sleeps, together with his male children" (37). This housing-system reflects the gendered-structure of traditional African families. Opposing common stereotypes, he acknowledges the relative power and privilege that women have in the African family. As he points out, on either side of the husband's principal building, "are the apartments of his wives, who have also their separate day and night houses" (37). This detailed description of his traditional home and of the privilege that women have in Essaka attests Equiano's respect for his African village and tradition.

Equiano's deference for African culture is also noticeable in his portrayal of the rituals such as totemism, animal sacrifices, and ancestor worships that were practiced in Essaka. He writes: "the day on which the sun crosses the line [the equator]" is the time when "the greatest offerings are made" in Essaka (41). The day when the sun crosses the equator is also the time when "any young animals are killed" as sacrifices for the spiritual health of the community (41). These statements suggest the importance of animal sacrifices in Igbo culture, where animals serve as intermediaries between the living and the spirits of ancestors and deities, the latter being the most frequent beneficiaries of these offerings. As John E. E. Njoku points out in "The Igbos of Nigeria," while in many African countries "sacrifice" means offerings made to spirits, in Igboland the word signifies offerings made to either Chukwu (God) or Ekwensy (Devil), who are both considered as "too high on the scale of being to be the recipients of any sacrificial offering," since they are "the master spirits of good and evil, with little time or inclinations to bother about petty humans" (76). Njoku's assertion reveals the Igbo opposition of the Western conception of the world as constituted of unconnected "good" or "evil" resources out of which one chooses only one. By blurring the boundaries between "good" and "evil," Igbo culture provided Equiano with a flexible worldview and a concept of morality that allowed him to maneuver his struggle for freedom in the West successfully.

In an attempt to create respect for Africa and Africans in the West, Equiano rejects racial and cultural stereotypes and dichotomies. Combining the African bard's practice of oracling with philosophy, he presents various theories, which are antecedents of the Jewish hypothesis of Igbo origin.[25] As David Ihenacho argues in *African Christianity Rises: A Critical Study of the Catholicism of the Igbo People of Nigeria* (2004), this theory holds that "like most other epithets in the Hebrew culture, the term Igbo was an epithet of an ancient Jewish city or deity that became independent as an Igbo clan that splintered off and migrated southwards across the Sahara Desert to the area of equatorial Africa. According to this strand of Igbo scholarship, the former nomadic Igbo tribe finally settled in Southern Nigeria where it shed its nomadic culture for a more sedentary lifestyle encouraged by its new tropical habitation" (6–7). As Ihenacho contends, this hypothesis continues Equiano's theory that "the Igbo ancestry is Jewish in origin" (6). In his narrative, Equiano develops a similar idea when he argues that the cultures of the Igbo and the Jews are similar. He explains that rituals such as circumcising children or naming them from some event or circumstance are practiced in the cultures of both the Igbo and the Jews (42). Later, he contends that the Igbo and the Jews share the use of ablution for physical and spiritual cleanliness (42).

Equiano's intercultural theories help him demonstrate that the Igbo and the Jews have a common origin. He tells us that, according to an eighteenth-century European physician known as Dr. Gill, "the Africans [come] from Afer and Afra, [and are] the descendents of Abraham by Keturah his wife and concubine" (44). Gill's theory, he continues, "alone would induce me to think that the one people had sprung from the other" (44). His analogy between the Igbo and the Jews reveals his attempt to show that Africans are descendants of the same Judeo-Christian heritage to which many Europeans trace their religious beliefs. By locating the ancestors of the Igbo among the offspring of Abraham, Equiano wants to demonstrate the ancient nature of African people and civilizations in an attempt to create admissibility and respect for them in the New World. In this sense, Equiano's theory of the Jewish origin of the Igbo helps him subvert the racist representation of Africans as inferior to Europeans. As Adam Potkay and Sandra Burr argue in *Black Atlantic Writers of the Eighteenth Century* (1995), Equiano's theory of race and culture "runs contrary to the common (though fantastic) taunt that blacks are the cursed descendants of Ham who are ordained to serve God's chosen people—here, white Europeans—as slaves" (12). Equiano's representation of himself as the product of an African culture that was influenced by Jewish tradition exposes a radical change in his perception of his African identity in the West. In representing his racial and cultural background as a hybrid blend of African and Jewish elements, he undermines the notion of pure African identity.

Equiano's perception of his racial identity as hybrid is also visible in how he later prefers to be seen as white rather than as black. In the fourth chapter of the *Narrative*, he describes the moment when he wanted to be white. Referring to Mary, who was the daughter of an Englishman in Guernsey, South Great Britain, he states: "I had often observed that when her mother washed her face it looked very rosy, but when she washed mine it did not look so. I therefore tried oftentimes myself if I could not by washing make my face of the same color as my little play-mate, Mary, but it was all in vain; and I now began to be mortified at the difference in our complexions" (64). Equiano's belief that he could wash off the color of his face attests a desire to be assimilated into a European culture in which one's ability to pass as white was a key to gaining social admissibility and political and economic success. Ironically, his use of "passing" is damaging, since it leads him to question his relationships with Africa. As Jesús Benito and Ana Manzanas argue in a 1999 study of Equiano's shifting identities in the Western world, "Equiano seems to forget that whiteness for the African equates 'otherness'" (50).

Another major theme in Equiano's *Narrative* is his involvement in the black emigration project. This idea germinated in England as a result of anxieties about the presence of blacks in England during the early seventeenth century, when, according to Lewis K. Gordon, the Elizabethan royal proclamation of 1601 complained about the high number of "Negroes and blackamoors" in the kingdom (21). To alienate these blacks, the British government proposed their deportation as a remedy at a time when "a noticeable black community had settled itself in Shakespeare's London, immediately occasioned by the royal encouragement of the triangular trade with West Africa and the new American lands and the return of absentee planters with their retinues of black retainers" (21).

Despite the racism they experienced, blacks in London received a degree of acceptance from the white abolitionist sympathizers such as Lord Chief Justice Mansfield and Granville Sharp. Mansfield settled the infamous Somersett Case of 1772 in favor of blacks. The case was about a slave named James Somersett that a planter wanted to return to Jamaica chained in irons. Lord Mansfield ruled that despite his proprietary claims, the master could not force James to leave England. In "Black Writers of the Eighteenth and Nineteenth Centuries" (1985), Paul Edwards asserts: "By 1701, an Englishman making his will could write of his black servant, 'I take him to be in the nature of my goods and chattels.' There were critical voices to be heard, but no serious focus of protest until the 1760s when Granville Sharp won a series of cases against slave-owners in Britain, culminating in Lord Chief Justice Mansfield's ruling of 1772 in the Somerset case that black servants in Britain had the right to refuse to return to service—that is, to slavery—in the Americas" (51). The Somersett case dealt a heavy blow to the interest of slavery advocates while giving blacks a significant, though unclear, legal status in Britain. As James Walvin contends, the Somersett case brought a beacon of hope to blacks in England who "bowed with profound respect to the judges, and shaking each other by the hand, congratulated themselves upon the recovery of the rights of human nature" (112).[26]

A pivotal change occurred in the aftermath of the Somersett case when English abolitionist lawyer Granville Sharp, who was a friend of both Cugoano and Equiano, took advantage of Mansfield's ruling to argue that slaves were free once they set foot on English soil. Though it was equally significant for blacks, Sharp's argument was somewhat compromised by the institutional racism in Britain. According to Helena Woodward, despite his support for blacks, Sharp knew that "'the Crown and the nobles—and the monied interests—and the church and the bench and the bar' consolidated to preserve an ideology of racial inferiority to protect slavery" (40). This institutional racism did not prevent Sharp from continuing to support the Anti-Slavery movement, especially when Equiano and Cugoano asked him to help black servants in England avoid deportation to the Caribbean (53).

Equiano was aware of the quagmire that the English faced when they did not know what to do with poor blacks in England. In an attempt to overcome this dilemma, Equiano was determined to help these blacks migrate to Africa. He strongly wanted to go to Africa to serve as a missionary. He dreamed of serving as an officer of the "select committee of gentlemen for the black poor," whose humanitarian goals he espoused at first (187). Equiano was a major witness of the British government's plan to emigrate these blacks to Sierra

Leone. Equiano writes: "On my return to London in August [1786], I was very agreeably surprised to find that the benevolence of government had adopted the plan of some philanthropic individuals, to send the Africans from hence to their native quarter; and that some vessels were then engaged to carry them to Sierra Leone, an act which redounded to the horror of all concerned in its promotion, and filled me with prayers and much rejoicing" (187). The emigration project had a few ill intentions that Equiano understood but could not disclaim immediately. The risk of being carried in ships where slavery was practiced and the likelihood of being resold into slavery, as was current in the late eighteenth century, repulsed Equiano and distanced him from a project he perceived as a secret plan to rid England of its black leadership. In his introduction to Equiano's narrative, Carretta argues that the ending of the first editions of Equiano's book was "where the genre of *apologia*, or justification and vindication of one's life, shows its influence. Having been accused in the newspapers by powerful opponents of having mismanaged his position as Commissary for the Sierra Leone project, Equiano defends himself with witnesses and evidence" (xxiv).

In his narrative, Equiano tells us that he resigned from the position of Commissary for the Sierra Leone Project because he had witnessed "flagrant abuses" committed by an agent of the British government whom he charged for the loss of 750 slops (necessaries) that were needed for 750 persons (188). Yet, though he quit his position of appointed Commissary, Equiano remained interested in the African trip and learned with disillusionment about its setbacks. He asserts: "Thus ended my part of the long talked of expedition to Sierra Leone; an expedition which, however unfortunate in the event, was humane and politic in its design, nor was its failure owing to government; everything was done on their part; but there was evidently sufficient mismanagement attending the conduct and execution of it to defeat its success" (189). The legitimate reasons for Equiano's resignation from the position of Commissary of the Sierra Leone Project include the fear of racism and exploitation of his public status and intellect that he had, especially when emigrationist projects were designed with cruel policies that gave little power to the black elite that was expected to carry them out.

Equiano's narrative reflects his ability to use trickster strategies and other covert tools of resistance in order to justify the liberation of slaves from their oppressive masters. He used Igbo folklore constructively in an attempt to demonstrate the humanity of the African slaves and demand the end of their bondage. In addition, his account shows his capacity to participate in the intellectual debates about race and slavery in the West. His own experiences with slavery and racism, and his familiarity with European writings that demonized blacks, allowed him to identify and confront racist theories about Africans.

Moreover, Equiano's book reveals his dualistic relationships with Africa. While he is occasionally ambivalent toward certain parts of his Igbo customs and the participation of some Africans in the enslavement of other blacks, he never shatters the core of his Igbo identity and his respect for the customs and values of his homeland. Yet his Igbo identity does not prevent him from embracing European Christianity, creating alliances with free-minded Western abolitionists, and affirming connections between the Jews and the Igbo. In this sense, he developed a Pan-Africanism that allowed him to gain a legitimate space in Western culture and promote his Igbo tradition at the same time.

CHAPTER FOUR

◀ ··

Africanism and Methodism in the Works of Elizabeth Hart Thwaites and Anne Hart Gilbert

Elizabeth Hart Thwaites (1771–1833) and Anne Hart Gilbert (1768–1834) were black Antiguan women and Methodist authors of the late eighteenth and early nineteenth centuries whose writings remained unknown until Moira Ferguson made them available in *The Hart Sisters: Early African Caribbean Writers, Evangelicals, and Radicals* (1993). This book contains two memoirs entitled "The History of Methodism" that the sisters wrote in 1804. Reading these memoirs carefully, one finds the sisters' opinions about the conditions of slaves in Antigua in the 1830s, their attitudes about Africa, the importance of African traditions in Antiguan slave culture, and the authors' resistance against slavery. Using Moravian and Methodist ideologies of sin and redemption, the sisters denounced slavery and supported Antigua's oppressed blacks. Yet, they developed condescending and prejudiced theories about these blacks and their African traditions, exposing contradictions and ambivalences in their representation of people of African descent.[1] In order to understand these inconsistencies and dualities, one must explore how the sisters employed the resistance strategies of trickster figures of West Indian and African folktales to represent their identity or fight against slavery. Like *Anancy*, *Leuk*, and *Bouki*, the sisters employ tools of survival that occasionally conflict with the African communal notions of loyalty and fairness. Yet, like the folk figures, they invent legitimate ways to survive in an unstable New World where *Boukism*, or the ideology of the "survival of the fittest," is ubiquitous, and where diversion, false deference, and disguise are necessary means of struggle. Though they were not slaves themselves and were part of a different social group, the Hart Sisters would have known some of these trickster strategies and the folktales in Antigua. First, they were born and reared in an early Antiguan society where oral narratives that are similar to those in Africa were prevalent. Second, they represent the cultures of Antiguan slaves in ways that suggest their familiarity with the African cultures in the island.

Thwaites and Gilbert were born to Barry Conyers Hart, an African Caribbean slaveholder and estate owner, and to Anne Clearkley, the daughter of Frances Clearkley (who was an African Caribbean Methodist), near St. John, Antigua.[2] Their parents were members of a small class of free and colored blacks who used their limited rights and relative wealth to fight for the emancipation of slaves. In *Women Writing the West Indies: 1804–1939: "A Hot Place Belonging to Us"* (2003), Evelyn O. Callaghan argues that the Hart Sisters were "educated colored women born into a network of small but powerful and propertied mixed race families in Antigua" (181). In a similar vein, Moira Ferguson's introduction to *The Hart Sisters: Early African Caribbean Writers, Evangelicals, and Radicals* traces the mixed race of the Hart Sisters to their maternal grandmother, Frances (5). Ferguson states: "Frances Clearkley must have been a free colored; otherwise her daughter would have been a slave, because in slave society the mother's status determined the children's. The original membership of the Hart family within the free colored community may, then, have come from this marriage [with Timothy Clearkley]" (5). As the other free blacks in Antigua, the Hart family obtained rights of British citizenship, voting, and owning land and slaves, which angered a white Anglican planter class that felt threatened by these liberties and by the Methodist religious affiliations blacks were gaining in the island.[3]

Despite the prejudice they encountered from whites, the Harts helped their fellow blacks achieve education and exercise civil liberties. Their father helped many slaves prepare their manumission documents without charge.[4] As Ferguson argues in *The Hart Sisters*, he "agonized over punishments and tried to act humanely toward his slaves" (5). The sisters themselves educated many free Antiguan slaves on the benefits of literacy for the development of their native island.[5] According to Mindie Lazarus-Black, in 1813, they opened the first school for free slaves in Antigua, where they taught "only 'moral' persons" (*Legitimate Acts*, 91). They blended Christian religiosity with racially conscious activism and intellectualism to improve the conditions of black Antiguans. They invoked the principles of universal equality and freedom of the Enlightenment in an attempt to convince educated or Christian Europeans to abolish slavery.

The abolitionist rhetoric of the sisters partly came from their exposure to Moravian Christianity through their mother's sister, Grace Clearkley Cable.[6] Moravianism in Antigua began in 1756, more than two decades after it was implanted in the Danish West Indies, in St. Thomas (now the Virgin Islands of the United States) in 1732.[7] Fearing that it would spur slaves to rebel against their masters, planters refused to spread Christianity among them. In "The Negro in the West Indies, Slavery and Freedom" (1932), Charles H. Wesley argues that the Moravians, as the Methodists and the Baptists did later, seized the planter's isolation of slaves to influence the latter (60). Thus, as James Latimer points out, Moravians taught slaves ideas of self- discipline, acceptance of the master's will, and full obedience to his orders (435). In this sense, the missionaries used religion as a means to control the behavior of slaves. This use of religion as a tool of control initially worked in favor of the planter, who benefited from the deference of slaves. Yet, it finally worked to the advantage of slaves, because they were the ones who were gaining knowledge from useful instructions about private estates and literacy that Moravians were giving them during personal conversations (known as speakings).[8]

Additionally, the Hart Sisters' exposure to Christianity came from their relationships with John Wesley (1703–1791), who was a cofounder of Methodism. In 1729, he and his brother Charles joined the Holy Club of Lincoln College, Oxford. The club members were called "Methodists" because, as an anonymous critic suggests, they adhered to religious precepts and practices such as visiting prisons and comforting the ill. As this critic shows, Wesley's theology was based on inner religion and the idea that each person was a child of God. In 1744, he convened the first conference of Methodist leaders who adopted the Articles of Religion stressing repentance, faith, sanctification, and full and free salvation.[9]

In *Slaves and Missionaries*, Mary Turner argues that the roots of Wesleyan Methodism in the Caribbean go back to 1789, when a Wesleyan preacher, who was the "first of a contingent of missionaries dedicated to teaching the slaves Christianity, began preaching in Kingston" (7). Yet the beginning of Methodism in the West Indies can also be traced to December 25, 1786, when Thomas Coke, an Anglican clergyman Wesley had ordained to administer sacraments in 1784, arrived in Antigua after his ship landed off course. By 1814, Coke had expanded Methodism in both the Caribbean and the rest of the world, leaving missions in Sierra Leone, Newfoundland, Nova Scotia, and in fifteen West Indian islands (7).

Wesleyan Methodism had strong influence on blacks of the diaspora because of its liberal and militant Evangelicalism. Francis Smith Foster explains in *Written by Herself*: "He encouraged them to speak publicly and to assume positions of leadership and responsibility. While Wesley's attitudes toward women were not always shared by other Methodists ministers, his sanctions did establish precedents" (69). The influence of Wesleyan Methodism on the diaspora is visible in Anne Hart Gilbert's own family history. As Ferguson points out in her introduction to *The Hart Sisters*, the Methodist minister Nathaniel Gilbert was the person who converted Anne Hart Gilbert's maternal grandmother Frances Clearkley (7). In the 1760s, Nathaniel met "the founder and spiritual father of Methodism, John Wesley, and was astounded when Wesley baptized two of his slaves . . . [Nathaniel] Gilbert was influenced by Wesley's teaching and brought his spiritual mentor's religious message back to Antigua as the Caribbean's first self-appointed missionary" (7). Nathaniel Gilbert was an assembly member from Antigua, who owned slaves. The conversion of his two slaves, which is also considered as the beginning of Methodism in Antigua, occurred in 1757 when he traveled to England to hear Wesley speak.[10] Nathaniel was the cousin of John, the man Anne Hart Gilbert married in 1798 only to spark what Ferguson calls "a clandestine racist backlash" among the elite of Antigua. Ferguson writes: "The couple returned from their honeymoon to find the door of his notary office painted half white and half yellow, their enemies' reminder of the couple's 'unholy union'" (*Nine Black Women*, 27).

The black population in Antigua grew substantially between the late seventeenth century and the early nineteenth century. In "With a Rod of Iron" (1999), Gaspar argues: "In 1678 the population of black slaves [in Antigua] was estimated at 2,172, compared with 2,308 whites. After this point, the number of slaves grew quickly and surpassed the number of whites, which increased much more slowly. By the 1690s there were probably close to 10,000 slaves and perhaps 2,500 whites" (358). Gaspar's statement shows Antigua's continuous dependence on the labor of slaves whose population increased from additional slave imports. In *Bondmen and Rebels*, Gaspar estimates the number of slaves brought to Antigua between 1671 and 1763 at 60,820 (75). As Lazarus-Black argues in *Legitimate Acts and Illegal Encounters: Law and Society in Antigua and Barbuda* (1994), in 1832, the total number of slaves in Antigua included 13,483 males and 14,971 females (97).

A considerable segment of Antigua's slave population came from Senegambia. According to *The Trans-Atlantic Slave Trade* database (Eltis et al., 1999), by the end of the slave trade, Western ships had brought 126,323 Africans to Antigua. As *The Trans-Atlantic Slave Trade* database shows, 14,579, or 11.5 percent of this population, came from the Gold Coast while 6,204, or 4.91 percent of it, derived from Senegambia. In addition, as the database suggests, 50,449 of the inhabitants, or 39.90 percent, came from unspecified parts of Africa. In "Antigua and Barbuda" (2006), John G. Hall clarifies the African presence in Antigua when he argues that four years after the island became a British colony in 1632, one-half of its population consisted of African slaves brought to the

Caribbean to produce tobacco, sugar, ginger, and indigo for export (37). According to Hall, "many of these slaves came from what is now called Guinea, a Coastal West African country bordered by Guinea-Bissau, Senegal, Mali, the Ivory Coast, Liberia, and Sierra Leone, but they were also brought from other places along Africa's west coast" (38). These numbers demonstrate the substantial migration of African people and culture from the Windward Coast, Senegambia, and other parts of Africa into Antigua during the slave trade.

Moreover, the forced migration of Senegambians to Antigua is examined in Daniel P. Manix's *Black Cargoes: A History of the Atlantic Slave Trade, 1518–1865* (1962). Manix describes how a ship called Charlestown, which anchored on the Gambia River on June 15, 1797, exchanged its cargo of rum and tobacco for a hundred and thirty slaves who were mostly Mandingos (155). Quoting Mungo Park, who served as a surgeon on the *Charlestown*, Manix writes: "After some objections on the part of the master, we directed our course for Antigua, and fortunately made that island in about thirty-five days after our departure from Goree" (156). The Senegambians in the vessel carried African folklore, spirit of resistance, and power of adaptation that helped them survive their painful conditions of servitude in the West Indies.

The transplantation of African folklore and survival skills into the black diaspora allows us to explore the relationships between trickster icons in West Indian culture and African folktales. These connections are apparent in Maureen Warner-Lewis's essay "Caribbean Verbal Arts" (2004), which examines the influence of the African-derived trickster figures in West Indian folktales (46). According to Warner-Lewis, the trickster in Caribbean tales "may be the Akan spider *Anansi*, after whom the folktales are generically named, the Senegambian rabbit-sized antelope variously called Rabbit or Hare, or the Yoruba tortoise. The trickster is called Malice in Haiti, his dupe being *Bouki*, the Wolof term for hyena. Among other dupes are Tiger, Elephant, Alligator, Dog, and Monkey" (46). As Warner-Lewis argues, the influence of these tricksters in West Indian oral tradition is perceptible in the tales of the Jamaican Big Boy Character, in which this figure "is a combination of trickster, dunce, and word magician" (46). Furthermore, Warner-Lewis argues that the African survival in Caribbean oral tradition is visible in the West Indian stories that contain "songs, sometimes cryptic, in which the audience participates" and "narrative devices [that] include the use of onomatopoeia and ideophones, hand and facial gestures, and opening and/or closing devices" (46).

In a similar vein, John W. Roberts points out in *From Trickster to Badman: The Black Folk Hero in Slavery and Freedom* (1989) that the transplanted blacks in the diaspora used African animal tricksters "to transmit a conception of behaviors appropriate and beneficial for protecting their values and well-being under the conditions faced in slavery" (33). According to Roberts, African slaves in the Americas inherited the African tricksters' egocentric and solitary approach to life and their view of the world as a jungle where the fittest survives in an attempt to "gain an advantage over forces in the social world inhibitive to material and social well-being" (33). Roberts's assessment conveys the philosophy of the survival of the fittest that justified the desperate actions of African slaves and their trickster icons who live in drastic conditions in which their owners' deceit and individualism compromise their honesty and communalism.

The relationships between African and Caribbean folktales are also evident in Keith Q. Warner's *Critical Perspectives on Leon Gontran-Damas* (1972) where the author represents the Guyanese tale "Sur un air de guitare" ("to a tune for guitar") as a narrative that reflects important ideas of Caribbean and African folklore (165).[11] According to Warner, this folk story "is a mythological motif which offers an explanation of why fowls kill roaches." As Warner argues, the Guyanese writer Léon Gontran-Damas elucidates this dilemma through a Guyanese proverb that says, "ravet pa jin gain réson divant poulailler poule" which literally means, "Cockroach is never in the right before the strong and powerful" (162). The unbalanced relationship between Cockroach and Fowl epitomizes the unequal power relations between slaves and slave masters that are obvious in Antiguan and Senegambian folktales.

Elizabeth Hart Thwaites's "History of Methodism"

Thwaites's "History of Methodism" demonstrates the influence of Christianity and African culture on her worldview and her analysis of the conditions of blacks in Antigua. She celebrates the culture of the enslaved Africans in Antigua. Yet, she occasionally makes negative remarks about these slaves, revealing the contradiction in how she fought for the freedom of blacks while repeating the Europeans' demeaning notions about blacks and Africa. Thwaites's quandary can, however, be understood as the recourse of a black writer who utilizes trickster resistance strategies such as ambivalence, false deference, masking, and adornments of multiple roles and positions in order to survive in the alienating world slavery created in Antigua. The use of false deference is visible in one Antiguan tale collected by John H. Johnson in 1925. In this tale entitled "The Three Questions," a servant disguised as a professor went to the King Pascha to answer questions that were to save his master's life. According to the narrator, "the servant told the monarch that the mountain might be filled with earth filling a basket the size of the mountain, or with two baskets one-half the size of the mountain, filled with earth. He gave the king's worth by citing Jesus' price as thirty pieces of silver. He said the king was thinking that he was the professor" (74).[12]

This tale provides the folkloric background that helps us understand the ways in which Thwaites represents herself as a frail character when she praises her white Methodist and abolitionist friends. The anecdote reflects power relations similar to those between Thwaites and her white friends. Like the man in the tale, Thwaites complies with the hegemony of the dominant group simply because she wants to gain the knowledge that can allow her to fight for her freedom. She seeks to be literate about Christianity and speak the message of freedom within it in order to gain her white patrons' support in her struggle for the recognition of her humanity and that of her race. In this sense, when she praises her Methodist and abolitionist friends, she is using the weapons of the weak in order to find refuge in an environment that is full of injustices. While she invokes Methodist ideas of religiosity and individual restraint, she conjures the African principle of social regulation in a community that occurs only when the will and power of individuals are subordinated to those of the group. This African-centered interpretation of Thwaites's worldviews allows us to fathom the Eurocentric allusions in her depiction of blacks. These allusions are eccentricities she creates to please and divert her white, Christian, and abolitionist supporters while developing subversive African worldviews and spiritualisms.

First, Thwaites's memoir indicates a blend of Methodist Christianity and African traditional religiosity. The influence of Methodism is visible in the rejection of earthly things that her Methodist parents taught her. She pays homage to her grandmother Frances Clearkley, "who was converted to God by the ministry of the Rev. Francis Gilbert and who died in the Faith, with my Dear Mother (gone to Glory)" (89). Thwaites thanks her parents who "were united to the Methodists and trained up the younger branches of the Family, myself among them, in the fear of God and the observance of religious duties" (89). This passage shows the Christian foundation that later attracted Thwaites and her sister to asceticism. In *The Hart Sisters*, Ferguson writes: "After their Methodist conversion, the sisters changed their habits, dressed plainly, and renounced what they considered worldly pursuits" (9).

Although it has Christian features, Thwaites's reference to her deceased mother also reflects the African idea that death is a passage into a world that is inseparable from that of the living. John S. Mbiti argues in *Introduction to*

African Religion (1991) that some African societies believe that "the departed remain in the neighborhood of their human homestead. They are still part of the family . . . Their surviving relatives and friends feel the departed are close to them" (122–23). The belief in the continuity between the worlds of the dead and that of the living was widely shared among blacks of Antigua. As Gaspar suggests in *Bondmen and Rebels*, this Akan worldview survived in Antiguan slave culture, where the Coromantee rebels took the oath "with grave dirt that signified that the world of the living was intertwined with that of the dead, that they were united with their ancestors, by whom they swore to be true to their solemn obligations or incur dreadful sanctions" (245).[13]

Later, Thwaites praises the genealogy of her family by celebrating the mother and father who gave her life. She writes: "I was also blest with an affectionate Father who ever watched with the tenderest solicitude over the morals of his Children, as did others of our near Relations, who by their kind attention prevented our feeling the want of Mother's care after her Death" (89). This statement introduces a concept of kinship based on the sanctity of the parents' love for their children that was central in traditional African societies. As Mbiti shows in *Concepts of God in Africa* (1970), both the Mende (of Sierra Leone) and the Nandi (of Kenya) viewed the parents' love for their offspring as the sole power that can ward off evil from them (201–2). This conception of parenthood as a shield against evil is consistent with Thwaites's representation of her parents as the most important protectors of their children.

Yet, in her memoir, Thwaites frequently displays ambivalence toward blacks. For instance, she expresses moral reprobation against slave women who "are raised to wealth" and, as a consequence, may become concubines (96). But she later defends black women that society represents in negative ways. In her "Letter from Elizabeth Hart to a Friend," she recounts an incident in which a black woman from her church was ridiculed and abused "for doing that which would have appeared strange in them not to do, as though she had committed a crime: the poor affrighted creature withdrew from her husband, to stop the clamour of this narrow-hearted *gentry*, and made haste out of the way" (107–8). By denouncing the *gentry*'s intolerance and prejudice against the black woman, Thwaites shows that she identifies with black Antiguan women, to whom she relates in a black womanist ideology. This philosophy is best described through Bernice Johnson Reagon's concept of a "mothering generation," that is "the way the entire community organizes itself to nurture itself and its future generations" (177). This theory of "mothering" is grounded on the Pan-Africanist conception of the black woman as the voice and protector of the children of Africa and the black diaspora whose lives were shattered by slavery.[14] Drawing from the African concept of motherhood, Thwaites uses the term "mothers" to refer to how the black sisters unite to fight against oppression. She describes Gilbert as "the only Person to whom I could communicate my Joys and Griefs. We walked hand in hand, and mutually helped each other on. Blessed be God, we are at this Day of one heart and soul" (92). This assertion indicates Thwaites's respect for a black womanhood that is grounded on "marronage."

The term "marronage" comes from the concept of "maroons," which identifies defiant African Caribbean slaves who escaped plantations to live up on hills and mountains where they were able to re-create communities similar to those in Africa. Although they existed in various parts of the diaspora, such as Brazil, Colombia, Cuba, Equador, Jamaica, Mexico, Suriname, Guadaloupe, Martinique, and Haiti, the maroons are particularly associated with Jamaica, where Cudjoe and Nanny led successful resistance against the British from the 1690s to the 1730s. Maroon women had major roles as leaders and priestesses of their community, similar to that Thwaites had in Antigua. One of these women was Nanny, who led a strong resistance against the English in 1734, which has become a symbol of the resilience of black women of the diaspora against colonialism.[15]

Nanny also embodies cultural connections between the black diaspora and Africa. The relationships are apparent in the African origin of Nanny's name. As Jenny Sharpe points out in *Ghosts of Slavery*, her name derived from the word "*Nana*," which is an Akan term of respect for ancestors and spiritual leaders and "*ni*," which means "mother." Yet the meaning of Nanny's name goes beyond its Akan roots of "ancestress" and "mother" to include a range of Asante words that encompass what Sharpe calls "the 'total complex' of her roles as a female leader: 'woman, mother, ancestor, leader, priestess, judge and legislator, healer of the breach and revolutionary' "(22).

Thwaites had social roles that were similar to Nanny's. She was a spiritual leader and a social advocate for Antiguan women. Like Nanny, she fought for the emancipation of slaves in the Caribbean and the improvement of the conditions of their children. Moreover, she wanted to create a free community of educated blacks who could use the education slaveholders denied them to reconstruct their lives. In order to uncover Thwaites's Nanny-like attributes, one must explore the dilemma in the ways in which she juxtaposes her primitivizing of Africans with her romanticizing and defense of them. Yet she remains conflicted, because she does not view Africans as the cultural equals of Europeans and her defense of Africans arises not from her awareness of their humanity but from her internalization of the Europeans' racist mission to civilize them. Paradoxically, she later criticizes the Europeans' misrepresentation of Africans and places the responsibility of the Africans' suffering during slavery on the Europeans' wrongdoings.

Thwaites's ambivalence about Africans is noticeable when she expresses compassion toward Antigua's slaves while showing utter revulsion for Africans. In "Letter from Elizabeth Hart to a Friend," dated October 24, 1794, but included in *The Hart Sisters*, she expresses sorrow for the harsh treatment slaves received from cruel Europeans. She says: "It is not uncommon to see old persons, who have spent their health and strength in this unreasonable service [slavery], and whose conduct merits every respect, receiving the utmost indignities at the hand of some untaught capricious little Master or Miss, who thinks nothing of lifting the hand or heel against them" (108). Thwaites's representation of Antigua's slaves as oppressed people contrasts with her depiction of Africans and blacks from Haiti and Martinique as exploited people who have become oppressors. She writes: "I have thought, that when the Almighty afflicts a people, for sin, they repent and are humbled before deliverance is brought near. But I believe the Africans remained in their original darkness when He [God] raised up men in Europe to espouse their cause" (110). This quotation reflects the hypocrisy in Thwaites's discourse about blacks. As visible in her representation of Africans as people who have "remained in their original darkness," she perceives Africans as inferior to Europeans, exemplifying the Eurocentrism that nineteenth-century black diasporan nationalists often revealed in their representation of Africa. In *UnAfrican Americans*, Tunde Adeleke describes this perception of Africa in the writings of nineteenth-century Pan-Africanists such as Martin Robinson Delany, Edward Blyden, and Alexander Crummel as a reflection of their "affection for European values and their disdain for African societies and indigenous African traditions and norms" (27). Thwaites exemplifies this ambiguous Pan-Africanism since she was indirectly involved in the mission to civilize Africa in which some of these nationalists participated.

In a correspondence to her cousin Miss Elizabeth Lynch, written in 1809, and also published in *The Hart Sisters*, Thwaites mentions a letter from Mr. Dawes of Antigua, a former Governor of Sierra Leone, who is an "agent of the Church Missionary Society in Antigua, showing the destitute condition of the young women growing up in the Island, virtuously and religiously, by means, under God, of Sunday schools" (112). Mr. Dawes's portrayal of Antiguan women as "destitute" was contiguous to his stereotyping of their African counterparts as impossible to civilize or Christianize. Dawes's stereotypes of blacks, which certainly influenced Thwaites's views of them, were part of the discourse white missionaries such as William Wilberforce often developed about Africans even when they were fighting to end slavery.[16] Seeking an alternative to African cultures that they saw as embodiment of the decadence of Africans, not of the English colonists in the continent, the British began asking black West Indians to begin a crusade of civilizing Africa during the 1830s and '40s. As Nemata Blyden posits in *West Indians in West Africa*, having initially opposed the use of blacks as missionaries to Sierra Leone, the Church Missionary Society finally agreed to let blacks be "agents as the panacea for all Africa's ills" and mediators who will "regenerate" the continent (37).

Another example of Thwaites's ambivalence toward blacks is visible in how she proposes the abolition of slavery while refusing to support the rise of slaves in St. Domingue and Martinique. She says: "Nor have we reason to suppose the Negroes in St. Domingo, Martinique, &c., are one whit better than ever they were. Concerning these we have strange accounts, many of them having taken their masters' places; and the oppressors are now the oppressed. I believe, with a good man, that 'present impunity is the deepest revenge'" (110). This passage indicates Thwaites's elitist distance from the Caribbean slaves whose use of violence as a means of resistance against tyranny she rejects. Thwaites's public detachment from the liberation struggle of Caribbean slaves creates serious limitations in her Pan-Africanism. Yet the detachment does not obliterate her Pan-Africanism because it stemmed from her calculated shifting attitudes about blacks. Thwaites's change of attitude toward blacks was a strategy of deception she utilized to fight for the freedom of blacks while publicly appearing, in front of whites, to do the contrary. For example, her public dismissal of the violence of blacks in the quote above could be a calculated tactic of warning the Europeans of the inevitability of slave uprising for freedom, which she secretly supports. She maintains that the violence slavery created in Antigua can end only when the institution itself ends. Answering the question of whether free blacks like her should not "rejoice in hope, and be thankful that we are not in bondage, either in a literal or spiritual sense?" (110), which her white penfriend asks her, Thwaites responds: "We should indeed rejoice in hope of this bright morning, be abundantly thankful that we are not in the chains of sin or slavery, and pray that God would hasten the time when 'violence shall no more be heard in our land, neither wasting nor destruction within our borders, but our walls be salvation and our gates praise'" (111).

In her rhetoric, Thwaites intersperses in her dream of peace in Antigua a prayer for the end of violence and destruction in the island (111). Yet, as is apparent in her wish that "God would hasten" this time, Thwaites is somewhat reluctant to let religion alone determine the end of slavery. In her next statement, she takes a bold step against slavery by calling for a restoration of justice in the island through reparation of the wrongs of the evil institution. She writes: "I was no sooner capable of thinking, than my heart shuddered at the cruelties that were presented to my sight; but more have I felt since I began to think seriously. I am, however, more concerned to have the evils within rectified, or rather cured; this will perhaps render some of those that are without less poignant, though I do not expect that religion will deliver me from fellow-feeling, nor do I desire it should; only I wish that I (and all who are in those things like-minded) may be enabled to live" (111). Thwaites attempts to leave the comfort zone of Methodist idealism and search for practical ways to make the benign teachings of the religion applicable to the restoration of justice for slaves. The anxiety and emotional distress that Thwaites experiences as she seeks to determine the role that religion should have in this restitution of human rights show her double consciousness toward Methodism and Antiguan slaves. In *Colonialism and Gender Relations from Mary Wollstonecraft to Jamaica Kincaid*, Ferguson writes: "She [Thwaites] draws attention to the pain she feels about the double standard she had exercised toward her pupils: her own hypocrisy in teaching slaves morality while not practicing what she preached" (52). As suggested in her call for a cure of the "cruelties" and "evils" of slavery, Thwaites somewhat corrects her hypocrisy toward slaves by developing a notable degree of radicalism. In order to avoid appearing as a belligerent or steadfast dissenter, she couches her radicalism in an idealist discourse of hope and salvation while endorsing practical actions that lead to freedom.

Thwaites's propensity to endorse some radicalism that can bring freedom reminds us of the ways in which trickster figures in Antiguan and Senegambian tales use violence to liberate themselves from oppressors. One example of this motif is the Antiguan tale "The Chosen Suitor," which, as Thomas A. Green argues in the *Greenwood Library of American Folktales* (2006), "is of African origin" (277). In this tale, Bro' Boar-Hog disguises himself as a man and pays a visit to the daughter of a very protective woman. As the storyteller says, the woman's son knows that Bro' Boar-Hog is a boar-hog, not a man, but he cannot convince his mother to share his suspicion. One day, the boy's mother asks him to take some food to Bro' Boar-Hog. When the boy arrives behind a tree near the suitor's home, he finds him on the ground. According to the narrator,

> While he [the boy] got behind da tree, he see dis boar-hog rootin' up de ground. An' dis boar-hog root all de ground, like ten men with forks.

Dis boy stay behind da tree an' see all he do. When da boy see him, he wait a little; den da boy say, "Ahem!"

> Boar-Hog jump around; he start to say,
> "Indiana, Indiana, um, um!
> Indiana, Indiana, um, um!
> Indiana, Indiana, um, um!

Dat caused his clothes to jump right on him accordin' as he sing da song. He step out, put his two hands in his pocket, an' say, "Boy, see how I plough up dis land!" He boast about da work he do on da field. (279)

When Boar-Hog returns to the boy's house to see his sister, the lad takes his fife and starts to play the same song that the suitor played in the field. Then "Bro' Boar-Hog say, 'What vulgar song dat boy singin'!' He start movin'. He not able to keep still, 'cause his tail comin' out fast. Quick he say, 'Stop it, stop it! Let's go out for a walk! Let's go out for a walk! I can't stay here.'" According to the narrator, the grandfather intervenes by asking his grandson to keep playing his music. As the boy continues to play his fife, the family begins to see change in Bro' Boar-Hog's attire and deportment. The storyteller says:

> His [Bro' Boar-Hog's] beaver [hat] drop off. Den he [the boy] play on again da same song: his coat drop, his shirt drop. All drop save his pants.
> Da ol' man tell him, "Play, boy! Play, play, play!" An' his pant drop off. Dey see his long tail show, an' he start to run. Da ol' man point da gun at him an' shoot him dead. (279)

This folktale has a motif of desperate use of violence to end the treachery of an oppressor that one also finds in a Senegambian tale entitled "La dernière prise" [the last catch]. According to the narrator, *Bouki* asked a poor and old woman-farmer to keep a skinny goat for him. Later, *Bouki* stole the goat and went to the farmer every day to ask for his missing property. The poor and defenseless farmer reluctantly allowed *Bouki* to pick one of her cows anytime he came to ask for his lost goat. One day, *Leuk* told *Gaïn*dé-the-Lion about *Bouki*'s offense. After telling the story to *Gaïn*dé-the-Lion, *Leuk* went to see the woman farmer and asked if she would let *Gaïn*dé-the-Lion eat her last cow and cover himself with its skin, so that *Bouki* would take him home unknowingly. When *Bouki* arrived at the farm, *Gaïn*dé-the-Lion had already eaten the cow, covered himself with the dead animal's skin, and was smoking his pipe. *Bouki* arrived at the woman's farm and took his last catch. Meanwhile, *Bouki*'s family was waiting for him for another feast. When *Bouki* arrived home, he decided to tie the cow to a post and keep it for one of his future big family gatherings. That night, *Gaï*ndé-the-Lion tore the rope which bound him to the post and went to knock at *Bouki*'s door. Realizing that he had brought *Gaï*ndé-the-Lion, not a cow, *Bouki* asked all the members of his family to climb up the ceiling of his house fast for their safety. *Gaï*ndé-the-Lion waited patiently below and crushed *Bouki* and every member of his family who fell to the ground (99–104).

The two folktales reflect a communality that is apparent in the ways in which a community gathers around a defenseless person in order to protect him/her from a domineering and transgressive force such as Bro' Boar-Hog and *Bouki*, whose foibles resemble those of slave masters. In the Antiguan tale, the communal solidarity is visible in the ways in which the grandfather, mother, and brother protect their young and female relative from Boar-Hog when they realize that he is an animal in disguise. This fear of strangers reflects the difficult context of slavery in the diaspora that prompted blacks to be cautious toward potential kidnappers and other deceivers. As the Antiguan tale suggests, blacks resisted authoritarian tricksters who symbolized domineering slave catchers by developing their own deceptive strategies against oppression. For instance, the family in the Antiguan narrative dupes Bro-Boar by forcing him to reveal his true identity and "shooting him dead" (279). This family appropriates the survival instinct of the trickster icons in slave culture and African tales who use wit to defeat the duplicity of their oppressors. A similar use of communality and wit against oppression is suggested in the clever and collaborative strategy that *Leuk* and *Gaï*ndé-the-Lion develop in order to protect the defenseless woman-farmer from *Bouki*'s transgression. This strategy shows *Leuk* and *Gaï*ndé-the-Lion's development of an African relational concept of society in which individual leaders devise perfect plans to protect the members of their community. This African respect for the intelligence and skills of leaders in the struggle for freedom is apparent in John Thornton's argument in *Africa and Africans in the Making of the Atlantic World, 1400–1800* (1999) that the African slaves in the New World carried notions of leadership from their homeland that strengthened the revolts of Caribbean slaves. Thornton writes:

> The African background may have figured in these plots in two ways. First of all, insofar as the national organizations preserved African cultural and political ideas, they would contribute to the leadership, organization, and goals of the future state. Second, insofar as Africans

with military or political experience participated in the plots, whether through national organizations or not, a state with strong leadership and continued inequality, such as was found in the runaway communities, was likely to be perpetuated. (303)

The survival of African concepts of leadership in the diaspora is also apparent in the Antiguan folktale above in which a Caribbean family uses relational diplomacy and negotiation to influence Bro' Boar-Hog into revealing his false identity and punish him. This tactic is similar to the "weapon of the weak" that Antiguan slaves used to protect their community against the duplicity of slave-owners by reversing the unequal power relations between masters and themselves through subtle countertricking. Discussing similar subversive tactics, David Barry Gaspar argues, in *Bondmen and Rebels: A Study of Master-Slave Relations in Antigua* (1985), that eighteenth-century Caribbean slaves devised "patterns of resistance that were accommodative and patently less dramatic than rebellion, flight to the interior, or attacks on whites and plantations" (257). These Caribbean slaves retained the African relational and diplomatic notions of resistance since they used the African concept of consensus to create a liminal space in their relationships with their owners. As Gaspar points out in *Bondmen and Rebels*, "the slave society itself, always unstable, always capable of being split apart by internal discord between masters and slaves, came to rely less upon coercion and more upon a mixture of coercion and consensus to preserve some semblance of order within which masters and slaves might pursue their interdependent and independent interests" (258). This diplomatic and relational resistance of Caribbean slaves evolved out of their reminiscence of the divisive power of European imperialism and trickery in Africa. Giving examples of the terrible historical circumstances that African slaves in the New World remembered, Rucker writes in *The River Flows On: Black Resistance, Culture, and Identity Formation in Early America* (2006):

> Thus, control over the production and distribution of food was one of the power-relationships binding peasants to the numerous polities in Atlantic Africa. Failure to pay tribute, personal debt, military service, or involuntary involvement in war led to many rural villagers becoming slaves in the Americas. The folklore they created, therefore, may have been a full reflection of conditions and concerns in Atlantic Africa. (204)

Thus, the New World African slaves used diasporan folktales as a means of imagining a world in which they re-created the wisdom and diplomacy of

African trickster icons in order to resist planter strategies such as kidnapping, punishment, prohibitions, and other legal restrictions that reminded them of the tactics that Europeans used in Africa to enslave them. As Gaspar shows in *Bondmen and Rebels*, the African-based environment was instrumental in the resistance of Antiguan slaves against their masters since it "reduced some of the force of attempts at domination, especially through legal controls that reflected the immediate necessities of the master class" (134). This re-creation of an African-based heritage in the black diaspora suggests the drastic economic and social contexts that required New World slaves to implement defensive resistance tactics that could surpass the cunning of their masters. One example of such strategies is the tactic of countertricking that the Antiguan family uses to subvert Bro-Boar. This strategy of countertricking conveys a resistance philosophy that resonates with that of blacks in antebellum America. This ideology is preserved in the South Carolina slave saying that Lawrence W. Levine cites in *Black Culture and Black Consciousness* (1978): "*De buckruh [whites] hab scheme, en de nigger hab trick, en ebery time de buckruh scheme once de nigger trick twice*" (81). This proverb reflects a belief in the importance of countertricking that Africans in America learned from animal folktales. These Africans preserved the pretence of innocence of the tricksters of these tales and used it as an effective tool of resistance against oppression. As is apparent in the writings of Thwaites and Gilbert, the Africans in Antigua knew the power of this strategy of deception and employed it to liberate themselves from their white oppressors.

Another trickster strategy that Thwaites uses is false deference. She uses this tactic by pretending to be thankful for the limited freedom she has as a free black while she rejects this freedom that is incomplete without the abolition of slavery. She pretends to be grateful to whites while she is conscious of being exploited by them. In this sense, she uses false deference since her routine compliance to the ideology of the dominant group betrays her true consciousness about the necessity to end this conformity through actual freedom. Thwaites's behavior reflects the exploited person's use of false deference as a means to protect herself/himself against further oppression. This theory is informed by James C. Scott's representation of false deference as the psychological state in which the exploited recognizes that he/she has been ill-treated and becomes conscious of the achievement and effort he/she has developed by swallowing his/her anger lest it endangers his/her livelihood (278–79). Thwaites employs this tactic by seeking alliance, not in false-consciousness but in the true conviction shared by abolitionists such as William Wilberforce, Mr. Pitt, Mr. Fox, Lord Grenville, Lord Lansdowne, and Lord Grey that slavery was ubiquitously immoral and needed to be replaced, not just by liberation but also by transformation of slaves into a free labor force. In *An Appeal to the Religion, Justice, and Humanity of the Inhabitants of the British Empire in Behalf of the Negro Slaves in the West Indies* (1823), William Wilberforce writes: "for let it be remembered, that, from the very first, Mr. Pitt, Mr. Fox, Lord Grenville, Lord Lansdowne, Lord Grey, and all the rest of the earliest Abolitionists, declared that the extinction of slavery was our great and ultimate object" (26). Wilberforce and his fellow abolitionists longed "for that happy day, when the yoke should be taken off for ever, when the blessed transmutation should take place of a degraded slave population into a free and industrious peasantry" (26). These abolitionists' revulsion for slavery was consistent with Thwaites's abhorrence of a system that she considered as exploitative. In "Antiguan Methodism and Antislavery Activity: Anne and Elizabeth Hart in the Eighteenth-Century Black Atlantic" (2000), John Saillant observes: "'Her [Thwaites's] comments on slavery reveal a tension between an older notion that enslavement was an unfortunate, though justifiable situation and a newer understanding that it was an immoral system designed to strip away from laborers the value of work and production" (95). Thwaites went beyond the ideological framework of the early abolitionists, since she believed that slaves needed land as much as they needed freedom. Thwaites writes: "Europeans who have not independent fortunes, for the most part labour with their hands; . . . while most of the free people in this part of the world, of all complexions, are supported, by the toils of the slaves, in every degree of idleness and excess. Slavery affords them a wide field for the indulgence of every diabolical disposition, in which they 'riot unscared'" (109).

Thwaites shows that slavery was a system that exploited the labor and humanity of slaves, denouncing the economic culpability of a Western plantocracy that took advantage of the labor of blacks without compensation. By denouncing slavery, Thwaites resists the racist ideology of this plantocracy through acquisition of Nanny's strength that Cynthia James describes as the purveyor of the resilience, partnership, familial bonding, and vengefulness that black women writers of the diaspora develop against patriarchal systems that threaten to destroy them (108). Contributing to this resistance of black women of the diaspora, Thwaites writes letters to her white friends in an attempt to oppose their stereotyping of Africans, in which she unconsciously participates. Replying to her white friend who asks her, "Is it not, at least, *permitted* by the all-wise Governor of the universe, and He will not do all things well? Might there not be some clue to it quite unknown to us, such as the sins of the Africans, as it was the case of the Israelites before their bondage in Babylon?" (108–9) Thwaites says:

"He doeth all things well." But we cannot take upon us to say, "This is the Lord's doing." I agree with you, that there might be some clue to it quite unknown to us; but this does not strike me as being the sins of the Africans; for, from all I can learn of them, according to their light, though barbarous and uncivilized, they are not so depraved as the generality of the Europeans, but more especially the West Indians; neither are they acquainted with so many methods of drawing down the vengeance of Heaven. (109)

Thwaites's discourse about Africans reflects a mix of reverence and disrespect toward them. On the one hand, she repeats her caricature of Africans who were involved in the slave trade by describing them as "barbarous and uncivilized." Yet she slightly counters such distortion of Africans by depicting them as being less evil and corrupt than European slaveholders, especially those in the West Indies, whom she blames for the kidnappings and suffering of Africans during the Atlantic slave trade. Early in her memoir, she discusses "the shocking practice of taking the Africans from their native land where—

The sable-warrior, frantic with regret
Of her he loves, and never can forget,
Loses in tears the far receding shore,
But not the thought that they must meet no more.
Deprived of her and freedom at a blow,
What has he left, that he can yet forego?
To deepest sadness suddenly resign'd,
He feels his body's bondage in his mind. (105)

Therefore, Thwaites somewhat identifies with the enslaved Africans whose physical suffering and alienation from Africa she laments. She grieves about the atrocity of the Middle Passage and attempts to feel compassion and respect for Africans she saw as people who lost their freedom when their terrible journey began on the shores of Africa. In this sense, she juxtaposes her condescending and primitivistic representation of Africans with a denunciation of slavery. Opposing her correspondent's theorizing of the cause of the enslavement of Africans, she represents this oppression not as the product of "the sins of the Africans, as it was the case of the Israelites before their bondage in Babylon," but as the consequences of the evil actions of Europeans on Africans. Seeking to know why Africans were enslaved, she says: "I readily allow their being in a state of servitude is permitted by the Almighty, and do not question but He may intend bondage for this race of men; but I account the abominations that follow to be purely the will and work of corrupt, fallen men, and displeasing to God" (109). This assertion exposes Thwaites's acceptance of the theory of Black Zionism, which, as David Jenkins argues in *Black Zion: The Return of Afro-Americans and West Indians to Africa* (1975), started when African slaves began to interpret their servitude as "a fixed term" and their deliverance from it as "inevitable" (13). This concept of slavery is evident in Thwaites's depiction of servitude as a temporal state during which God tests the faith of a people before freeing it for better times. She asserts: "When the Almighty afflicts a people, for sin, they repent and are humbled before deliverance is brought near" and adds, "a brighter scene is approaching" (110). Here, Thwaites counters the stereotypes she developed earlier about Africans and represents slavery as only a transient experience to be followed by salvation.

Thwaites's portrayal of slavery resonates with traditional African folklore, where captivity is theorized as a rite of passage and exile from where one gains knowledge. One example is the Antiguan tale "Leaf Disguise," collected by John H. Johnson in 1921, which is comparable to an Akan story Rattray collected in 1930. In "Leaf Disguise," the Rabbit becomes a captive when he is caught stealing from a field; yet he escapes when the owners of the field, who have thought about violent options such as burning him, drowning him, or hanging him, finally throw him in a "briar-bush" from where he escapes (55). This tale represents captivity as an ephemeral state from which the weak becomes free and strong through cleverness and supernatural miracles. The transient nature of captivity is an African concept that permeates the Akan tale "How Abosom, the Lesser-Gods, Came into the World," in which a young boy called Number Eleven escapes the prison where a woman called Death had confined his ten brothers and him. As the narrator suggests, after escaping multiple traps built by both the Sky-God and Death, the boy finally asks his captor "to go and take a calabash full of holes and go and splash water in it, and boil some food for me to eat."[17] The young brother takes advantage of Death's absence to escape with his brothers. Like Thwaites's narrative, this tale conceptualizes bondage as a temporary exile leading to deliverance, revealing the strong link between the representation of slavery in Antiguan and Akan cultures.

Elizabeth Hart Thwaites's "History of Methodism" reveals her ambivalent and complicated relationships with Africa. She represents the cultures of the enslaved Africans in Antigua in dualistic terms that reveal a blend of neutrality, bias, and frustration about their conditions and cultures. Yet Thwaites overcomes her ambiguous feelings, prejudices, and relationships toward Africans by developing a tacit and genuine Pan-Africanism that is apparent in her denunciation of slavery and her support of education for blacks in Antigua. The covert ways in which she denounces European oppression of blacks in colonial Antigua resonates with the concealed resistance tactics of trickster icons in Caribbean and African folktales.

Anne Hart Gilbert's "History of Methodism"

Like Thwaites, Gilbert was ambivalent in her representation of Antiguan slaves. She was unable to maintain her loyalty to Wesleyan Methodism without repeating its missionaries' perception of slaves as heathen to convert into Christianity. As Mary Turner points out in *Slaves and Missionaries*, the missionaries believed "that Christianity would civilize the slaves and prepare them for the gift of freedom rather than politicize them and encourage them to demand it" (59). Indoctrinated into this belief, Gilbert thanks the Moravian church for establishing a Mission in Antigua in 1756 in order to fight the "darkness" among slaves (58). In her sustained attempt to fathom this darkness that she demonizes, Gilbert paradoxically reveals the strong impact of African cultures on Antigua's slave culture. While she demeans this culture, she ironically demands the emancipation of slaves and their integration as free and educated workers, revealing contradictions in her representation of blacks.

In her resistance against slavery, Gilbert uses strategies such as indirection and false deference, which are similar to those that tricksters in African and Antiguan tales employ to subvert oppression. Two examples are the Antiguan tale, "He Sings to Make the Old Woman Dance," and the Senegalese tale, "Le Taureau de Bouki" [The Bull of Bouki], which both reveal the importance of playfulness and oratory as weapons of resistance against oppression. In the Antiguan tale, "Bra Nancy was able to steal from a woman's provision grounds by singing a song and making the woman dance. She danced eleven miles to town. He robbed her this way four times. Sometimes she danced to the north, and sometimes to the south. After that he took his mother with him regularly to rob."[18] This tale conveys the playfulness, diversion, and musicality of tricksters in folktales that Antigua's slaves carried from Africa to survive in a hostile environment where they were landless and poor. Similar aspects are noticeable in the Senegalese tale, "Le Taureau de Bouki" [The Bull of Bouki], in which *Leuk* steals a bull *Bouki* had robbed from the shepherd Paté Diambar. According to the narrator, *Leuk* moved the booty close to his home by distracting *Bouki* with the irresistible sound of riti (Fulani violin) tunes and songs. When he arrived near his hometown in Senene, *Leuk*, who had been shamefully discharged by *Bouki* as a helper, asked his people to march behind *Bouki* and pretend that they were a flock of bulls being led by Paté to catch the robber. *Bouki* fled, leaving the bull to *Leuk* and his people (126–36).

Like the Antiguan tale, the Senegalese story centers on the cleverness that a puny character such as *Leuk* can develop upon necessity to procure the food that can sustain his family. Both *Nancy* and *Leuk* draw from "the weapon of the weak" motif and the African traditions of songs, dance, and oration that pave the road to power. Like the woman in the Antiguan tale, "[who] dance to de nart', [and] mek a gran' wheel," *Bouki* can't resist the power of songs. He tells *Leuk*, "Sing again! Stealing away from a dance step he just made."¹⁹ *Bouki*'s dance steps mark the trickster's ability to manipulate the actions of the oppressor, shifting power and creating a sense of equality. This power change would have been impossible had the trickster not employed the language of the oppressor to feed his/her ego and project a false sense of deference toward him/her.

In her memoir, Gilbert uses tactics similar to those of the above tricksters to shift the balance of power between planters and slaves. Speaking on behalf of slaves, she describes the West Indies as "this benighted land" where "I will however venture; hoping at least to profit my own soul by calling to mind the wonders God has wrought" (57). The imagery of "benighted land" reflects Gilbert's implicit condemnation of slavery as a practice that morally and spiritually corrupts both planters and slaves in Antigua. She describes a black woman whose master required "that by such and such day (which he named) if she did not bring him a Shirt free from Stains, & equally as good as that she had spoil'd, he would give her fifty lashes" (59). This passage denounces the whites' cruel treatment of slaves in Antigua and shows the connection between the moral corruptibility of the planters and their violence against blacks.

Gilbert's memoir is permeated with Africanisms. One early example is when she describes the manner in which slaves in Antigua treated the deceased members of their community by playing music and performing various death rituals. She writes:

> Their Dead were carried to the grave attended by a numerous concourse, some of them beating upon an instrument they call a "Shake Shake." (This is a large round hollow Calabash fixed upon the end of a stick,

with a few pebbles in it) and all singing some heathenish account of the Life & Death of the deceased; invoking a perpetuation of their friendship from the world of Spirits with their Surviving friends and relations, & praying them to deal destruction among their enemies; especially if they thought their death had been occasion'd by the power of Witchcraft. (59)

It is ironic that Gilbert, who pretends to dislike slave culture, knows so much about it to the point that she can describe the central "emic" value that insiders attach to it. As Clifford Geertz points out in *The Interpretation of Cultures* (1973), the "emic" view of a culture refers to the significance that people give to their own culture and experience (15). As Geertz suggests, this "emic" view should "be cast in terms of the constructions we imagine 'that they [the members of the culture] use to define what happens to them'" (15). Gilbert's representation of the way of life of Antiguan slaves gives us an "emic" view of their culture, since it attempts to portray it as realistically as possible. Her representation of this culture suggests her familiarity with the African remnants in this culture. Her genuine knowledge of this culture is apparent in the African origin of the elements that she identifies, in the above quotation, in the music of Antiguan slaves. The "Shake Shake" that Gilbert describes is an African musical instrument that the slaves in the Americas used as a symbolic protest against their owners. This instrument played the same function that Tommie Lee Jackson and John Lowe ascribe to the African drum, which was played "in defiance of the slavers" who believed that the slave would "serve" them better if they brought him from Africa "naked and thing-less."[20] The "Shake Shake" performs a similar subversive role by fueling the stamina and communality of slaves against their oppressors.

In addition, Gilbert's description of the death rituals of slaves reveals African elements: the participant's singing an account of the departed person's life and their testimony about his/her good relationships with the community of the living and the deceased ancestors are parts of traditional funerals in Africa. In *Introduction to African Religion* (1975), John S. Mbiti describes these rites as "rituals of death" that "are intended to send off the departed peacefully, to sever his links with the living, and to ensure that normal life continues among the survivors. People, especially women, wail and weep, lamenting the departure of the dead person, recalling the good things he said and did, and reminding themselves that he lives on in the next world" (121).

These funerals are usually accompanied by feasts and songs of mourning that last a day or two after the burial (121). Music and dance play an important part in funerals because they allow the living to accompany the deceased to their new world. As Mbiti states, "By ritualizing death, people dance it away, drive it away, and renew their own life" (122). These rituals of death continue through yearly anniversaries, tributes, and prayers for the deceased that are similar to the yearly celebration of the spirit of the departed among Antiguan slaves that Gilbert describes. She writes:

> The Grave yards & burying places, both in Town & Country, would be crowded on Christmas mornings with the friends & relatives of deceased persons, strewing quarters of boiled, and roasted, meat; or fowls & yams, & pouring bottles of Rum, upon the graves of their departed friends. The Obeah men & women of that day were very rich people; possessed of large sums of money; being kept in constant pay, by those that could afford it, to prevent their enemies from injuring their persons or properties, to procure, & keep the favor of their owners, to give their children good luck, and to make them prosperous in every thing. (59)

All these rites, including the libation, which can be done with either water or liquor, exist across Africa where various spiritual leaders who perform services to the family of the deceased and their guests play the role of the Caribbean Obeah man. While they rarely demand money beforehand, most African spiritual leaders expect it. Like Antiguan slaves, Africans use the services of their spiritual guides to protect their families and themselves. In *Concepts of God in Africa* (1970), Mbiti traces this worldview to the culture of the Mende of Sierra Leone, in which God's power and protective work are considered as being mediated through ancestors (201).

Additional Africanisms in Gilbert's study are visible in her references to Obeah men and women who serve as leaders in Antigua's slave community. Obeah is, like Vaudou, Hoodoo, Santería, Myalism, and other diaspora religious traditions, a practice rooted in traditional African societies where the use of magic, countermagic, and witchcraft was common in death or birth rituals, wars, and daily activities. These cultural forms survived in the Caribbean, where they became part of both the slaves' rebellions against planters and their lifestyle.[21] The term "Obeah" derived from either the Twi word *Obeye* (a minor god) or the Ashanti terms *Obboney* (malicious deity) or *obayifo*, meaning "witch or wizard," and later corrupted into Obeah, Obiah, or Obia.[22] In *Roots* (1993), Brathwaite defines practitioners of Obeah as "the religious leaders" that helped the African Caribbean slaves continue to be "cultured beings" despite their transportation to the New World (169). He later argues that, as "depositories" of African culture, Obeah men helped slaves speak the master's language while adhering to their own culture (169).[23]

Gilbert is an Obeah woman because she speaks the master's language to help preserve knowledge about Africa's influence on Antigua. As a literary Obeah woman, she uses literature to provide an ethnographic portrayal of the cultural resistance in Antigua's slave culture. For example, she says that the slave woman, whose white owner had ordered her to be beaten, went to see an Obeah man who tried to help her conjure the planter. The Obeah man gave the woman powder wrapped up in paper "with directions to blow through a quill, into a crevice in the window, at the head of the Managers bed; & she was to blow till he sneezed three times." The woman's African-derived means of resistance worked because, after she followed the instructions, her owner inflicted no more punishment on her (60). By using Obeah to protect herself, the black woman has employed an Africanism as a means of subversion of the planter's power.

Despite her useful representation of the African retentions in Antigua's slave culture, Gilbert is, like her sister, habitually very condescending toward these African elements. She continued to view them as evil. For example, she associates the death rituals of slaves as opportunities for witchcraft, "Debauchery, Drunkenness, [and] Duelling" (59), revealing her attempt to detach herself from her African heritage. As Ferguson points out in *Colonialism and Gender Relations from Mary Wollstonecraft to Jamaica Kincaid* (1993), Gilbert "distances herself and her constituency from cultural practices like Obeah" (41). This argument makes sense because Gilbert and her sister lived in a predominantly white world that, as O'Callaghan suggests in *Women Writing the West Indies, 1804–1939*, "aimed at converting blacks and colored" to Christianity (181). This attempt to convert black and colored populations of Antigua from their African traditions was a colonialist enterprise since its goal was to prevent these people from rebelling against whites. In "Cultural Formations in the Caribbean" (2004), Lennox Honychurch writes:

> The African religions and beliefs were outlawed from the earliest days of plantation slavery, not merely because they were seen to be pagan, primitive and generally unchristian but more so because the plantocracy feared these practices were a cover for revolt. Paranoia against any form of African religious spiritualism rose sharply after the Haitian revolution, during which messages and plans of insurrection were passed on during such gatherings. However, despite these restrictions certain forms of traditional religious practices survived under a blanket of secrecy. (162)

From this perspective, Gilbert's demeaning remarks about Obeah and other aspects of slave culture might be her attempt to keep African traditions in Antigua "underground" by representing them as trivial so that whites would not see them as threats to their plantocracy. These whites were prone to punish slaves who used their African traditions to plot rebellion against their owners. This European censure of resistance in slave culture is apparent in the ways in which the English punished slaves in Antigua who used Akan customs as parts of their planned rebellion against their masters in 1736. As Ronald Segal points out in *The Black Diaspora: Five Centuries of the Black Experience Outside of Africa* (1995), in 1736, a group of Antiguan slaves planned "to blow up with gunpowder the assembly rooms on a night when the leading whites were to be at a ball there" and to make this incident be a signal for rebellion (131). The slave rebellion failed when two siblings reported its existence to anxious slave owners. In *Slave Women in Caribbean Society: 1650–1838* (1990), Barbara Bush says that the plot was discovered "as a result of 'voluntary information' given by one Phillida who was 'taken up on suspicion of some virulent Expressions, used upon her Brother's Account', and subsequently revealed the existence of secret Saturday-night meetings" (67). In the same vein, Segal argues that the conspiracy was frustrated "after the disclosure of the design by one of the conspirators, who had been arrested for a minor offense and confessed in his panic" (131). These accounts suggest the fear and coercion that Antiguan slave owners used to foil a well-organized slave resistance in which Akan tradition had an important role.

A key instrument in the failure of the 1736 slave rebellion in Antigua was a General Report entitled *A Genuine Narrative of the Intended Conspiracy of the Negroes at Antigua* that three British judges (J.V., A.W., and N.G.) wrote in 1737 to describe the possible causes of the planned slave uprising in Antigua. Reading this report, one notices the strong influence of Akan traditions in Antiguan slave culture. The Akan presence is blatant in the passage of the report that describes the oath-taking rituals of Antiguan slaves who were considered as masterminds of a conspiracy against whites. According to the report, one of the major suspects of the rebellion "was *Court*, alias *Tackey*, a Coromantee Negroe Man-Slave, belonging to *Thomas Kerby, Esq*; and at the head of the latter was *Tomboy*, a *Creole* born in *Antigua*, a Master-Carpenter, belonging to Mr. *Thomas Hanson*" (3). The report also says that Court, Tomboy, and a group of Coromantee slaves took an oath (patterned after the customs of their African country) to defeat their white oppressors and protect each other (6). By this oath,

> A new Government was to be established, when the white Inhabitants were intirely extirpated: *Court*, amused and flattered by all with being

King of the Island; but the *Creoles* had resolved unknown to him, and his *Coromantees*, to settle a *Common-wealth* and to make Slaves of the *Coromantees*, and Negroes of all other Nations, and to destroy *Court*, and all such who should refuse to submit to the Terms the *Creoles* should please to prescribe or impose. (6)

The above rite suggests the capacity of Antiguan slaves to organize a rebellion against their masters despite the internal competition that existed between them. Despite their plan to colonize the Coromantee, the Creoles joined hands with the latter in order to end the oppression of the Europeans in Antigua. This unity transcended the Creoles' rivalry with the Coromantee and demonstrated the two groups' ability to collaborate against a common enemy. Mindie Lazarus-Black writes in *Legitimate Acts and Illegal Encounters: Law and Society in Antigua and Barbuda* (1994): "The conspiracy demonstrates that by the early eighteenth century, Antiguan slaves possessed a creole political/legal sensibility capable of prosecuting a revolution. This awareness included practical knowledge about the extent to which the existing legal codes could be circumvented, a desire for freedom, a charter for a different social order . . . and a plan that redirected individual acts of resistance into a united force" (41–42). Therefore, Antiguan slaves created a Pan-African relationship that allowed them to overcome their ethnic differences in order to attack the common enemy: slavery. The subversive ritual in which Court and Tomboy participated in order to legitimize the rebellion derived from traditional Ghanaian folklore in which the Ashanti used it to declare their loyalty to their leaders and people before wars. The three judges' report describes this oath-taking ritual as a tradition in which an Ashanti prince dances to the rhythm of drums playing the *Ikem beat*. As the report suggests, the Prince has a cutlass in his hand and moves with a whirling motion of his body while dancing and leaping round about at the same time. Later, the prince takes an oath in which he swears to fight and die by the side of the general of his army and to be willing to have his head cut off "should he fail in his oath."[24] This ritual resonates with an Ashanti ceremony that Bush describes in *Slave Women in Caribbean Society* as an eighteenth-century rite in which a Coromantine male slave named Court participated before the Antiguan conspiracy of 1737 (72–73). Bush writes, "He [Court] was said to have 'a good saber by his side with a red scabbard' and a 'peculiar cap' made of green silk . . . Court was dressed in accordance with Coromantine rites performed when a king has resolved upon war" and "conducted his affairs 'under an umbrella or canopy of state'" (72–73). According to Bush, Rattray recorded the use of "similar ceremonial apparel at the courts of the Ashanti (Coromantine) kings" in Africa (73).

The ceremony in which Court participated in 1737 is very similar to the one that Gilbert describes in the passage cited earlier as a graveyard ritual in which the slaves "both in Town & Country" were involved in 1830 Antigua (59). Graveyards, alcohol, money, and festivities were key elements of both Antiguan and Gold Coast Coromantine rituals in which they anticipated oath-taking ceremonies. Like the Coromantee in Gilbert's story who pour bottles of rum on the graves of their deceased friend (59), those in 1737 Antigua made a libation to the departed members of their community in a ritual that included fowl sacrifice. In *A Genuine Narrative*, the authors describe how Court, Tomboy, and the other conspirators began the oath-taking ceremony with dancing, gaming, feasting, consuming liquor, and commemorating some deceased friend "by throwing Water on his Grave, or christening a House, or the like, according to the Negroe Customs" (5). This ritual of the Antiguan Coromantee is similar to that of their Gold Coast counterparts. The latter is portrayed in the following passage from *A Genuine Narrative*: "The manner of administring the Oath, was by drinking a Health in Liquor, either Rum, or some other kind, with Grave-Dirt, and sometimes Cock's Blood infused, and sometimes the Person swearing, laid his Hand on a live Cock: The Words were various, but the general Tenor, was to stand by, and be true to each other, and to kill the Whites, Man, Woman, and Child" (13). By interpreting the oath of the early Coromantee as an attempt to kill both the white planters and their families, the authors of *A Genuine Narrative* represent Africans as savages. This racism shows that the three British judges wanted to incriminate Court, Tomboy, and their conspirators not simply as participants in a revolt for equality but as instigators of a serious mutiny against their white masters. Therefore, English law used colonial mentality and racism as means for accusing and punishing Court and Tomboy outside of European conventions and respect for natural liberty, righteousness, and resistance against tyranny.

Despite its racist portrayal of blacks, *A Genuine Narrative* is a useful book because it presents rare evidence of Africanisms in eighteen-century Antiguan culture. The narrative's depiction of Coromantee oath-taking ritual helps us interpret the custom of feasting, drinking, and libation in Gilbert's narrative as tricks or, as the three judges say about the rite of the slave rebels, as activities that are "always coloured with some innocent Pretence" (5). This pretence of innocence is an act of resistance that mirrors the small and covert actions that tricksters develop to defeat tyranny. James C. Scott's *Weapons of the Weak: Everyday Forms of Peasant Resistance* (1998) identifies these tactics as tools that "a small and weak creature who survives and triumphs over far more powerful beasts by his wits, his deceit, and his cunning" uses to subvert domination

(300). Such weapons of liberation are consistent with the pretense of innocence and weakness that the religious worshippers in Gilbert's narrative and *A Genuine Narrative* employ to subvert the domination of their white oppressors. These tools are similar to the means that tricksters in African folktales use to resist oppression. One example is the Senegambian tale "The Lion's Treasured Goat" in which the motif of playing dead is a subjugated group's covert tool of resistance against domination. According to the narrator, the hyena steals Lion's goat, kills it, and shares it with his family. When he finds out about the robbery, Lion weeps until Hare and Deer come to console him. In an attempt to appease Lion's sorrow, Deer sings the following lyric

ANTELOPE, ANTELOPE, THE RASCAL HAS
MUDDIED IT FOR ME.
ANTELOPE DID NOT DIG THE WELL,
THE RASCAL HAD MUDDIED IT FOR ME,
STOP DRINKING, WE DUG THE WELL. (67)

Hearing this song helps Hare realize that Deer is implicitly telling him that hyena, the "rascal" who had been punished by other animals for not guarding Antelope, may be the same rogue who has stolen Lion's property. In the song, Deer is prompting Hare to trick Hyena in the same way Antelope had duped him. As Magel says, "When the hyena spies the antelope on the ground, his desire for revenge leads him to drop his defenses and fall into the trap" (69). Therefore, in order to trap Hyena, Hare lures him at a time when he is not expecting trouble. Having understood Deer's message, Hare tells Lion, "Uncle Lion, deer and I will bring the hyena back to you . . . what will you grant us?" to which Lion replies, "I will protect you from all the hyena's threats" (67). Hare tells Lion, "Uncle Lion, now we are going to use the deer in a trap. He will lay down and pretend that he is dead. Assemble all of the criminals you can and tell them to lay down in the middle of the bush as if they too were dead. When you do this, I will bring the hyena back to you" (67). As the narrator suggests, Deer, Jackal, and all other kinds of animals lay on the ground pretending to be dead as Hare goes towards the village while singing this song:

ALL THE ANIMALS ARE DEAD, ALL, ALL, ALL, ARE DEAD!
THEY SAY I SHOULD INHERIT ALL OF THEM,
BUT I CANNOT INHERIT ALL OF THEM,
SINCE UNCLE HYENA IS THE OLDEST. (67–68)

As soon as he hears the song, Hyena jumps up and tells his family to prepare for a feast. Then Hyena takes his family to the place where the animals are lying dead and refuses to touch the Lion who is also resting on the ground. When Hyena's wife asks him to eat Lion, he says, "Ah, you come and see for yourself." When he realizes that Lion is not dead, Hyena farts and runs for his safety. Lion catches him and kills him (68).

The story suggests the Senegambians' abhorrence of injustice and immorality against hardworking and vulnerable people. In this tale, Hyena is a symbol of tyranny and corruption since, as the narrator suggests, whenever he goes without eating, "he always attacks the hare" (67). This predicament compels Hare to trick Hyena and reject the unfair and unethical behavior he exhibits through robbery and weakness. Hare's victory against Hyena conveys the Senegambians' preference of the former's duplicity over the latter's deceit. As Dorothy Blair asserts in her introduction to Birago Diop's *Tales of Amadou Koumba* (1989), Senegambians portray Hare as a "cunning and malicious" character "whose conscience is as mobile as the pair of old, worn-out slippers which he has been wearing clipped on to his head" (viii). On the other hand, the Senegambians depict Hyena as "that chief and coward, whose hind-quarters always seem to be sagging beneath a shower of blows" (viii). The contrast between Hare's conscience and Hyena's decadence is a disparity that allowed the enslaved Africans to recognize the distinction between slave owners and themselves. The slave owners resembled Hyena, whose cruelty and cowardliness toward other animals parallel their evil treatment of slaves. On the other hand, the slaves looked like Hare, whose compassion and heroism toward other animals match their mercy for other human beings.

Despite her possible familiarity with slave culture in Antigua, Gilbert continues to represent blacks in the island in condescending terms. This inconsistency makes one wonder, did she secretly cherish the culture she pretends to dislike? Was she playing tricks on her white readers by giving them the false impression that she supports the missionaries' attempt to substitute the slaves' traditional customs with Christian and European mores? This last hypothesis is not far-fetched since Gilbert visibly draws the attention of Mr. [John] Wesley, the father of Methodism, whose *Arminian Magazine* she credits for publishing a piece entitled, "Baxter's Certainty of the World of Spirits; fully evinced by unquestionable Histories of Apparitions & Witchcrafts," where she allegedly found references about the slaves' common transaction of witchcraft. Gilbert's reference to this text shows that she was widely read and was consistent with the scholarship Methodists were using to support their intent to convert Antigua's slaves to Christianity. These Methodists did not seem to know that Christianity and traditional African religions were intertwined in Antiguan slave culture. This syncretism is evident in Gilbert's own observation that slaves selected Christmas as the day to celebrate the memory of their departed (59). Christmas provided slaves with a cover where they could practice their African religions underneath their Christian mores.

Gilbert's inconsistent representation of slave culture is also perceptible in the way in which she shows some familiarity with the slave culture she claims to abhor. This intimacy is evident when Gilbert criticizes the practice of slavery while continuing to describe the cultures of slaves in demeaning ways. Listing cultural practices slaves devised to resist their oppressors, she insinuates her conflicted relations with African survivals by describing how many slaves were

> Applying to fortune-tellers to know what lot they were to have in life, and for every trivial loss sprinkling grave-dirt & mixing it for the people about the house to drink. This grave-dirt is procured by sending a piece of money which we call a dog* by some faithful hand to a grave, over which the person prays the dead not to be offended; & tells of the loss that has happened in the family, and that in order to discover the offender they are going to give all round a drink of this dirt mix'd thin enough with water to be drunk. They pray that in three days the guilty person may be swell'd to an enormous size, & the innocent preserved in perfect health. (61)

Here, Gilbert shows her "emic" knowledge of Antigua's slave culture. That knowledge came from intimate relations she had with the culture that she now views as "heathen." Gilbert's use of the subjective and collective pronoun "we" and her detailed analysis of the cultural, spiritual, and psychological values the worshippers of Obeah attach to conjuring show her genuine knowledge of the practice of Obeah. She chooses not to take part in Obeah for fear of losing her reputation as a devout Methodist Christian and free person of color in Antigua. As Ferguson points out in *Colonialism and Gender Relations from Mary Wollstonecraft to Jamaica Kincaid*, "In Gilbert's day it was much less easy to incorporate old practices in light of univocal Methodist beliefs" (150). This Methodist intolerance of old traditions prevented Gilbert from recognizing her connections with Antigua's slave culture and its African heritage. Therefore, Gilbert's representation of blacks expresses a double voice that attempts to please the Methodists while demanding equality for blacks. Imitating the tricksters *Nancy* and *Leuk*, who are good at pleasing the ears of those in power while denouncing their subjugating means of control, she tells the Methodists what they want to hear while criticizing the sins of slaveholders of Antigua. Using these tricksters' allegorical, oral, and imitative language, she subverts the inequality between blacks and whites by disparaging it implicitly, thereby clearing the path for the emancipation of slaves.

Gilbert lampoons the views of whites about blacks by reproducing them in trickster acts of mimicry that are similar to what Abrahams describes in *Singing the Master* as the tools that allowed slaves to create "a world of imitational possibilities that became a part of the cultural process of breaking out" (88). These tools include the imitative and satiric use of songs and allusions to signify the overpowering social forces or overbearing surveillance in the plantation (110–11). Like a trickster, Gilbert praises Europeans by making lavishing remarks about John Wesley's crusade for converting slaves to Christianity. She describes Wesley as a "sincere" man with "zeal & impartiality" (71), reflecting the Wesleyan notion that humanity is measurable by faith and not by creed or race. She credits the increase of her congregation to the ministry of Dr. Thomas Coke, who helped the Methodist society in Antigua begin "to be regulated more according to Mr Wesley's mode of discipline" (66). Later, Gilbert congratulates the "leaders both in Town & Country [who] co-operated heartily with those preachers, that adhered more strictly to Mr. Wesley's rules" (70). These statements show Gilbert's act of "singing the master" through reiteration of the Wesleyan notion that conversion and indoctrination into Methodist self-discipline and faith are pathways to salvation. Using this theory as a shield, Gilbert fights for the liberation of Antigua's slaves and reflects her sincere beliefs in the power of Wesley's philosophy to bring positive change to the island.

On the one hand, Gilbert expresses prejudice about blacks of Antigua when she criticizes the slavery that Methodism abhorred. She complains about the practice of conjure among the African slaves by saying: "I am sorry to say that too much of this diabolical work still exists in the West Indies and am of opinion that our preachers in general not being aware of it, pass too lightly over the sin of witchcraft" (60). Later, she criticizes the "great Heathenism among the free people of Colour" that she portrays as "beings endued with the same understandings faculties & powers that were in the white people; tho by blood most or many of them, as nearly allied to the whites as to the blacks. Among the upper classes those called white people, excepting a few that had been educated in Europe, there was great ignorance & superstition" (60–61). The two passages reflect the negative impact of racism and ethnocentrism on Gilbert's perception of her fellow blacks. She suffers from a racism that influences her to create a nonsensical hierarchy of blacks based on the level of their white ancestry.

On the other hand, Gilbert criticizes the culture of whites of Antigua by representing some white missionaries as hypocrites. She represents Antigua as a land where "the clouds of sin and error" and "darkness" were dispersed among slaves by the instrumentality of white ministers such as W. Edmundson from Ireland, who "carefully" hid "the torch of Moral and divine truth" from them (58). Later, she describes corrupt white ministers who indulge in playful activities instead of preaching. She writes: "I understand that to this day, the time of Horseracing is time of great imolument to these Ministers of Satan; having to supply Ointments, to rub the Horses, & Riders, & materials to bury under the ground over which the Horses run; and (shame to tell) some of the owners concur, or connive, at it, & furnish money to pay these Factors for the Prince of darkness" (60). Gilbert's religious worldview suggests a blend of Methodism and Obeah. Her perception of the horse racers as "Ministers of Satan" derives from the Methodist belief in the existence of this being. Unlike Christianity, traditional African religions do not believe in the existence of Satan. Yet, like Christianity, these religions and Obeah believe in the existence of evil power. In this sense, Gilbert's representation of the rituals of preparing for horse racing as involving cunning and the power of the "Prince of darkness" is a result of a syncretism between the European concept of the "Devil" and the African notion of "evil." As Maureen Warner-Lewis argues in *Guinea's Other Suns: The African Dynamic in Trinidad Culture* (1991), Caribbean slaves carried the Africans' belief that evil exists through either malevolent spiritual power or the evil eye (176). This ideology lies within Gilbert's hybrid culture, which intertwines with Christian lore about Satan.

Later, Gilbert promotes a militancy aimed at improving the conditions of slaves. Working with Thwaites, she offered instruction to hundreds of slaves and their children. In "Antiguan Methodism," John Saillant writes: "In 1809, they established a Sunday school open to slave and free children alike. In 1813, the Hart sisters' proposal to instruct enslaved children in literacy spurred adult slaves to build the sisters a school, which Anne named Bethesda. In 1815, the sisters established the Female Refuge Society, devoted to the instruction and moral education of slave women" (89). The educational work Gilbert and Thwaites did for blacks in Antigua is a black womanist effort that fits into Pan-Africanism's search for ways to improve the conditions of blacks. Like Thwaites, Gilbert encouraged women of color to take positions of leadership and responsibility in the effort to help blacks achieve freedom in Antigua. Like Thwaites, Gilbert created a type of bonding between black Antiguan women by speaking in favor of the improvement of their conditions. Though, like her sister, she was unable to avoid trivializing her fellow blacks, Gilbert fought for their emancipation. Regarding efforts made by free black female slaves to build their own church in Antigua, she writes:

> The most decent, and creditable of the black women did not think it a labour too servile to carry stones and marl, to help with their own hands to clear the Land of the rubbish that lay about it, & to bring ready-dressed victuals for the men that were employed in building the House of God. They now rejoiced to sell their Ear-rings & bracelets and to buy Lumber & pay Carpenters, to forward this blessed work; and at last they got a comfortable little Chapel, which soon became too small. (64–65)

The support of the Hart Sisters empowered the black women of Antigua to develop a Pan-African sense of collective organizing. Thanks to this solidarity, Mary Alley and Sophia Campbel, two black women, built a chapel in Antigua from a spot of land for which they had to pay the cash down (64). After Nathaniel Gilbert's death, these two women led the Methodist Society of Antigua between 1774 and 1778 and became the realization of Gilbert's vision of a conscious and educated black womanhood that could overcome prejudices between the mixed and the nonmixed blacks. She praises all the women of the society for helping slave members of the society achieve a "purity & love of the cross in only one half of our greatly increased Society now [which numbered about 600 by 1779]," although, she condescendingly adds, "it cannot be said, that they [the black women] abounded in knowledge, brightness of reason or soundness of speech" (63). This statement epitomizes the ambivalence and elitism in Gilbert's representation of slaves that contradicts the black womanist supports she gives them.

Other agencies in which Gilbert was active were the English Harbour Sunday School and the Female Refuge Society. Ferguson points out that Mrs. Gilbert cofounded these societies, which were not the only

> charitable institutions which Mrs. Gilbert was engaged in [and cofounded]—there were several others. She kept a weekly school, to teach writing and arithmetic. She superintended, and had the direction of, a large Infant School, supported by the Ladies' Society in London. She was the dispenser of blessings through the poor's fund for many years; visiting the sick, comforting the afflicted, clothing the naked, and feeding the hungry. (*Nine Black Women*, 28)

Ferguson's statement attests to Gilbert's dedication to improving the conditions of the poor and oppressed black women in Antigua despite the frequent ambivalence that she expressed about their slave culture and African traditions. Gilbert's philanthropy and her secretive ways of resisting slavery through trickster tactics allowed her to outweigh her Methodist-influenced condescension toward the Africanisms in slave culture.

Gilbert played multiple roles of activist, public leader, advocate, and humanitarian in Antigua. She helped slaves and other poor people of Antigua by developing a Pan-African solidarity based on the same concept of collective organizing that her sister, Thwaites, also promoted. Both women employed the resistance strategies within slave folklore to subvert the power of slave owners. Like Nanny and the Obeah men and Obeah women who protected the slave community, Gilbert and Thwaites drew from the powers of African tricksters and ancestral mothers by caring for blacks and other poor, uneducated, or colored people in the island and working for the emancipation of slaves.

CHAPTER FIVE

African and Caribbean Patterns in Mary Prince's Resistance

The studies about Mary Prince tend to disassociate early black diasporan literature from Africa. While some critics have interpreted Prince's work and life merely as individual struggles against slavery and sexism, others have overlooked the African cultural survivals and Pan-Africanist sensibilities in them. In *Nine Black Women: An Anthology of Nineteenth-Century Writers from the United States, Canada, Bermuda, and the Caribbean* (1998), Moira Ferguson describes Prince as "the first black British woman to 'walk away' from slavery and claim her freedom" and hails her narrative as "the first known recorded autobiography by a freed West Indian slave" (48).

The fact that Prince was the first black woman to free herself from slavery shows her central position in the canon of New World blacks who used the strength of their African past to resist European racial, cultural, and economic supremacy. Critics who do not perceive Prince as having any significant ties with Africa are unable to gauge the Pan-Africanism and African womanism in her work. In *The Maroon Narrative: Caribbean Literature in English across Boundaries, Ethnicities, and Centuries* (2002), Cynthia James writes: "Although she is of African descent, she [Prince] knows neither Africa nor African parentage, and can cite no African comparisons, traditions, and customs. In her case, the famous freedom narrative opening, 'I was born,' records a Caribbean parentage that opens its eyes on slavery as practice and tradition" (44). Later, James asserts: "In addition to being cut off at root from her African legacy, Mary Prince knows the dislocated, loveless, and unstable existence of being moved from island to island" (45). These assertions assume that Africa is absent in Prince's narrative and minimize the complex ways in which African cultures survived in the Caribbean in ways that can be analyzed only through reinterpretation of Caribbean literature. Brathwaite explains:

> I cannot maintain that African continuities are as easily traced in our literature as in the socio/ideological world I have so far described. This does not mean there is no African presence in Caribbean/New World writing. It simply means that, because of its almost inevitable involvement with the establishment through education, communication and sales processing (mercantilism), much of what we have come to accept as "literature" is work which ignores, or is ignorant of, its African connection and aesthetic. (*Middle Passages*, 204)

Brathwaite's rationale suggests the necessity for reinterpreting Caribbean literature from new perspectives. In an attempt to answer this call, I interpret Prince's narrative as a story of individual achievements and resistance that gives credit to the collective sacrifices of an African community in Antigua that spiritually and ideologically influenced her actions. In "The Heartbeat of a West Indian Slave: The History of Mary Prince" (1992), Sandra Pouchet Paquet urges critics to understand Prince's struggle in a brutal world as "an individual and collective state of mind. It is an ideology of survival and resistance. It is the well of being. It engenders a new literary tradition rooted in the values of a transplanted and transformed African community in the Caribbean" (142).

While it has continually reinvented itself in order to adjust to new situations, the African community of Prince was not devoid of stability, continuity, agency, and hope. Its resistance against oppression was inspired by age-old wisdom preserved in African and Caribbean folktales. This wisdom is apparent in *Anancy*'s resistance tactics, language, worldviews, and search for an African community that mirrors Prince's fight against racism in Bermuda, Antigua, and England. A comparison of Prince's narratives with folktales from Bermuda, Antigua, and Africa will reveal implicit denunciation of the physical and material domination that Caribbean slaveowners perpetrated against Prince and her community. Like Prince, the trickster figures of *Anansi* and *Leuk* in West Indian and African tales invoke African traditions in order to survive in a world in which terror and divisions replaced love and unity.

Though its history of colonization and its tropical climates are similar to those of many countries in the West Indies, Bermuda is geographically not a part of the Caribbean. Bermuda is a British dependent territory that consists of an archipelago of about 150 islands in the [North] Atlantic Ocean, and is located 70 miles off the coast of South Carolina. In 1510, the islands were named after the Spanish explorer Juan de Bermudez, who discovered them in 1503. They remained uninhabited until 1609 when the English ship *Sea Venture*, which carried 150 people under the command of Sir George Somers, wrecked on one of its reefs. Bermuda became a British colony in 1612 and was included into the third charter of the Virginia Company.[1]

According to Virginia Bernhard, the first record of slaves in Bermuda was made in February 1616 when "the Somers Islands Company's instructions to Governor Daniel Tucker included orders to send to the West Indies for 'sundrye thinges . . . as Cattle Cassadoe Sugar Canes, negroes to dive for pearles'" ("Beyond the Chesapeake," 546). As Bernhard argues, "in May of that year the ship *Edwin* arrived from the West Indies" and "brought with her also one Indian and a Negroe . . . More blacks soon followed, and by 1619, when Virginia's 'twenty negars' arrived, Bermuda already had at least twice that number cultivating tobacco" (546–47). In a similar vein, Oscar Reiss contends in *Blacks in Colonial America* (1997) that slavery existed in Bermuda in 1616 before it was introduced on the American mainland in 1619 (9).[2] Reiss also says that slaves of Bermuda "were seized from other West Indian islands as well as from Spanish and Portuguese ships" (8). Bernhard's and Reiss's arguments show the significant role Bermuda had in the early history of the black Atlantic world when Africans of diverse origins and locations were brought to develop Western economy. The Antiguan slavery that predated its American counterpart demonstrates the crucial importance of the neglected history of enslavement and race relations in Antigua and Bermuda that Prince's narrative reinscribes into the study of early black Atlantic cultures.

Slave culture in Bermuda was hybrid since its inception. This heterogeneity is visible in *Sketches of Bermuda* (1835), where an English woman named Suzette Harriet Lloyd describes her 1829 travel to the island. Lloyd says that the English supplied Bermuda with "Negroes" who derived "partly from the coast of Africa, and partly from the West Indies, which had been previously settled" (93). According to Lloyd, in 1829, Bermuda's population consisted "of about 10,000 souls, of which the proportions of white and coloured" were nearly equal (93). In this sense, Bermuda had a demographic and cultural diversity that was traceable to slavery when the transplanted Africans in the colony mixed Christianity with their traditional religions in an attempt to create a creolized identity. Describing the culture of slaves in Bermuda, Lloyd writes, "The gleam of Christianity which penetrated the dreary dungeon of their African superstition, was at first so faint that it served rather to discover the gloom than to dispel the darkness which shrouded them; and having embraced the profession of the gospel, they adopted its name without receiving its influence in their heart" (94). Lloyd develops a Eurocentric perspective on Bermudan slave culture that is apparent in her depiction of the religion of the Africans in the island as "superstition" with a "darkness" that resisted the "gleam of

Christianity" (94). Lloyd's portrayal of slave religion as gloomy "superstition" resonates with the condescension that Europeans in Bermuda expressed toward the spirituality of African slaves in the West Indies. In *Slave Women in Caribbean Society* (1990), Barbara Bush argues that these Europeans "could conceive of African spirituality only in the 'other-worldly' context of European Christianity" because their own experiences with witchcraft led them to develop aversion for religious practices such as "obeah," which they perceived as "irrational" (75). The slaves' retention of African spirituality allowed them to preserve their ethnic roots while opposing the indoctrinating message of the Christianity that their masters wanted to impose on them. These slaves were part of the community of the early black Atlantic world that, as Ira Berlin points out in *Generations of Captivity*, "resisted Christianity for more than two centuries to embrace it and make it their own" (15–16).[3]

Moreover, Bermudan slave culture was replete with African folkloric elements. An example of such African patterns was the slaves' use of lampooning. This device is visible when Lloyd discusses how a Bermudan female slave named Piny subjected a male slave she did not like by making a deriding song about him (91–92). Although she does not quote a passage of the song, Lloyd says that its verses "are of course very uncouth, but possess a great deal of wit" (92). This anecdote shows the Bermudan slaves' knowledge of the verbal art of lampooning a person through songs. This strategy which originated from West Africa is similar to the tactic that Levine describes in *Black Culture and Black Consciousness: African-American Folk Thought from Slavery to Freedom* (1977) as a rhetorical tactic that slaves in antebellum America called "puttin somebody down on the banjo." According to Levine, Priscilla McCullough, a black woman from the southern United States, remembered the time when male slave musicians sang about women who misbehaved on plantations: "When dey play dat night, dey sing bout dat girl and dey tell all bout uh. Das putting uh on duh banjo. Den ebrybody know an dat girl sho bettuh change uh ways" (10). This punitive verbal form is akin to the rhetorical strategy that Roger D. Abrahams identifies in *Deep Down in the Jungle: Negro Narrative Folklore from the Streets of Philadelphia* (1963) as the "dozen" or the adult discursive technique of "The Dialectic of Insult" (53). Both rhetorical techniques are similar to the Wolof discursive strategy known as *xass*, which is a direct or an indirect verbal derision of a person. Like the dozen, *xass* helps someone ridicule a person while showing oral dexterity.[4]

Another African-derived tradition in Bermudan slave culture was Gombey. Eighteenth-century slaves in Bermuda and the Leeward islands in the West Indies invented this ritual of dance, music, and storytelling as a form of resistance against planters. In its December 2005 newsletter, The Bermuda National Library describes Gombey as a word of Bantu origin meaning "rhythm." In this ceremony, "the 'Captain' leads the dance; he carries a whip and a whistle. His cape is the only one with bits of mirror and ribbons fixed to it. The 'Wild Indian' carries a bow and arrow. The 'Trapper' carries a rope. The 'Chiefs' carry tomahawks and shields while the 'Warriors' carry small hatchets." This ritual is a creolized performance in which Africans and Indians in Bermuda used pantomime and music as ways of telling a story about their resistance against European colonization of the island. The references to weapons such as "tomahawks," "shields," and "small hatchets" show the Native American contributions to Bermudan slave culture. These rudiments allowed slaves in Bermuda to join the other Africans in the West Indies in communal revolts against planters throughout the seventeenth and eighteenth centuries.[5]

Further African influences in Bermudan culture are apparent in the remnants of slave folktales in the island. In the 1925 essay "Bermuda Folklore," Elsie Clew Parson presents four tales told by descendants of slaves in Bermuda (239–42). Two of these stories have parallels in Africa. The first one is entitled "What Darkens the hole" and deals with a greedy Wolf trickster who enters through a small hole, steals food, and is subsequently found and beaten by the rightful owner of the victuals. The tale is as follow: "Fox and Wolf, they were working together. Fox told Wolf he knew where there was some meat. So they went there, and Wolf ate and ate and ate and got bigger and bigger. And there was only a little hole to get in. So when the farmer came with his gun Fox crept out of the little hole, but Wolf could not get out, he was so fat, and the farmer shot him" (240). This story is similar to three folktales that appear in May Augusta Klipple's *African Folktales with Foreign Analogues* (1992). The three narratives that Klipple found in the Hottentot, East African Cattle, and East Horn areas of Africa share the following plot: "The fox persuades the wolf to enter a cellar (smokehouse or kitchen) and steal food. The wolf eats so much that he cannot escape through the hole he has entered by. He is killed" (28–29). This plot is similar to the ones that exist in numerous Senegambian folktales in which Hyena is punished for gluttony. One instance is a Gambian tale that Emil A. Magel has collected in *Hare and Hyena: Symbols of Honor and Shame in the Oral Narratives of the Wolof of Senegambia* (1977). As the narrator suggests, one day, Hare and Hyena decide to walk on separate paths. Hare sees a tree where an ostrich has left many eggs (380). The ostrich lets Hare stay inside and gives him the passwords "Tree open" and "Tree close" for entering and leaving the refuge (381). When Hyena sees Hare, he asks that he share his secret with him so that he can become fat like him (381). Hare gives him the password (381). Hyena enters the tree, eats too many eggs, and refuses to leave the shelter (382–83). The ostrich returns to the tree and beats Hyena (383).

The plot of this story is identical to the one in the Senegalese tale "Bouki rossé par les aveugles" ("How Bouki was Beaten by the Blind People"), which appears in Senghor and Sadji's *La Belle Histoire de Leuk-le-Lièvre* (*The Beautiful Story of Leuk-the-Hare*). In this narrative, *Bouki* forces *Leuk* to give him a password so that he can enter a little hole in a tree (63). Once he enters the hole, *Bouki* eats so voraciously that the blind people who live there begin to hit him with their sticks. *Bouki* hurries out and mistakenly says, "Tree close" (63). The tree almost squeezes him to death (63).

The two above stories in which a trickster enters a hole and consumes so much food that he/she forgets to leave are analogous to the Bermudan tale "What Darkens the hole." This same type of plot is apparent in an Antiguan folktale that is recorded in William Bascom's *African Folktales in the New World* (1992). As the narrator of this Antiguan story says, one day, *Nancy* manages to enter a cow's belly from a small hole by saying the password "Open, Toukouma, Open" (98). Once he is inside, *Nancy* begins to eat the cow's meat and forgets to go away (98). When he learns what has happened to his cow, the owner cuts the belly of the animal and beats *Nancy* to death (98). These African tales have the motif of the password, which, as Bascom remarks, "is [also] common in the tales from the New World." Bascom refers to an African story with a password motif that Stith Thompson found among the Temne people of Sierra Leone (84, 109). This Temne version of the tale has a plot that resonates with those of the two Senegalese legends discussed above, suggesting the possible Senegambian origin of the tale type.

In a similar way, there are correspondences between the Bermudan tale "Playing Godfather," which Parson found in Bermuda, and numerous African narratives. The tale Parson collected is as follows:

> Cyat and Dawg buy a keg of butter fe a reserve fe the winter. Well, they was in a puzzle to find place whe' to put it. They agree to put it in a church which it will be safe. A week or two after, Cyat make an alarm that he has to go to church and stan' godfather for a child. When he returned back, Dawg asked him what is the name of the child. "Top-Off." Well, he keep on until the last child he stan' for he name "All-Gone." Butter was finished then. Winter sets in. Agree to go and get the butter home. Cyat didn't like to go. Dawg alone go to get de butter. When he found out keg of butter was all finished he returned back in a

has' (haste). Cyat flee before him. He ketch Cyat by de neck and break his neck. And dat is why today Dawg hate Cyat. (240–41)

This Bermudan story belongs in the category of Tar-Baby narratives, since it shares the motif of "The Theft of the Butter by Playing Godfather" that Richard Dorson identifies in *American Negro Folktales* as a recurring element of African American tales (1956).[6] In *The Myth of The Negro Past* (1941), Herskovits argues that the Tar-Baby tale "is so characteristic of West Africa that Africanists have themselves long used Joel Chandler Harris's version of this Negro tale from the United States as a point of comparative reference" (272). Describing the common plot of the Tar-Baby story, Herskovits writes: "A trickster-thief is himself tricked by the device of erecting in a field a figure made out of tar or some other sticky substance, to discover who is stealing the produce. Coming in the dark, the trickster speaks to the figure, and when it fails to reply, rebukes it for the lack of good manners it shows (A significant Africanism!)" (272).

Two Senegambian analogues of this plot exist in the extant collections of black folktales. One parallel is visible in Emil A. Magel's *Hare and Hyena* (1977), in which Hare tricks Hyena into killing his seven cows and sharing them with him. As the narrator suggests, when the seventh cow is almost ready to be eaten, Hare proposes that Hyena and he go up a tree and braid and tie each other there. Hare ties Hyena to two strong branches and requests that he himself be bound to a small branch since he is small. As soon as he is fastened to a small tree, Hare jumps down and eats the entire cow. When the rainy season comes, Hare gathers some mud from an anthill, rubs the wet and red clay over his skin, and goes to visit hyena. Hyena puts Hare in a house where the walls and roofs have holes. The next day, Hyena finds Hare without the mud on his skin and gets ready to punish him. Hare suggests that Hyena put him in a bag with a knife and some food called *Mudaka*. When Hyena does as he says, Hare escapes from the bag and disappears (368–72).

A similar version of this tale is apparent in Senghor and Sadji's *La Belle Histoire de Leuk-le-Lièvre*, in which *Leuk* covers himself with the skin of a dead animal and claims to be a big termite when he goes to visit *Bouki*. As the narrator says, *Bouki* puts *Leuk* in a separate house and finds him there the next morning without his skin. Cricket tells *Bouki* that the best punishment for *Leuk* is to put him in wet grassland. *Bouki* does what Cricket says and sees *Leuk* run away from him (80–91). This story shows a trickster's successful attempt at duping another one by pretending to do something good for him/her and eating his/her food. The deceptive strategies of resistance in the above folktales are subversive tactics of resistance that help us interpret the dissident manners in which Prince countered the oppression of her owners and gained her freedom.

Mary Prince was born into slavery in about 1788 at Brackish Pond, in Devonshire Parish, in Bermuda, which was then a part of the British colony. She grew up in many households, including those of the Darrels, the Williamses, and the Prudens. Later, she was sold to Captain and Mrs. I——, at Spanish Point, and then to Mr. D——, in Turks Island. In 1810, she retuned to Bermuda and lived there for eight years before she was sold to Mr. and Mrs. John Wood in Antigua, where she met and married a free black carpenter and cooper named Daniel James. In 1827, Prince accompanied her owners to England, where she established connections with the Anti-Slavery Society in Aldermanbury in November 1828. She refused to return to Antigua with her owners and was backed by the abolitionist lawyer Thomas Pringle, who was the secretary of the English Anti-Slavery Society. Shortly before her death, she told Susanna Strickland her story of the brutality of slavery in Bermuda, Turks Island, Antigua, and England. Her narrative was first published in 1831 in England, under the title, *History of Mary Prince, A West Indian Slave, Related by Herself*, as a tract for the English Anti-Slavery Society.[7]

In her narrative, Prince denounces the exploitation, exile, deprivations, anxieties, and legal barriers against African Caribbeans during the first part of the nineteenth century. Her story participates in the Pan-Africanist intellectual tradition by fighting against racist contexts in which the legal support that could improve the conditions of the enslaved Africans in Antigua and Bermuda were nonexistent. Although it is a personal account, the narrative is relevant to the lives of millions of blacks of the Caribbean who were directly impacted by the racial prejudice, classism, and sexism of their slaveowners.

Early in her narrative, Prince gives us useful information about her parents. She says, "my mother was a household slave; and my father, whose name was Prince, was a sawyer belonging to Mr. Trimmingham, a ship-builder at Crow-Lane. When I was an infant, old Mr. Myners died, and there was a division of the slaves and other property among the family" (187). Later, she states, "my little brothers and sisters were my play-fellows and companions. My mother had several fine children after she came to Mrs. Williams,—three girls and two boys" (187). These assertions show that Prince was born in a large family of slaves in which she had the opportunity to develop strong relationships with her siblings. Prince's allusion to "several" children of her mother supports Moira Ferguson's argument, in "The Literature of Slavery and Abolition" (2004), that she had "at least ten siblings" (247).

Later, Prince describes her horrible experiences in Turk's island when Mr. D purchased her and took her there to work in salt ponds. In her book, Prince describes how she and Mr. D's other slaves worked "from four o'clock in the morning till nine, when we were given some Indian corn boiled in water, which we were obliged to swallow as fast as we could for fear the rain should come on and melt the salt." (198). She also says, "We were then called again to our tasks, and worked through the heat of the day; the sun flaming upon our heads like fire, and raising salt blisters in those parts which were not completely covered. Our feet and legs, from standing in the salt water for so many hours, soon became full of dreadful boils, which eat down in some cases to the very bone, afflicting the sufferers with great torment" (198). Prince's description attests to the barbarity of slavery in Turk's Island, a system that had ties with slavery in North America. As Walter Brownell Hayward argues, from 1678 to 1741 and after, Turk's Island was a site where Bermudans manufactured salt and stored it either in the island or in "Virginia, Maryland, Pennsylvania, New York, and New England, receiving in exchange corn, bread, flower, pork, and lumber" (32). Hayward's assertion shows that Bermuda was part of a transnational economy that rendered white slaveowners in the island prosperous at the expense of the black producers of salt who lived in horrible conditions.

Moreover, Prince bears witness to the daily violence that her owner Mr. I—— perpetrates against three slaves from different geographic origins. The first victim is "a French Black woman called Hetty, whom my master took in privateering from another vessel, and made his slave" (193). Prince describes how Hetty is tortured beyond imagination when her owner beats her to death while she is pregnant. She was repeatedly flogged by both her master and mistress and "Ere long her body and limbs swelled to a great size; and she lay on a mat in the kitchen, till the water burst out of her body and she died . . . I cried very much for her death. The manner of it filled me with horror" (195). The second victim of the owner's torture is a biracial slave called Cyrus, and the third one is an African man from the Guinea coast named Jack whom a sailor had sold to Prince's master (194). The owner tortures Cyrus and Jack in the most inhumane ways. Prince writes: "Seldom a day passed without these boys receiving the most severe treatment, and often for no fault at all. Both my master and mistress seemed to think that they had a right to ill-use them at their pleasure; and very often accompanied their commands with blows, whether the children were behaving well or ill. I have seen their flesh ragged and raw with licks" (194).

Representing the brutality that white planters committed against African slaves in the Caribbean, Prince's account shows that these slave owners oppressed blacks of different national origins or gender in an attempt to maintain supremacy over them. The strategies Prince uses to resist the tyrannical attitudes of her slave owners are similar to those that frail characters in Antiguan folktales use to defend themselves against domineering figures. One of these stories is "Bone for a Stump," which John H. Johnson collected in "Folk-lore from Antigua, British West Indies" (1921).[8] In this story, a watchman catches Ramgoat, who has stolen food from a field and has fled into a hole, and cuts his horns (57). Noticing the horns of Ramgoat that are sticking from the ground, the watchman takes an axe and severs them. Suffering from this agonizing experience, Ramgoat said: "Lord, Lord, Lord! I can't stand it. It too much" (57). Ramgoat and *Nancy* were arrested and taken to court where *Nancy* denied being involved in any robbery. Shocked by this news, Ramgoat fought fiercely with *Nancy*. As the storyteller says, "Ramgoat get mat at *Nancy*. Mad, so dat dey begin to fight. Ramgoat an' Nancy is fightin' all over de place. Ramgoat catch Bro' Nancy one butt. He knock him so hard, dat Nancy run an' go in de cassy-tree" (57).

This tale reflects a dynamic in which a person of higher authority (the overseer of the planter) accuses a subordinate character for a crime he/she did not commit and punishes him/her severely for it. The Watchman's act of cutting the Ramgoat's horn for "the act of stealing," which he and *Nancy* allegedly committed, is a metaphor for the planter's power to subjugate slaves arbitrarily. *Nancy*'s denial of his participation in the theft is a metaphor for the desperate position in which slaves were compelled to use tricks to resist the planter's tyranny. This denial epitomizes the moment that Andrew Salkey describes in *Caribbean Folk Tales and Legends* (1980) as the moment when even "the Spider-man, trickster of tricksters, is himself outwitted" (8). Yet, the subjugation of *Nancy* is never final because African pranksters always bounce back to overturn the guile of their oppressors.

The African trickster's ability to rebound from subordination is visible in the tactics that Prince uses to protect herself from the violence of her owners. She devises tactics of resistance that are similar to those that the Spider and Rabbit figures in folktales of Antigua, Bermuda, and West Africa use to protect themselves against the repression and ruse of their enemies. Prince's initial resistance strategy is to create a family based on parenthood, racial solidarity, and gender unity.

When she had run away from her drunken owner, Mr. I——, who had severely beaten her to the point of death, her mother hid her in a hole and brought her food at night (196–97). This example shows the sanctity of filial bonds in Prince's family. Having been separated from her mother, two sisters, and two brothers, she had to re-create this family by seeking refuge among members of her kinfolk. Her reconnection with her mother is a search for kinship that resonates with the primordial importance that slaves in Antigua placed on their black community. In *The History, Civil and Commercial, of the British Colonies in the West Indies* (1793), Bryan Edwards, who was a British traveler to the West Indies, admits that the African slaves shared a special spirit of solidarity and affection with each other, especially with people from the same countries as theirs.[9] The African unity among Antiguan slaves is apparent in the bonding Prince's parents create in order to protect their daughter from Mr. I——'s oppression.

Prince's re-creation of family bonds shares parallels with the ways in which characters in Bermudan and Antiguan folktales reestablish threatened kin groups. In some of these tales, female and male characters demonstrate true affections toward their children and each other during peculiar moments of hardships. In a variant of the Antiguan tale, "The Ordeal," which was collected by Elsie Clews Parsons between 1933 and 1943, a woman saves her children from death. Helen L. Flower summarizes the tale as follows: "Three children ate the grain of rice and the fish bone which their mother left. She went to the well to drown them, but pulled them out before they sank" (456). The anecdote attests to the affection that black Antiguans had for their children, for whom they had special filial bonds and motherly instincts, despite the cruelty of slavery, which sometimes led them to wish their offspring were dead and free. This intimate relationship is apparent in the manner in which Prince's parents rescued her from her abusive owners. One example of this rescue is the Antiguan tale, "Under the Green Old Oak Tree," (collected by John H. Johnson in 1920) that Flower also summarizes as follows: "A boy killed his sister to get her flower bucket. He buried her under an oak tree where a shepherd boy later picked up a flute made of bone. It played only one tune until the mother played it. She fainted. When the brother played it, it sang, 'It is you that killed me.' He fainted and died" (257). This tale reveals the African belief in the resurrection of the spirit of dead persons, whose ghosts return to do either good or evil. One example occurs when Prince describes the ramble in and around the home of her owners that occurred when she was being beaten by Mr. I——. Prince writes:

> He beat me again and again, until he was quite wearied, and so hot (for the weather was very sultry), that he sank back in his chair, almost like to faint. While my mistress went to bring him drink, there was a dreadful earthquake. Part of the roof fell down, and every thing in the house

went—clatter, clatter, clatter. Oh I thought the end of all things near at hand; and I was so sore with the flogging, that I scarcely cared whether I lived or died. The earth was groaning and shaking; every thing tumbling about; and my mistress and the slaves were shrieking and crying out, "The earthquake! the earthquake!" It was an awful day for us all. (196)

African cosmology has a strong influence on Prince's interpretation of the impact of spiritual interventions on natural and physical calamities. Her allusion to the "groaning," "shaking," and "tumbling" of things in her owner's home indicates her belief that such ramblings are driven by supernatural forces that attempt to end the injustice of her owner. The intervention of spirits into the world of the living for good or bad purposes is not unfamiliar in the African cosmology. In *Introduction to African Religion* (1975), John S. Mbiti asserts: "The spirits can do both good and evil to people, just as people do both good and evil to their fellow human beings" (79). The Caribbean equivalents of these ambivalent spirits are the *Rada* and *Petro* deities of Haitian vodun, who can do either good or bad, depending on the situation at hand. The *Rada* are "a pantheon of loa [deities] who originated in Africa, named after the Dahomean town of Arada" (12), while the *Petro* are "the pantheon of loa who originated in Haiti" (Cleaver 14).

The "clatter" Prince has described can be interpreted as a divine intervention of *Rada* and *Petro* deities who combine supernatural forces to free her from slavery. This intervention of African and diasporan spirits is evident in the shrieks and cries of the slaves, which appear as ritualistic incantations for the ominous interference of the "living-dead." As Mbiti explains it in *Concepts of God in Africa* (1970), in African religions, the "living-dead" are conceived as "the departed who are still remembered personally by someone in their family" and in whose names the family makes sacrifices and offerings as a symbol of fellowship, respect, and the recognition that "the departed are still members of their human families" (179). From the African worldview, the cries and shrieks of the Antiguan slaves can be interpreted as African and African diasporan lamentations and prayers for the end of oppression.

Other African elements in Prince's narrative are noticeable in the ways in which she mimics the African tricksters' skill at overcoming oppression in unpredictable ways that the oppressor could not foresee. When her new owner, Mr. John A. Wood, took her to the town of St. John in Antigua after the horrible years she spent with her drunken master of Turks' Island (203), Prince refused to be treated as a slave any longer. Using the importance that language had in traditional African societies as a means of gaining status in a relational context, she presented her reasons that it was time for her to be free.[10] Being conscious of the profit that Mr. Wood was making from his legal ownership of her, Prince drew the attention of antislavery advocates by saying: "I then took courage and said that I could stand the floggings no longer; that I was weary of my life, and therefore I had run away to my mother . . . He [Mr I———,] told me to hold my tongue and go about my work . . . He did not, however, flog me that day" (197).

Prince uses African folkloric and rhetorical devices that allow her to denounce the planter's inhuman treatment of slaves without appearing to be a threat to his authority. She appropriates the defiance of authority of the Monkey figure in Antiguan and Senegambian tales. In the Antiguan tale "Monkey Husband" (1936), collected by Elsie Clews Parsons, the Monkey character demonstrates bravery and rebelliousness toward the power of the oppressor at the risk of losing his own life.[11] In this tale, the Monkey goes to the field of a wealthy man to steal bananas. One day, the guard hides behind a tree and shoots the Monkey to death (310).

This story shows the inequitable power relations between the watchman and Monkey, which mirror the imbalance of authority between Prince and her constraining masters and overseers. The historical context of the Antiguan tale coincides with that of Prince's narrative, since both stories signify the unequal power relations between blacks and whites during slavery. Like Prince, the Monkey challenges the forces that limit the social and physical movements of individuals. Both Prince and the Monkey trickster use language as a rhetorical and cultural tool of resistance against this domination.

The connection between Prince and the Monkey trickster icon is also noticeable in the relationships between their rhetorical strategies. Monkey's communication style derives from the African Caribbean vernacular tradition out of which Prince's language was crafted. This impact is noticeable in the song that Bra Monkey improvises to laugh at the irony of an existence in which one is compelled to don a mask in order to survive in an alienating world that was identical to that of the Caribbean slave. The song goes as follows:

> Since God we mek ah we
> Ahl below
> See Monkey wear a jacket
> Ahl below. (310)

Songs and laughter were, then, subtle African Caribbean defense strategies against the slave owner's brutality. As Edward Brathwaite contends in

"Roots" (1963), it is one of the devices West Indian blacks have used throughout history as a relief from "this dichotomy [which] expresses itself . . . though a certain psychic tension, an excitability, a definite feeling of having no past, of not really belonging (which some prefer to call adaptability)" (10). Brathwaite perceives this anxiety of the West Indian as a result of "a spiritual inheritance from slavery and the long story before that of the migrant African moving from the lower Nile across the desert to the Western ocean, only to meet the Portuguese, and a history that was to mean the middle passage, America, and a rootless sojourn in the Caribbean sea" (10). In order to relieve their pain from this traumatic history, Monkey and Prince use the power of words to comment on the irony of the slaveowner's denial of the humanity of the slaves. Through laughter, they create a temporary therapeutic device for soothing the pain of their economic and social alienation in the watchman's fields. Their predicament resonates with the historical situation in which slaveowners exploited thousands of slaves in Antigua and Bermuda who toiled in their fields daily.

The determination of Prince and the Monkey figure in Caribbean literature is traceable to that of the Monkey icon *Golo* in Senegambian folklore, in which this trickster resists domination through various means such as ideological defiance and linguistic dexterity. In a Wolof tale entitled "The Dog and Monkey Build a Town," collected by Emil Magel, Monkey confronts barriers similar to those that the Antiguan Brar Monkey confronted. In the Wolof version, the Monkey icon influenced his people to defy the rules of Dog by using the latter's well, which had been forbidden to his community. The storyteller says:

> So the dog went and constructed his own town. He dug a well between his town and the temporary settlement of the monkey. He dug the well between his town and the monkey's. That is where he built it.
> One day the monkeys secretly left their villages and went to the well. They wanted to do their washing in the well. They washed their clothes until they were clean. They drew some water and began to wash. (141)

When the dogs find out that the monkeys had used their well, they killed them as soon as they got down a tree. Yet the Monkeys had not died without insubordination. They said: "Let us wash here. Any dog that comes here, we will beat him to death until his ass looks like a bitter tomato" (142). The retort of *Golo* [the Wolof word for Monkey] provides the background for the invectives that the Monkey figures in the black diaspora use to denounce the oppressions of slavery and racism.

A comparable discursive device is apparent in the tale, "The Signifying Monkey and the Lion," (collected by Abrahams) in *Deep Down in the Jungle*, in which the Monkey in African American folklore challenges the Lion's authority in ways similar to how Prince and the Monkey figure in Antiguan folklore do it. In the African American tale, the Monkey provokes Lion by insulting him and signifying his lack of courage for not fighting against the Elephant. The Lion gets angry and rushes to the Elephant, who beats him. After several attempts, the Lion catches the Monkey and was on the point of beating him when the Monkey says, "Please, Mr. Lion, I apologize" shortly before he dies (153–56).

This tale reflects the importance of signification as a defensive strategy of powerless characters against strong ones in black folktales. The Monkey's use of invective language to prompt strong, egotistical, and power-driven characters, such as the dog and the lion, is a resourceful communicative tactic that helped slaves like Prince criticize the immorality and injustice of their oppressors explicitly or implicitly at the risk of losing their own lives. The Monkey's employment of a subversive language as a means of resistance permeates black cultures. In *The Signifying Monkey*, Gates describes the Monkey as "a hero of black myth, a sign of triumph of wit and reason," that reflects "the black person's capacity to create" rich and complex poetry and rituals that confront "domination" (77). A key example of this subversive use of the Monkey's language occurs when Prince vituperates her white oppressors for their physical and economic exploitation of their black laborers and, above all, for their immorality. Describing how she confronted Mr. D's violence in Turks Island, Prince writes: "One time I had plates and knives in my hand, and I dropped both plates and knives, and some of the plates were broken. He struck me so severely for this, that at last I defended myself, for I thought it was high time to do so. I then told him I would not live longer with him, for he was a very indecent man—very spiteful, and too indecent; with no shame for his servants, no shame for his own flesh" (202–3).

One can only imagine the dexterous ways in which she verbally challenges her owner in the form of speech that Sandra Pouchet Paquet describes as follows: "She takes their [the slaveowners'] private space and makes it a public space in a speech act that mocks their ownership in a series of verbal assaults. Whether you call this *signifying* (as an African American would) or ramachez (as a Trinidadian would), such a speech performance is a ritual feature of black talk, and Prince is a practiced performer" (*Caribbean Autobiography*, 39).

Prince's use of subversive language occurs within the context of the African relational concept of identity. In traditional African societies, identities were primarily determined by the individual's abilities to invent himself/herself in relational contexts in a community in which elders had supreme decision-making power. In "The Integrities of History in Africa" (2005), Joseph C. Miller states: "Thus 'truth' is experienced as validated social position, the 'self' constructed relationally, thus once again locating experience rather than observed externalities as the site of continuity, as stability" (33). Miller's rationale suggests that traditional Africans believed that an individual could alter social consensus internally by influencing the members of the group that made such agreement to change their rules and regulations when it was necessary to do so. This individual had the power to invoke and utilize the wisdom of the collective as an ideological resource to achieve freedom.

The conception of truth as a relationally and culturally constructed consensus is noticeable in the subtle ways in which Prince negotiates her freedom in Antigua and England through argumentation. When Mr. D—— beats her for dropping utensils, Prince goes to seek support. She says: "So I went away to a neighbouring house and sat down and cried till the next morning, when I went home again, not knowing what else to do" (203). Prince received the support of the other slaves in Antigua. When her owner who hired her to work at Cedar Hills beats her, a white woman named Mrs. Greene calls an old slave woman to help heal her wounds. Revealing the impact of biracial support in her survival, Prince says: "The old slave got the bark of some bush that was good for the pains, which she boiled in the hot water, and every night she came and put me into the bath, and did what she could for me: I don't know what I should have done, or what would have become of me, had it not been for her" (203–4). The support Prince receives from both a white woman and a black woman reveals connections in her search for interrelated gender-based and race- based communities against slavery. The relationships between these communities are apparent in the manner in which Prince domesticates both the succor of Mrs. Green and the assistance of the black woman to regain the strength she needs to survive the sexism and racism of her white owners. In this sense, her narrative makes her what critic Marjorie Thorpe describes as the pioneer of a woman's literature that explores "the complex dynamics of intersecting race, class, and gender relations in our transplanted colonial and postcolonial island societies" ("Keynote," 530).

Yet the interracial solidarity between Mrs. Greene and Prince should not be overemphasized, because it can relegate the systemic racial oppression against Prince and the slave woman to the background by overlooking the participation of white women in the oppression of black women during slavery. In *Slave Women in Caribbean Society, 1650–1838* (1990), where she shows the triple oppression slave women faced in the Caribbean, Bush points out: "In common with women in virtually all cultures, the slave woman was subordinate to all men and hence suffered sexual as well as economic oppression. In this sense, her white European counterpart fared little better than she did herself. However, the slave woman, subjected to both black and white patriarchy, in addition to experiencing class exploitation was a victim of racism" (8). While each of these oppressions is important to study, the one that affected the lives of black women the most was the racial one from which white women benefited economically and socially. Deborah Gray White explains: "Black and white womanhood were interdependent. They played off one another. The white woman's sense of herself as a woman—her self-esteem and perceived superiority—depended on the racism that debased black women. White women were mistresses *because* black women were slaves" (6). White's thesis shows the importance of class in the framework in which the achievement of slave women must be assessed. Both critics point out the interracial relationships between black and white women that are relevant to the study of Prince's narrative. Yet in Prince's narrative, the relationships between black and white women are not more important than the relationships between black women.

In her narrative, Prince shows that finding a strong community of black women is not easy because class and color differences between slave women often interfere with her search for a Pan-African family. She tells events that occurred when she worked for the Woods, who had hired a mulatto woman named Martha to nurse their child. Prince talks about how she perceived the biracial woman: "She was such a fine lady she wanted to be mistress over me. I thought it very hard for a coloured woman to have rule over me because I was a slave and she was free. Her name was Martha Wilcox: she was a saucy woman, very saucy; and she went and complained of me, without cause, to my mistress, and made her angry with me" (204). Colorism interferes in the resistant black womanhood that Prince is trying to create. She perceives Martha as a free black woman who is exempt from the brutal labor of slaves and is given the illusion of a class and race-based superiority over the darker-skinned slaves. She says: "Mrs. Wood told me that if I did not mind what I was about, she would get my master to strip me and give me fifty lashes . . . The mulatto woman was rejoiced to have power to keep me down. She was constantly making mischief; there was no living for the slaves—no peace after she came" (204). This statement is doubly relevant. First, it corroborates the theories Bush and Gray developed earlier about the inequities between white women and black women during slavery. As visible in Mrs. Wood's power to flog Prince at her ease, the quotation reflects the dominance of white women over black women during slavery. White women possessed the same power to restrict the movement of blacks and punish black women at the pretext of any alleged transgression of orders that white men had. Second, the quotation shows Prince's attempt to portray Martha as a person that slaveowners in Antigua are using to create color-based stereotypes and class stratifications among blacks. These manipulations, that are apparent in Martha's and Mrs. Wood's attitudes toward slaves, lead Prince to view Martha as a participant in the oppression against slaves rather than as one of the recipients of this subjugation.

In order further to understand the relationships of Martha, Mrs. Wood, and Prince, one must analyze black folktales in which trickster characters utilize wicked means to dominate each other. In such folktales, the more privileged figures use guile, ruse, and mischief in order to overpower the disadvantaged ones. One instance is the Antiguan tale, "The False Message: Annancy makes Fox his Ridding Horse" in which *Nancy*, who is the "watchman" of a field of nuts owned by a wealthy "nobleman," tortures Rabbit and Fox for stealing from the farm. One day, Rabbit went to *Nancy*, who is the watchman of the field of a rich nobleman and tells him that the master has ordered him [*Nancy*] to tie the Rabbit to a tree in the field. At night, the Rabbit unties the knot and steals nuts from the field. The Rabbit tells his secret to Fox who attempts to do the same thing and is caught. *Nancy* castrates Fox.[12]

First, the tale signifies the inhumanity of slavery. *Nancy*'s act of burning the genitals of the Rabbit and Fox are metaphors for the agonizing physical and psychological scarring that the violence of slavery inflicted on blacks. This sexualized and ritualized violence recalls the captivity, branding, and psychological castration of African slaves during and after the Middle Passage. This violence reflects the chauvinist and sexist attitude of planters and overseers over the enslaved Africans.

Second, the folktale comments on the interactions between slaves and their owners and overseers in the West Indies, which are also alluded to in the interactions of Prince, Mrs. Wood, and Martha. Like Prince, the oppressed tricksters Rabbit and Fox are victims of the hegemony of a plantocracy. In the tale, this plantocracy is represented by the "nobleman," who orders that Rabbit be punished for having allegedly stolen from his field, and by *Nancy*, who performs the punishment. Like Mrs. Wood and Martha, *Nancy* becomes a trickster who dominates individuals who are denied the same freedom he is seeking. All three pranksters exhibit the guile and selfishness of their oppressor. Their domineering behavior contrasts with the peacefulness of Rabbit and Fox, whose suffering in the hands of the planter class resonates with the predicament Prince experienced in Antigua.

The correspondence between the experiences of Rabbit, Fox, and Prince is noticeable in the Antiguan tale's motif of incarceration and punishment of individuals who transgress the authority of the dominant planter class. The predicament of Rabbit, Fox, and Prince corroborates Orlando Patterson's theory in *Slavery and Social Death* that slavery "is the permanent, violent domination of natally alienated and generally dishonored persons" (13). Patterson interprets slavery "as a parasitic relationship in which masters seek total domination of slaves through symbolic and ideological as well as legal and violent means. Most original and interesting is his use of the concept of social death to analyze the slave as a natally and liminally incorporated marginal person who is dishonored and degraded" (Bolland 249). Although he centers the constant dehumanization that marked the life of slaves throughout history, Patterson gives the wrong impression that the slaves had no means to subvert the forces that alienated them. Critiquing Patterson's thesis, Adéékè Adééko points out in *The Slave's Rebellion: Literature, History, Orature* (2005) that its definition of the enslaved "as the 'socially' dead casts in sociological terms Hegel's allegorical notion that the slave's consciousness is a 'dead' one." As Adééko argues, Patterson's thesis does not recognize "the possibility of the slave restarting the battle for self-consciousness and extracting freedom from slavery's barbarity" (17). Alternatively, Adééko proposes a reading of black literature that explores "the efforts of black slaves who dared to 'kill' their masters and break the norms of subjection." This interpretation is based on the premise "that the central contention in the making of modern black intellectual history concerns how to gauge the meaning of the attempts which black folks have made to cut the normative strings that bound their fate to the will of those who claim to be their masters" (12).

The possibility of radical slave rebellion against their masters is noticeable in the way in which Prince is able to use the diplomatic and relational skills of *Anancy* to bounce back from oppression and chart her road to freedom. Despite the terrible experiences she goes through in the land of Mr. I——, Mr. D——, and the planter in Cedar Hills, she is not a totally powerless character. Despite the constant floggings and threats of the Woods (204), she is able to use the power of English law on her behalf, subvert the economic dominance of the Woods, and reach out for freedom. When, following the complaints of his wicked wife, Mr. Wood asked Prince to go find a new owner, Prince said:

> I went to a Mr. Burchell, showed him the note, and asked him to buy me for my own benefit; for I had saved about 100 dollars, and hoped, with a little help, to purchase my freedom. He accordingly went to my master:—"Mr. Wood," he said, "Molly has brought me a note that

she wants an owner. If you intend to sell her, I may as well buy her as another." My master put him off and said that he did not mean to sell me. I was very sorry at this, for I had no comfort with Mrs. Wood, and I wished greatly to get my freedom. (205)

We notice that Prince uses the same tactic of divide and conquer that Europeans employed to conquer Africans. Her strategy of bargaining her way to freedom by challenging Mr. Burchell to purchase her reveals her understanding of the African conception of identity as a process emerging from negotiations occurring in a relational group. In this process, one's fate is determined by the skills that one can utilize to win the consensus of elders. In "Oral Tradition and History: An Agenda for Angola" (1997), Miller describes the importance of oral performance and communal gathering in decision making in traditional Kongo societies as "this social, or collective aspect of thinking [which] may be utilized in oral cultures to compensate for the fallibility of the individual human memory" (20).

The centrality of communal conversation prior to the finalization of agreement was an African custom that Prince was certainly familiar with in the Caribbean. This tradition was integral in the organizational process that accompanied the passive and active resistance of slaves in Bermuda against their masters. In *Nine Black Women: An Anthology of Nineteenth-Century Writers from the United States, Canada, Bermuda and the Caribbean* (1998), Moira Ferguson argues that Prince might have well heard from family members about early black inhabitants who organized plots and revolts in Bermuda in the late seventeenth century and in the eighteenth century (48). Her memory of the rebelliousness of her ancestors must include an awareness of African resistance against oppression through negotiation.

Prince draws her power from a number of cultural icons whose efforts she intertwines for the struggle against oppression. The immediate figure is the Caribbean *Anancy*, whose strength, like that of the Rabbit and the Monkey characters in black folktales, lies in the ability to use wits and diplomatic talent to counter the dominance of the oppressor. The survival tactics of the Caribbean *Anancy* are traceable to Africa, because they recall the resistance strategies of the Akan *Anancy* character whose power in traditional Akan culture derives from his ability to use diplomatic skills to win the favors of God. The wisdom of the Akan *Anancy* comes from the power of his wife Aso. This power is African diasporan because it resurfaces in the sagacity and toughness of Prince toward her oppressors.

The negotiation skills of the Caribbean *Anancy* is noticeable in the Antiguan tale "Hurricane Coming," collected by Parsons, in which *Nancy* tricks

Lion, the cattle-robber, and brings him to God, who has promised to pay him "ten pound, give him three kile of rope an' set up de cloud black" (309). *Anancy*'s power to use small steps in order to achieve big results is a technique that Prince employs to develop a strong sense of entrepreneurship and feminist consciousness that sustains her rebellion against white sexism and her fight for freedom. She develops a rebellion that supports her war against economic, racial, and gender oppression. She garners the strength embodied in the concept of "maronnage" which, as Rosalyn Terborg-Penn argues in "Black Women in Resistance," epitomizes the survival strategies that small groups of women fugitive slaves used in an attempt to "subsist on the fringes of plantations located near swamps." In this feminist ideological framework, "Survival was said to be based upon an illegal trade they maintained with whites living on the borders of the swamp. The women who were part of these communities helped to plan insurrection" (201).

Prince uses a similar tactic in her development of a black womanhood by creating an autonomous economic freedom built on the liminal space she has in spite of her status as a slave of the Wood family. She writes: "I took in washing, and sold coffee and yams and other provisions to the captains of ships. I did not sit still idling during the absence of my owners; for I wanted, by all honest means, to earn money to buy my freedom. Sometimes I bought a hog cheap on board ship, and sold it for double the money on shore; and I also earned a good deal by selling coffee. By this means I by degrees acquired a little cash" (205). Prince is able to use her own wits to develop a form of "maronnage" in which she assembles incremental economic strength to create radical social transformation in her world. Her acts of washing clothes and selling coffee, yams, and hogs, which her master perceives as insufficient means to buy her freedom, are gigantic steps. These acts are crucial developments in Prince's creation of her own space and agency in the New World. They are indicative of the subversive consciousness that James C. Scott represents in *The Weapons of the Weak* (1985) as a tool that allows oppressed peasant societies to disrupt the power of the hegemony. In Scott's rationale, "Behind the façade of symbolic and ritual compliance," members of subordinate classes such as peasant societies demonstrate "innumerable acts of ideological resistance" (304), one being the power of these individuals "to penetrate and demystify the prevailing ideology" (317). Though its context is Malaysia in the 1970s, Scott's theory helps us understand the manner in which Prince's attempts to buy her freedom are powerful means of rebellion that allow her incrementally to disrupt her subaltern position in servitude.

Prince's accumulation of strength to buy her freedom develops in a mechanical manner that recalls the calculated process in which *Ananse* plotted to stop the lion from stealing God's cattle. Knowing that they were physically and socially at the mercy of the adversary, both *Anancy* and Prince relied on their wits and ingenuity to turn the immediate elements within their environment to their benefit. The most important part of such environment is the cultural and ideological legacy of Aso, *Ananse*'s wife on *Ananse* himself. This influence is noticeable in the Akan tale "How it Came About That the Sky-God's Stories Came to be Known as 'Spider-Stories,'" collected by Rattray, in which *Ananse* performs different tasks, allowing him to purchase "the Sky-god's stories" from the Akan God Nyankonpon. In this narrative, *Ananse* tricked "the Onini creature the Python; Osebo, the Leopard; Mmoatia, the Fairy; (and) Mmoboro, the Hornets" (55) that the Sky-God wanted to have by using the same wit and sense of measurement, balance, and consciousness that allowed the Caribbean *Anancy* and Prince to achieve liminal freedom despite their subaltern position. This folktale is highly relevant because *Ananse*'s knowledge of how to succeed in his plots came from his wife Aso, who gave him specific directions that he followed precisely. The cooperation between *Ananse* and his wife shows that tricksters transcend gender binaries and work toward the same goal of using diplomacy to get what they want. One example of such cooperation is when Aso gives instructions to *Ananse* on how to catch Onini the Python. In this tale, a woman teaches *Anansi* how to catch the Python. The woman tells *Anansi* to cut a branch of a palm tree and lay it in a stream, to wait until Python stretches himself on the branch and tie him around it (57).

This oral narrative reflects plot elements and motifs that are identical to those in the Antiguan tale "Hurricane Coming." In both tales, the spider figure pretends not to know about the Lion's and the Python's presence and acts disinterested when the two figures show up after hearing statements that concern them directly. Both spider tricksters are adept at provoking the Lion or the Python by influencing them to do something that they might have refused to do if they had been asked to do so. They both employ indirection in order to talk strong characters into being duped in their games. In addition, both tales reveal parallels in the use of motifs such as the meeting of the trickster and the act of being tricked in a naturally secluded area, the use of rope to tie the tricked, and the trickster's final confession of his actual motives.

These motifs and the plot they support suggest the sophisticated nature of black folktales in which tricksters have complex roles that are matched only by the dexterity and creativity of Prince. For example, in order to gain her freedom, Prince had to venture into alien worlds in which she had to protect herself against the sexism of the white men she encountered on the ships where she was selling her hogs. Ships were the only means for slaves to cross the oceans that separated them from one another. As Gilroy points out in *The Black Atlantic*, these ships "were the living means by which the points within that Atlantic world were joined. They were mobile elements that stood for the shifting spaces in between the fixed places that they connected. Accordingly they need to be thought of as cultural and political units rather than abstract embodiments of the triangular trade" (16–17). In Prince's narrative, ships acquire an ambiguous and troubling cultural and political significance. On the one hand, they allow her to take advantage of a capitalistic economic venture in which people were selling and buying items for profits in relational terms. Yet ships are unsafe environments for Prince, because they are the dangerous zones where she encounters prejudiced white Englishmen sailors who express promiscuous desires toward her. A clear example is Captain Abbot's attempts to exploit Prince's sexuality in exchange for money (225). In this sense, ships were not safe places for black women, who could, however, achieve relative economic power from selling items there.

In the case of Captain Abbot, prejudice is primarily driven by a stereotyping of black women, because his audacity to approach Prince for sexual favors results from his association of black femininity with a sexual libertinage and socioeconomic inferiority. Discussing white men's misconceptions of the sexuality of black female slaves in the West Indies, Bush identifies different representations, including, 1) the "Sable Queen," which "reflected a common and often near-obsessional interest in the 'exotic charms' of African womanhood"; 2) childbearing; and 3) "sexual duties performed for white masters" (11).

The ways in which whites perceived blacks in Antigua are apparent in the stereotypes that Captain Abbot develops around Prince. By conditioning his financial support for Prince's legal freedom on her willingness to be "free" for his sexual urges, Captain Abbot enacts the obsession and hypocrisy of nineteenth-century Englishmen toward black women. Discussing this duality, Louis James argues in *Caribbean Literature in English* (1999) that *The History of Mary Prince* offers insights not only into the courageous personality of Prince but also into "the conflicting attitudes of her owners, who liked her, yet fiercely resented her independent spirit" (22). This double standard, which Bush theorizes as the West Indian white society's "hypocritical double standard (chastity for women, sexual licence for men" (1), reflects deep contradictions in how nineteenth-century Englishmen viewed black people. This paradox is visible in the possessive and patronizing attitudes Mr. Wood projects on Prince when she marries Daniel James, who is a free black carpenter and cooper and a member of the Moravian Church. Prince explains: "When Mr. Wood heard of my marriage, he flew into a great rage, and sent for Daniel, who was helping to build a house for his old mistress. Mr. Wood asked him who gave him a right to marry a slave of his? My husband said, 'Sir, I am a free man, and thought I had a right to choose a wife'" (207–8). Here, Prince condemns the limitations against marriage between free and enslaved blacks in 1820s Antigua despite the existence of a political climate that was in favor of the liberation of blacks. In 1833, the Emancipation Act was signed two years before the publication of Prince's narrative, marking the time when blacks in Antigua and in Barbados were legally freed but were not allowed to have a portion of the land they used to cultivate. In *Capitalism and Slavery* (1944), Eric William writes: "It never dawned upon them [abolitionists] that the Negro's freedom could be only nominal if the sugar plantation was allowed to endure . . . the slaves [were] now raised to the dignity of landless wage earners [and were] paid twenty-five cents a day" (191).

The continuity of exploitation of blacks despite the passage of the Emancipation Act is anticipated in Prince's narrative through the legal hassles that prevent her and her husband to marry without Mr. Wood's interference. Prince faced a myriad of planter manipulations such as Mrs. Wood's ill treatment of her in front of Daniel, her indifference toward Prince's inability to do chores owing to rheumatism, and, above all, her refusal to let Prince entertain the notion of being free. When Prince attempts to borrow money from Mr. Burchell to buy her freedom, she realizes her mistress's anxieties about the very concept of black freedom. Prince says: "Mrs. Wood was very angry—she grew quite outrageous—she called me a black devil, and asked me who had put freedom into my head. 'To be free is very sweet,' I said: but she took good care to keep me a slave. I saw her change colour, and I left the room" (208). Mrs. Wood shares the whites' association of blackness and rebelliousness with inferiority or evil. As both Bush and White point out, during their initial encounters with Africa, Europeans formed impressions that blacks were sensual beings, primitive, idle, and of lower intelligence than Europeans.[13]

In the same vein, Europeans were prone to see African slaves in the West Indies as evil whenever they suspected them of preparing to rebel against their masters. In "A True and Extract History of the Island of Barbadoes" (1673), Richard Ligon, who wanted to justify violence as a legal way of protecting whites from the enslaved blacks of Barbados, described Africans as naturally tyrannical people who should be controlled. He writes: "It has been accounted a strange thing, that the *Negroes*, being more than double the numbers of the Christians that are there, and they accounted a bloody people, where they think they have power or advantages; and the more bloody, by how much they are more fearful than others: that these should not commit some horrid massacre upon the Christians, thereby to enfranchise themselves, and become Masters of the island" (54). Ligon's representation of blacks as rebellious is consistent with Bryan Edwards's depiction of a 1760 slave uprising in Jamaica in his *The History, Civil, and Commercial, of the British Colonies in the West Indies* (1793). Edwards describes how "At Ballard's Valley they [slaves] surrounded the overseer's house about four in the morning, in which eight or ten White people were in bed, everyone of whom they butchered in the most savage manner, and literally drank their blood mixed with rum" (67). Edwards's representation of slaves shows his association of rituals of resistance with evil. This connection is the worldview that prompted Mrs. Wood to be anxious when Prince announced her desire to be free.

Moreover, the exchange between Mrs. Wood and Prince reveals the oral and ideological strategies that Prince uses against her mistress in order to express her right to be free and equal to her. This freedom began to loom when Prince traveled with the Woods to England, where they were bringing their son to his new school. Three months after she arrived in England in 1828, Prince started to demand her freedom by refusing to do the work Mrs. Wood expected her to perform. In one scene, she refuses to wash a pile of clothes Mrs. Wood gave her. Prince says: "I told her I was too ill to wash such heavy things that day. She said, she supposed I thought myself a free woman, but I was not; and if I did not do it directly I should be instantly turned out of doors. I stood a long time before I could answer, for I did not know well what to do. I knew that I was free in England, but I did no know where to go, or how to get my living; and therefore, I did not like to leave the house" (210). Prince is increasingly aware of her human rights that were denied to her in the West Indies. Yet, knowing that she was alone and new to England, she sought relations that could authenticate the recognition of such rights in England. Prince's search for authentication is an African cultural survival, because it represents the African's quest for a community that is larger than the one he/she knew in the past. In "Claiming an Identity: Caribbean Women Writers in English" (1994), Brenda F. Berrian says that Prince had two major communities. On the one hand, "Prince has her mother and supportive women from the Anti-Slavery Movement." Yet, as Berrian points out, "Prince understood clearly that she was owned and viewed as property by the white plantation owners. She also had alternatives to go back to the 'slave quarters' after working hours to reclaim her identity with fellow enslaved Africans, to voice her displeasure over being exploited economically by her owners, and to choose to obtain her freedom in England" (213–14). Berrian's argument that Prince could have chosen to return to her community of enslaved Africans that shared "displeasure over being exploited" shows the importance of collective identity for the black West Indian community in which Prince was a part.

The slave community that provided support for Prince during her disillusionment with plantation society is identical to traditional African societies that gave succor to their members at times of need. An example of these African communities is the Sande traditional women society of Sierra Leone and Ivory Coast that Levin portrays as a close-knit community in which the members supported each other for friendship and used artistic elements such as the Sowo mask, combined with chickens or birds, to represent "the certainty and inevitability of struggle, and the probability of a stalemate at best" (33–34). The Sande's representation of struggle as an unavoidable process is consistent with the black Antiguan's perception of resistance against slavery as a necessary course of action. In this sense, although she lived in the West, Prince was part of a radical and transnational black tradition of resistance that is rooted in Africa.

In the same vein, Prince was part of a black tradition rooted in the West. She spent time in England, where she had gone to escape slavery. Contrasting the West Indies with England, she writes: "Work—work—work—Oh that Turk's Island was a horrible place! The people in England, I am sure, have never found out what is carried on there. Cruel, horrible place!" (199). This passage shows that, like her predecessors, Prince knew that in order to obtain her freedom, she needed to travel to places where ideals of natural liberty were espoused and form alliances with members of different races there. Prince's exile into England is an Africanism, because it recalls the process of displacement that African trickster figures such as *Leuk* and *Ananse* went through at numerous times in their search for knowledge and a better life. Yet being away from their original homeland, these figures learned to form alliances and return home with practical knowledge from divinities that give them special privilege. Like these icons, Prince travels far to seek the support of elders. In her case, the elders are members of the Anti-Slavery Society such as Hill and the Pringles, who offer to help her find a shelter and secure her rights to be free in England. Prince writes: "The gentlemen of the Society took me to a lawyer, who examined very strictly into my case; but told me that the laws of England could do nothing to make me free in Antigua. However, they did all they could for me: they gave me a little money from time to time to keep me from want; and some of them went to Mr. Wood to try to persuade him to let me return a free woman to my husband; but though they offered him, as I have heard, a large sum for my freedom, he was sulky and obstinate, and would not consent to let me go free" (212).

Prince's refuge in England is historically important, because this is a country where in the 1820s the freedom of blacks had to be secured through trials despite the existence of laws that theoretically guaranteed such liberty. Before and during 1828, the status of blacks in Britain had been legally transformed through the activism of Anti-Slavery advocates such as Granville Sharp (1735–1813), Thomas Clarkson (1760–1846), William Wilberforce (1759–1833), the French abolitionists' group the Société des Amis des Noirs (Society of the Friends of Blacks) founded in 1788, and the Pennsylvania Quaker missionaries who forced the English government to abolish slavery. Thanks to the goodwill of these individuals and institutions, slavery was abolished in Britain in 1807 and in the British West Indies in 1808. While slavery lasted till 1863 in its territories, the United States had begun campaigning for the abolition of the trade since 1830. That year, "the United States sent three war vessels to the African coast to aid in the suppression of the slave trade; but the appropriation of $100,000, made by Congress in 1819, for enforcing the Act, was reduced to $50,000 in 1823, and soon after was reduced to a few ineffective thousands."[14]

Slavery heavily influenced how blacks of the diaspora saw themselves and their relations with blacks worldwide. For example, in her narrative, Prince planned to spend her future speaking about the traumatic experiences of other blacks. This Pan-Africanist stance echoes loudly in her narrative when she says that she will continue telling English people about the truth in slavery "till all the poor blacks be given free, and slavery done up for evermore" (215). Prince's resolve to continue denouncing slavery shows her use of the black literary trope of the "talking book."[15] Prince takes her rightful place in this literary tradition by pledging to defend constantly the freedom of blacks. She was a Pan-Africanist who believed that slavery needed to end so that blacks could be treated as workers with the same rights and dignity accorded to whites. Speaking about the conditions of blacks in England, she writes: "What's the reason they can't do without slaves as well in England? No slaves here—no whips—no stocks—no punishment, except for wicked people. They hire servants in England; and if they don't like them, they send them away: they can't lick them. Let them work ever so hard in England, they are far better off than slaves. If they get a bad master, they give warning and go hire to another. They have their liberty. That's just what we want" (214–15). Prince's struggle for the freedom of blacks across the globe and their right to be treated as human beings is a Pan-Africanist resistance that led her to search for allies in the court action that the Anti-Slavery Society had initiated on her behalf. Key information about Prince's trial is given in the addendum piece where Mr. Pringle discusses his response to Mr. Wood's arguments against her freedom. In a letter he wrote on October 20, 1830, to his secretary, Mr. Taylor, Mr. Wood accused Prince of taking her freedom without his consent. He writes: "I'll say nothing of the liability I should incur, under the Consolidated Slave Law, of dealing with a free person as a slave" (221). Here Mr. Wood is invoking a law that traditionally allowed planters to reject the claims of freedom of their slaves; the law was no longer valid in England in 1830. Mr. Pringle explains: "Is not this pretext hypocritical in the extreme? What liability could he possibly incur by voluntarily resigning the power, conferred on him by an iniquitous colonial law, of re-imposing the shackles of slavery on the bondwoman from whose limbs they had fallen when she touched the free soil of England?—There exists no liability from which he might not have been easily secured, or for which he would not have been fully compensated" (224).

With the support of Mr. Pringle's convincing arguments and the legal team of the Anti-Slavery Society, a petition attached to sections of Mary's statements was submitted to the British Parliament to help bring a bill that will "provide for the entire emancipation of all slaves brought to England with the owner's consent" (218). While she was later declared as free to stay in England, Prince could not return to Antigua without jeopardizing her liberty, because "it was found that there existed no legal means of compelling Mary's master to grant her manumission; and that if she returned to Antigua, she would inevitably fall again under his power, or that of his attorneys, as a slave" (217).

The History of Mary Prince reflects the defiant strategies that a courageous black woman from Bermuda and Antigua used to resist the violence, racism, sexism, and prejudices that slavery imposed on her. She fought against such oppressions by using the survival tactics of trickster figures in West Indian and African folktales. She fought for the end of slavery in England and abroad and contributed significantly in the Pan-Africanist intellectual tradition of resistance. In this sense, Prince's narrative is a story of both trauma and healing since, as Moira Ferguson suggests in "The Literature of Slavery and Abolition" (2004), the tale is "one of suffering endured, but ultimately of the human spirit triumphant" (248).

Conclusion

In an attempt to trace the history of Pan-African resistance in early black diasporan literature to Africa, this book has explored specific traditional African oral narratives and cultures in which the spirit of individual and collective resistance against tyrannical authority are pervasive. The cultures of the Wolof of Senegambia, the Fanti of Ghana, the Igbo of Nigeria, and those of the Africans in the Caribbean, the United States, and England, had complex traditions and ideas about god, spirituality, family, ancestors, lineage, kinship, life, and death that gave enslaved blacks the ideological and emotional tools to overcome slavery and rebuild their lives. These blacks infused the African spirit of resistance and cosmologies into the early literature and cultures of the diaspora. Uncovering this Pan-African culture and spirit of resistance requires a new framework in which critics compare classic black narratives of slavery with African folktales. This comparative study allows us to interpret the ideologies and actions in the works of pioneer black authors of the diaspora as derisions and rejections of the unequal race and power relations between Africans and Europeans during the Atlantic slave trade. This framework can exist only when critics begin to analyze the oral narratives of blacks from both sides of the Atlantic Ocean as cultural and ideological resources that help us understand the rich history of resistance and the hybrid identities of Western blacks.

Moreover, as I will show in my next book project, the early black narratives of slavery provide us with a historical and cultural background that allows us to know the roots of the Pan-Africanism in which many black writers and intellectuals from the United States and the Caribbean of succeeding centuries played important parts. These black diasporan writers and intellectuals who emerged between the 1820s and the end of the twentieth century included David Walker, Maria W. Stewart, Robert Campbell, Edward Wilmot Blyden, Martin Robinson Delany, Frances E. W. Harper, W. E. B Du Bois,

Marcus Garvey, Richard Wright, Malcolm X, C. L. R. James, Frantz Fanon, Lorraine Hansberry, Maryse Condé, Alice Walker, and Toni Morrison. These black writers of the diaspora were concerned with the same issues of injustices and struggle for liberation from slavery, repression, and exploitation that preoccupied their predecessors. The black writers of later generations grappled with the same question of freedom from the despairing legacies of slavery and imperialism that Wheatley, Cugoano, Equiano, the Hart Sisters, and Prince had confronted in their writings. Therefore, the early black diasporan writers' interest in Africa was a seminal Pan-Africanism, since it inspired future black authors to have the intention to help Africa and its diaspora achieve political, economic, and intellectual independence from the legacies of slavery and imperialism.

On the one hand, the early black writers represented Africa, in demeaning terms, as a location of savage and barbaric ways that they did not want to associate with. This misrepresentation of Africans perpetuates the European mythologizing of Africa as a "Dark Continent," contradicting the black diasporan writers' invocation of Africa's great civilizations in their resistance against European slavery and racism. On the other hand, the early black writers portrayed Africa as a source of ethnic pride, freedom, and identity that they wanted to reclaim in order to affirm their humanity, dignity, and race consciousness. In spite of their ambivalent relations to Africa, these black writers occasionally depicted Africa as a homeland and a source of inspiration and cultural rebirth. These writers' positive representation of Africa outweighed their negative perception of the continent and opposed their Eurocentric and racist representation of blacks as inferior or primitive people.

Furthermore, despite their hesitancy toward Africa, the pioneer black authors of the diaspora fiercely defended Africa by denouncing the effects of Western racism and imperialism on Africa and its diaspora. They traced the problems confronting Africa to the loss of resources that slavery brought about on the continent and in the diaspora and showed convergences between the conditions of blacks from both sides of the Atlantic Ocean. The process in which the black writers represented Africa in positive terms established the foundation of a Pan-Africanist intellectual and cultural tradition that needs to be revisited so that Africa's significance in the diaspora's theorizing of slavery, racism, and imperialism can be properly understood.

The major goal of this book is to suggest the importance of African and diasporan folktales in the study of black literature. This objective stems from my conviction that African tales are the oral traditions that gave birth to black diasporan folktales and literature. The distinctive rhetorical features of black diasporan folktales discussed in this book originated in the African oral narratives and epics that only *griots* could preserve and tell with rare dexterity and appeal. Therefore, it is no wonder that the African writers such as Léopold Sédar Senghor, Birago Diop, and Djibril Tamsir Niane, who wanted to discover the traditional folktales of their independent nations, turned to the *griot* in the same way American folklorists such as Elsie Clews Parsons, Lawrence W. Levine, Zora Neale Hurston, and Roger D. Abrahams turned to slave culture in quest of black New World folktales.[1] These major scholars of different background, and many others that I have acknowledged in the introduction of this book, have collected a large number of black folktales that await more scholarly research and analysis. By drawing from this invaluable treasure of black folktales and analyzing them in juxtaposition with early diasporan narratives of slavery, I want to inspire a new method of comparing black literature from the two sides of the Atlantic Ocean. This comparative study suggests the strong influence of traditional African discursive strategies—such as those of the *griot* and the tricksters in black folktales—on the ways in which early diasporan writers fought for liberation and acknowledgment of their humanity.

Other influences of African folktales in the black diaspora are those in Pan-African popular culture that also await scholarly research and analysis. African oral narratives could be effective tools for studying the discursive and rhetoric devices and the ideologies of resistance that permeate Pan-African cultural expressions such as break-dance, rap, hip hop, and reggae-muffin. The African and diasporan tales are ethnographic and anthropological data that can also help scholars examine African survivals in spirituals, jazz, blues, calypso, ska, and reggae. The enslaved Africans who remembered African oral narratives planted the seeds of these vibrant black cultural forms in the Western world.

Listening to the African American poet Saul Williams as he read a part of his writings to a college audience that was highly fascinated by his oratorical skills, I could not help remembering the pioneer black writers who served as major links of transmission of Africanisms into his identity and hip-hop poetry. Acknowledging this legacy, Williams writes in his autobiography, *The Dead Emcee Scrolls* (2006): "The more I read the more I began to believe that these words had been written by someone African in origin. Perhaps some sort of shaman who foresaw slavery and the calculated oppression of African people and had planted this text to guide us through a crucial moment in our history, our future, our present. I thought intensely about the power of hip-hop. Had it, also, been planted by these African shamans as some sort of seed that would not blossom until four generations after slavery?" (xxiv). Williams's inquiries prompt us to ask the following questions: What are the relationships between the tricksters in black folktales and those in African American popular culture? Did Williams receive the art of talking, "Signifying," and negotiating freedom from the tricksters of Pan-African culture? Did his powerful mastery of the word come from early black diasporan writers who passed it to him through other black writers and artists? From where did the black diaspora's expert, subtle, and powerful mastery and usage of words as tools of resistance come? Asking these questions will help us recognize Africa's contributions in the development of the rich oral traditions of resistance and negotiation that enslaved Africans carried into the Western world. Therefore, contrary to E. Franklin Frazier's "Tabla Rasa" thesis, Africans did not come to the New World empty-handed (*Negro Family in the United States*, 35). They arrived in the West with stories of survival on their mind and in their bodies and hearts. They came to the black diaspora with subversive tactics of resistance and negotiation such as "Signifying," disguise, irony, praise, diversion, false deference, ambivalence, masking, and adornments of multiple roles and positions, which were and remain indispensable means of confronting tyrannical power.

Notes

Introduction

1. For a discussion of the elite status of early black diasporan writers such as Wheatley, Martin Robinson Delany, and Robert Campbell, see Toppin, *A Biographical History of Blacks in America*, 59; Blackett, "Martin R. Delany and Robert Campbell," 1.

2. Other studies of this homogenization of Africa are Miller, "History and Africa," 6; Gooden, Review of *Africanisms in American Culture*, 733.

3. For a study of these functions, see Dundes, "Making and Breaking," 171–85; Okpewho, *African Oral Literature*, 176.

4. See Geiss, "Pan-Africanism."

5. See Geiss, *Pan-African Movement*, 8.

6. See Martin, *Pan-African Connection*, vii.

7. For the original source of this quotation, see Wiltse, *David Walker's Appeal*, 29–30.

8. See Bonnett and Watson, *Emerging Perspectives*, 2; Segal, *Black Diaspora*, xiii.

9. Claudel and Carrière, *Three Tales*, 39; Fortier, *Louisiana Folk-Tales*, 94.

10. Faine, *Philologie Créole*, 214; Claudel and Carrière, *Three Tales*, 38.

11. Claude and Carrière, *Three Tales*, 38–39.

12. Examples of this binary are visible in Erickson, Review of *Contes Africains*, 67; Cartwright, *Reading Africa*, 110–13.

13. See Erickson, Review of *Contes Africains*, 67; Mortimer, *Contes Africains*, x.

14. See Bascom, *African Folktales*, 1–16, 22–29, 29–31, 40–70, 71–82, 83–103, 104–7, 107–13, 114–36, 137–44, 144–54, 155–200, 201–6, 206–8, 208–11, 211–14, 214–20, 221–27, 228–35.

Chapter One

1. For studies of this African practice, see Peel, Murray, and Heald, *Islamic and Caste Knowledge Practices among Haalpulaar'en in Senegal*, 124; Akyeampong, "Alcohol in Africa," 61.

2. See Goboldte, "Laying on Hands," 244; Jones, *Teaching African American Religions*, 162–63.

3. See Dove, "African Womanism," 515–39; Davies and Fido, *Out of the Kumbla*, xii; John, *Clear Word and Third Sight*, 55, 58–61, 71; Hoving, *In Praise of New Travelers*, 5, 17, 43–44, 47, 56, 116, 241, 298.

4. For studies of Puritanism and Methodism in colonial New England, see Fischer, *Albion's Seed*, 13–205; Parrington, *Main Currents in American Thought*, vii–128; Haller, *Rise of Puritanism*, 5, 17, 24, 302, 79, 177, 191, 265, 331; Miller, *Errands into the Wilderness*, 9, 48–98, 141–83; Hudson, *Religion in America*, 7–9, 13, 14–16, 27–30, 96–103, 111, 115, 134, 281.

5. Bassard, *Spiritual Interrogations*, 45.

6. See Gates, *Trials of Phillis Wheatley*, 17; Shields, "Phillis Wheatley."

7. See Mason, "Introduction to the Poems of Phillis Wheatley," 48, 50.

8. Also see Mason, *Poems of Phillis Wheatley*, 8–10; Robinson, *Phillis Wheatley in the Black American Beginnings*, 19.

9. See Robinson, "On Phillis Wheatley and Her Boston," 47.

10. See Kafka, *Great White Way*, 40; Robinson, *Phillis Wheatley in the Black American Beginnings*, 23

11. See Sylla, *La Philosophie*, 9.

12. See Leymarie, *Les Griots*, 22.

13. See Boulègue, *Les Anciens Royaumes Wolof*, 22.

14. For examples of these contacts, see Connolly, *Social Life in Fanti-Land*, 132; Sarr, "Les Guêlawars," 143–44; Sylla, *La Philosophie*, 10.

15. See Gamble, *Wolof of Senegambia*, 12, 16, 17.

16. See Searing, *West African Slavery*, 113; Boulègue, *Les Anciens Royaumes Wolof*, 50–72; Leymarie, *Les Griots*, 23–38.

17. See Boulègue, *Les Anciens Royaumes Wolof*, 135; Barry, *Senegambia and the Atlantic Slave Trade*, 108–9.

18. Bacon, *Puritan Promenade*, 31.

19. See Rodney, "African Slavery," 431.

20. See Eltis et al., *Trans-Atlantic Slave Trade*.

21. See Lambert, "'I Saw The Book Talk,'" 193; Bennett, "Phillis Wheatley's Vocation," 72; Shields, "Phillis Wheatley," 775; Robinson, *Phillis Wheatley in the Black American Beginnings*, 60.

22. See Achebe, "Image of Africa" 2; Achebe, "Named for Victoria," 23.

23. Terence, whose full name was Publius Terentius Āfer, was a successful writer of Roman comedies and dramas (c. 195 or 185–159 B.C.) of African descent who was brought to Rome as a slave. His owner, Terentus Lūcānus later educated him and freed him in Rome on account of his literary talents. See Harvey, *Oxford Companion to Classical Literature*, 416.

24. The term "poetics of ascent" derives from the title of Shields's dissertation, "Phillis Wheatley's Poetics of Ascent," written in 1978. See Shields, "Phillis Wheatley's Use of Classicism," 99.

25. For more information about this eighteen-page broadside, see Dunlap, *Poems*, 4; Robinson, *Critical Essays on Phillis Wheatley*, 19; Cima, "Black and Unmarked," 483.

26. See the discussion on opening formulas in Kesteloot, *Contes*, 5; Knappert, *Myth and Legends*, 2, 20; Armah, *Healers*, 2.

27. See Piersen, *Black Yankees*, 56–57; Berlin, *Many Thousands Gone*, 139.

28. For a study of the rhetorical strategies of African griots, see Okpewho, *African Oral Literature*, 26; Okpewho, *Epic in Africa*, 27; Diop, *Oral History and Literature*, 107–8.

29. See Steele, "Figure of Columbia," 266; Williams, "Phillis Wheatley," 245–59; Napierkowski, "To His Excellency"; Vera Camden, conversation with author, September 10, 2007.

Chapter Two

1. See Carretta, Introduction *Unchained Voices*, 11.
2. See Adams and Sanders, "Ottobah Cugoano," 43.
3. Pettinger, Introduction to "Ottobah Cugoano," 14.
4. *Ibid.*; Carretta, Introduction *Thoughts and Sentiments*, xiv.
5. In the preface to *Oral Traditions of Fante States*, John Fynn lists these groups as follows: the Shama, Komenda, Elmina, Anomabo, Mankessim, Ayanmain, Ayam Denkyera, Ayam Abasa, Esiam, Ajumako, Esikuma, Gomoa Assin, Gomoa Ajumako, Agona and Efutu (Winneba) (I).
6. Fage, *Ghana*, 29.
7. See Piersen, *Black Legacy*, 4–12; Alan Rice, "'Who's Eating Whom,'" 107–21.
8. See Ransford, *Slave Trade*, 73–74; Richburg, *Out of America*, xvi-xv, 161–62; Carretta, Introduction to *Unchained Voices*, 2.
9. See Lovejoy, *Ideology of Slavery*, 13; Meillassoux, *The Anthropology of Slavery*, 7; Thornton, *Africa and Africans*, 74, 76.
10. See Meillassoux, *Anthropology of Slavery*, 7; Lovejoy, *Ideology of Slavery*, 13; Kopytoff and Miers, *Slavery in Africa*, 3–4.
11. See Miller, *Way of Death*, 42; Thornton, *Africa and Africans*, 74, 76; Kopytoff and Miers, *Slavery in Africa*, 3–4.
12. See Lovejoy, *Great Chain of Being*, 59–61.
13. For analyses of the denial of black humanity in Western literature and culture, see Jefferson, *Notes on the State of Virginia*, 138, 140, 143, 146; Jordan, *White Over Black*, 309–10; Gates, "Critical Remarks," 323, 319–29; Eze, *Race and the Enlightenment*, 1–9, 33; Gates and McKay, "From Phillis Wheatley to Toni Morrison," 96–97.
14. For a study of the representation of these elements in Western intellectual tradition, see Ikuenobe, *Philosophical Perspectives*, 3–5, 11–16, 19–22, 24–32, 42–43, 84, 93–99, 105–8, 268, 318.
15. According to Carretta, this forced migration of Canaanites occurred circa 60 B.C.E. and 21 C.E. (158). See Carretta, "Explanatory Notes," 158.
16. Other studies of the negative construction of blackness in Western intellectual history include Johnson, "(Re)Conceptualizing Blackness," 173–202; Hood, *Begrimed*, 73–180; Pandian and Parman, *Making of Anthropology*, 171–74.
17. See the excerpt from James Beattie's *An Essay on the Nature and Immutability of Truth, in Opposition to Sophistry and Skepticism* (1770) that Eze included in *Race and the Enlightenment*, 34–37. In this passage, Beattie expresses disagreements with both Hume's and Aristotle's views on blacks.
18. For readings on Judeo-Christian representation of God as personable, see Woodard, *Holy Spirit and Prayer*, 58; Stein, *Claude Goldsmid Montefiore on the Ancient Rabbis*, 31; King, *Passion Heart*, 99.
19. See 173 and note 170 in Cugoano, *Thoughts and Sentiments*, 173–74, 176–77.
20. See Christensen, *Double Descent*, 34.

21. Rattray, *Akan-Ashanti*, 5.

22. See Adi and Sherwood, *Pan-African History*, 27; Shyllon, *Black People in Britain*, x; Campbell, Review of *Black People in Britain*, 14–16; Westhauser, "Revisiting the Jordan Thesis," 113–14.

23. Adams and Sanders, "Ottobah Cugoano," 43; Keough, "Ottobah Cugoano or John Stewart."

24. See Christensen, *Double Descent*, 4, 11, 77, 80.

25. For reading on the importance of the King in Fanti culture, see John Mensah Sarbah's *Fanti Customary Laws*, 11–12, 73–74, 92, 278.

Chapter Three

1. Carretta, "Three West Indian Writers," 73–87.

2. Carretta, "Olaudah Equiano or Gustavus Vassa?" 96–105. See also Carretta, "Three West Indian Writers," 73–87; Kelleter, "Ethnic Self-Dramatization," 72–73, 68; Stein, "Olaudah Equiano"; Rice, Review of *Romanticism and Slave Narratives*.

3. Carretta, Introduction to *Olaudah Equiano*, ix; Pettinger, Introduction to *Ottobah Cugoano*, 17; Berson, *Young Heroes in World History*, 42–43.

4. Potkay and Burr, Introdcution to *Black Atlantic Writers*, 160; Berson, *Young Heroes in World History*, 92–93; Worger et al., *Africa and the West*, 42.

5. See Milsome, *Olaudah Equiano*, 1–59.

6. Carretta, "Three West Indian Writers."

7. In *Exchanging Our Country Marks*, Gomez also argues that 17 percent of Virginia's population was from Senegambia in the middle of the eighteenth century (150).

8. For readings about the Igbo slaves' spirit of resistance and survival, see Benton, "Grace Nichols"; Chambers, "Tracing the Igbo into the African Diaspora"; McKoy, "Limbo Contest."

9. See Nwankwo, "Igbo," 5; Ejidike, "Human Rights," 81–82.

10. See also Njoku, *Igbos of Nigeria*, 32–33.

11. For more information on the impact of the Atlantic slave trade on the status of the Osu [cult slaves] of Igbo society, see Lovejoy, *Transformations in Slavery*, 84–86; Oriji, *Traditions of Igbo Origin*, 32–33; Njoku, *Igbos of Nigeria*, 32–36.

12. This Igbo cosmology is taken from Okeke, *Tales of Land of Death*, xii.

13. In *Exchanging Our Country Marks*, Gomez says: "Faced with the prospect of slavery in a strange land, some Igbo began to think the unthinkable, and to act upon it. In Igboland, suicide was a violation of omenela and an abomination; the offender was denied a place in the ancestral burial grounds, 'the worst social humiliation for any Igbo'" (133). According to Gomez, the Igbo slaves resorted to suicide not as a choice but as a means to go "back to Africa" to "renegotiate the next life, and return to the soil of the ancestors, far from the shores of America" (134).

14. Additional definitions of "marronage" are in Sharpe, *Ghosts of Slavery*, 4, 5; Campbell, *Maroons of Jamaica*, 2.

15. See Gates and Appiah, *Dictionary of Global Culture*, 440; Terborg-Penn, "Black Women in Resistance," 198.

16. See Allen, "Serious and Alarming Daily Evil," 21, 37.

17. See Oriji, *Traditions of Igbo Origin*, 33.

18. Okeke, *Tales of Land of Death*, 24–25.
19. See Basil Davidson's analysis, in *The African Slave Trade*, of Thomas Carlyle's racist theory about blacks (xvii).
20. See Engerman, Review of *The Slave Community*; Genovese, *Roll, Jordan, Roll*, 76.
21. Okeke, *Tales of Land of Death*, 32, 35.
22. *Ibid.*, 22.
23. For further discussion of this ambivalence, see Gruesser, "Afro-American Travel Literature," 5–20.
24. See Robertson, "Africa into the Americas?" 10.
25. For discussion of this thesis, see Oriji, *Traditions of Igbo Origin*, 25–27.
26. For more analysis of the James Somersett case, see Williams, *Capitalism and Slavery*, 45.

Chapter Four

1. Ferguson hints at this ambivalence in her introduction to *The Hart Sisters*, 44.
2. See Ferguson, Introduction to *Nine Black Women*, 3; Ferguson, *Hart Sisters*, 1, 5.
3. Ferguson, *Hart Sisters*, 1–2; Lazarus-Black, *Legitimate Acts*, 31–32.
4. Ferguson, *Nine Black Women*, 3.
5. Saillant, "Antiguan Methodism," 89; Paquet, *Caribbean Autobiography*, 24.
6. Ferguson, *Hart Sisters*, 9.
7. See Kohnova, "Moravians and their Missionaries," 351–52.
8. See Latimer, "Foundation," 435; Gaspar, *Bondmen and Rebels*, 132–34; Reyes, *Mothering across Cultures*, 121.
9. "Wesley, John"; "Methodism."
10. Dayfoot, *Shaping of the West Indian Church*, 126.
11. See Damas, *Veillées Noires*, 19–23.
12. This synopsis of "The Three Questions" is taken from Flowers, *Classification of the Folktale of the West Indies by Types and Motifs*, 74.
13. See also Senior, "Ancestral Poem," 320; Stuckey, *Slave Culture*, 30.
14. For readings about this theory, see Reagon, "African Diaspora Women," 177; Wilentz, *Binding Cultures*, xxi; Reyes, *Mothering across Cultures*, 9.
15. In *The Maroons of Jamaica*, Campbell writes: "In Jamaican Maroon communities women played a multifaceted role. African fashion, they were the agriculturalists, thus giving them nutritional power over the menfolk . . . But some of these women were also great warriors" (4). See Sharpe, *Ghosts of Slavery*, 1–43; Campbell, *Maroons of Jamaica*, 4, 5, 51–52, 174–79; James, *Maroon Narrative*, 105–9.
16. For readings about these stereotypes, see Turner, "Limits of Abolition," 328; Wilberforce, *Appeal*, 47.
17. Rattray, *Akan-Ashanti Folk-Tales*, 195.
18. The summary of this tale comes from Flowers, *Classification of the Folktale of the West Indies*, 210; a full version of the tale is in Parsons, "He Sings to Make the Old Woman Dance," 314–15.
19. See Parsons, "He Sings to Make the Old Woman Dance," 314; Diop, "Le Taureau de Bouki," 125.
20. See Jackson, *Invincible Summer*, 40; Lowe, *Jump at the Sun*, 18.

21. See Olmos and Paravisini-Gebert, *Sacred Possessions*, 6; Benítez-Rojo, *Repeating Island*, 160; Gaspar, *Bondmen and Rebels*, 246; Pittman, "Fetishism," 652–53.

22. See Bush, *Slave Women in Caribbean Society*, 74; Olmos and Paravisini-Gebert, *Sacred Possessions*, 6.

23. For more studies on the role of Obeah in the Caribbean and in black-white relations, see Brown, "Spiritual Terror" 24–53; Brown, *Reaper's Garden*; Engerman, Review of *New Studies in the History of American Slavery*;

24. The authors (J.V., A.W, and N.G, *A Genuine Narrative*) define the Ikem as "a shield composed of Wicker-skins, and two or three small pieces of thin Board," 7.

Chapter Five

1. See Robinson, "Bermuda"; Howard, "About Bermuda," 7–8; Lloyd, *Sketches of Bermuda*, 92–93; Morgan, *American Slavery, American Freedom*, 82.

2. See also Manning, *Black Clubs in Bermuda*, 10.

3. See also Bush, *Slave Women in Caribbean Society*, 156.

4. For more discussion of the use of "xass" in Wolof society and its influence in slave culture, see Wilson-Fall and Sow, "Kimoh, dar you are!" 24, 33, 34.

5. See "Bermuda Gombey," 1–2; See also Greenberg, *Bermuda Alive*, 215. For studies on the relations between Native Americans and Bermuda slaves, see Boissevain, "Whatever Became of the New England Indians Shipped to Bermuda," 103–14; Smith, *Slavery in Bermuda*, 23–25; Mason, "Bermuda's Pequots," 616–20; Sands, "Carnival Celebrations," 79, 80; Hayward, *Bermuda Past and Present*, 30. On communal revolts against planters, see Ferguson, "The Literature of Slavery and Abolition," 238–54; Ramphal, *Time For Action*, 276–77; "Bermuda Gombey," 1–2; Segal, *Black Diaspora*, 43.

6. See "Who Ate Up the Butter," "Who Ate Up the Food," "The Tar Baby," and "Stealing the Butter, Hiding in the Log," in Dorson, *American Negro Folktales*, 68–79.

7. See Ferguson, "The Literature of Slavery and Abolition," 247; Rice, *Radical Narratives of the Black Atlantic*, 21; Prince, *History of Mary Prince*, 187; Ferguson, *Nine Black Women*, 49–52; Woodward, *African-British Writings*, 135; Paquet, *Caribbean Autobiography*, 28–29; Packwood, *Chained on the Rock*, 63; Lazarus-Black, *Legitimate Acts*, 34–35.

8. For a summary of this tale, see Flowers, *Classification of the Folktale of the West Indies*, 476.

9. Edwards writes: "The Negroes in general are strongly attached to their countrymen, but above all, to such of their companions as came in the same ship with them from Africa. This is a striking circumstance: the term shipmate is understood among them as signifying a relationship of the most endearing nature; perhaps as recalling the time when the sufferers were cut off together from their common country and kindred, and awakening reciprocal sympathy, from the remembrance of mutual affection" (*History*, 73).

10. For reading about this relational context of status acquisition in traditional African societies, see Miller, "Integrities of History in Africa," 23; Miller, "Oral Tradition and History," 20.

11. For a summary of the tale, see Flowers, *Classification of the Folktale of the West Indies*, 401.

12. For a summary of the tale, see Flowers, *classification of the folktale of the West Indies*, 507–8.

13. See Bush, *Slave Women in Caribbean Society*, 12; White, *Ar' n't I a Woman*, 29.

14. Postma, *Atlantic Slave Trade*, 66–67; Williams, *Capitalism and Slavery*, 47, 149, 191; Turner, *Slaves and Missionaries*, 141, 143.

15. See Gates and Andrews, Introduction to *Pioneers of the Black Atlantic*, 4.

Conclusion

1. See Blair, Introduction to *Tales of Amadou Koumba*, v.

Bibliography

Aardema, Verna. *Misoso: Once upon a Time Tales from Africa*. New York: Alfred A. Knopf, 1994.

Aarne, Antti. *The Types of the Folk-Tale: A Classification and Bibliography*. 1928. Edited by Stith Thompson. New York: Burt Franklin, 1971.

Abarry, Nana. "Teaching Akan Oral Literature in Ghanaian Schools." *Journal of Black Studies* 24, no. 3 (1994): 308–28.

Abrahams, Roger D. *Deep Down in the Jungle: Negro Narrative Folklore from the Streets of Philadelphia*. 1963. Chicago: Aldine, 1970.

———. "Preface." In *Afro-American Folktales: Stories from the Black Traditions in the New World*, edited by Roger D. Abrahams, xxii. New York: Pantheon Books, 1985.

———. "The Signifying Monkey and the Lion." In Abrahams, *Deep Down in the Jungle*, 153–56.

———. *Singing the Master: The Emergence of African-American Culture in the Plantation South*. New York: Penguin Books, 1993.

———. *Talking Back*. Rowley, Mass.: Newbury House, 1976.

———, and John F. Szwed, eds. *After Africa: Extracts from British Travel Accounts and Journals of the Seventeenth, Eighteenth, and Nineteenth Centuries Concerning the Slaves, their Manners, and Customs in the British West Indies*. New Haven, Conn.: Yale University Press, 1983.

Achebe, Chinua. "An Image of Africa: Racism in Conrad's *Heart of Darkness*." In *Hopes and Impediments: Selected Essays, 1965–1987*, edited by Chinua Achebe, 1–14. London: Heinemann, 1988.

———. "Named for Victoria: Queen of England." In *Hopes and Impediments: Selected Essays, 1965–1987*, edited by chinua Achebe, 20–26. London: Heinemann, 1988.

———. "The Writer and His Community." In *Hopes and Impediments: Selected Essays: 1965–1987*, edited by Chiua Achebe, 32–41. London: Heinemann, 1988.

Acholonu, Catherine Obianuju. *The Igbo Roots of Olaudah Equiano: An Anthropological Approach*. Owerri, Nigeria: AFA Publications, 1989.

Ackah, Christian Abraham. *Akan Ethics: A Study of the Moral Ideas and the Moral Behaviour of the Akan Tribes of Ghana*. Accra, Ghana: Ghana University Press, 1988.

Adams, Francis D., and Barry Sanders. "Ottobah Cugoano (1757–?)." In *Three Black Writers in Eighteenth Century England*, edited by Francis D. Adams and Barry Sanders, 43–106. Belmont, Calif.: Wadsworth, 1971.

Adéèkó, Adélékè. *The Slave's Rebellion: Literature, History, Orature*. Bloomington: Indiana University Press, 2005.

Adeleke, Tunde. *UnAfrican Americans: Nineteenth-Century Black Nationalists and the Civilizing Mission*. Lexington: University Press of Kentucky, 1998.

Adi, Hakim, and Marika Sherwood. *Pan-African History: Political Figures from Africa and the Diaspora since 1787*. London: Routledge, 2003.

———. "Quobna Ottobah Cugoano: 1757–?" In *Pan-African History*, 26–28.

Agyeman, Opoku. *The Panafricanist Worldview*. Independence, Mo.: International University Press, 1985.

Akoma, Chiji. *Folklore in New World Black Fiction: Writing and the Oral Traditional Aesthetics*. Columbus: The Ohio State University Press, 2007.

Akyeampong, Emmanuel. "Alcohol in Africa." In *Africana: The Encyclopedia of the African and African American Experience*, edited by Henry Louis Gates Jr. and Kwame Anthony Appiah, 60–62. New York: Basic Civitas, 1999.

Allen, Richard B. "A Serious and Alarming Daily Evil: Marronage and Its Legacy in Mauritius and the Colonial Plantation World." In *Slavery and Resistance in Asia and Africa*, edited by Edward A. Alpers, Gwyn Campbell, and Michael Salman, 20–37. London: Routledge, 2005.

Allison, Robert J. "Introduction: Equiano's Worlds." In *The Interesting Narrative of the Life of Olaudah Equiano, Written by Himself*, by Olaudah Equiano, 1–26. Boston and New York: Bedford Books, 1995.

———. "Olaudah Equiano: An African in Slavery and Freedom." In *The Human Tradition in Colonial America*, edited by Ian Kenneth Steele and Nancy Lee Rhoden, 291–304. New York: Rowman & Littlefield, 1999.

Amadiume, Ifi. *Male Daughters, Female Husbands: Gender and Sex in an African Society*. London and New Jersey: Zed Book, 1987.

Anyanwu, U. D. "Gender Question in Igbo Politics." *The Igbo and the Tradition of Politics*, edited by U. D. Anyanwu and J. C. U. Aguwa, 113–20. Uturu, Nigeria: Centre for Igbo Studies of Abia State University, 1993.

Apap, Christopher. "Caught between Two Opinions: Africans, Europeans, and Indians in Olaudah Equiano's *Interesting Narrative*." *Comparative American Studies: An International Journal* 4, no. 1 (2006): 5–24.

Armah, Ayi Kwei. *The Healers*. Portsmouth, N.H.: Heinemann, 1979.

Arthur, James, et al. "Slave, Subject and Citizen." In *Citizenship through Secondary History*, 151–58. London: Routledge, 2001.

Ashcraft-Eason, Lillian. "'She Voluntarily Hath Come': A Gambian Woman Trader in Colonial Georgia in the Eighteenth Century." In *Identity in the Shadow of Slavery*, edited by Paul E. Lovejoy, 202–21. London and New York: Continuum, 2000.

Awuyah, Chris Kwame. "Nationalism and Pan-Africanism in Ghanaian Writing: The Examples of Ottobah Cugoano, Joseph E. Casely-Hayford, and Ayi Kwei Armah." In *Challenging Hierarchies: Issues and Themes in Colonial and Postcolonial African Literature*, edited by Leonard A. Podis and Yakubu Saaka, 203–30. New York: Peter Lang, 1998.

Bacon, Martha Sherman. *Puritan Promenade*. New York: Houghton Mifflin, 1964.

Baker, Houston A., Jr. *Blues, Ideology and Afro-American Literature: A Vernacular Theory*. Chicago: University of Chicago P, 1984.

———. *The Journey Back: Issues in Black Literature and Criticism*. Chicago and London: University of Chicago Press, 1980.

———. *Modernism and the Harlem Renaissance*. Chicago: University of Chicago Press, 1987.

Balkun, Mary McAleer. "Phillis Wheatley's Construction of Otherness and the Rhetoric of Performed Ideology." *African American Review* 36, no. 1 (Spring 2002): 121–35.
Baraka, Imamu Amiri. "The Revolutionary Tradition in Afro-American Literature." In *The Leroi Jones/Amiri Baraka Reader*, edited by Imamu Amiri Baraka, 311–22. New York: Thunder's Mouth Press, 1999.
Barry, Boubacar. *Senegambia and the Atlantic Slave Trade*. New York and Melbourne: Cambridge University Press, 1998.
Barskile, Zawadi Iyanjura. "Carrying Our Spirit with Us: Gold Coast Spiritual Continuities in Eighteenth-Century Suriname and North America." M.A. Thesis. The Ohio State University, 2005.
Bascom, William. *African Folktales in the New World*. Bloomington: Indiana University Press, 1992.
Bassard, Katherine Clay. *Spiritual Interrogations: Culture, Gender, and Community in Early African American Women's Writing*. Princeton, N.J.: Princeton University Press, 1999.
Bauman, Richard, and Joel Sherzer. "The Ethnography of Speaking." *Annual Review of Anthropology* 4 (1975): 95–119.
Beattie, James. "An Essay on the Nature and Immutability of Truth, in Opposition to Sophistry and Skepticism." (1770). In *Race and the Enlightenment: A Reader*, edited by Emmanuel Chukwudi Eze, 34–37. Malden, Mass.: Blackwell, 2001.
Benítez-Rojo, Antonio. *The Repeating Island: The Caribbean and the Postmodern Perspective*. Durham and London: Duke University Press, 1996.
Benito, Jesús, and Ana Manzanas. "The (De) Construction of the 'Other' in *The Interesting Narrative of the Life of Olaudah Equiano*." In *Black Imagination and the Middle Passage*, edited by Maria Diedrich and Henry Louis Gates Jr., 47–56. New York and Oxford: Oxford University Press, 1999.
Bennett, Paula. "Phillis Wheatley's Vocation and the Paradox of the 'Afric Muse.'" *PMLA* 113, no. 1 (January 1998): 64–76.
Benton, Jacquelyn. "Grace Nichols' *I is a Long Memoried Woman* and Julie Dash's *Daughters of the Dust*: Reversing the Middle Passage." In *Black Women Writers across Cultures: An Analysis of Their Contributions*, edited by Valentine Udoh James, et al., 221–32. Lanham, N.Y., and Oxford: International Scholars Publications, 2000.
Bercovitch, Sacvan. *The Puritan Origins of the American Self*. New Haven: Yale University Press, 1975.
Berlin, Ira. *Generations of Captivity: A History of African-American Slaves*. Cambridge, Mass.: Cambridge University Press, 2003.
———. *Many Thousands Gone: The First Two Centuries of Slavery in North America*. Cambridge, Mass.: Belknap Press, 1998.
"The Bermuda Gombey." *Newsletter of the Bermuda National Library*, December 2005, 1–2.
Bernhard, Virginia. "Beyond the Chesapeake: The Contrasting Status of Blacks in Bermuda, 1616–1663." *Journal of Southern History* 54, no. 4 (November 1988): 545–64.
Berrian, Brenda F. "Claiming an Identity: Caribbean Women Writers in English." *Journal of Black Studies* 25, no. 2 (1994): 200–216.
Berson, Robin Kadison, ed. *Young Heroes in World History*. Westport, Conn.: Greenwood Press, 1999.
Blackett, Richard. "Martin R. Delany and Robert Campbell: Black Americans in Search of an African Colony." *Journal of Negro History* 62, no. 1 (January 1977): 1–25.

Blair, Dorothy. "Introduction" to *Tales of Ahmadou Kumba*, by Birago Diop, v-xvi. 1959. Essex, England: Longman. 1989.
Blakey, Michael L. "Bioarchaelogy of the African Diaspora in the Americas: Its Origins and Scope." *Annual Review of Anthropology* 30 (2001): 387–422.
Blassingame, John W. *The Slave Community: Plantation Life in the Antebellum South*. New York: Oxford University Press, 1979.
Bloom, Harold. "Phillis Wheatley c. 1753–1784." In *Black American Poets and Dramatists before the Harlem Renaissance*, edited by Harold Bloom, 119. New York: Chelsea House Publishers, 1994.
Blyden, Nemata Amelia. *West Indians in West Africa, 1808–1880: The African Diaspora in Reverse*. Rochester, N.Y.: University of Rochester Press, 2000.
Boahen, A. Adu. *African Perspectives on Colonialism*. Baltimore: John Hopkins University Press, 1987.
Bogues, Anthony. *Black Heretics, Black Prophets: Radical Political Intellectuals*. New York and London: Routledge, 2003.
Boissevain, Ethel. "Whatever Became of the New England Indians Shipped to Bermuda to be Sold as Slaves." *Man in the Northwest* 11 (Spring 1981): 103–14.
Bolland, O. Nigel. Review of *Slavery and Social Death: A Comparative Study*, by Orlando Patterson. *Ethnohistory* 33, no. 2 (Spring 1986): 248–49.
Bonnett, Aubrey W., and G. Llewellyn Watson. *Emerging Perspectives on the Black Diaspora*. Lanham, Md.: University Press of America, 1990.
Boulègue, Jean. *Les Anciens Royaumes Wolof (Sénégal). Vol. 1: Le Grand Jolof (XIIIe-XVIe SIÉCLE)*. Paris: 1987.
Brathwaite, Kamau. *Middle Passages*. 1992. New York: New Directions, 1993.
———. "Roots." *Bim* 10, no. 37 (1963): 10–21.
———. *Roots*. Ann Arbor: University of Michigan Press, 1993.
Brauer, Gerald C. "Types of Puritan." *Church History* 56 no. 1 (March 1987): 39–58.
Brown, Vincent. *The Reaper's Garden: Death and Power in the World of Atlantic Slavery*. Cambridge, Mass.: Harvard University Press, 2008.
———. "Spiritual Terror and Sacred Authority in Jamaican Slave Society." *Slavery & Abolition* 24, no. 1 (April 2003): 24–53.
Bryan, Judith. "The Evolution of Black London." *Black British Writing*, edited by Victoria R. Arana and Lauri Ramey, 63–71. New York: Palgrave, 2004.
Burnett, Mark Thornton. *Masters and Servants in English Renaissance Drama and Culture: Authority and Obedience*. London and New York: Macmillan Press, 1997.
Bush, Barbara. *Slave Women in Caribbean Society: 1650–1838*. Bloomington and Indianapolis: Indiana University Press, 1990.
Callaghan, Evelyn O. *Women Writing the West Indies: 1804–1939: "A Hot Place Belonging to Us."* London: Routledge, 2003.
Campbell, James. *Middle Passages: African American Journeys to Africa, 1787–2005*. New York: Penguin Press, 2006.
Campbell, Mavis C. *The Maroons of Jamaica 1655–1796: A History of Resistance, Collaboration and Betrayal*. Trenton, N.J.: Africa World Press, 1990.
———. Review of *Black People in Britain 1555–1833*, by Folarin Shyllon. *ASA Review of Books* 5 (1979): 14–16.

Carretta, Vincent. *Equiano The African: Biography of a Self-Made Man*. Athens: University of Georgia Press, 2005.
———. "Explanatory Notes." In *Thoughts and Sentiments*, 151–98.
———. "Introduction" to *Olaudah Equiano: The Interesting Narrative and Other Writings*, by Olaudah Equiano, edited by Vincent Carretta, ix-xxx. New York and London: Penguin Books, 2003.
———, ed. "Introduction" to *Thoughts and Sentiments on the Evil of Slavery*, by Quobna Ottobah Cugoano, ix-xxviii. New York: Penguin Books, 1999.
———. "Note 170." In *Thoughts and Sentiments*, 173.
———. "Olaudah Equiano or Gustavus Vassa? New Light on an Eighteenth-Century Question of Identity." *Slavery and Abolition* 20, no. 3 (1999): 96–105.
———. "Strangers in Strange Lands." *Eighteenth-Century Studies* 36, no. 2 (2003): 255–58.
———, ed. *Thoughts and Sentiments on the Evil of Slavery*, by Quobna Ottobah Cugoano. New York: Penguin Books, 1999.
———. "Three West Indian Writers of the 1780s Revisited and Revised." *Research in African Literatures* 29, no. 4 (1998): 73–87.
———, ed. *Unchained Voices: An Anthology of Black Authors in the English-Speaking World of the Eighteenth Century*. 1996. Lexington: University Press of Kentucky, 2004.
———, and Philip Gould, eds. *Genius in Bondage: Literature of the Early Black Atlantic*. Lexington: University Press of Kentucky, 2001.
Carson, Clayborne, Emma J. Lapsansky-Werner, and Gary B. Nash. *The Struggle for Freedom: A History of African Americans*. New York: Longman Pearson, 2005.
Cartwright, Keith. *Reading Africa into American Literature: Epics, Fables, and Gothic Tales*. Lexington: University Press of Kentucky, 2002.
Chambers, Douglas B. *Murder at Montpelier: Igbo Africans in Virginia*. Jackson: University of Mississippi Press, 2005.
———. "Tracing the Igbo into the African Diaspora." In *Identity in the Shadow of Slavery*, edited by Paul E. Lovejoy, 55–71. New York: Continuum, 2000.
Chantler, Clyde. *The Ghana Story*. London: Linden Press, 1971.
"The Chosen Suitor." *Greenwood Library of American Folktales. Vol. 2: The South, the Caribbean*, edited by Thomas A. Green, 277–79. Westport, Conn.: Greenwood Press, 2006.
Christensen, Abigail M. H. *Afro-American Folk Lore*. 1898. Freeport, N.Y.: Books for Library Presses, 1971.
Christensen, James Boyd. *Double Descent among the Fanti*. Edited by Genevieve A. Highland. New Haven: Human Relations Area Files (HRAF), 1954.
Christian, Barbara. *Black Feminist Criticism: Perspectives on Black Women Writers*. New York: Pergamon Press, 1985.
Cima, Gay Gibson. "Black and Unmarked: Phillis Wheatley, Mercy Otis Warren, and the Limits of Strategic Anonymity." *Theatre Journal* 52 (2000): 465–95.
Claudel, Calvin, and J.-M. Carrière. "Three Tales from the French Folklore of Louisiana." *Journal of American Folklore* 56, no. 219 (1943): 38–44.
Cleaver, Carole, and Selden Rodman. *Spirits of the Night: The Vaudun Gods of Haiti*. Dallas: Spring Publications, 1992.
Collins, Terrence. "Phillis Wheatley: The Dark Side of the Poetry." *Phylon* 36, no. 1 (1975): 78–88.

Collins-Sibley, G. Michelle. "Who Can Speak? Authority and Authenticity in Olaudah Equiano and Phillis Wheatley." *Journal of Colonialism and Colonial History* 5, no. 3 (2004).

Colvin, Lucie Gallistel. "Islam and the State of Kajoor: A Case of Successful Resistance to Jihad." *Journal of African History* 15, no. 4 (1974): 587–606.

Connolly, R. M. *Social Life in Fanti-Land*. New Haven, Conn.: Human Relations Area Files (HRAF), 1954. (HRAF Microfiche 12: Connolly. G-5).

Courlander, Harold. "Africa's Marks in the Western Hemisphere." In *A Treasury of African-American Folklore*, edited by Harold Courlander, 1–7. 1976. New York: Marlowe and Company, 1996.

Crooks, John Joseph, (Major). *Records Relating to the Gold Coast Settlements from 1750 to 1874*. Belfast, Cork, and Waterford, Dublin: Browne and Nolan Limited, 1923.

Cugoano, Quobna Ottobah. *Thoughts and Sentiments on the Evil of Slavery*. Edited by Vincent Carretta. New York: Penguin Books, 1999.

Curtin, Philip D. *Economic Change in Precolonial Africa: Senegambia in the Era of the Slave Trade*. Madison: University of Wisconsin Press, 1975.

Dabydeen, David, ed. *The Black Presence in English Literature*. Oxford: Manchester University Press, 1985.

Damas, Léon-Gontran. *Veillées Noires*. Ottawa: Leméac, 1972.

Dash, Julie. *Daughters of the Dust*. New York: Dutton, 1997.

Davidson, Basil. *The African Slave Trade: Precolonial History, 1450–1850*. Boston: Brown and Company, 1961.

Davies, Carole Boyce, and Elaine Savory Fido. *Out of Kumbla: Caribbean Women and Literature*. Trenton, N.J.: Africa World Press, 1990.

Davis, David Brion. *The Problem of Slavery in Western Culture*. 1966. New York: Oxford University Press, 1988.

Dayfoot, Arthur Charles. *The Shaping of the West Indian Church: 1492–1962*. Gainesville: University of Florida Press, 1999.

Deandrea, Pietro. *Fertile Crossings: Metamorphoses of Genre in Anglophone West African Literature*. Amsterdam: Rodopi, 2002.

DeCorse, Christopher R. *An Archeology of Elmina: Africans and Europeans on the Gold Coast, 1400–1900*. Washington and London: Smithsonian Institution Press, 2001.

Delany, Martin R. *Official Report of the Niger Valley Exploring Party (1860)*. In *Search for a Place: Black Separatism and Africa*, edited by Howard H. Bell, 27–148. 1860. Ann Arbor: University of Michigan Press, 1969.

Dial, Abdoulaye. *Apprentissage Rapide Du Wolof: Jàng Wolof*. Saint Louis, Sénégal: Abdoulaye Dial, 1994.

Diouf, Sylviane. *Servants of Allah: African Muslims Enslaved in the Americas*. New York and London: New York University Press, 1998.

Diop, Abdoulaye-Bara. *La Famille Wolof: Tradition et Changement*. Paris: Editions Karthala, 1985.

Diop, Birago. "The Flying-Fox." In *Tales of Ahmadou Kumba*, by Birago Diop, edited by Dorothy Blair, 87–92. 1959. Essex, England: Longman, 1989.

———. "Le Taureau de Bouki." In *Les Nouveaux Contes D'Amadou Kumba*, 123–36. Paris: Présence Africaine, 1964.

———. *Mother Crocodile* [Maman-Caïman]. 1961. New York: Delacorte Press, 1981.

Diop, Samba. *The Oral History and Literature of the Wolof People of Waalo, Northern Senegal: The Master of the Word (Griot) in the Wolof Tradition*. Ontario: Edwin Mellen Press, 1995.
Doak, Robin S. *Phillis Wheatley: Slave and Poet*. Minneapolis: Compass Point Books, 2006.
"The Donkeys of Jolof." In *Folktales from the Gambia: Wolof Fictional Narratives*, edited by Emil A. Magel, 154–58. Washington, D.C.: Three Continents Press, 1984.
Dorson, Richard M. *American Negro Folktales*. 1956. New York: Fawcett World Library, 1970.
Dove, Nah. "African Womanism: An Afrocentric Theory." *Journal of Black Studies* 28, no. 5 (1998): 515–39.
Dundes, Alan. "Foreword." In *African Folktales in the New World*, edited by William Bascom, vii-xx. Bloomington: Indiana University Press, 1992.
———. "The Making and Breaking of Friendship as a Structural Frame in African Folk Tales." *Structural Analysis of Oral Tradition*, edited by Pierre Maranda and Elli Kongas Marandas. Philadelphia: University of Pennsylvania Press, 1971.
———. Ed. *Mother Wit from the Laughing Barrel*. 1973. Jackson: University Press of Mississippi, 1990.
Dunlap, Jane. *Poems, Upon Several Sermons, Preached by the Rev'd, and Renowned, George Whitefield, While in Boston*. Boston: Early American Imprints, 1771.
Edeh, Emmanuel M. P. *Toward an Igbo Metaphysics*. Chicago: Loyola University Press, 1985.
Edwards, Bryan. *The History, Civil and Commercial, of the British Colonies in the West Indies*. In *After Africa: Extracts from British Travel Accounts and Journals of the Seventeenth, Eighteenth, and Nineteenth Centuries Concerning the Slaves, their Manners, and Customs in the British West Indies*, edited by Roger D. Abrahams and John F. Szwed, 64–76. New Haven, Conn.: Yale University Press, 1983.
Edwards, Paul. "Three West African Writers of the 1780s." In *The Slave's Narrative*, edited by Charles T. Davis and Henry Louis Gates Jr., 175–98. Oxford and New York: Oxford University Press, 1985.
———, and David Dabydeen. "Black Writers of the Eighteenth and Nineteenth Centuries." In *The Black Presence in English Literature*, edited by David Dabydeen, 50–67. Oxford: Manchester University Press, 1985.
———. "Ottobah Cugoano (John Stuart)." In *Black Writers in Britain 1760–1890: An Anthology*, 39–40. Edinburgh: Edinburgh University Press, 1994.
Ejidike, Okey Martin. "Human Rights in the Cultural Traditions and Social Practice of the Igbo of South-Eastern Nigeria." *Journal of African Law* 43, no. 1 (1999): 71–98.
Elsbree, Oliver Wendell. "Samuel Hopkins and His Doctrine of Benevolence." *New England Quarterly* 8, no. 4 (December 1935): 534–50.
Eltis, David, et al., eds. *The Trans-Atlantic Slave Trade: A Database on CD-ROM Set and Guidebook*. New York: Cambridge University Press, 1999.
Emenanjo, E. Nolue. "Introduction." *Omalinze: A Book of Igbo Folk-Tales*, vii-xx. Ibadan: Oxford University Press, 1977.
Engerman, Stanley L. Review of *The Slave Community: Plantation Life in the Antebellum South*, by John W. Blassingame. *Journal of Political Economy* 81 (1973): 1476.
———. Review of *New Studies in the History of American Slavery*, by Edward E Baptist and Stephanie MH Camp. *Civil War History* 53, no. 2 (June 2007): 203–5.
Ephirim-Donkor, Anthony. *African Spirituality: On Becoming Ancestors*. Asmara, Eritrea, and Trenton, N.J.: Africa World Press, 1997.

Equiano, Olaudah. *The Interesting Narrative of the Life of Olaudah Equiano, Written by Himself.* Edited by Robert J. Allison. Boston and New York: Bedford Press, 1995.
Erickson, John. Review of *Contes Africains*, by Mildred P. Mortimer. *Modern Language Journal* 58, no. 1–2 (1974): 67.
Erkkila, Betsy. "Ethnicity, Literary Theory, and the Grounds of Resistance." *American Quarterly* 47, no. 4 (December 1995): 563–94.
———. "Phillis Wheatley and the Black American Revolution." In *A Mixed Race: Ethnicity in Early America*, edited by Frank Shuffelton, 231–32. New York and Oxford: Oxford University Press, 1993.
———. "Revolutionary Women." *Tulsa Studies in Women's Literature* 6, no. 2 (Autumn 1987): 189–223.
Estell, Kenneth, ed. *The African-American Almanac.* Detroit: Gale Research, 1994.
Eze, Emmanuel Chukwudi, ed. *Race and the Enlightenment: A Reader.* Malden, Mass.: Blackwell, 2001
Fage, J. D. *Ghana: A Historical Interpretation.* Madison: University of Wisconsin Press, 1966.
Faine, Jules. *Philologie Créole: études historiques et étymologiques sur la langue créole d'Haïti.* Port-au-Prince, Haïti: Imprimerie de l'État, 1937.
Ferguson, Moira. *Colonialism and Gender Relations from Mary Wollstonecraft to Jamaica Kincaid.* New York: Columbia University Press, 1993.
———. *The Hart Sisters: Early African Caribbean Writers, Evangelicals, and Radicals.* Lincoln and London: University of Nebraska Press, 1993.
———. "The Literature of Slavery and Abolition." In *The Cambridge History of African and Caribbean Literature, vol. 1*, edited by F. Abiola Irele and Simon Gikandi, 238–54. Cambridge, England: Cambridge University Press, 2004.
———, ed. *Nine Black Women: An Anthology of Nineteenth-Century Writers from the United States, Canada, Bermuda, and the Caribbean.* New York and London: Routledge, 1998.
Festa, Lynn M. *Sentimental Figures of Empire in Eighteenth-Century Britain and France.* Baltimore: Johns Hopkins University Press, 2006.
Fischer, David Hackett. *Albion's Seed: Four British Folkways in America.* New York and Oxford: Oxford University Press, 1989.
Fisher, Humphrey J. *Slavery in the History of Muslim Black Africa.* London: Hurst & Company, 2001.
Flowers, Helen Leneva. *A Classification of the Folktale of the West Indies by Types and Motifs.* New York: Arno Press, 1980.
Fortier, Alcée. *Louisiana Folk-Tales in French Dialect and English Translation, vol. 2.* Boston and New York: American Folklore Society, 1895.
Foster, Frances Smith. *Written by Herself: Literary Production by African American Women, 1746–1892.* Bloomington: Indiana University Press, 1993.
Frazier, E. Franklin. *The Negro Family in the United States.* 1939. Chicago and London: University of Chicago Press, 1968.
Fynn, John Kofi. *The Fante of Ghana c. 1600–1874.* Legon, Ghana: J. K. Fynn, 1989.
———. *Oral Traditions of Fante States.* Legon, Ghana: University of Ghana, Institute of African Studies, 1974.
Gamble, David P. *The Wolof of Senegambia: Together with Notes on the Lebu and the Serer.* London: International African Institute, 1967.

———. *Wolof Stories from Senegambia Mainly From Old Published Sources*. Gambian Studies Series; no. 10b. Edited by David P. Gamble. San Francisco: San Francisco State University, 1987.

Gaspar, David B. *Bondmen and Rebels: A Study of Master-Slave Relations in Antigua, with Implications for Colonial British America*. Baltimore and London: John Hopkins University Press, 1985.

———. "With a Rod of Iron: Barbados Slave Laws as a Model for Jamaica, South Carolina, and Antigua, 1661–1697." *Crossing Boundaries: Comparative History of Black People in Diaspora*, edited by Darlene Clark Hine and Jacqueline McLeod, 343–66. 1999. Bloomington: Indiana University Press, 2001.

Gates, Henry Louis, Jr., ed. *The Classic Slave Narratives*. New York: New American Library, 1987.

———. "Critical Remarks." *Anatomy of Racism*, edited by David Theo Goldberg, 319–29. Minneapolis: University of Minnesota Press, 1990.

———. "The Day When America Decided that Blacks Were of a Species that Could Create Literature." *Journal of Blacks in Higher Education* 5 (Autumn 1994): 50–51.

———. "Introduction." *The Classic Slave Narratives*, xvi. New York: New American Library, 1987.

———. *The Signifying Monkey: A Theory of Afro-American Literary Criticism*. New York and Oxford: Oxford University Press, 1988.

———. *The Trials of Phillis Wheatley: America's First Black Poet and Her Encounters with the Founding Fathers*. New York: Basic Civitas, 2003.

———, and William L. Andrews, eds. "Introduction." *Pioneers of the Black Atlantic: Five Slave Narratives from the Enlightenment*, 1–29. Washington, D.C.: Civitas, 1998.

———, and Charles T. Davis. "Introduction." *The Slave's Narrative*, xxvii. Oxford and New York. Oxford University Press, 1985.

———, and Kwame Anthony Appiah, eds. *The Dictionary of Global Culture*. New York: Alfred A. Knopf, 1997.

———. and Nellie Y. McKay. "From Phillis Wheatley to Toni Morrison: The Flowering of African American Literature." *Journal of Blacks in Higher Education* 14 (Winter 1996): 95–100.

———. and Maria Wolff. "An Overview of Sources on the Life and Work of Juan Latino, the 'Ethiopian Humanist.'" *Research in African Literatures* 29, no. 4 (98): 14–51.

Geiss, Immanuel. *The Pan-African Movement: A History of Pan-Africanism in America, Europe and Africa*. New York: Africana Publishing, 1974.

———. "Pan-Africanism." *Journal of Contemporary History* 4, no. 1 (January 1969): 187–200.

Genovese, Eugene D. *Roll, Jordan, Roll: The World the Slaves Made*. New York: Vintage, 1976.

Gilbert, Anne Hart. "History of Methodism." In *The Hart Sisters: Early African Caribbean Writers, Evangelicals, and Radicals*, edited by Moira Ferguson, 56–75. Lincoln and London: University of Nebraska Press, 1993.

Gilroy, Paul. *Against Race: Imagining Political Culture Beyond the Color Line*. Cambridge, Mass.: Harvard University Press, 2000.

———. *The Black Atlantic: Modernity and Double Consciousness*. Cambridge, Mass.: Harvard University Press, 1993.

Goboldte, Catharine. "Laying on Hands: Women in Imani Faith Temple." In *My Soul Is a Witness: African-American Women's Spirituality*, edited by Gloria Wade-Gayles, 241–52. Beacon Press, 2002.

Gomez, Michael A. *Exchanging our Country Marks: the Transformation of African Identities in the Colonial and Antebellum South*. Chapel Hill: University of North Carolina Press, 1998.

———. *Reversing Sail: A History of the African Diaspora*. New York: Cambridge University Press, 2005.

Gooden, Rosemary D. Review of *Africanisms in American Culture* by Joseph E. Holloway. *Journal of Southern History* 57, no. 4 (November 1991): 733.

Gossman, Norbert J. "William Cuffay: London's Black Chartist." *Phylon* 44, no. 1 (1983): 56–65.

Graham-White, Anthony. *The Drama of Black Africa*. New York: Samuel French, 1974.

Green, Thomas A, ed. *Greenwood Library of American Folktales, vol. 2: The South, the Caribbean*. Westport, Conn.: Greenwood Press, 2006.

Greenberg, Harriet. *Bermuda Alive: Hunter Travel Guide*. Walpole, Mass.: Hunter Publishing, 2000.

Greene, Lorenzo Johnston. *The Negro in Colonial New England*. New York: Atheneum, 1968.

Gruesser, John Cullen. "Afro-American Travel Literature and Africanist Discourse." *Black American Literature Forum* 24, no. 1 (Spring 1990): 5–20.

———. *Black on Black: Twentieth-Century African American Writing about Africa*. Lexington: University Press of Kentucky, 2000.

Hale, Thomas A. *Griots and Griottes: Masters of Words and Music*. Bloomington: Indiana University Press, 1998.

Hall, Gwendolyn Midlo. *Africans in Colonial Louisiana: The Development of Afro-Creole Culture in the Eighteenth Century*. Baton Rouge: Louisiana State University Press, 1992.

Hall, John G. "Antigua and Barbuda." *The Greenwood Encyclopedia of African American Folklore, vol. 1: A-F*, edited by Anand Prahlad, 37–41. Westport, Conn.: Greenwood Press, 2006.

Haller, William. *The Rise of Puritanism*. New York: Harper, 1957.

Hammon, Jupiter. "An Address to Miss Phillis Wheatley [sic], Ethiopian Poetess, in Boston, who Came from Africa at Eight Years of age, and Soon Became acquainted with the Gospel of Jesus Christ." In *The Vintage Book of African American Poetry: 200 Years of Vision, Struggle, Power, Beauty, and Triumph from 50 Outstanding Poets*, edited by Michael S. Harper and Anthony Walton, 3–10. New York: Vintage, 2000.

Handler, Jerome S. "Survivors of the Middle Passage: Life Histories of Enslaved Africans in British America." *Slavery and Abolition: A Journal of Slave and Post-Slave Studies* 23, no. 1 (2002): 24–56.

Harrow, Kenneth W. *Faces of Islam in African Literature*. London: Heinemann, 1991.

Harvey, Paul, ed. *The Oxford Companion to Classical Literature*. Oxford: Clarendon Press, 1969.

Haskins, Jim, Clinton Cox, and Brenda Wilkinson, eds. *Black Stars of Colonial and Revolutionary Times*. Hoboken, N.J.: J. Wiley, 2002.

Hayward, Walter Brownell. *Bermuda Past and Present: A Descriptive and Historical Account of the Somers Islands*. New York: Dodd, Mead, & Company, 1922.

"He Sings to Make the Old Woman Dance." *A Classification of the Folktale of the West Indies by Types and Motifs*, edited by Helen Leneva Flowers, 210. New York, NY: Arno Press, 1980.

Henry, Paget. *Caliban's Reason: Introducing Afro-Caribbean Philosophy*. London: Routledge, 2000.

Herskovits, Melville J. *The Myth of the Negro Past*. Boston: Beacon Press, 1941.

———. *Suriname Folklore*. New York: Columbia University Press, 1936.

Honychurch, Lennox. "Cultural Formations in the Caribbean." *Introduction to the Pan-Caribbean*, edited by Tracey Skelton, 154–72. London: Arnold Publishers, 2004.

Hood, Robert E. *Begrimed and Black: Christian Traditions on Blacks and Blackness*. Minneapolis: Augsburg Fortress, 1994.
Hoving, Isabel. In *Praise of New Travelers: Reading Caribbean Migrant Women's Writing*. Stanford, Calif.: Stanford University Press, 2001.
Howard, Blair. "About Bermuda: History and Government." *Bermuda (Adventure Guide)*, 7–12. Walpole, Mass: Hunter Publishing, 2004.
Hudson, Winthrop S. *Religion in America*. New York: Scribner's, 1965.
Hurston, Zora Neale. "Big Talk." In *Mules and Men*, 77–79. New York: Harper & Row, 1990.
———. *Dust Tracks on a Road*. 1942. New York: Harper Perennial, 1991.
———. *Mules and Men*. New York: Harper & Row, 1990.
"The Hyena Engages the Hare as a Gewel." In *Folktales from the Gambia: Wolof Fictional Narratives*, edited by Emil A. Magel, 53–57. Washington, D.C. Three Continents Press, 1984.
Ihenacho, David. *African Christianity Rises Volume One: A Critical Study of the Catholicism of the Igbo People of Nigeria*. New York: iUniverse, 2004.
Ikuenobe, Polycarp. *Philosophical Perspectives on Communalism and Morality in African Traditions*. Oxford: Lexington Books, 2006.
Irele, F. Abiola. *The African Imagination: Literature in Africa and the Black Diaspora*. New York and Oxford: Oxford University Press, 2001.
Isani, Mukhtar Ali. "Far from 'Gambia's Golden Shore': The Black in Late Eighteenth-Century American Imaginative Literature." *William and Mary Quarterly* 36 (July 1979): 353–72.
———. "'Gambia on My Soul': Africa and the African in the Writings of Phillis Wheatley." *MELUS* 6, no. 1 (1979): 64–72.
Jackson, Tommie Lee. *An Invincible Summer: Female Diasporan Authors*. Trenton, N.J.: Africa World Press, 2001.
Jagne, Siga Fatima. "Mariama Bâ," In *Postcolonial African Writers: A Bio-Bibliographical Critical Sourcebook*, edited by Siga Fatima Jagne and Pushpa Naidu Parekh. London: Greenwood Press, 1998.
James, Cynthia. *The Maroon Narrative: Caribbean Literature in English across Boundaries, Ethnicities, and Centuries*. Portsmouth, N.H.: Heinemann, 2002.
James, Louis. *Caribbean Literature in English*. London and New York: Longman, 1999.
Jefferson, Thomas. *Notes on the State of Virginia*. 1787. Edited by William Peden. Chapel Hill and London: University of North Carolina Press, 1982.
Jehlen, Myra, and Michael Warner. *The English Literatures of America, 1500–1800*. London: Routledge, 1997.
Jenkins, David. *Black Zion: The Return of Afro-Americans and West Indians to Africa*. London: Wildwood House, 1975.
John, Catherine A. *Clear Word and Third Sight: Folk Groundings and Diasporic Consciousness in African Caribbean Writing*. Durham and London: Duke University Press, 2003.
Johnson, Clarence Sholé. "(Re)Conceptualizing Blackness and Making Race Obsolescent." In *White on Black/Black on Black*, edited by George Yancy, 173–202. Landham, Md.: Rowman & Littlefield, 2005.
Johnson, John H. "Bone for a Stump." In John H. Johnson. "Folk-lore from Antigua, British West Indies." *Journal of American Folklore* 34, no. 131 (1921): 56–57.
———. "Folk-lore from Antigua, British West Indies." *Journal of American Folklore* 34, no. 131 (1921): 40–88.

———. "Leaf Disguise." In John H. Johnson. "Folk-lore from Antigua, British West Indies." *Journal of American Folklore* 34, no. 131 (1921): 55–56.

———. "The Three Questions." In John H. Johnson. "Folk-lore from Antigua, British West Indies." *Journal of American Folklore* 34, no. 131 (1921): 74.

———. "Under the Green Oak Tree." In John H. Johnson. "Folk-lore from Antigua, British West Indies." *Journal of American Folklore* 34, no. 131 (1921): 70–71.

Jones, Carolyn M. *Teaching African American Religions*. New York: Oxford University Press, 2005.

Jones-Jackson, Patricia. *When Roots Die: Endangered Traditions on the Sea Islands*. Athens: University of Georgia Press, 1987.

Jordan, Winthrop D. *White over Black: American Attitudes toward the Negro, 1550–1812*. Chapel Hill: University of North Carolina Press, 1968.

Jusdanis, Gregory. *Belated Modernity and Aesthetic Culture: Inventing National Literature*. Minneapolis and Oxford: University of Minnesota Press, 1991.

Kafka, Philipa. *The Great White Way: African American Women Writers and American Success Mythologies*. New York and London: Garland Publishing, 1993.

Kane, Mohamadou. *Essai sur les contes d'Amadou Kumba*. Dakar: Nouvelles Éditions Africaines, 1981.

Kanneh, Kadiatu. *African Identities: Race, Nation and Culture in Ethnography, Pan-Africanism and Black Literature*. London: Routledge, 1998.

Kelleter, Frank. "Ethnic Self-Dramatization and Technologies of Travel in *The Interesting Narrative of the Life of Olaudah Equiano, or Gustavus Vassa, the African, Written by Himself* (1789)." *Early American Literature* 39, no. 1 (2004): 67–84.

Keough, Leyla. "Olaudah Equiano." *Africana: The Encyclopedia of the African and African American Experience*. New York: Basic Civitas, 1999. 684.

———. "Ottobah Cugoano or John Stewart." *Microsoft Encarta Africana*. Microsoft Corporation, 1999.

Kesteloot, Lilyan. *Contes et Mythes du Sénégal*, trans. Ellen Conroy Kennedy. Philadelphia: Temple University Press, 1972.

King, Cameron, and Louis James. "In Solitude for Company: The Poetry of Derek Walcott." In *The Islands in Between: Essays on West Indian Literature*, edited by Louis James, 86–99. Ibadan, Nairobi and London: Oxford University Press, 1968.

King, Janice. *A Passion Heart: The Journey Begins*. Carson City, Nev.: Elm Publishing, 2005.

Klein, Herbert S. *The Atlantic Slave Trade*. Cambridge: Cambridge University Press, 1999.

Klinkowitz, Jerome. "Early Writers: Jupiter Hammon, Phillis Wheatley, and Benjamin Banneker." In *Black American Writers: Bibliographical Essays, vol. 1*, edited by Thomas Inge, Maurice Duke, and Jackson R. Bryer, 1–20. New York: St. Martin's Press, 1978.

Klipple, May Augusta. *African Folktales with Foreign Analogues*. New York: Garland Publishing, 1992.

Kludze, A Kodzo Paaku. *Chieftaincy in Ghana*. Lanham, New York, and Oxford: Austin & Winfield Publishers, 2000.

Knappert, Jan. *Myth and Legends of the Congo*. Nairobi and London: Heinemann, 1971.

Knight, Janice. "Learning the Language of God: Jonathan Edwards and the Typology of Nature." *William and Mary Quarterly* 48, no. 4 (October 1991): 531–51.

Knowles-Borishade, Adetokunbo. "Paradigm for Classical African Orature: Instrument for a Scientific Revolution?" *Journal of Black Studies* 21, no. 4 (June 1991): 488–500.

Kohnova, Marie J. "The Moravians and their Missionaries: a Problem in Americanization." *Mississippi Valley Historical Review* 19, no. 3 (1932): 348–61.
Kopytoff, Igor, and Suzanne Miers, eds. *Slavery in Africa: Historical and Anthropological Perspectives*. Madison: University of Wisconsin Press, 1977.
"Kumba the Orphan Girl." In *Folktales from the Gambia: Wolof Fictional Narratives*, edited by Emil A. Magel, 90–95. Washington, D.C. Three Continents Press, 1984.
"La dernière prise" [the last catch]. In *La Belle Histoire de Leuk-le-Lièvre*, by Léopold Sédar Senghor and Abdoulaye Sadji, 96–105. Paris: Classique Hachette, 1953.
Lambert, Frank. "'I Saw The Book Talk': Slave Readings of the First Great Awakening." *Journal of Negro History* 77, no. 4 (Autumn 1992): 185–98.
Langford, Peter. *Modern Philosophies of Human Nature: Their Emergence from Christian Thought*. Boston: Martinus Nijhoff Publishers, 1986.
Langley, April C. E. *The Black Aesthetic Unbound: Theorizing the Dilemma of Eighteenth-Century African American Literature*. Columbus: The Ohio State University Press, 2008.
Langley, J. Ayodele. *Pan-Africanism and Nationalism in West Africa, 1900–1945: A Study in Ideology and Social Classes*. Oxford: Clarendon Press, 1973.
Latimer, James. "The Foundation of Religious Education in the British West Indies." *Journal of Negro Education* 34, no. 4 (1965): 435–42.
Lauter, Paul, ed. *The Heath Anthology of American Literature*, vol. 1. Lexington and Toronto: D. C. Heath and Company, 1994.
Lazarus-Black, Mindie. *Legitimate Acts and Illegal Encounters: Law and Society in Antigua and Barbuda*. Washington, D.C., and London: Smithsonian Institution Press, 1994.
"Le Lapin Devant Dieu" [The Rabbit Standing before God]." *Wolof Stories from Senegambia Mainly from Old Published Sources*, edited by David P. Gamble, 67–68. San Francisco: San Francisco State University, 1987.
"Le Taureau de Bouki" [The Bull of Bouki]. In *Les Nouveaux Contes D'Amadou Kumba*, by Birago Diop, 123–36. Paris: Présence Africaine, 1964.
Levecq, Christine. "Sentiment and Cosmopolitanism in Olaudah Equiano's Narrative." *African and Black Diaspora: An International Journal* 1, no. 1 (January 2008): 13–30.
Levernier, James A. "Phillis Wheatley and the New England Clergy." *Early American Literature* 26 (March 1991): 21–38.
Levin, Amy K. *Africanism and Authenticity in African-American Women's Novels*. Gainesville: University Press of Florida, 2003.
Levine, Lawrence W. *Black Culture and Black Consciousness: African-American Folk Thought from Slavery To Freedom*. Oxford, London, and New York: Oxford University Press, 1977.
Lewis, Gordon K. *Slavery, Imperialism, and Freedom: Studies in English Radical Thought*. New York and London: Monthly Review Press, 1978.
Leymarie, Isabelle. *Les Griots Wolof du Sénégal*. Paris: Maisonneuve & Larose, 1999.
Ligon, Richard. "A True and Extract History of the Island of Barbadoes." In *After Africa: Extracts from British Travel Accounts and Journals of the Seventeenth, Eighteenth, and Nineteenth Centuries Concerning the Slaves, their Manners, and Customs in the British West Indies*, edited by Roger D. Abrahams and John F. Szwed, 51–64. New Haven, Conn.: Yale University Press, 1983.
"The Lion's Treasured Goat." In *Folktales from the Gambia: Wolof Fictional Narratives*, edited by Emil A. Magel, 66–69. Washington, D.C.: Three Continents Press, 1984.
Lloyd, Suzette Harriet. *Sketches of Bermuda*. 1829. London: James Cochran and Company, 1835.

Logan, Shirley W. *We Are Coming: The Persuasive Discourse of Nineteenth-Century Black Women.* Carbondale: Southern Illinois University Press, 1999.

Lorimer, Douglas A. "Black Resistance to Slavery and Racism in Eighteenth-Century England." In *Essays on the History of Blacks in Britain: From Roman Times to the Mid-Twentieth Century,* edited by Jagdish S. Gundara and Ian Duffield Brookfield, 58–80. Vermont: Ashgate, 1992.

Lovejoy, Arthur P. *The Great Chain of Being: A Study of the History of an Idea.* Cambridge, Mass.: Harvard University Press, 1964.

Lovejoy, Paul E. "Identifying Enslaved Africans in the African Diaspora." *Identity in the Shadow of Slavery,* edited by Paul Lovejoy, 1–29. London and New York: Continuum, 2000.

———, ed. *The Ideology of Slavery.* Beverly Hills, Calif.: Sage, 1981.

———. *Transformations in Slavery: A History of Slavery in Africa.* 1983. Cambridge, England: Cambridge University Press, 2000.

Lowe, John. *Jump at the Sun: Zora Neale Hurston's Cosmic Comedy.* Urbana: University of Illinois Press, 1994.

Magel, Emil A. "The Dog and Monkey Build a Town." *Folktales from the Gambia: Wolof Fictional Narratives,* 141–43. Washington, D.C. Three Continents Press, 1984.

———. ed. *Folktales from the Gambia: Wolof Fictional Narratives.* Washington, D.C.: Three Continents Press, 1984.

———. *Hare and Hyena: Symbols of Honor and Shame in the Oral Narratives of the Wolof of Senegambia.* Ph.D. Thesis. University of Wisconsin, 1977.

———. "The Hare Seeks Endowments from Allah." *Folktales from the Gambia: Wolof Fictional Narratives,* 179–81. Washington, D.C.: Three Continents Press, 1984.

———. "The Hyena Engages the Hare as a Gewel." *Folktales from the Gambia: Wolof Fictional Narratives,* 53–57. Washington, D.C.: Three Continents Press, 1984.

Manix, Daniel P. *Black Cargoes: A History of the Atlantic Slave Trade, 1518–1865.* New York: Viking Press, 1962.

Manning, Frank E. *Black Clubs in Bermuda: The Ethnography of a Play Word.* Ithaca, N.Y.: Cornell University Press, 1973.

Margulis, Jennifer. Review of *An African's Life: The Life and Times of Olaudah Equiano, 1745–1797,* by James Walvin. *African Studies Review* 43, no. 2 (September 2000): 174–75.

Marshall, Barbara J. "Kitchen Table Talk: J. California Cooper's Use of Nommo—Female Bonding and Transcendence." In *Language and Literature in the African American Imagination,* edited by Carol Aisha Blackshire-Belay, 91–102. Westport, Conn.: Greenwood Press, 1992.

Martin, Toni. *The Pan-African Connection: From Slavery to Garvey and Beyond.* Dover, Mass.: Majority Press, 1983.

Mason, Julian D. "Introduction to the Poems of Phillis Wheatley." In *Modern Critical Views: African-American Poets: Phillis Wheatley Through Melvin B. Tolson,* edited by Harold Bloom, 47–68. Philadelphia: Chelsea House Publishers, 2003.

———. *The Poems of Phillis Wheatley.* Chapel Hill: University of North Carolina Press, 1989.

Mason, Van Wyck. "Bermuda's Pequots." *Harvard Alumni Bulletin* 39 (1937): 616–20.

Matson, R. Lynn. "Phillis Wheatley--Soul Sister?" *Phylon* 33, no. 3 (1972): 222–30.

Mazama, Ama. "The Afrocentric Paradigm." In *The Afrocentric Paradigm,* edited by Ama Mazama, 3–34. Trenton, N.J.: Africa World Press, 2002.

Mbiti, John S. *Concepts of God in Africa.* New York: Praeger Publishers, 1970.

———. *Introduction to African Religion.* 1975. Oxford, England: Heinemann Educational Books, 1991.

McKoy, Sheila Smith. "The Limbo Contest: Diaspora Temporality and Its Reflection in 'Praisesong for the Widow' and 'Daughters of the Dust.'" *Callaloo.* 22, no. 1 (Winter 1999): 208–22.

McKnee, Lisa. "The Black and the White: Race and Oral Poetry in Mauritania." In *The Desert Shore: Literatures of the Sahel,* edited by Christopher Wise, 127–38. Boulder, Colo.: Lynne Rienner, 2001.

———. *Selfish Gifts: Senegalese Women's Autobiographical Discourses.* Albany: State University of New York Press, 2000.

Meillassoux, Claude. *The Anthropology of Slavery: The Womb of Iron and Gold.* Chicago: University of Chicago Press, 1991.

"Methodism." *The Columbia-Viking Desk Encyclopedia,* 692. New York: Viking Press, 1968.

Miller, Joseph C. "The Integrities of History in Africa." Working Paper, 22 March 2005.

———. "Oral Tradition and History: An Agenda for Angola." Seminário Construindo a História Angolana: As Fontes e a sua Interpretação. Luanda-4–8 de agosto de 1997. Arquivo Histórico Nacional (Comissão Nacional para as Comemorações dos Descobrimentos Portugueses), 1997.

———. "History and Africa/Africa and History." *American Historical Review* 104, no. 1 (February 1999): 1–32.

———. *Way of Death: Merchant Capitalism and the Angolan Slave Trade, 1730–1830.* Madison: University of Wisconsin Press, 1988.

Miller, Perry. *Errands into the Wilderness.* 1956. New York: Harper & Row, 1964.

Milsome, John R. *Olaudah Equiano: The Slave Who Helped End the Slave Trade.* London: Longmans, 1969.

Mintz, Sidney, and Richard Price. *An Anthropological Approach to the Afro-American Past: A Caribbean Perspective.* Philadelphia: Institute for the Study of Human Issues, 1976.

Morgan, Edmund S. *American Slavery, American Freedom: The Ordeal of Colonial Virginia* 1975. New York and London: Norton, 1995.

Mortimer, Mildred P. *Contes Africains.* Boston: Houghton, 1972.

N'Diaye, Diana Baird, and Gorgui N'Diaye. "Creating the Vertical Village: Senegalese Traditions of Immigration and Transnational Cultural Life." In *The New African Diaspora in North America: Trends, Community Building, and Adaptation,* edited by Kwadwo Konadu-Agyemang, Baffour K. Takyi, and John Arthur, 96–106. Lanham, Md.: Lexington Books, 2006.

Napierkowski, Marie Rose. "To His Excellency General Washington: Introduction." *Poetry for Students: Presenting Analysis, Context and Criticism,* vol. 13, edited by Marie Rose Napierkowski, 211–18. Detroit: Gale, 1998.

Njoku, John E. Eberegbulam. *The Igbos of Nigeria: Ancient Rites, Changes and Survival.* Lewiston, N.Y., Queenston, and Ontario. Edwin Mellen Press, 1990.

Nobles, Wade W. "African Philosophy Foundations for Black Psychology." In Seeking *the Sakhu: Foundational Writings for an African Psychology,* edited by Wade W. Nobles, 5–22. Chicago: Third World P, 2006.

Nwankwo, Arthur. "The Igbo and the Tradition of Politics: An Overview." In *The Igbo and the Tradition of Politics,* edited by U. D. Anyanwu and J. C. U. Aguwa, 3–8. Uturu, Nigeria: Centre for Igbo Studies, Abia State University, 1993.

Nwokeji, G. Ugo. Review of *Equiano the African: Biography of a Self-Made Man,* by Vincent Carretta. *Journal of American History* 93, no. 3 (December 2006): 840–41.

Odell, Margarita Matilda. *Memoir and Poems of Phillis Wheatley: A Native of Africa and a Slave.* Boston: George W. Light, 1834.

Offiong, Daniel A. "The Status of Slaves in Igbo and Ibibio of Nigeria." *Phylon* 46, no. 1 (1985): 49–57.

Ojo-Ade, Femi. "Africa and America: A Question of Continuities, Cleavage, and Dreams Deferred." In *Of Dreams Deferred, Dead of Alive: African Perspectives on African-American Writers,* edited Femi Ojo-Ade, 1–27. Westport, Conn.: Greenwood Press, 1996.

Okafor, Dubem. "'Over-Determined Contradictions': History and Ideology in Achebe's *A Man of the People.*" In *Meditations on African Literature,* edited by Dubem Okafor, 89–100. Westport, Conn.: Greenwood Press, 2001.

Okeke, Uche. *Tales of Land of Death: Igbo Folktales.* New York: Doubleday, 1971.

Okpewho, Isidore. *African Oral Literature: Backgrounds, Character, and Continuity.* Bloomington: Indiana University Press, 1992.

———. *The Epic in Africa: Towards A Poetics of the Oral Performance.* New York: Columbia University Press, 1979.

Olmos, Margarite Fernández, and Lizabeth Paravisini-Gebert. *Sacred Possessions: Vodou, Santería, Obeah and the Caribbean.* New Brunswick: Rutgers University Press, 1997.

O'Neale, Sondra. "A Slave's Subtle War: Phillis Wheatley's Use of Biblical Myth and Symbol." *Early American Literature* 21, no. 2 (September 1986): 144–65.

Orban, Katalin. "Dominant and Submerged Discourses in the Life of Olaudah Equiano (or Gustavus Vassa?)" *African American Review* 27, no. 4 (Winter 1993): 655–64.

Oriji, John Nwachimereze. *Traditions of Igbo Origin: A Study of Pre-Colonial Population Movements in Africa.* New York: Peter Lang, 1994.

Osabu-Kle, Daniel Tetteh. "The African Reparation Cry: Rationale, Estimate, Prospects, and Strategies." *Journal of Black Studies* 30, no. 3 (January 2000): 331–50.

Packwood, Cyril Outerbridge. *Chained on the Rock: Slavery in Bermuda.* New York and Bermuda: Eliseo Torres & Sons, 1975.

Palmer, Colin. "The African Diaspora." *Black Scholar* 30, no. 3/4 (2000): 56–59.

Pandian, Jacob, and Susan Parman. *The Making of Anthropology: The Semiotics of Self and Other in the Western Tradition.* New Delhi, India: Vedams, 2004.

Paquet, Sandra Pouchet. *Caribbean Autobiography: Cultural Identity and Self-Representation.* Madison: University of Wisconsin Press, 2002.

———. "The Heartbeat of a West Indian Slave: The History of Mary Prince." *African-American Review* 26, no. 1 (1992): 131–46.

———. Review of *The Hart Sisters: Early African Caribbean Writers, Evangelicals, and Radicals,* by Moira Ferguson. *African American Review* 29, no. 3 (Autumn 1995): 517–19.

Pandian, Jacob, and Susan Parman. *The Making of Anthropology: The Semiotics of Self and Other in the Western Tradition.* New Delhi, India: Vedams, 2004.

Park, Mungo. "Document 2: Mungo Park Accompanying a Slave Coffle in West Africa, 1797." In *The Atlantic Slave Trade: Greenwood Guides to Historic Events, 1500–1900,* ed. Johannes Postma, 110–17. Westport and London: Greenwood Press, 2003.

Parrington, Vernon Louis. *Main Currents in American Thought, Volume 1: The Colonial Mind, 1620–1800.* 1927. Norman and London: University of Oklahoma Press, 1987.

Parsons, Elsie Worthington Clews. "Bermuda Folklore." *Journal of American Folklore* 38, no. 148 (April-June 1925): 239–66.

———. *Folk-lore of the Antilles, French and English.* New York: American Folklore Society, 1933.

———. "He Sings to Make the Old Woman Dance." In *Folk-lore of the Antilles, French and English*, 314–15.

———. "Hurricane Coming." In *Folk-lore of the Antilles, French and English*, 309–10.

———. "Monkey Husband." In *310*. New York: American Folklore Society, 1933.

———. "The Ordeal." In *Folk-lore of the Antilles, French and English*, 310–11.

Patterson, Orlando. *Slavery and Social Death: A Comparative Study*. Cambridge, Mass.: Harvard University Press, 1982.

Peel, J. D. Y., Colin Murray, and Suzette Heald, eds. *Islamic and Caste Knowledge Practices Among Haalpulaar'en in Senegal*. Edinburgh: Edinburgh University Press, 2004.

Pettinger, Alasdair. Introduction to "Ottobah Cugoano." In *Always Elsewhere: Travels of the Black Atlantic*, edited by Alasdair Pettinger, 14–16. London and New York: Cassell, 1998.

Phillips, Caryl, ed. *Extravagant Strangers: A Literature of Belonging*. New York: Vintage Books, 1997.

Piersen, William D. *Black Legacy: America's Hidden Heritage*. Amherst: University of Massachusetts Press, 1993.

———. *Black Yankees: The Development of an Afro-American Subculture in Eighteenth-Century New England*. Amherst: University of Massachusetts Press, 1988.

Pittman, Frank Wesley. "Fetishism, Witchcraft, and Christianity among the Slaves." *Journal of Negro History* 11, no. 4 (1926): 650–68.

"Playing Dead." In "Folk-lore from Antigua, British West Indies" by John H. Johnson. *Journal of American Folklore* 34, no. 131 (1921): 58–59.

Pollard, Verma. "To The Children." *Anansesem: A Collection of Caribbean Folk Tales, Legends and Poems for Juniors*, vii–viii. Kingston, Jamaica: Longman Jamaica, 1985.

Postma, Johannes. *The Atlantic Slave Trade: Greenwood Guides to Historic Events, 1500–1900*. Westport and London: Greenwood Press, 2003.

Potkay, Adam, and Sandra Burr. Introduction to *Black Atlantic Writers of the Eighteenth Century: Living the New Exodus and the Americas*, edited by Adam Potkay and Sandra Burr, 1–20. New York: St. Martin's Press, 1995.

Prince, Mary. *The History of Mary Prince: A West Indian Slave. Related by Herself*. 1831. In *The Classic Slave Narratives*, edited by Henry Louis Gates Jr., 183–242. New York and Scarborough: New American Library, 1987.

Puckett, Newbell Niles. *Folk Beliefs of the Southern Negro*. London: University of North Carolina Press, 1926.

Pudaloff, Ross J. "No Change without Purchase: Olaudah Equiano and the Economies of Self and Market." *Early American Literature* 40, no. 3 (September 2005): 499–527.

Quarles, Benjamin. "A Phillis Wheatley Letter." *Journal of Negro History* 34, no. 4 (October 1949): 462–64.

Ramphal, Shridath. *Time for Action: Report Of The West Indian Commission*. Kingston, Jamaica: University of West Indies Press, 1993.

Ransford, Oliver. *The Slave Trade: The Story of the Transatlantic Slavery*. London: Fakenham and Reading, 1971.

Rattray, Robert Sutherland Capt. *Akan-Ashanti Folk-Tales (Collected and Translated by Capt. R. S. Rattray and Illustrated by Africans of the Gold Coast Colony)*. 1930. New Haven: Human Relations Area Files [HRAF], 1953. (HRAF Microfiche 15: Rattray. E-5).

Rawley, James A. "The World of Phillis Wheatley." *New England Quarterly* 50, no. 4. (December 1977): 666–77.

Reagon, Bernice Johnson. "African Diaspora Women: The Making of Cultural Workers." In *Women in Africa and the Diaspora*, edited by Rosalyn Terborg-Penn, Sharon Harley, and Andrea Benton Rushing, 167–80. Washington, D.C.: Howard University Press, 1987.

Reindorf, Rev. Carl Christian. *History of the Gold Coast and Asante: Based on Traditions and Historical Facts, Comprising A Period of More Than Three Centuries from About 1500 to 1860*. 1895. Cape Coast and Accra: the Gold Coast District Book Depot, 1966.

Reiss, Oscar. *Blacks in Colonial America*. Jefferson, N.C.: McFarland & Company, 1997.

Reyes, Angelita. *Mothering across Cultures: Postcolonial Representations*. Minneapolis and London: University of Minnesota Press, 2002.

Rice, Alan. *Radical Narratives of the Black Atlantic*. New York: Continuum, 2003.

———. "'Who's Eating Whom': The Discourse of Cannibalism in the Literature of the Black Atlantic from Equiano's Travels to Toni Morrison's *Beloved*." *Research in African Literature* 29, no. 4 (1998): 107–21.

Rice, Alan J. Review of *Romanticism and Slave Narratives: Transatlantic Testimonies*, by Helen Thomas. *Criticism* 43, no. 4 (2001): 454–58.

Richburg, Keith B. *Out of America: A Black Man Confronts Africa*. New York: Basic Books, 1997.

Roberts, John W. *From Trickster to Badman: The Black Folk Hero in Slavery and Freedom*. Philadelphia: University of Pennsylvania Press, 1989.

Robertson, Claire. "Africa into the Americas?: Slavery and Women, the Family, and the Gender Division of Labor." *More than Chattel: Black Women and Slavery in the Americas*, edited by David Barry Gaspar and Darlene Clark Hine, 3–42. Bloomington: Indiana University Press, 1996.

Robinson, Lisa Clayton. "Bermuda." *Microsoft Encarta Africana*. Microsoft Corporation, 1999.

Robinson, William H. *Black New England Letters: The Uses of Writings in Black New England*. Boston: Boston Public Library, 1977.

———. *Critical Essays on Phillis Wheatley*. Boston: G. K. Hall, 1982.

———. "On Phillis Wheatley and Her Boston." *Phillis Wheatley and Her Writings*, 3-86. New York and London: Garland Publishing, 1984.

———. *Phillis Wheatley in the Black American Beginnings*. Detroit: Broadside Press, 1975.

———, and Phillip Richards. "Phillis Wheatley." In *The Heath Anthology of American Literature*, vol. 1, edited by Paul Lauter, 1060. Lexington and Toronto: D. C. Heath and Company, 1994.

Rodney, Walter. "African Slavery and Other Forms of Social Oppression on the Upper Guinea Coast in the Context of the Atlantic Slave-Trade." *Journal of African History* 7, no. 3 (1966): 431–43.

Rogal, Samuel J. "Phillis Wheatley's Methodist Connection." *Black American Literature Forum* (Spring and Summer 1987): 85–95.

Ross, Eric. "Touba: A Spiritual Metropolis in the Modern World." *Canadian Journal of African Studies* 29, no. 2 (1995) 222–59.

Rucker, Walter C. *The River Flows On: Black Resistance, Culture, and Identity Formation in Early America*. Baton Rouge: Louisiana State University Press, 2006.

Sabino, Robin, and Jennifer Hall. "The Path Not Taken: Cultural Identity in the Interesting Life of Olaudah Equiano." *MELUS* 24, no. 1 (1999).

Saillant, John. "Antiguan Methodism and Antislavery Activity: Anne and Elizabeth Hart in the Eighteenth-Century Black Atlantic." *Church History* 69, no. 1 (March 2000): 86–115.

Salkey, Andrew. *Caribbean Folk Tales and Legends*. London: Bogle-L'Ouverture Publications, 1980.
Sallah, Tijan. *Wolof*. New York: Rosen Publishing Group, 1996.
Samuels, Wilfred D. "Disguised Voice in *The Interesting Narrative of Olaudah Equiano, or Gustavus Vassa, the African*." *Black American Literature Forum* 19, no. 2 (Summer 1985): 64–69.
Sands, Rosita M. "Carnival Celebrations in Africa and the New World: Junkanoo and the Black Indians of Mardi Gras." *Black Music Research Journal* 11, no. 1 (Spring 1991): 75–92.
Sarbah, John Mensah. *Fanti Customary Laws: A Brief introduction to the Principles of the Native Laws And Customs of the Fanti and Akan Districts of the Gold Coast with a Report of Some Cases thereon Decided in the Law Courts*, ed. Hollis R. Lynch. London: Cass, 1968.
Sarr, Alioune. "Les Guêlawars." W*olof Stories from Senegambia Mainly From Old Published Sources*. Gambian Studies Series; no. 10b, edited by David P. Gamble, 143–44. San Francisco: San Francisco State University, 1987.
Scott, James C. *Domination and the Arts of Resistance: Hidden Transcripts*. New Haven, Conn.: Yale University Press, 1990.
———. *Weapons of the Weak: Every Forms of Peasant Resistance*. New Haven: Yale University Press, 1985.
Searing, James F. *West African Slavery and Atlantic Commerce: The Senegal River Valley, 1700–1860*. New York: Cambridge University Press, 1993.
Seeber, Edward D. "Phillis Wheatley." *Journal of Negro History* 24, no. 3 (July 1939): 259–62.
Segal, Ronald. *The Black Diaspora: Five Centuries of the Black Experience Outside Africa*, New York: Noonday Press, 1995.
Senghor, Léopold Sédar, and Abdoulaye Sadji. "Bouki rossé par les aveugles." In *La Belle Histoire de Leuk-le-Lièvre*, 62–63.
———. *La Belle Histoire de Leuk-le-Lièvre*. Paris: Classique Hachette, 1953.
———. *Les Aventures de Leuk-Le-Lièvre*. 1953. Dakar and Abidjan: Les Nouvelles Editions Africaines, 1975.
Senior, Olive. "Ancestral Poem." In *The Penguin Book of Caribbean Verse in English*, edited by Paula Burnett, 320–21. New York: Penguin, 1986.
Sharpe, Jenny. *Ghosts of Slavery: A Literary Archaeology of Black Women's Lives*. Minneapolis and London: University of Minnesota Press, 2003
Shields, John C., ed. *The Collected Works of Phillis Wheatley*. New York and Oxford: Oxford University Press, 1988.
———. "Phillis Wheatley's Struggle for Freedom." In *The Collected Works of Phillis Wheatley*, edited by John C. Shields, 229–70. New York and Oxford: Oxford University Press, 1988.
———. "Phillis Wheatley." In *African American Writers*, edited by Valerie Smith et al., 773–92. New York: Scribner, 2001.
———. "Phillis Wheatley's Use of Classicism." *American Literature* 52, no. 1 (March 1980): 97–111.
———. "Wheatley, Phillis (Peters)." In *Black Women in America: An Historical Encyclopedia*, edited by Darlene Clark Hine, 1251–55. Brooklyn, N.Y.: Carlson, 1993.
Shyllon, Folarin. *Black People in Britain 1555–1833*. London, New York, and Ibadan: Oxford University Press and the Institute of Race Relations, 1977.
Smith, James E. *Slavery in Bermuda*, New York: Vantage Press, 1976.

Smitherman, Geneva. *Talking and Testifying: The Language of Black America*. Boston: Houghton Mifflin Company, 1977.

Socé, Ousmane. *Contes et Légendes d'Afrique Noire*. Paris: Nouvelles Editions Latines, 1962.

Steady, Filomina Chioma. "The Black Woman Cross-Culturally: An Overview." In *The Black Woman Cross-Culturally*, edited by Filomina Chioma Steady, 7–41. Rochester, Vt.: Schenkman Books, 1985.

Steele, Thomas J. "The Figure of Columbia: Phillis Wheatley plus George Washington." *New England Quarterly* 54, no. 2 (June 1981): 264–66.

Stein, Joshua B. *Claude Goldsmid Montefiore on the Ancient Rabbis: The Second Generation of Reform Judaism in Britain*. Providence, R.I.: Brown Judaic Studies, 1977.

Stein, Mark. "Olaudah Equiano: Representation and Reality: An International One-Day Conference." *Early American Literature* 38, no. 3 (2003): 543–45.

Stewart, James. "Transdisciplinary African American Studies Approaches and Implications: A Collective Interview with James Stewart," by Itibari M. Zulu and Karanja Keita Carroll. *Journal of Pan African Studies* 2, no. 2 (March 2008): 85–95.

Stuckey, Sterling. *Going Through the Storm: The Influence of African American Art in History*. New York and Oxford: Oxford University Press, 1994.

———. *Slave Culture: Nationalist Theory and the Foundations of Black America*. New York and Oxford: Oxford University Press, 1987.

Sylla, Assane. *La Philosophie Morale des Wolof*. Dakar, Sénégal: Sankoré, 1978.

Terborg-Penn, Rosalyn. "Black Women in Resistance: A Cross-Cultural Perspective." In *Resistance: Studies in African, Caribbean, and Afro-American History*, edited by Gary Y. Okihiro, 188–209. Amherst: University of Massachusetts Press, 1986.

Thatcher, B. B. (Benjamin Bussey), ed. *Memoir of Phillis Wheatley, a Native African and a Slave* (Electronic Edition), 1–36. 1834. Chapel Hill: University of North Carolina Press, 2001.

Thompson, Stith. *The Folktale*. New York: Dryden Press, 1946.

Thornton, John. *Africa and Africans in the Making of the Atlantic World, 1400–1800*. Cambridge, England: Cambridge University Press, 1998.

Thorpe, Marjorie. "Keynote Address: Second Conference of Caribbean Women Writers." *Callaloo* 13, no. 3 (1990): 526–31.

"The Three Questions." *A Classification of the Folktale of the West Indies by Types and Motifs*, edited by Helen Leneva Flowers, 280. New York: Arno Press, 1980.

Thwaites, Elizabeth Hart. "History of Methodism," "Hymns and Verse," and "Letter to A Friend." In *The Hart Sisters: Early African Caribbean Writers, Evangelicals, and Radicals*, edited by Moira Ferguson, 89–111. 1804. Lincoln and London: University of Nebraska Press, 1993.

"To The Public." In *Poems of Phillis Wheatley: A Native African and A Slave*. Bedford, Mass.: Applewood Books, 1995.

Toppin, Edgar A. *A Biographical History of Blacks in America Since 1528*. New York: David McKay, 1971.

The Trans-Atlantic Slave Trade: A Database on CD-ROM Set and Guidebook. Edited by David Eltis et al. New York: Cambridge University Press, 1999.

Turner, Lorenzo D. *Africanisms in the Gullah Dialect*. Chicago: University of Chicago Press, 1949.

Turner, Mary. *Slaves and Missionaries: The Disintegration of Jamaican Slave Society, 1787–1834*. Urbana: University of Illinois Press, 1982.

Turner, Michael J. "The Limits of Abolition: Government, Saints and the 'African Question,' c. 1780–1820." *English Historical Review* 112, no. 446 (1997): 319–57.

Turner, Prince. *Slaves and Missionaries: The Disintegration of Jamaican Slave Society, 1787–1834.* Urbana, Chicago, and London: University of Illinois Press, 1982.

Uchendu, Victor Chikezie. *The Igbo of Southeast Nigeria.* New York: Rinehart and Winston, 1965. New Haven, Conn.: HRAF, 2003. (Computer File. "As seen in the eHRAF Collection of Ethnography on the Web, [July 14, 2005].")

V., J., A. W., and N. G. *A Genuine Narrative of the Intended Conspiracy of the Negroes at Antigua.* 1737. New York: Arno Press, 1972.

Walker, David. *Walker's Appeal, in Four Articles; Together with a Preamble, to the Coloured Citizens of the World, but in Particular, and Very Expressedly, to Those of the United States of America, Written in Boston, State of Massachusetts, September 28, 1829.* 1830. Electronic Edition. Chapel Hill: University of North Carolina, Academic Affairs Library, 2001.

Walker, Sheila S. *African Roots/American Cultures: Africa in the Creation of the Americas.* Landham, Md.: Rowman & Littlefield, 2001.

Walvin, James. *Making the Black Atlantic: Britain and the African Diaspora.* London and New York: Cassell, 2000.

Wamba, Philippe. *Kinship: A Family's Journey in Africa and America.* New York: Dutton Book, 1999.

Warner, Keith Q. *Critical Perspectives on Leon Gontran Damas.* Boulder, Colo.: Lynne Rienner Publishers, 1988.

Warner-Lewis, Maureen. "Caribbean Verbal Arts." *African Folklore: An Encyclopedia*, edited by Philip M. Peek and Kwesi Yankah, 45–47. New York: Routledge, 2004.

———. *Guinea's Other Suns: The African Dynamic in Trinidad Culture.* Dover, Mass.: Majority Press, 1991.

Wesley, Charles H. "The Negro in the West Indies, Slavery and Freedom." *Journal of Negro History* 17, no. 1 (1932): 51–66.

"Wesley, John." *Microsoft Encarta Reference library.* CD-ROM. Microsoft Corporation. 1993–2004.

Westhauser, Karl E. "Revisiting the Jordan Thesis: 'White over Black' in Seventeenth-Century England and America." *Journal of Negro History* 85, no. 3 (2000): 113–14, 112–22.

"What Darkens the Hole." In "Bermuda Folklore," by Elsie Clews Parsons. *Journal of American Folklore* 38, no. 148 (April-June 1925): 241.

Wheatley, Phillis. *The Collected Works of Phillis Wheatley*, edited by John C. Shields. New York: Oxford University Press, 1988.

Wheeler, Roxann. "Betrayed By Some of My Own Complexions." In *Genius in Bondage: Literature of the Early Black Atlantic*, edited by Vincent Carretta and Philip Gould, 17–38. Lexington: University Press of Kentucky, 2001.

White, Deborah Gray. *Ar' n't I a Woman: Female Slaves in the Plantation South.* New York and London: W. W. Norton & Company, 1999.

Wilberforce, William. *An Appeal to the Religion, Justice, and Humanity of the Inhabitants of the British Empire in Behalf of the Negro Slaves in the West Indies* (*Slavery in the West Indies*), edited by William Wilberforce and Zachary Macaulay, 1–56. 1823. New York: Negro University Press, 1969.

Wilcox, Kirstin. "The Body into Print: Marketing Phillis Wheatley." *American Literature* 71, no. 1 (March 1999): 1–29.

Wilentz, Gay. *Binding Cultures: Black Women Writers in Africa and the Diaspora.* Bloomington: Indiana University Press, 1992.
Williams, Adebayo. "Of Human Bondage and Literary Triumph: Hannah Crafts and the Morphology of the Slave Narrative." *Research in African Literatures* 34, no. 1 (Spring 2003): 137–50.
Williams, Eric Eustace. *Capitalism and Slavery.* 1944. New York: Capricorn Books, 1966.
Williams, Kenny J. "Phillis Wheatley: 1754-December 5, 1784." *Dictionary of Literary Biography, Volume 50: Afro-American Writers before the Harlem Renaissance*, edited by Trudier Harris, 245–59. Chapel Hill: University of North Carolina and the Gale Group, 1986.
Williams, Saul. *The Dead Emcee Scrolls: The Lost Teachings of Hip-Hop and Connected Writings.* New York: MTV Books/Pocket Books; London: Turnaround. 2006.
Williamson, Sidney George. *Akan Religion and the Christian Faith: A Comparative Study of the Impact of Two Religions.* Accra, Ghana: Ghana Universities Press, 1965.
Wilson-Fall, Wendy, and Charles Sow. "Kimoh, dar you are!" *Journal of Pan-African Studies* 1, no. 11 (November 2007): 19–40.
Wiltse, Charles, ed. *David Walker's Appeal.* New York: Hill and Wang, 1965.
Woodard, Judith A. *The Holy Spirit and Prayer.* Longwood, Fla.: Xulon Press, 2006.
Woodward, Helena. *African-British Writings in the Eighteenth Century: The Politics of Race and Reason.* Westport and London: Greenwood Press, 1999.
Worger, William H., et al., eds. *Africa and the West: A Documentary History from the Slave Trade to Independence.* Phoenix, Ariz.: Oryx Press, 2001.
Yankah, Kwesi. *Speaking for the Chief: Okyeame and the Politics of Akan Royal Oratory.* Bloomington and Indianapolis: Indiana University Press, 1995.
Yarak, Larry W. "The Kingdom of Wasa and Fante Diplomacy in Eighteenth-Century Ghana." *Ghana in Africa and the World*, edited by Toyin Falola, 141–54. Trenton, N.J.: Africa World Press, 2003.
Young, Robert J. C. *Postcolonialism: An Historical Introduction.* Malden, Mass.: Blackwell Publishing, 2001.

Index

abolitionists: black, and slavery, 91, 95, 102, 106, 159, 160; Cugoano and, 69, 71–72; Equiano and, 106, 128, 130; P. Wheatley and, 56, 60; white, and slavery, 82, 101–2, 106, 130, 159–60, 201, 204
Achebe, Chinua, 131–32
Acholonu, Catherine O., 108, 109, 132–33, 136
Adeleke, Tunde, 89, 91, 153
adornments: defined, 149, 210; in *Poems*, 43
Africa: in African American literature, 4, 11–12; in black Atlantic studies, 6; in *Interesting Narrative*, 3, 11, 106, 115, 130, 133–40; in *Poems*, 3, 11, 21, 22, 24, 33–38, 60–61; in *Thoughts*, 3, 76, 78, 79, 80, 81–94, 97–100, 102–4; Western blacks and, 3, 90–93
African American folklore: and African folklore, 13, 14–15, 23
African-centered method, 7, 112
African diaspora, 3, 10, 72, 86, 108, 189, 197. *See also* black diaspora
African folktales: and black diasporan folktales, 16–17, 18, 19, 56–57; and black popular culture, 209–10; importance of, ix, 6, 14, 209
Africanism: in black diaspora, 5–6, 13, 181–82; defined, 9–10; in Gilbert's "History," 163–64, 165, 166, 167, 168, 171–73, 177; in *History of Mary Prince*, 187, 188–90, 192–93, 195–99, 203, 205; in *Interesting Narrative*, 112–15, 119–22, 124–39, 142–43; in *Poems*, 22, 23, 38–46, 51–68; in *Thoughts*, 77–78, 87, 93–104; in Thwaites's "History," 150–52, 155–56, 158, 162–63

Against Race (Gilroy), 11
Akan: and African American folklore, 13; in black diaspora, 72, 93; concept of "*mfe-hoekyir*," 102–3; filial bonds, 97; representation of individuals, 99; representation of whites, 76–77, 78; Sky God (*Nyankonpon*), 93, 100–1, 199; verbal negotiations, 98–99
alternative perspective, 127
ambiguity, 16, 29, 33, 124, 133
ambivalence: of *Anansi*, 101; of black diasporan writers, 3, 5, 12; in Gilbert's "History," 163, 173, 175–77; in Igbo folklore, 135–36; in *Interesting Narrative*, 106, 115, 117, 133, 134; in *Poems*, 21, 33–36, 64; in Thwaites's "History," 149, 151, 152–53, 154, 155, 161, 162–63
analogue, 8. *See also* parallel
Anancy (trickster figure), 4, 17, 72–73; compared with *Leuk* and *Bouki*, 144; and freedom, 103, 195; influence of, in black diasporan cultures, 17; survival tactics of, 102, 164, 179, 196, 197–98, 199. *See also Ananse*; *Anansi*; *Annancy*; *Nancy*; Spider
Ananse (trickster figure), 4, 16, 17, 73, 95, 100–1, 198–99, 203. *See also Anancy*; *Anansi*; *Annancy*; *Nancy*; Spider
Anansi (trickster figure), 17, 72, 94, 95, 96–97, 100, 101, 102, 103, 104, 148, 179, 199. *See also Anancy*; *Ananse*; *Annancy*; *Nancy*; Spider
Annancy (trickster figure), 17, 195. *See also Anancy*; *Ananse*; *Anansi*; *Nancy*; Spider
Antelope (trickster figure), 148, 171
Anthropological Approach, An (Mintz), 7

241

Antigua: Akan influence in, 151, 168–70; Senegambians in, 147–48; slaves in, 147, 201. *See also* Bermuda; Caribbean
apologia, 142
appropriation: in black diasporan narratives, 3–4; as resistance strategy, 11, 16, 35, 37, 40, 45, 51, 52, 56, 65, 91, 93, 120, 122, 125, 126, 132, 133, 138, 149, 157, 190

Babo: and Brer Rabbit, 16; Senegalese origin of, 14
Baker, Houston, 11–12, 37, 51, 117, 123
Barber, Francis, 95
Berlin, Ira, 107, 181
Bermuda: colony of, 179–80; slaves in, 180. *See also* Antigua; Caribbean
"Ber Rabbit, Ber Wolf, and the Butter," 112
"Big God in the Sky," 108
"Big Talk," 57
Black Aesthetic Unbound, The (Langley), 21–22
Black Atlantic, The (Gilroy), 11
Black Culture and Black Consciousness (Levine), 18, 56, 159, 181
black diaspora, 10. *See also* African diaspora
Black Heretics (Bogues), 3, 71, 81
black voice: of Equiano, 130; of Gilbert, 173–74; of Prince, 202; and slavery, 101; and "Talking Book," 129; of Thwaites, 151
Black Yankees (Piersen), 29, 30, 31
black Zionism, 162
Bogues, Anthony, 3, 71, 72, 81, 82
"Bone for a Stump," 187
Bouki (trickster figure): as alter ego of *Leuk*, 65; and black folklore, 4, 14, 16; compared with *Anansi*, 148; compared with Thwaites and Gilbert, 144; as deceptive dancer, 164; as glutton, 183; origin of, 14; as symbol of authoritarian violence, 64; as symbol of indeterminacy, 15; as symbol of strength, 66; as transgressor, 53, 156–57. *See also* Deer; Hyena
"Bouki rossé par les aveugles" ("How Bouki was Beaten by the Blind People"), 183
Boukism, defined, 144
Brathwaite, Kamau, 166–67, 178–79, 190–91

"Brave Mbabaa!," 62–63
Brer Mockingbird (trickster figure), 13, 14
Brer Rabbit (trickster figure): and black literature, 4; as defender and punisher, 16. *See also* Cunnie Rabbit; Hare; *Leuk*; Rabbit
Bro' Boar-Hog (trickster figure), as disguised suitor, 155–56
"Bur Rabbit in Red Hill Churchyard," 13

Caribbean: African folklore in, 17, 18, 72–73; blacks of, 3; women authors of, 20; slavery in, 106, 115–16. *See also* Antigua; Bermuda; slavery
Caribbean Autobiography (Paquet), 192
Carretta, Vincent, 5, 52, 70, 71, 80, 84, 91–92, 95–96, 105, 107, 111, 142
Chambers, Douglass, 107, 108, 109–10, 124
"Chosen Suitor, The," 155–56
Christianity: Cugoano and, 87, 88, 89, 90, 92, 93; Equiano and, 121–22, 128, 133; Gilbert and, 145–46, 147; Thwaites and, 145–46, 147, 149; P. Wheatley and, 24, 35–36, 38, 45, 55–56
Clarkson, Thomas, 101, 204
Cockroach (trickster figure), 149
colonialism, 7, 10, 64, 152
Committee for the Relief of the Black Poor, 91, 95, 96; Cugoano and, 92–93
communality: in Akan culture, 85–86, 97; of blacks in colonial New England, 48, 68; defined, 46; in Igbo culture, 113; of New World blacks, 96; in pawnship, 81; in Senegambian folktales, 46–47
countertricking, as resistance strategy, 158–59
Courlander, Harold, 7–8
Cricket (trickster figure), 184
Crummel, Alexander, 7–8, 91, 153
Cugoano, Quobna Ottobah: abduction of, 76, 78–79; compared with *Anansi*, 102, 103, 104; and European culture, 86, 87, 89; on Hume, 81, 82, 84, 85; Pan-African consciousness of, 69; as pioneer of black Atlantic literature, 70, 71–72; as slave in England, 73, 86
Cunnie Rabbit (trickster figure), 55. *See also* Brer Rabbit; Hare; *Leuk*; Rabbit

Dash, Julie, 110, 111
Daughters of the Dust (Dash), 110, 111
Deer (trickster figure), 14, 15, 171. See also *Bouki*; Hyena
dehomogenization, 7. *See also* homogenization
Delany, Martin R., 11, 83, 84, 89, 91, 153, 207
Demane, Harry, 95
"de rabbit an' de elephan' tushes," 65–66
"dernière prise, La" [the last catch], 156–57
diaspora, 10
diffusionism: defined, 89, 91; of New World blacks, 90–91; in *Thoughts*, 89–90, 91
Diop, Birago, 19, 54, 58, 172, 209
Diop, Haja Mbana, compared with P. Wheatley, 63–64
diplomacy: in Antiguan folklore, 158; Equiano's use of, 121, 129; of *griots*, 24; in slave culture, 158; P. Wheatley's use of, 64, 66, 87
disguise: in Antiguan folklore, 149–50, 155, 157; in black diasporan narratives, 210; and *Boukism*, 15, 144; Equiano's use of, 120; P. Wheatley's use of, 24, 54; in Wolof folklore, 53, 54
diversion, 144; in black diasporan narratives, 163, 210
Dog (trickster figure), 57, 58, 121, 148, 173, 191, 192
"Dog and Monkey Build a Town, The," 191
"Donkeys of Jolof, The," 46–47
double voice: as Africanism, 41; as signifying, 41
Dundes, Alan, 7, 8, 19

Edwards, Paul, 70, 71–72, 93, 141
Elephant, 12, 64, 65, 66, 148, 192
England, blacks in, 71, 91, 92, 95, 102. *See also* Cugoano, Quobna Ottobah; Equiano, Olaudah; Prince, Mary; Wheatley, Phillis
Enlightenment, 81, 84–85, 145
Equiano, Olaudah: abduction of, 106, 119; and Richard (Dick) Baker, 115, 120–21, 122, 123; birthplace of, 105–6; cosmopolitanism of, 118–19, 123; hired to Dr. Charles Irving, 118; involvement of, in slavery, 116–19; opinion of, on African slavery, 115–16; on relations between Igbo and Hebrew people, 139–40; as seaman in England, 106, 118, 119; as self-made man, 117; significance of, in black literature, 105; as slave of Captain Doran, 125; as slave of Robert King, 106, 116, 117, 126, 127; as slave of Michael Henry Paschal, 105–6, 119, 120, 122; as soldier, 120, 122
Erkkila, Betsy, 37, 64, 119, 130
Esu Elegbera (trickster figure), 15
Ethiopianism: of Cugoano, 83; defined, 49; of P. Wheatley, 49
European depiction: of Africa, 153–54; of Antigua, 153–54, 201–2, 208; of Bermuda, 180–81; of blacks, 82, 84–85, 106, 112, 135–36; of Igbo people, 137–38, 153–54
Exchanging Our Country Marks (Gomez), 5–6, 107, 109, 114

false deference: defined, 159; as resistance tactic, 144, 146, 149, 159, 163, 164, 210
"False Message: Annancy makes Fox his Ridding Horse, The," 195
Fanti: concept of individual power, 97; filial bonds, 94–95; involvement in Atlantic slavery, 75–76; notion of collective good, 97; origin of, 74; relations with Ashanti, 74–75; slavery, 80–81, 85, 86; worship of *abusa* (God), 97–98
Ferguson, Moira, 5, 144, 145, 147, 150, 155, 167, 173, 176, 177, 178, 185, 197, 205
folklore, 7
"Food Drum, The," 121–22, 131
Fowl (trickster figure), 149
Fox (trickster figure), 182, 195, 196
free blacks: in Antigua 5, 145, 159, 173, 174, 175, 176, 185, 200; in England, 73, 101–2; in United States, 29, 30, 128, 130
freedom: Cugoano and, 85, 89, 91, 94, 95, 97; Equiano and, 114, 118–19, 120, 128, 129, 130, 133, 134, 137; Gilbert and, 145, 163, 175; Prince and, 194, 201, 204; Thwaites and, 145, 149, 150, 152, 154–55, 159, 160, 161, 175; P. Wheatley and, 34, 35, 36, 45–46, 48, 49, 51, 52, 54, 56, 59–60, 61, 64, 66, 67–68

From Trickster to Badman (Roberts), 4, 16, 148–49

Gaïndé-the-Lion (trickster figure), 156–57. See also Lion
Gamble, David P., 14, 19, 40, 64
Gates, Henry Louis, Jr., 4, 15, 22, 25, 26, 41, 52, 105, 129, 192
Geiss, Immanuel, 8–9
Gendered Africanism, 45
gender relations: in *History of Mary Prince*, 194–95, 200–1; in *Interesting Narrative*, 136–38
Generations of Captivity, 107
Gilbert, Anne Hart: birthplace/birthdate of, 144, 145; as educator of free slaves, 145, 175, 176; family of, 145, 147; relations of, with Methodists, 163, 172, 173, 174, 175, 176
Gilroy, Paul, 11, 200
Going through the Storm (Stuckey), 14, 16
Golo (trickster figure), 66; influence of, in Caribbean literature, 191; and Signifying Monkey, 58–59. See also Monkey; Signifying Monkey
Gomez, Michael A., 4, 103, 107, 109, 114, 214
griots: functions of, 24; rhetorical strategies of, 41–43, 59

Hare (trickster figure), 14, 15, 17, 18, 55, 65, 112, 148, 171, 172, 182–83, 184. See also Brer Rabbit; Cunnie Rabbit; *Leuk*; Rabbit
"Hare Seeks Endowments from Allah, The," 12
Hart Sisters, The (Ferguson), 5, 144, 145, 147, 153
heaven: in Judeo-Christian worldview, 40; in Senegambian Islamic worldview, 39–40
Herskovits, Melville J., 13, 184
"He Sings to Make the Old Woman Dance," 163
hidden transcript, 52, 58, 123–24. See also weapon of the weak
History of Mary Prince, The (Prince), 4, 185, 200, 205
"History of Methodism" (Gilbert), 4, 144, 163
"History of Methodism" (Thwaites), 4, 144, 149, 162
homogenization, 6–7, 211. See also dehomogenization

"How Ananse, The Spider, Became Poor," 100–1
"How it Came About That the Sky-God's Stories Came to be Known as 'Spider-Stories,'" 199
"How it Came that Wisdom Came among the Tribe," 95
Hume, David, 81, 84, 85, 94
"Hurricane Coming," 197–98
Hurston, Zora Neale, 19, 31, 57, 59, 209
hybridity: of *Anancy*, 72; in Bermudan slave culture, 180; in Gilbert's Christianity, 175; Gilroy's theory of, 11; in Igbo identity, 108, 140; in Pan-Africanism, 86–87; in slave culture, 6; of Western blacks, 207; in P. Wheatley's Methodism, 38
Hyena (trickster figure), 4, 14, 44, 148, 171–72, 182–83, 184. See also *Bouki*; Deer
"Hyena Engages the Hare as a Gewel, The," 53

Igbo: in black diaspora, 108–10, 112; communal identity, 112, 131–32; oral traditions, 109–10, 129; relations with gods, 132–33; and slavery, 109, 111, 113–14, 115; in Virginia, 107
Igbo Roots of Olaudah Equiano, The (Acholonu), 108, 132, 136
imperialism: and black literature, 3–4, 33, 71, 89, 91, 92, 93, 112, 158, 208; defined, 10. See also Pan-Africanism
impersonation, as storytelling strategy, 43
indirection: in black literature, 54, 56, 59–60, 128; in Wolof language, 53–54
"Integrities of History in Africa, The" (Miller), 193
Interesting Narrative of the Life of Olaudah Equiano, The (Equiano), 4, 105, 112; Igbo society in, 114–15, 136–38; place of, in Pan-Africanism, 112
irony, as resistance tactic, 14, 33, 59, 126

Jackal (trickster figure), 171
Jeremiad: defined, 52; in *Poems*, 55
Johnson, John H., 19, 149, 162, 187
Journey Back, The (Baker), 11, 37, 51

Kane, Mohamadou, 15
Keita, Sunjata, 64

Kumba (character), 44; compared with P. Wheatley, 45, 46
"Kumba the Orphan Girl," 44–45

Langley, April C. E., 21, 22
Langley, J. Ayodele, 9
"Lapin devant Dieu, Le [The Rabbit Standing before God]," 64–65
"Leaf Disguise," 162
Leuk (trickster figure): compared with *Bouki*, 65; compared with Brer Rabbit, 66; role of, in black literature, 4; as symbol of cleverness and diplomacy, 64. *See also* Brer Rabbit; Cunnie Rabbit; Hare; Rabbit
Levin, Amy K., 9–10, 45, 203
Levine, Lawrence, 18, 19, 56, 159, 181, 209
liberation strategies: in Gilbert's "History," 164; in *History of Mary Prince*, 178, 185, 187–92, 193, 196–97, 198, 199, 202, 203; in *Interesting Narrative*, 116, 118, 119–20, 125–27, 126, 128–29, 133, 139, 142; in *Poems*, 3, 20, 21, 23, 24, 27, 32–33, 35, 36, 37, 45–46, 52, 55, 56, 59, 60, 64; in *Thoughts*, 73, 78, 99–100, 102, 103; in Thwaites's "History," 149, 159–60. *See also* Obeah; trickster strategies
Lion (trickster figure), 29, 44, 45, 46, 171, 172, 192, 198, 199. *See also Gaïndé*-the-Lion
"Lion's Treasured Goat, The," 171–72
Lovejoy, Paul, 10, 29, 80

Magel, Emil, 12, 14, 19, 32, 44, 53, 58, 62, 171, 182, 184, 191
Manichean worldviews, 15–16, 91, 139
Mansfield, Lord Chief Justice, 141
marronage: as black female resistance, 198; defined, 123, 152, 214; as hidden transcript, 123–24
mask: in black literature, 55, 190; in Igbo folklore, 120; in Sowo culture, 203. *See also* masking
masking, in black literature, 149, 210. *See also* mask
Mbe (trickster figure), 4, 16, 120, 121, 122, 131, 132, 133
Methodism: and Antigua, 146–47; British, 146; Calvinist, 38; and Gilbert, 163, 172, 174, 175; and Thwaites, 150, 155; and P. Wheatley, 24–25
Middle Passage, 6, 7, 12, 22, 28, 45, 46, 72, 73, 99, 105, 161, 191, 195
Middle Passages (Brathwaite), 179
Middle Passages (Campbell), 5
Miller, Joseph C., 77–78, 81, 193, 197
Mintz, Sidney W., 7
Monkey (trickster figure), 59, 190, 191, 192, 197. *See also Golo*; Signifying Monkey
"Monkey and the Dog Court the Same Girl, The," 58–59
"Monkey Husband," 190
Moravianism, and Antigua, 145–46
mothering, 151, 152
Mules and Men (Hurston), 19, 31, 57
Murder at Montpellier (Chambers), 107, 124

Nancy (trickster figure), 4, 17, 163, 164, 173, 183, 187, 195, 197. *See also Anancy; Ananse; Anansi; Annancy*; Spider
Nanny, as Maroon leader, 152, 160, 177
New England: African folktales in colonial, 28–29; Africans in colonial, 29, 47, 48; election day (ceremony) in colonial, 12; Pan-African influence in colonial, 12; Senegambian folklore in colonial, 28–29, 30, 31
Nine Black Women (Ferguson), 147, 176, 178, 197
Njaaye, Njajaan, 64
Nnabe (trickster figure), 112
"Nnabe and the Fruits," 112

Obeah: defined, 166, 173; Gilbert's depiction of, 173, 175; role of, in slave resistance, 96, 167, 168, 177. *See also* liberation strategies; trickster strategies
Okolo (trickster figure), 124, 125, 126
opening formula: in African storytelling, 32; in *Mules and Men*, 31; and testifying, 31–32
oral tradition: African, in New World, 16, 17, 19, 22, 28, 30, 31, 62, 72, 108, 109–10, 148; importance of, 3, 15, 16, 109, 197, 208
"Oral Tradition and History" (Miller), 197
"Ordeal, The," 188
Owl (trickster figure), 13, 14

Pan-Africanism: and black literature, 3; defined, 8–9; and Middle Passage, 6, 79. *See also* imperialism
Paquet, Sandra Pouchet, 5, 179, 192
parallel, defined, 8. *See also* analogue
patrilineality, in Akan culture, 95, 97
pawnship, 81
personas, 15, 29, 43, 46
Petro (concept), defined, 189
Piersen, William D., 29, 30–31, 77, 78
"Playing Godfather," 183–84
Poems (P. Wheatley), 4, 26
Prince, Mary: birthplace/birthdate of, 185; in England, 185, 202, 205; family of, 185; as slave in Turks island, 186; slaveowners' abuse of, 185, 186, 188, 189, 200, 201
Puritan cosmology: compared with Senegambian Islamic cosmology, 51; and *Poems*, 50–55
Puritan elegy: compared with Senegambian Islamic elegy, 39; and *Poems*, 38, 39, 40, 43

Rabbit (trickster figure): as captive, 162, 195; compared with *Anancy*, 197; compared with *Leuk*, 64, 65, 66; compared with *Mbe*, 121; importance of, in black literature, 4, 13–14, 16–17, 18, 29, 112, 187, 196; in Senegambian culture, 14, 15, 16, 55, 148. *See also* Brer Rabbit; Cunnie Rabbit; Hare; Leuk
racism: and black literature, 3, 4, 84, 127, 208; in European representations of blacks, 3, 81, 122, 170
Rada (concept), defined, 189
Ramgoat (trickster figure), 187
Rattray, Robert Sutherland, 19, 72, 100, 162, 169, 199
relational identity: in Antiguan folklore, 158; in *History of Mary Prince*, 189–90, 191, 196, 197, 200; in Senegambian folklore, 157; in traditional Africa, 7, 81, 103, 192–93, 197, 216
Reversing Sail (Gomez), 6, 103
River Flows On, The (Rucker), 16, 73, 158
Roberts, John W., 4, 16, 44, 102, 148, 149
Rucker, Walter C., 16

Sancho, Ignatius, 71, 95, 105
Senegambia: cultural influence of, in Atlantic world, 12–13, 14, 22–23, 148–49, 182–84; exportation of slaves from, to Americas, 29–30, 39–40
Senghor, Léopold Sédar, 8, 14, 19, 54, 183, 184, 209
sexism, 20, 178, 185, 193, 198, 199, 205
Sharp, Granville, 95, 101, 141, 204
Shields, John C., 28, 39
Sierra Leone Project, 91, 92, 95, 96, 141, 142, 154
signifying: in black diaspora, 192; defined, 52; in *Poems*, 52; and "Wax," 53
Signifying Monkey (trickster figure), 59, 192. *See also Golo*; Monkey
Signifying Monkey, The (Gates), 15, 41, 52, 192
"Signifying Monkey and the Lion, The," 192
Slave Culture (Stuckey), 9, 12, 13, 79
slave narratives, as political criticism and critique, 3
slave resistance: in Caribbean, 158, 159, 168, 169, 175, 188, 198; in England, 96, 106, 202–3, 204; during Middle Passage, 102, 103; in United States, 6, 48, 66, 106, 159, 196
slavery: African systems of, 80–81; Cugoano on, 79, 80–81, 85, 86; Equiano on, 109–10, 113–14, 115; Gilbert on, 164, 172–74, 175; Prince on, 185–86, 187, 188, 189, 190, 193, 194, 196–97, 198, 200–1, 202, 203, 204; Thwaites on, 154, 155, 159, 160; P. Wheatley on, 3, 54, 55, 56–61, 66, 67, 68
slaves: culture of, in Antigua, 165, 166, 167, 173, 174, 175; culture of, in Bermuda, 180–82, 185–88; culture of, in United States, 5–6, 12, 13, 29, 30, 79, 107–8; status of, in Africa, 45, 80, 81, 86, 97, 157, 193; status of, in Americas, 12, 203, 205; as viewed by white abolitionists, 106, 141, 143, 159–60, 201, 203, 205; as viewed by white slaveowners, 106, 127, 195, 200–1, 202, 203, 204–5
Socé, Ousmane, 14
Somersett Case, 141
"Sons of Africa," 95, 96, 101
Spider (trickster figure), 4, 17, 18, 72, 94, 96, 100, 101, 112, 148, 187, 199. *See also Anancy; Ananse; Anansi; Annancy; Nancy*

Stewart, James, 6
Stuckey, Sterling, 4, 9, 12, 13, 14, 16, 79

taasu (concept), defined, 22
tagg (concept): defined, 41–42; example of, 62; and P. Wheatley's poetry, 42, 62, 63, 64; and *xass*, 59
Tales of Ahmadou Kumba, The (Diop), 54
tale-type, 8
"Talking Book," 129, 134, 204
"Taureau de Bouki, Le" [The Bull of Bouki], 163–64
"Theft of the Butter by Playing Godfather, The," 184
Thompson, Stith, 8, 183
Thoughts and Sentiments (Cugoano), 4, 5, 69, 70, 71, 72, 75, 77, 81, 82, 91, 95, 103
"Three Questions, The," 149–50
Thwaites, Elizabeth Hart: birthplace/birthdate of, 144, 145; family of, 145, 147; and free slaves, 145, 175, 176; and Methodists, 150, 154–55; and Nanny, 152–53; and white abolitionists, 150, 153–54, 159–60
Tortoise (trickster figure), 4, 18, 112, 120, 121, 126, 127–28, 129, 148
tricksters: in black folktales, 4, 18, 121; and freedom, 54, 66, 127, 129, 130, 208
trickster strategies: in African American tales, 59, 184, 192; in African folktales, 45–46, 59, 64, 102; of *Anansi*, 96–97, 100, 103, 199; of *Bouki*, 164; in Caribbean tales, 149–50, 157, 182, 183, 184, 190–91; of *Mbe*, 121; of Okolo, 125, 126; of Rabbit, 66, 162. *See also* liberation strategies; Obeah
"Twin Gongs, The," 124–25

"Under the Green Old Oak Tree," 188
United States: African folklore in, 4, 17, 18; Africanisms in, 5–6, 23
Usu (trickster figure), 121, 134–35

Way of Death (Miller), 77–78, 81
"Wax" (concept), 53, 54
weapon of the weak, 52, 58, 158, 164. *See also* hidden transcript
Wesley, John, 146, 147, 172, 174
Wesleyan Methodism: and Antiguan slaves, 163; in Caribbean, 146–47
Western blacks, and Sierra Leone Project, 141–42
"What Darkens the hole," 182
Wheatley, Phillis: compared with Kumba, 44–46; in England, 26, 46; as *griotte*, 24, 43, 62; and her white examiners, 25–26; and New England blacks, 28, 29, 47–48, 49; as Sankofa bird, 21; Senegambian roots of, 25, 27, 28, 54–55; as slave, 25; on George Washington, 67–68; and George Whitefield, 26–27, 37
Wheatley, Susanna: death of, 27; and P. Wheatley, 26, 27, 41–42, 43, 44, 46
Wilberforce, William, 154, 159–60, 204
Wolf (trickster figure), 182
Wolof: funeral elegy, 39; origin of, 27–28; as slaves from Senegambia, 29
womanism: in black diaspora, 24, 194, 200; of Gilbert, 176–77; of Prince, 198; of Thwaites, 151–52; of P. Wheatley, 24

"Xass" (concept), 59, 181; P. Wheatley's use of, 59–60

Zulu, Chaka, 64